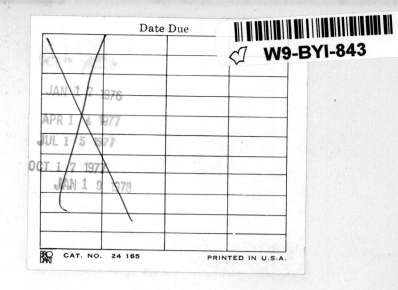

Early Russian Architecture

Hubert Faensen · Vladimir Ivanov

EARLY RUSSIAN ARCHITECTURE

Photographs by Klaus G. Beyer

G. P. PUTNAM'S SONS · NEW YORK

Introduction by Dr Hubert Faensen, Kleinmachnow
Commentary by Dr Faensen and Dr Vladimir Ivanov, Moscow
Photography by Klaus G. Beyer

Originally published in German copyright © 1972 by Union Verlag
(VOB) Berlin
This translation copyright © 1975 by Paul Elek Ltd., London
SBN: 399-11293-6
Library of Congress Catalog Card Number: 73-87578
Graphic design: Joachim Kölbel
Production: Druckerei Fortschritt Erfurt
Photo-setting by ČGP Delo, Ljubljana
Printed in Germany (East).

less conception of silhouette, the instinct for decorative effect, the richness of formal invention, in a word, all the architectural virtues are to be found everywhere and unremittingly in the course of the history of Russian art, so that we are compelled to believe that the Russian people possess a fully formed architectonic gift.' The birth of this gift did not have to wait until the need for a monumental art arose with the foundation of the first state of the East Slavs, Kievan Rus, and the introduction of Christianity. It is true that histories of the subject customarily begin with the first masonry churches. It is also true that the Byzantine legacy was one pole of the fertile tension within which early Russian architecture developed. But the history of its origins goes back further than that, even though hardly any tangible archaeological evidence has survived. Its roots lie in the centuries-old traditions of folk art. The other pole consists of the forms of the indigenous wooden architecture and the native handicrafts.

When Kievan Rus adopted the craft of building with stone and brick from the Byzantine empire, it already possessed extensive experience of building with timber. This skill had left its mark on the stylistic sense of the whole race and by the end of the tenth century it had reached a high level technically, structurally and aesthetically. The first churches were still made of wood. They may well have looked like the houses with their lofty 'terema' described by Arabic and later Russian writers. They were built by the same carpenters as built the pagan sacrificial shrines, tombs and temples. It is known from the early Russian chronicles that Prince Igor had Christian followers who confirmed a treaty with the Byzantine Empire by taking an oath in the wooden church of St Elijah in Kiev as early as 945. As well as ordering the mass baptism of the population of Kiev in the Dnepr in 988–89, Vladimir the Great Prince is said to have had wooden churches erected on sites previously occupied by heathen idols. The Cathedral of St Sophia, built in Novgorod in 989, is believed to have been constructed of oak, and to have had thirteen domes. Between 1020 and 1026 a group of five wooden churches in the form of towers was built in Vyshgorod near Kiev, above the grave of the first Russian saints, Boris and Gleb. The astonishing speed with which the unfamiliar techniques of building in stone and brick were assimilated, and the creative originality shown in the adaptation of the Byzantine forms can be explained only by the strength of the East Slav traditions. They were an essential source of architectural fantasy which was kindled anew by the models of mature Christian, Byzantine art and gave rise to an original, independent, national formal language.

Even the Byzantine architects who were summoned to Kiev had to submit to the autochthonous stylistic principles. The first stone churches of Rus, which they built, the so-called Desyatinnaya ('tithe') Church (989–96) and the Cathedral of St Sophia (from 1037), both displayed characteristics of pre-Christian wooden architecture: the pyramidal construction, the exterior galleries, the large number of towers, the additive repetition, the use of decoration to give optical relief to the mass of the building. Similar modifications arose from the influences of other neighbouring cultures, whether transmitted directly or via Byzantium, especially from the Balkans, Western Europe, Transcaucasia and Islam. The monumental masonry architecture of medieval Russia was created and developed in the constant process of cross-fertilization between external influences and internal circumstances.

Constantinople —
the 'Versailles of
the Middle Ages'

If the need exists and the conditions are right, every indigenous culture will seize on the products of a more highly developed one, not in order to imitate them blindly but to assimilate them in its own practices. This kind of appropriation and adaptation is a selective and creative process. It is in this sense that the terms Carolingian Renaissance and the Ottonian *Renovatio Romanorum Imperii* were coined. The relationship of Kievan Rus to Byzantium, the legitimate spiritual heir of Rome, is to be understood in the same light. Right up to the present century attempts have been made to deny Russia an independent artistic development, because of this process of adaptation. Early Russian art was categorized as barbarian variation, or epigonal imitation of the Byzantine formal canon. It is true that for a long time the intellectual and spiritual content of Byzantine art forms fulfilled a particular religious, political and aesthetic need of the Middle Ages, but it played the same role in Western Europe as well. The fusion of elements from Roman, Hellenistic and Oriental culture in a feudal society and under the aegis of Christianity as the official state religion, gave rise to an imperial art which was the model for the whole of Europe. Constantinople was the 'Versailles of the Middle Ages'. The young barbarian races were hungry for culture, and their princes encouraged the appropriation of Byzantine art because they wanted to surround themselves with the same aura of 'Roman' majesty and power as the Basileus, the Byzantine emperor, who appeared as God's deputy on earth. The combination of secular and spiritual power, court ceremonial and religious ritual, sophisticated culture and brutal despotism, which had already characterized the rule of the 'divine' emperors of pagan Rome, was preserved in the Eastern empire in a Christian form. Even in the fifteenth century, after the fall of Constantinople, tsarist absolutism derived strong support from the notion of 'Moscow, the third Rome'. Ivan III was hailed, at his own behest, as the new Constantine, a claim that had also been made by his forebear Vladimir, and by Charlemagne in the West. The sublime, superhuman dignity of the emperor was emphasized by splendid ceremonial and expressed in artistic forms which were intended to compel awe and fear simultaneously, and both to represent and to strengthen the authority of the state. In its content and in its forms, Byzantine art developed as a relatively integrated system, recognized as the most comprehensive, the most consistent and the most enduring of the Middle Ages. As such it received official sanction, and as a constituent part of the ruling ideology it wielded great stylistic influence, particularly upon the early feudal monarchies, as they advanced from a state of barbarism.

What is meant nowadays, often presumptuously, by the term Western culture is inconceivable without the legacy of the empire of the East. On the other hand, the significance of Byzantium in the emergence of medieval Russia is still often overrated. In Kievan Rus the Byzantine influence, with its claim of tutelage, was transformed: 'from above' by the rulers and their courts, in the struggle for political and ecclesiastical independence, and 'from below' by the creative energy of the popular folk tradition and the legacy of paganism and magic. Both Western Europe and Russia had a 'Byzantine question' to solve, but they found different solutions. In the culture that built itself up on the remnants of the destroyed empire of the West, the pope successfully asserted himself as the highest ecclesiastical authority at the side of the secular ruler, while the empire of the East survived the onslaught of the barbarian hordes, to pass on to the East Slavs the political theory of the emperor as God's deputy, who was therefore necessarily head of the church as well.

Basilical and Centrally-Planned Churches

Otto Demus has called the icon the prototypal form of the European picture. Similarly, forerunners of Christian building types can be discovered in the Byzantine forms of the basilica and the centrally-planned structure. The pre-Romanesque revived basilical forms and in the tension between *regnum* and *sacerdotium*, between the imperial throne and the altar, there developed the practice of two choirs, two patronal dedications and an altar to the Saviour in the westwork. Early Russian architecture, born some two centuries later and growing up in the thick of the Great Schism between the Catholic and Orthodox churches, opted for the middle Byzantine type of the cruciform plan. The long rectangle of the basilical plan leads the congregation from the entrance at the west end towards the 'Holy of Holies', a directional impulse which is not weakened by the intersection of the transepts before the apse. The Orthodox plan is quite different in character: the form of a Greek cross (with all four arms of equal length) draws all attention towards the central area. Attempts have been made to explain the architectural difference, over and above the confessional and theological significance, by the difference between a linear and a cyclic sense of time, an irreflective and a reflective conceptual capacity, supposedly typical of the West or of the East as the case may be. But the evidence of this is based on speculation. The fundamental decisive factor is the difference in the two concepts of the *Imperium Christianum*. The crossing with the dome above it by no means lacks direction. One could say that it serves as a 'stage' for divine service, on which the 'actors', the priests, perform their cyclic movements, as a place of repose in which the *vita contemplativa* can be lived, and as a place providing a vertical dynamic for the *vita activa,* although the upward impetus cannot be achieved in real terms. The central positioning is the important factor in all three interpretations: in the 'sacred drama', in mediative circles of mystic submersion, and in the play of forces between 'below' and 'above'.

Kievan Rus did not simply adopt the ideas and forms of Byzantine art in slavish imitation, but subjected them to a process of Russification which, again, did not imply a primitive reversion into barbarism, but rather the rise of a new, major culture. Even the old Russian chronicles betray a critical attitude towards neighbouring cultures, as in the accounts of the 'examination of religions' by Vladimir Svyatoslavovich, the Great Prince of Kiev (930–1015). First he listened to missionaries from the Volga Bulgars, who were Muslims, from the pope in Rome, from the Khazar Jews, and from the Byzantine church; then he sent ten esteemed and clever men abroad 'to study each kind of worship, and how each one serves God'. On their return the emissaries described their impressions: the Muslim faith lacked consolation, the Roman Catholic ritual lacked sufficient beauty. Only in the Hagia Sophia in Constantinople did they find a liturgy that enraptured them, and to which their native aesthetic sense made them particularly susceptible: ' . . . we did not know if we were in heaven or on earth: for we have never experienced anything of the kind on earth, nor ever seen anything so wonderful.'

The Adoption of Christianity

Undoubtedly the aesthetic aspect of the Byzantine ritual and a theology that extended to architectural forms played a part in Vladimir's decision. The chronicles mention additional reasons – the legend of how he miraculously regained his sight after conversion, his acceptance in the 'family of kings' through his marriage with the Byzantine princess, Anna – but they touch only briefly upon the historically important reason: the significance of the concept of the *Imperium Christianum* for the process of feudalization and the foundation of the state in Russia. In 988–89 Vladimir ordered his subjects to be baptized and – as Hilarion put it in his *Discourse on Law and Grace* – 'he who did not do it for love, did it for fear of him who had commanded it, because both were united in him – true belief and power'. The exact circumstances in which the Byzantine form of Christianity was adopted and made the official religion remain unknown. It is known to have made inroads in the territory of the East Slavs by various routes long before Vladimir's mass baptism, and to have taken a long time to be fully accepted among the population.

Vladimir's grandmother, the Great Princess Olga, had been baptized in Constantinople after the death of her husband Igor, as early as 957. It must have been at about the same time that the first priests and liturgical books entered from Bulgaria, then still independent. Some scholars have seen Moravian influences at work, since early Russian chroniclers, writing the history of the ninth century, mention the activities of Cyril and Methodius, the 'apostles of the Slavs', and one of the many wives Vladimir had while still a heathen was a Moravian princess. At all events the Great Prince of Kiev, later canonized and venerated as highly as the evangelists and the apostles, was not pursuing solely religious goals in his decision, even though his gifts and interests as a soldier and an administrator were augmented by a personal piety which conjured up the vision of a state where social justice would prevail. His reign saw the end of 'glorious barbarism', of the obsolete forms of pagan society, and created the circumstances in which the land could be united 'under his right hand' and feudalism could be firmly established. Christianity served as an ideological implement to legitimize and affirm his sovereignty and the feudal hierarchy, and also to introduce the East Slavs, long despised by the Greeks as 'nordic barbarians', into the European family of nations on an equal footing, both culturally and politically. In the year 1000 Rus stretched from the Baltic coast to the lower reaches of the Dnepr, from the Carpathians to the Volga, and occupied the largest area after the Holy Roman Empire.

Subsequently the same system of land tenure grew up in Russia as in Western Europe, with land held by inheritance or as military fiefs (votchina and pomestye), and a social hierarchy, with forms of vassalage and serfdom, and a guild system in the towns. The formation of large estates and the exaction of feudal dues increased social inequalities, strengthened the autocratic and aristocratic institutions, and diminished the importance of the 'Veche' (popular assembly), except in a few commercial centres, like Novgorod, Smolensk, Polotsk and Pskov. The social and economic variations were reflected in architecture: in the contrast between courts and palaces and the hovels of lowly peasants and craftsmen, the wooden churches found mostly in the villages and the masonry churches of the towns and larger monasteries, the simple churches of the parishes and monasteries and the monumental cathedrals built by the princes. The feudal hierarchy found the construction of churches and other buildings for sacred uses an expedient, an expression of its social self-confidence, a means of conveying the 'divine sanction' on which the privileges and forms of its authority were based. Church building was financed by the uppermost levels of the hierarchy from the very first. The old *Vita* of Vladimir recounts that, nine years after his baptism, the Great Prince passed a statute (ustav), making over 'to the church of the Holy Virgin a tithe of his estate' – hence the name by which it is usually known. It is not certain as to whether this tithe is to be understood in the Western or in the Byzantine sense, but from then on a regular contribution to the priesthood and the erection and maintenance of churches was exacted from the people. Similar actions on the part of Vladimir's successors are also recorded. Ecclesiastical institutions, especially the great monasteries founded, or richly endowed at some later stage, by the princes, themselves became landlords and were constantly increasing the size of their estates. In the fifteenth century probably as much as a third of the entire soil of Russia was in clerical hands.

The architecture of the time symbolized the self-confidence and aspiration of the Russian state, representing the general interest in the struggle for national unity and independence, and the relatively unanimous religious attitude of the people, who had become the bastion of Christianity, 'Holy Russia' (Svyataya Rus) in Hilarion's phrase. In this sense architecture suffered as much from the invasions of the Mongols and Tartars, and the Lithuanians and Poles, as it helped to prepare the way for the national awakening. Nevertheless, in various stylistic periods and variations, it also reflected the differing social roles and motivations of those who initiated the individual buildings – the tsars and the princes, the hereditary and service nobility, the higher clergy, the monastic orders, then merchants and well-to-do craftsmen, either as individuals or groups, down to humble congregations. It was a seismograph of the social tensions, revealed in the divisive effects of feudalism, the centralization of government, the controversy about monastic possessions, the political reforms of Ivan IV and the ecclesiastical reforms of the Patriarch Nikon, the peasant uprisings and the flight from the country to the towns, and the unrest of the townspeople. In this sense the complex history of ideas and social evolution in medieval Russia can be read in the development of architectural style.

Social status also affected attitudes to the autochthonous traditions and the adoption of Byzantine models, which were by no means uniform. The simplicity of the architectural principles of the Christian Orient, to which Russian monasticism inclined, was vastly different from the complexity of the court school of Constantinople, of which St Sophia in Kiev was the clearest expression, though not a pure recreation of the Byzantine principles. What was accepted, in what circumstances, and when, are questions which must be asked anew in the case of each building. One must remember at the same time the dichotomy of purpose which affected the contrasts in architectural forms: the differences that existed in the Byzantine empire between the simplicity of monastic services and the theatrical ritual in the cathedral of the court, and between the popular and the imperial concepts of the Kingdom of God, were repeated under different conditions in Russia, while Russia's separate stage of development prescribed different methods of confronting or solving the problems.

Early Russian architecture developed and evolved in the seven hundred years between the advent of Christianity and the accession of Peter I in accordance with these fundamental tensions, although they were not normally expressed directly, due to the strongly individual character of the formal traditions. The decisive historical events created nothing absolutely new in the style of the architecture, but they activated ideological and psychological reflexes which affected the way in which existing and selected models were adapted and developed. Stylistic evolution followed social evolution only in a restricted sense, since the conventionally formed patterns of expectation constantly needed the stimulus of new and unfamiliar artistic data, yet at the same time the continuity of the specific Russian tradition was not to be broken. The principal factor determining the course of developments was the centrally-focused plan, which was based as much on traditional timber architecture as on the domed cruciform models of Byzantium.

The Predominance of the Central Plan

The hierarchic arrangement of the interior of the Byzantine church was an expression of the spirit of theocracy. Even pagan Rome had rejected the real three-dimensionalism of Greek architecture in favour of the government of space by optical effects. And the basilicas of the early Church – by contrast with the ancient temples – had drawn attention away from the exterior of the building to the interior where the congregation actually gathered, as well as separating clergy from the laity, the baptized from catechumens and men from women. The tendency to indicate distinctions of rank in spatial terms was intensified in Byzantine churches. The differences in the social categories were emphasized in visual, tangible terms.

The Hagia
Sophia
The symbol of the theocracy and the spiritual heart of the Byzantine empire was the church and patriarchal cathedral in Justinian's palace in the imperial capital, Constantinople: the domed basilica of Hagia Sophia (532–37/558–62). It created an image of the concept of the world governed 'from above', to which every individual existence had to subject itself, by virtue of its incommensurable proportions, which brook no anthropomorphic comparisons, and the 'overlapping forms' of its volume and its physical structure (H. Sedlmayr). The colossal domed canopy seems to bathe every section of the interior in a flood of light, to abrogate all spatial relationships and to dematerialize all solid three-dimensional forms. The rectangular central area immediately beneath the dome is surrounded by arcaded screens with surfaces that seem to evaporate when seen from within the square but which constitute proper boundaries when seen from the aisles, the vestibule and the tribunes. The central area is surrounded by this two-storeyed 'cloak' of relatively separate, half-lit subsidiary areas from which the 'audience' could watch services proceeding on the well-lit 'stage' beneath the dome. The 'canopy principle' led to

the optical and spatial illusionism, dissolving all forms, which Konrad Onasch has examined in connection with the hierarchical metaphysics of light of Dionysios the Areopagite.

The Byzantine liturgy has been spoken of as something so totally transfused with dramatic and aesthetic effects as to 'disenfranchise' the congregation. It was intended to bring about the union of earthly and heavenly existence: God, in the person of his priests, appeared in the church, symbolizing the universe, as an unapproachable, impersonal ruler, like the Basileus. He approached the faithful from the altar in the apse, and embraced and encircled them, descending from heaven in the bright central space beneath the dome, where the actions of the priests symbolized his passage through time and space. The congregation played a passive role, not remaining still in one spot, but standing, with arms hanging down, only occasionally bowing their heads or making the sign of the cross. They were also silent, the texts spoken and sung by the congregation in the early Church here being taken over by the choir.

A specific court liturgy with elaborate theatrical effects developed in the Hagia Sophia, which differed from the forms of service used in parish and monastic churches and predominating in Russia, too, until the eleventh century. The Basileus enjoyed the privilege of taking part in the eucharist as an 'actor', like the ordained priests. In the ceremonial of some of the great church festivals, such as the rite of washing the feet on Maundy Thursday, or the commemoration of the Entry into Jerusalem on Palm Sunday, he even represented the person of Christ. When he did not have an active part to play in the service he sat in the well-lit tribunes with his attendants. He was literally raised up above the people and placed directly in the light. Tribunes were built wherever the political concepts and the architecture of the Byzantine court were taken as models: in the imperial rotundas and westworks of Western Europe and in the princely cathedrals of Russia. The 'sacred stage' and the hierarchic arrangement of the interior reflected the claims of the governing class, which considered itself alone able and justified to take actions that were denied to the common people.

The domed stone vault had been used 'since time immemorial in the East, where wood is scarce, as the primitive utilitarian form' (Philipp Schweinfurth). From being used to roof martyrs' shrines (martyria) and baptisteries it was taken over in the structure of churches and gained a mystical significance as a symbol of the dome of heaven, the dwelling-place of God. To this end it was of course necessary to alter the original construction so as to replace the effect of oppressive mass with one of floating weightlessness, and the task was further complicated by the fact that the dome was being built over a basilica, and not a rotunda. The transition from the circle to the square or rectangular groundplan was another Eastern invention: it was accomplished by means of pendentives, spandrels in the form of spherical triangles, at each corner, of which second and third-century examples have survived in Syria and which probably originated in Egypt, or of squinches, a kind of corbelled fan-vaulting, of Persian origin. Both methods were used in Byzantine buildings and were adopted by early Russian architects; though, as in the Hagia Sophia, pendentives remained the general rule, as the more effective method.

The theocratic spirit and the observation of the court hierarchy in the performance of services in the 'Great Church' exercised a strong influence on the spatial structure of the monumental cathedrals in Kiev, Novgorod and Polotsk, dedicated, like their model, to Divine Wisdom. They display the same spatial and social differentiations, the same majestic proportions. N. Brunov, who has helped to clarify the connection between the spatial interplay and the character of the 'sacred stage', estimates that the predominance of solid three-dimensionalism over optical and spatial illusionism, already observable

1 *Kiev, Cathedral of St Sophia. Nave, central dome and altar, 11th century, seen from the west tribune; iconostasis, mid 18th century*

in St Sophia in Kiev, is due to the influence of the architectural principles of the Christian East. As a result of that influence the structural elements and surfaces were comprehended in their solid mass and cubic weight and were incorporated into the whole as independent forms.

The Development of the Domed Cruciform Plan

Early Russian architecture did not derive directly, as is often thought, from the early Byzantine model of Hagia Sophia, but from the later, middle Byzantine, domed cruciform plan, which amalgamated the formal models of Hagia Sophia with those of other archetypes in the capital city or elsewhere in the east. Even in Constantinople experiments were made in the time of Justinian with other means of illuminating and separating the central area and linking it with the dome: the 'ambulatory church' (SS Sergios and Bacchos, 527–32) and the cruciform, domed church (Church of the Apostles, 536–46). In them, as in the Hagia Sophia, principles of the basilica and of the central plan intermingled, and the architectonic character was governed by whichever of the two predominated. The definitive form of the domed cruciform plan finally developed in the eighth and ninth centuries under the influence of the eastern frontier provinces. The capital city was invaded by the popular, solid, three-dimensional provincial style, which ran counter to optical and spatial illusionism. It characterized in equal measure the basilicas of Syria, the barrel-vaulted, cruciform churches of Armenia, and the broad churches of Mesopotamia. The complex spatial unity of early Byzantine architecture broke up into ensembles of additive 'cells', without the 'stage' beneath the central dome being abandoned.

The domed cruciform plan combined the 'classical' traditions upheld by the court bureaucracy with the popular and monastic traditions of the Oriental school. After the Iconoclastic Controversy of 726–843 had been settled by the Empress Theodora, and after the resolutions of the Seventh Ecumenical Council (787) condemning iconoclasm had once again been confirmed, monasticism was able once more to spread without hindrance. The monks were the most ardent and successful champions of the popular iconolatry. The victory of the orthodox over the iconoclasts ushered in the 'age of monastic renown' – as contemporaries called this period of Byzantine history. It is true that with the empire's inner decay and the continuous erosion of its frontiers by Turkish onslaughts even the governing class had to moderate its pretensions. A process of de-monumentalization took place in architecture. By contrast with the immensity of Hagia Sophia the domed cruciform plan settled for small, intimate dimensions. The average length of buildings was about 40 feet and the diameter of the principal dome between 16 and 17 feet. The prototype was the Nea Ekklesia ('new church') of Basileios I in Constantinople, consecrated in 881, though this was actually rather larger than the average. It has not survived but the detailed description by the Patriarch Photius may refer to it. The Hagia Sophia, for all its imposing size, remained almost entirely free of exterior decoration or articulation. The domed cruciform church accorded some importance to its external appearance, though without relieving its mass. It took on a low, wide and heavy form under the dictates of a frugal, geometric style. The simpler, ascetic requirements of the monks and their liturgy altered the proportions and forms of the 'dominant' design: as the dimensions shrank the length of the nave was reduced in favour of the central space, the basilica was swallowed up by the centripetal form.

The victory of the domed cruciform plan over all other types, which survived only in the provinces or as noticeable exceptions, also represented an ideological resolution of the same period: the dispute that centred on Patriarch Photius aggravated the differences between the Roman Catholic and the Orthodox churches, leading to the Great Schism

2 Kiev, Cathedral of St Sophia. Mosaic in the main dome, mid 11th century: Pantocrator

of 1054 which endures to the present day. The plan of the central circular dome above a square base became a characteristic of the whole Orthodox area while the long basilica oriented on a single axis became the rule in Western Europe – though there were exceptions to suit particular functions in both halves of Christendom. But just as the popular and monastic influence did nothing to diminish the mystery of the liturgical drama but rather only added elements of the monastic offices to it, so in middle Byzantine architecture there was still a counterpoise to the solid three-dimensional character even if it was not actually reduced. The mass of a building was still dominated by the same linear frontality as is found in painting of the period, until a renewed sublimation of style took place in the eleventh and twelfth centuries.

The balance of the relationship between space and mass was only changed permanently in early Russian architecture. Like the Germanic tribes, the East Slavs had a preference for the stern, massive composition, more in sympathy with their own folk art, and – in the decorative arts – for the ornamental stylization of the Oriental school. It is believed that even so early a building as the Desyatinnaya church in Kiev showed this influence. But it was the effect of autochthonous traditions that brought an end to the primacy of the interior and, above all, the principle of dematerialization. The proportions became susceptible to anthropomorphic comparison. The structure was dominated by an organic massiveness and verticality, so that the geometric tensions were also relaxed. The effect of the walls is of thick shells. And when the interior gained importance once more – as with the rise of Moscow in the fifteenth century and during the process of secularization in the seventeenth – it retained nonetheless a relatively enclosed, stable composition. Even the vertical dynamic seems to be rooted in the earth and to be bound in the thickness of the walls. While outer shapes were decoratively articulated with the numerous variants of different stylistic periods, interiors usually retained the character of 'spatial mass' (Brunov).

The Structure of the Domed Cruciform Church

The basic groundplan of the domed cruciform church is an assemblage of three times three square 'cells', separated by arcades. It is a Greek cross (that is, with the arms of equal length) placed within a square or rectangular frame. The principal dome rises above the central crossing, supported on the arches between the pillars and on a drum furnished with windows, the transition from square to circle being made by pendentives or squinches. The four arms of the cross are roofed by barrel vaults. The four corner areas between them have barrel vaulting (which may lie either east-west or north-south), groin vaulting, corbelled vaulting, a segmental vault or a higher domical vault, so that the appearance from the outside is either of one central dome or of a group of four smaller domes encircling the higher, central one. According to the positioning of the arches and the type of vaulting, the cells can merge to form a single area enlivened by the play of light and shade, rigidify as sectional spaces enclosed on every side, or a dynamic gradation towards the main dome can create an upward thrust, whereby the possibilities are multiplied.

The basic directional flow is that of the vertical elements of the central area. All the surrounding cells are subordinated in greater or lesser degree to the principal dome above the crossing. But the other spatial co-ordinates are not without influence. There is a rudiment of basilical form at ground level in the movement from the west end towards the apses at the east, where the bema (sanctuary and presbytery) is housed. The naos, the space for the congregation, takes the form of a central nave flanked by side aisles. A transept is formed at right angles by the crossing and the north and south arms of the cross. The arms of the cross are normally the length of the radius of the principal dome. The apses are added to the basic plan of the nine cells, but occasionally form part of it, taking the place of the eastern arm of the cross and the east corner cells. The bays of the vaulting correspond to the cells. The supports are usually square, octagonal or cruciform. The horizontal thrust is countered structurally not only by the strength of the crossing arches and pillars but also by the conjunction of the barrel vaults. The arms of the cross are often given further support by the corner cells being raised less high – a trend which originated in the Oriental school and became a characteristic of the Russian style.

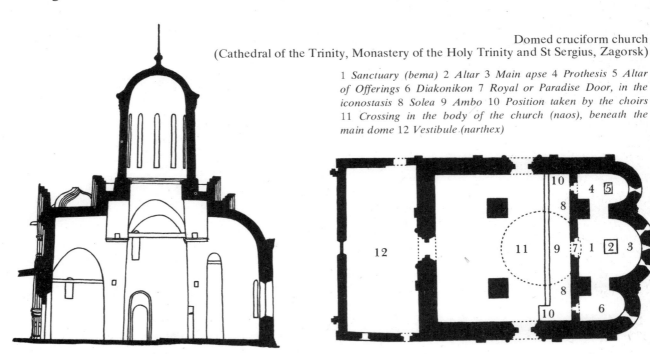

Domed cruciform church
(Cathedral of the Trinity, Monastery of the Holy Trinity and St Sergius, Zagorsk)

1 *Sanctuary (bema)* 2 *Altar* 3 *Main apse* 4 *Prothesis* 5 *Altar of Offerings* 6 *Diakonikon* 7 *Royal or Paradise Door, in the iconostasis* 8 *Solea* 9 *Ambo* 10 *Position taken by the choirs* 11 *Crossing in the body of the church (naos), beneath the main dome* 12 *Vestibule (narthex)*

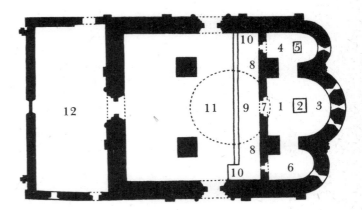

The bema, which can be identified with the chancel, opens from the crossing as a high, wide area, while, if the east corner cells are low in construction, the pastophoria (prothesis and diakonikon) within them, coming at the ends of the side aisles, almost escape notice. In five-domed churches and in the three-domed buildings found in the Moscow region, on the other hand, each of these cells has a dome over it, more in keeping with their liturgical importance. The movement from west to east is interrupted by the altar screen or the iconostasis, which stands directly in front of the east arch of the crossing, the Triumph Arch. The bema may be restricted to the main apse, but it usually extends into the east arm of the cross, with no sense of a division from the apse itself. Similarly the side apses form single units with the corner cells. The prothesis and the diakonikon behind the screen are linked to the bema by archways and sometimes form an unbroken spatial unit with it. The church may be extended by three additional cells at the west end, creating the vestibule (narthex), which, if it is divided off by an arcaded screen rather than a wall, raises the number of supports to six. There are sometimes as many as five relatively separate areas along the west-east axis: the exterior porch or gallery, the (outer) exo-narthex, the (inner) eso-narthex forming the pro-naos, the aisle and the sanctuary (as in the katholikon of Hosios Lukas). A widening of the church to five aisles occurs in association with a narthex at the west end and a total of twelve pillars. The tribunes are placed at the west end or are arranged in a horseshoe round the west arm of the cross. A kind of vaulting without any sharp-angled ridges or groins is common in Russia, especially in exterior galleries and vestibules, which can be described as a barrel vault with intersecting segments of vaulting at the narrow ends and flattened in the centre, and with spandrels over the doors and windows, and which is known as a somknuty svod (closed vault).

The interior, lit by the narrow windows in the drums below the domes but more effectively by candles in holders fixed to the walls or in chandeliers, is luxuriantly decorated. In addition to the colours of the polished stone of the floors and the base of the walls and supports, and the ornamentation on the pillars, columns and archways, there are the mosaics, frescos and icons, which normally cover every surface with large, grandiose compositions or small-scale intimate images. As well as subjects of Christian iconography there are elaborate patterns of flowers and foliage and painting which emphasizes structural elements by brilliant colouring or gilding. Pot-shaped cavities lined with clay, called golosniki (resonators), are often incorporated in the vaulting to lessen the weight, and in the upper part of the walls to improve the acoustic resonance. They had already been described by Vitruvius in Book 5, Chapter 5 of his *De architectura* and were known in the West, from the fourth century (Sankt Gereon, Cologne) to the late Carolingian period. Arranged in rows, their effect is both to relieve mass and tension and to decorate (for instance in Grodno and Pskov), if they do not disappear altogether in the rest of the ornamentation.

The nine-cell nucleus forms a cube or flatter square block. At particular periods in the history of early Russian architecture relatively independent spatial units were added: chapels, galleries, a refectory (trapeznaya), a bell-tower. The principle of symmetry was gradually replaced by asymmetry, until the stage was reached of the multifarious silhouettes, with their delightful intersections, typical of the seventeenth century. Sometimes the external appearance reveals the nature of the inner structure: in other cases it is a decorative disguise. This exemplifies two tendencies in the stylistic development of Russian architecture. One tendency is, generally speaking, in the direction of simultaneous and linear, 'classical' formations, the other towards successive and painterly, 'baroque' formations. The lesenes and pilasters may correspond to the positions of the interior supports, the gables and blind arches may echo the forms of the vaulting or, as H. Weidhaas has shown, they and other elements may be distributed without regard to space, mass, function or technics, so that structural forms are actually turned into something unstructural. The 'wavy roof' is characteristic of this: in order to give the building as a whole an appearance of regularity and consistency, rounded gables (zakomari) were given even to those sections of the wall that, to agree with the form of the vault, should have had angular gables with straight edges. These 'pseudo-zakomari' are found, for example, on the exterior of barrel-vaulted corner cells, on an east-west or a north-south line, according to the direction of the ridge of the vault.

Where the influences of the Byzantine capital or of the Italian Renaissance were felt (as in St Sophia in Kiev, or the Cathedral of the Assumption in the Kremlin in Moscow), the structure of the building is a regular casing surrounding the interior space, but where the influence of the native timber architecture asserted itself, the organic structural thickness is worked from within to provide an irregular shell. (There is a powerful contrast in the wooden churches between the squat, low spatial cells and the gigantic towers.) The transference of the forms of wooden architecture to stone was an effortful, complicated process. Incongruities arose constantly, not in the relationship of exterior and interior alone, but also in that of structure to decoration. The overemphasis given to the decoration and to the visible evidence of the articulation of the façades and the lavish ornamentation led to the abandonment of structural unity, witnessed by the interruption of pilasters by niches, the presence of a string course where there was no corresponding horizontal division on the interior, the erection of towers over wide vaults, the decorative effect of the surfaces of the roof, the tiers of blind or purely ornamental gables, the notching of arches at the most prominent point of the curve.

Numerous different kinds of fabric are found in the walls. The oldest churches in south Russia are built in the *opus mixtum,* alternating courses of brick, rubble and quarry stone;

then there is pure brick and mortar, the latter sometimes in very thick layers; rubble; ashlar-cut tuff and limestone, as in Vladimir-Suzdal and Moscow; quarry stone, as in Novgorod and Pskov; there is tile inlay in brickwork, as in Yaroslavl; and there is the white plaster commonly used in the later centuries. A typical feature of building in Novgorod from the fourteenth century onwards is the contrast of pilasters, pillars and decorative elements in brick with the stone walls, while in Moscow these elements are done in white hewn stone that contrasts with the brick walls. Stones vary in shape and size from place to place. The mortar is usually mixed with fragments of brick or brick dust, so that it looks pink. This is a relic of an old Roman technique, that has also been found in the region of Aachen, whereby the water retained by the fragments of brick bound the lime in the correct proportions.

The polychrome building materials added to the ornamentation: since the walls were not originally plastered the striped fabric made its full effect. Apart from where ashlar-cut limestone was used, courses of brick or stone or both usually alternate with layers of pink-tinged mortar. The variation of light and shade, according to the weather or degree of sunlight, is modified or intensified by the colour contrasts, as well as by the numerous niches, friezes, windows, nalichniki, other ornaments and reliefs. The ornamental style of the sixteenth and seventeenth centuries was based on the contrast between the carved limestone and the red masonry, and even bricks were moulded. Roofing materials included lead, planks and wooden shingles, tiles, and later, particularly, sheet tin. The gleaming gold or deep blue of the domes contributed to the play of colour and light over the whole fabric of the building.

Historical and Stylistic Periods

The 'dominant' type of sacred building in medieval Russia was the type of the socially dominant class: the cathedrals built by and for the courts and the princes. Their great size alone was intended to overawe the common people. They were erected on sites where they represented the identification of church and state authority, or commemorated 'Christian' military campaigns and victories. In the 'Golden Age' of Kievan Rus, Yaroslav the Wise (1019–45) himself laid the foundation stone of the Cathedral of St Sophia in 1037, on the spot where he had defeated the asiatic Pechenegs, and the light of 'divine wisdom' had dispersed the clouds of 'heathen darkness'. The fate of St Sophia in Novgorod (1045–52) was so closely associated with that of the townspeople that the first of the city's chronicles declares: 'Where St Sophia is, there is Novgorod also.' Even the warcry was 'For St Sophia!'. The Cathedral of the Assumption in Vladimir (1158–60/1185–89), like the famous icon of the Virgin it housed and the newly instituted feast of the Virgin of the Intercession, served the claims of Andrey Bogolyubsky and Vsevolod III to supremacy in Russia and the independence of the Russian state. The cathedral in Kolomna, also dedicated to the Assumption (1379–82), was commissioned by Dmitry Donskoi. It became the monument to the victory over the Mongolian and Tartar hordes of Mamai on the field of Kulikovo in 1380. The principal cathedral of Russia, the Cathedral of the Assumption in the Kremlin in Moscow (1475–79), was built to celebrate the subjugation of Novgorod, the overtures of peace made by the Khan, Ivan III's success in centralizing the government and international recognition of his rule. The Cathedral of the Icon of the Virgin of Smolensk in the New Convent of the Virgin in Moscow was built by Vasily III in 1524–25 to celebrate the liberation of Smolensk from the Poles and Lithuanians.

It was the 'tent-roof' style of the sixteenth century in particular that represented the political ambitions of the young power of the tsars and the rising national consciousness of the independent and unified Russian empire. The Church of the Ascension in Kolomenskoye (1530–32) was built in honour of the birth of the long-awaited heir to Vasily III, the future Ivan IV, the Church of St John the Baptist in Dyakovo (1547) on the occasion of Ivan IV's official coronation and his marriage to Anastasia Romanov, the Cathedral of the Virgin of the Intercession (St Basil the Blessed) on Red Square (1555–60) as a monument to the taking of Kazan, the conclusive victory over the asiatic invaders, and as a symbol of the Heavenly Jerusalem, a parallel to the conception of 'Moscow, the third Rome'. The same idea continued to dominate the court architecture of the seventeenth century: the rebuilding of the Moscow Kremlin, the projects instigated by the tsar outside Moscow, Patriarch Nikon's Monastery of the New Jerusalem. The ecclesiastical reforms instigated by Nikon (1652–67) with the full support of Tsar Alexey, which were the cause of the Raskol, the schism within the Russian Orthodox church, were not merely a matter of conforming to late Byzantine practices in church and reviving Byzantine ceremonial at court: they also involved the introduction of drastic new building regulations which, in the austere monumental shape of the five-domed Cathedral of the Assumption in Moscow, re-affirmed the spirit of theocracy. Nikon only fell from power because he attempted to assert the pre-eminence of the spiritual authority.

Quite apart from the fact that, as became particularly clear in the seventeenth century, the official buildings of the state and the state church drew on the riches of folk art and their symbolic function would be unimaginable without the co-operation and acceptance of the people, there were other, no less important trends, originating 'from below', even as early as the eleventh century. They were represented by the monks of the Orthodox church, who were close to the common people and advocated reformist movements to them. The asceticism of monastic rules, in particular, demanded a simpler, more intimate style of building. The early Russian chroniclers make a distinction between the monasteries founded by princely donors and those built by hermits: 'There are many monasteries erected by kings or boyars or with great wealth, but they are not like those which are founded with tears and fasting and prayer and watching.' Nevertheless even the monasteries endowed by princes had to be more modest and austere in their style.

Architectural Types of Kievan Rus

Thus the structure of St Sophia in Kiev, with its many domes, five aisles and twelve pillars, the first form assumed by the court art of medieval Russia and the prototype for an architectural school (Novgorod, Polotsk), was overtaken by another pattern: the Cathedral of the Assumption (1073–78) in the Kiev Monastery of the Caves, founded by Prince Svyatoslav Yaroslavovich, with its six pillars and three aisles and a tauter handling of the space, became the model for a very large number of other court, monastic and urban cathedrals. St Sophia was the seat of the metropolitan, who was appointed by the patriarch in Constantinople, was usually a Greek and represented Byzantine interests, while the Monastery of the Caves developed into a centre of opposition to him, representing national, Russian interests. The monastery did not even shrink from opposing the princes, when they placed dynastic disagreements above the interests of the realm and the well-being of the people. The patriotism and identification with the common people had some influence on the tendency towards realism, which also found expression in the literature and icon painting of the Monastery of the Caves. It can be traced throughout the subsequent development of Russian architecture up to the seventeenth century. The plain dimensions and harmonious proportions, conforming to a human scale, are typical of it. The articulation of façades and spatial units is clearer. The decoration afforded by arcaded galleries constantly occurs, but the more complicated methods of ornamentation (belts of stepped niches and meander friezes) disappear, leaving only blind arcades and dwarf galleries. The tower enclosing the stairs up to the interior galleries often shrinks to a doorway in the thickness of the west or north wall. The baptisteries previously added to the exterior of churches were transferred inside.

A simultaneous development was the spread of a more intimate type of parish church, with four pillars and a single dome, originating in the smaller monasteries, whose monks were members of the lower classes. The type is found in two basic variants: a 'linear' variant, cuboid, weightily proportioned, with a 'wave roof' and additive space (as in the Cathedral of the Transfiguration in Pereslavl-Zalessky, 1152–57); and a painterly variant with graceful, slender proportions, a pyramidal shape thanks to stepped gables, corbelled vaulting and a general impression of spatial unification (as in the Pyatnitsa Church in Chernigov); the distinctions arose from the relative strength of the influence of the Oriental school of Byzantine architecture, and that of Russian timber architecture. In the former case there was an almost total absence of ornament, in the latter folk-art motifs were used abundantly.

The divisive effect of feudalism from the mid eleventh century onwards moved the province of the simpler, de-monumentalized type from the monasteries and parishes to such of the princely courts as had to be careful in their expenditure (SS Boris and Gleb in Kideksha, 1152, built during the rise of the princes of Vladimir-Suzdal, and the Church of the Saviour in Nereditsa, 1198, built during the decline of the princes of Novgorod). On the other hand it was taken up, in a new concern for restraint, by a new source of opposition, the urban middle classes who, in Novgorod, even deposed their ruler in 1136. Feudalism brought territorial schools of architecture in its train, each modifying the legacy of Kiev: Chernigov, Volynia and Galicia, Polotsk and Smolensk, Vladimir-Suzdal, Novgorod and Pskov.

Churches of the Princes of Vladimir-Suzdal

The six-pillar type and the two variants of the four-pillar type together indicated the course of development in the eleventh and twelfth centuries. The same development was pursued at other levels, historical and social. The desire of princes to build monuments to their own wealth and power was challenged as time went by by a similar desire on the part of the patrician class, which later combined with the taste of the Posad (the lower middle class occupants of town suburbs) and the peasants. Andrey Bogolyubsky (1157–75) and, after his assassination, his brother Vsevolod III (1177–1212), known as the Mighty Thicket on account of his many sons, tried to move the Russian capital to their principality 'beyond the forests', to Vladimir on the Klyazma. They set in motion an ambitious building programme, under which the town grew rapidly, in an attempt – vain, as it turned out – to create a metropolis that would be independent of Constantinople. From Vladimir, in an alliance with the citizens, they waged war against the particularist ambitions of the old hereditary nobility, the boyars, and against the divisiveness of the feudal system. The Cathedral of the Assumption, built on the six-pillar model of the Monastery of the Caves in Kiev, was conceived as the centre, not of the city only, but of the whole of Russia. On the other hand, the little court church on the River Nerl, dedicated to the Virgin of the Intercession (1165), was representative of the single-dome, four-pillar type, with three apses and a west tribune; the slenderer, elongated form of the building, the raising of the dome, the slim, harmonious proportions and a vertical rhythm in the ornamentation produced an elegant, poetic effect, an impression of reaching upwards. The theocratic illusionism of the interior was repeated on the exterior. In the skilled hands of local and foreign masons, and with the assimilation of Romanesque, Byzantine and Transcaucasian influences, façades were transformed into a relief tapestry, with iconographic programmes that represented Vsevolod's concept of government and interpreted religious dogmas in popular terms (Cathedral of St Demetrius in Vladimir, 1194–97). At the same time the articulation became more elaborate and more ornamental.

The architecture of Vladimir-Suzdalian Rus seems to have undergone a process of change between the middle of the twelfth century (Cathedral of the Transfiguration in Pereslavl-Zalessky, SS Boris and Gleb in Kideksha) and the early thirteenth century (St George in Yuryev-Polsky, 1230–34), comparable to the transition from Romanesque to Gothic. But the evolution from the simple to the complex never led to the transcendency of Gothic architecture, the veiling of the structure and the dissipation of the surfaces of the walls. It is true that the ogee arch is found in St George in Yuryev-Polsky, and that the sculptural decoration of this cathedral marks the beginning of a new stylistic period, but the articulation of the structural forms came to a standstill. Even the term 'Russian Romanesque', which some historians have used on the grounds of the common Byzantine legacy and similar developmental trends, should be approached with caution. Gothic constructional processes remained totally alien to medieval Russian architecture, which was more inclined to the massive than to the skeletal.

The independent and powerful feudal city-republic of Novgorod and its satellite Pskov preserved their architectural traditions intact during the Tartar invasions, for the thaw in the spring of 1238 forced the hordes of Batu Khan's cavalry to turn back when they were a hundred versts away. The other parts of the country suffered severely under the foreign rule, which lasted until the end of the fifteenth century, though it was unable to suppress the creative energy of the Russian people. The Cathedral of St Sophia (1045–52), a somewhat simplified version of the Kievan model, with twelve pillars, five aisles but only five domes, was less typical of the Novgorod style than the two cathedrals in the monasteries of St Anthony (1117–19) and St George (1119–30), both with six pillars and three aisles, characterised by the asymmetrical arrangement of the three domes (over the crossing, the south-west corner and the tower added at the north-west corner), and by the objectivity, simplicity and clarity of their articulation and ornament. These were all still the monumental foundations of princes, but with the shift in the distribution of power from the thirteenth century onwards, an increasing number of churches were commissioned by the merchants, the guilds and the street communities. Their wishes, in full appreciation of the more modest monastic forms and influenced by Central and Northern European models, were met by the small, intimate type of the cuboid church, built on an almost square groundplan, with four pillars, one dome, one apse, a west tribune, no articulation of the façades and little mural decoration. The kind of roofs that had been common hitherto, with a 'wave' profile following the round gables (zakomari) or blind arches, now gave place to a trefoil profile, corresponding to the vaulting: barrel vaulting over the arms of the cross, flanked in each corner by the arc of a quarter of a circle (St Nicholas, Lipna, 1292). The extensive cellarage was used partly for services in winter and partly as storage space.

After the repulsion of the Swedes (in 1240) and the Teutonic Knights (in 1242) by Alexander Nevsky, trade and commerce—in which the Golden Horde was also interested—were able to develop freely. The citizens of Novgorod were known throughout Russia for their shrewdness, diligence, enterprise and prosperity. They undertook the colonization of the vast regions between the Baltic and the White Seas, with their immense animal and mineral resources, and created the economic and political basis of a city-state of the kind that in Western Europe first arose in Italy. The archbishop of Novgorod enjoyed a unique position, as head of the city government, as the most powerful feudal lord, and in the church, from 1165, ranking second only to the metropolitan, whom he often challenged. The combination of religion and a citizen culture gave birth to a simple, prosaic and vigorous architectural style. The churches of Novgorod resembled her citizens: sturdy and strong, confident and shrewd. When the desire to make a more positive

The Churches of Novgorod and Pskov

3 *Novgorod, Cathedral of St Sophia in the Kremlin, 1045–52: view of the south front with the staircase-tower adjoining to the west*

assertion of civic pride was felt, a rich decorational effect was achieved economically by the outlines of porches, blind arches, tiers of niches and windows, friezes, crosses and rosettes (St Theodore Stratilates, 1360–61). Somewhat later the roof with a trefoil profile was replaced by pointed gables, giving eight sloping surfaces (Church of the Transfiguration in the Street of Elijah, 1374), without profoundly affecting the overall appearance. The heretical movement of the Strigolniki, which arose in artisan circles and had an influence, through its social protest and de-mythologizing, on icon and mural painting, has left no traces in church architecture. On the other hand, the resistance of the patrician class to the Great Prince of Moscow's claim to his 'ancestral inheritance' produced a conservative reversion to the forms that had been current during the city's rise to power (St John the Baptist 'on the rock', 1453).

In theory the legislative power in Great Novgorod, until its incorporation into Muscovy in 1478, lay in the Veche, but in practice the city-state was governed by the 'Lords' Council' of boyars and patricians, under the presidency of the archbishop. Pskov, which became independent of Novgorod in 1348, was more truly democratic, and the craft and trade guilds exercised real influence. The little churches built by the citizens were in a popular style, with the snugness of the people's wooden houses: a cube in shape, four pillars, one dome, simple ornamentation on the apses and the drum (a typical pattern was a frieze of three bands of square and triangular depressions). In spite of the modesty of aspiration, painterly effects were achieved through the 'soft' treatment of the forms (the walls and the decorated stonework are of porous Permian limestone), numerous asymmetrical additions and the striking Pskov bell-gables. The subsidiary apses that had disappeared in Novgorod were re-introduced, as were a relatively spacious vestibule and lateral chapels and exterior galleries, under the influence of wooden architecture. They had the effect of enlarging the small area of the church by the addition of extra spatial compartments (St Basil 'on the hill', 1413; Church of the Epiphany, Zapskovye, 1496). A new method of vaulting that dispensed with pillars by the construction of corbelled and intersecting arches (St Nicholas 'by the wall', c1500), served the same purpose. The type of bell-gable that first developed in Novgorod is a more monumental structure than is usually meant by the term. It is built on to the vestibule, or is free-standing (Church of the Assumption 'by the ferry', 1521), and the bells are hung in the openings of a stone arcade, depending from a crossbeam, the whole under a pitched roof. Although Pskov was absorbed by Muscovy in 1510, the city preserved its independent architectural tradition until the seventeenth century. Its architects were famous over a wide area and were even summoned to Moscow to help in the rebuilding of the Kremlin.

The Gathering of the Russian Land

Ever since Ivan Kalita (1325–40) secured a position of privilege under the Golden Horde by his skilful policies, and Dmitry Donskoi (1359–89) registered the first decisive defeat of the Tartar overlords at the battle of Kulikovo, the Great Princes stood at the head of the national struggle for liberation and the 'Gathering of the Russian Land'. Their importance was underlined by the removal of the metropolitan see in 1328 to Moscow from Vladimir, where it had moved from Kiev thirty years before. The hierarchy of the Russian clergy and the coenobite monks, closely allied to the Muscovite princes for patriotic and theocratic reasons, helped them in the establishment of a centralized state. The fate of Sergius of Radonezh (1314–92) and the Monastery of the Holy Trinity that he founded to the north-east of Moscow in about 1340 is typical: the anchorite was made the patron saint of Moscow, blessed the army of Dmitry Donskoi and supported the repression of the feudal revolts. The little hermitage

4 Novgorod, Church of St Nicholas, Lipna, 1292: view from the south-east

became a 'lavra', one of the great monasteries, and devoted itself to propagating the ideas of the Great Princes.

The national resurgence demanded a new architecture. It developed between the 1360s and the 1420s, mainly in the monasteries (Cathedral of the Trinity in the Monastery of the Holy Trinity and St Sergius, Zagorsk, 1422–23). The architects employed by the Muscovite rulers picked up the threads of the Vladimir-Suzdalian tradition, in accordance with official policy, and injected it with the greater simplicity and dynamic energy of folk art. The twelfth century provided them with both the four pillar type of court church, with one dome and three apses, after the model of the Cathedral of St Demetrius in Vladimir, and the pyramidal vaulting and roofing of the Pyatnitsa Church in Chernigov. The silhouette of the body of the church, with its fronts given the traditional three vertical divisions, was graduated in a manner that could even dissipate the cuboid form altogether (as in the Cathedral of the Saviour in the Andronikov Monastery of the Saviour in Moscow, 1422–23): stepped rows of round and blind arches correspond to, or disguise, corbelled arches in the interior. The arches of the crossing rise above the intersections of the barrel vaults, which are in turn higher than the vaulting over the apses and the corners of the building. The west tribune and rigid spatial divisions went, and a unification of space was achieved, with central orientation and a dynamic, upward movement. The pillars supporting the dome were moved slightly to the east and the central drum, the principal source of light, grew in diameter. A new form of portal also evolved: three pairs of columns with 'melons' in the middle of the shafts alternated with squared pillars in the recessed door surround. The ogee arch started to become the predominant decorative element.

'Moscow, the Third Rome'

Ivan III, the Great (1462–1505), pursued the policy of unification. After he had annexed Rostov, Yaroslavl and Novgorod and had signified his intention of paying no more tribute to the Golden Horde, which was gradually disintegrating through internal dissension, in 1480, he was able to sign himself 'Tsar and Autocrat of all Russia'. Through the autocephaly proclaimed by the episcopal synods in Moscow in 1448 and 1459, and the final collapse of the Byzantine empire (1453), he not only won full spiritual power in his own church, but also became the head of the whole Orthodox church. He used his marriage to Sophia Paleologos, the niece of the last Basileus, in 1472, to give genealogical legitimacy to his assumption of the theocratic inheritance. The adoption of the Byzantine double eagle in the Muscovite arms and the revival of Byzantine court ceremonial were parallel acts.

The central power was made even more secure and given further religious sanction under Vasily III (1505–33). Joseph of Volokolamsk (1439–1515), an abbot and an aristocrat, declared that the tsar was 'placed upon his throne by God . . . his power like the power of God', and that his authority was final even in spiritual matters. And the monk Filofei of Pskov (died 1547) claimed that the first Rome had been doomed to fall because of its heresies, the second because it formed a union with the first (Union of Florence, 1439); the third, Moscow, would alone stand firm 'and there will never be a fourth'. This clerical exaltation of the ruler was not mere sycophancy but an exhortation to protect the church's traditional status, which seemed to be imperilled by bitter social dissensions. The uprisings (such as the one of 1547 in Moscow), the first intimations of the early Enlightenment, the heretical movement of the 'Judaizers' and the opposition of 'disinterested' ascetics to the monasteries, ownership of property and state regimentation, led the established church to demand – and to get – an efficient inquisition, set up by the tsar.

From the fifteenth century onwards the development of Russian architecture was led by Moscow. It was a melting-pot for the widest possible variety of influences, but imposed its own culture on the other provinces with ever increasing energy. An all-Russian style evolved as a consequence of the political centralization. Even its inception in the fifteenth century was affected by the theocratic principle, which subjected the simple forms of early Muscovite monastic building to differentiation and heroic sublimation. The basement-storey was important, raising the churches up on a podium, surrounding them on three sides with terraces or galleries and creating an effect of awe-inspiring isolation. Probably under the influence of Sophia, Ivan III summoned a large number of Italian architects (such as Rodolfo – known as Aristotle – Fioravanti, Pietro Solario, Alovisio Novo), who were all known as fryazi (Franks) in Russia and who contrived to master the new style. The first 'patrons' arose among the native architects, a class of building contractors (such as V. D. Yermolin), who contributed to the gradual replacement of stone by brick, as the quicker and cheaper building material.

Immense resources were drawn upon in the building of the Kremlin, the fortress-palace, in Moscow. In its early phase the new court style in sacred architecture married the monumental line of the Vladimir-Suzdalian tradition (Cathedral of the Assumption) to the principles of the Italian Renaissance, and achieved the stern, majestic solemnity and the spaciousness of the six-pillar type with three aisles and five domes (Cathedral of the Assumption in the Moscow Kremlin). The style was repeated in the monumental palace buildings, and the monastery cathedrals, with the Quattrocento ornamentation of the Cathedral of the Archangel Michael (1505–08), notably the arrangement of pilasters, the horizontal division of façades and the form of the windows. The four-pillar type was not abandoned: it is found with one dome and no tribunes in the metropolitan's palace church, dedicated to the Miracle of the Virgin's Veil (1484–86), and with five domes and a west tribune in the tsar's palace church, the Cathedral of the Annunciation (1484–89). The harmonious integration and solidity, relieved only minimally by vertical forces, prevalent in Novgorod and Pskov, underwent an organic invigoration in

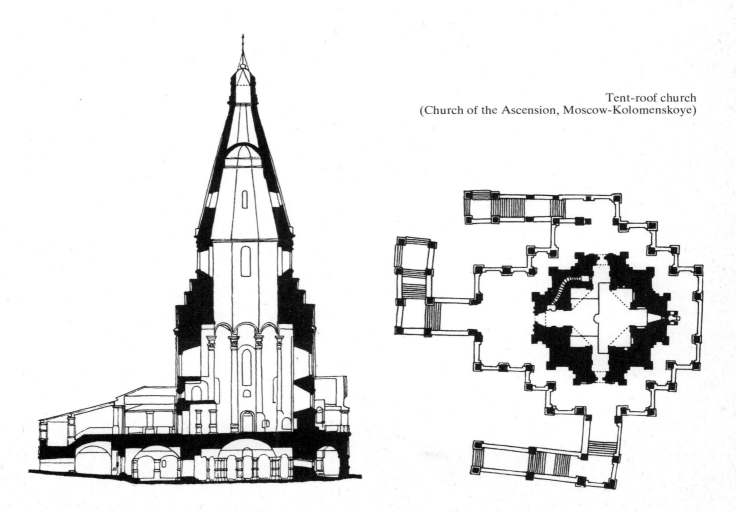

Tent-roof church
(Church of the Ascension, Moscow-Kolomenskoye)

early Muscovite monastic building, which was further enhanced by the decorative style of the school of Moscow court architects. The pedestal raising the central dome, the triple division of the facades by lesenes or pilasters, the columnar surrounds of recessed doorways were all adopted, but much enriched by ornamental details: blind gables, blind arcades, cornices, friezes, coffering. The ogee arch form asserted a strong influence, transforming the heavy, helmet-shaped dome that had been usual in Russia, into the lively 'onion', and drawing the round arch up to a point. It also shaped the blind gables that formed the outer casing to the new corbelled vaulting—called kokoshniki after a halfmoon-shaped women's hairstyle. They are arranged around the pedestal at the base of the dome in several, gradually diminishing tiers, so that the roofing displays a painterly disregard of the boundaries of form and rises pyramidally.

The Tent-Roof Church

The decisive stage in dynamic intensification through the strengthening of vertical forces came only in the sixteenth century, with the evolution of the type of the masonry tent-roof church, which achieved a spatial upsurge analogous to the political rise; and a spatial unification analogous to the 'Gathering of the Russian Land'. Early Russian architecture was revolutionised by a completely new style. Under the influence of wooden architecture, the body of the church was drawn up, as if by suction, by the tower, which rose with a rhythmic impetus and a wide variety of visual diversification to as much as 200 feet (for example the Church of the Ascension in Kolomenskoye, 1530–32). The interior, a single spatial entity, covered a relatively small area of ground, and the graduations of the vertical rhythm symbolized the play of 'lower' and 'upper' forces, between earthly and heavenly powers, between the social ethic and patriotic ideals of the people and the caesaropapism of the tsar. The affinity to the Gothic style is not the outcome of dematerialization or spiritualization, but lies in the urge to imitate nature as an organizing power. Thus the play of forces is to be understood as an embodiment of the Kingdom of God on earth, as a natural organism, and not as transcendent perfectionism, devaluing this world. The vertical structure spreads itself massively over the ground and grows upwards with the strength and natural vigour of a plant.

Ivan IV, called the Terrible or the Stern (grozny) (1533–84), began to reform the structure of the state from 'above'. He skilfully exploited the divisions within the church, playing off the ascetics against the 'Josephites' who supported ecclesiastical ownership of property. At first he made a pact with the representative of the latter, the Metropolitan Makary, where the interests of church and state coincided. Several councils met under Makary between 1547 and 1554, to discuss fundamental questions of church organization, ritual, theology, morals and art; the most important was the Synod of a Hundred Chapters, the Stoglav, of 1551. Administration and forms of worship were systematized, a list of new national saints was drawn up with Lives, the moral degeneracy of the monks and simony were decried, heretics and reformers (Matvey Bashkin and Feodosy Kossoy) were condemned.

Just as the tent-roof style broke open the traditional architectural canons, so 'sacred' painting was invaded by historical and contemporary subject matter (icons of the 'Church Militant') and portraits of individuals (especially of Ivan IV), with the official sanction of the conciliar decisions. The prime requirement of church art was that it should serve the glorification of the ruling house. The sumptuous Cathedral of the Virgin of the Inter-

5 *Suzdal, Kremlin, Cathedral of the Nativity of the Virgin. Four damascened panels on the west door, c. 1227–37: above left, the Raising of Lazarus; above right, Christ's Entry into Jerusalem; below left, Christ's Descent into Hell; below right, the Whitsun Miracle, the Descent of the Holy Ghost*
6 *(overleaf) Moscow, Kremlin, 15th–19th centuries. View from the south-east, over the Moskva, showing the fortifications, palace, cathedrals and bell-tower*

cession in Moscow attempted to reach a compromise between Byzantine, Oriental, Italian and traditional Russian architectural principles: between the dome and the tent roof, between vertical aspiration and ponderous massivity, between a painterly dissolution of outline and simultaneous linear forms, between 'earthly' and 'heavenly' symbolism.

The open conflict which broke out between Ivan IV and the church under Metropolitan Filip II, who was consequently deposed (1568), illustrates the rapidity with which the concepts and the operation of power were secularized. The cause was the division of the state into the Zemshchina, left to the old class of boyars, and the Oprichnina, directly subject to the tsar, and administered by the new service nobility. This did not so much upset the long-held theocratic theory of the unity of the state and government, as obstruct the ambitions of the church to hold land, which had also been opposed by Ivan III. In his correspondence with Prince Andrey Kurbsky (1564–79), who had fled to Poland to escape him, Ivan IV still used the term 'Holy Russia' in its traditional sense and claimed that God had given him unlimited power, for which he was accountable to no one. But his reform of the state was an act of secular absolutism, which was also evident in his political ideology, for instance, in his claim to linear descent from the Caesars.

Ecclesiastical architecture reflected the encroachment of secular influences. The churches built for the imperial court are distinguished by features that originated in fortress architecture (St John the Baptist in Dyakovo, Moscow, 1547), while the Posad quarter transmitted ideas originating in folk art and domestic architecture. There is a large number of different sixteenth-century types, but they can no longer be categorized by geographical distribution. In spite of their stylistic variations they are all stamped with a uniform, national character, known as the tsarist imperial style. In 1583 the tsar set up an office to supervise the steadily increasing number of masonry buildings being erected for the state; for even the cathedrals in the cities and the monasteries in the country were now being commisioned by the central government in Moscow. The forms officially approved were permeated 'from below' by the intimate popular style of buildings in the suburban quarters of Moscow, which influenced the churches not only of the monasteries and the landowners but even those of the court: exteriors, with a single dome and generally either a trefoil roof of the Novgorod type or a pyramid of blind gables, were attractive and domestic, and the specifically Russian form of the kreshchaty vault (a combination of barrel vaulting over a cruciform base and domical vaulting over the corners) made the small interiors a pillar-less spatial entity (Church of Triphon in Moscow-Naprudnoye, late fifteenth century).

The Painterly Style of the Seventeenth Century

After the Time of Troubles (1605–13), the uprising of the lower classes, the struggle for power among the aristocracy, and the Intervention of Poland, Lithuania and Sweden, it was not until the second quarter of the seventeenth century, at the end of the reign of Michael Romanov, that a new architectural style was able to evolve that swept away the traditional Byzantine schema once and for all. Elements that had already appeared individually in tent-roof churches and suburban churches in the sixteenth century, unfolded with the secularization of the national culture into a decorative, dynamic and painterly formal language that was quite original and modern in its tone. Ecclesiastical architecture was permeated by vigorous popular forces from the Posad and the peasantry, transmitted by means of wooden architecture. Popular taste was active even earlier in the construction of palaces for the governing classes. The increased privileges awarded to the new nobility, those who had been rewarded for service to the tsar, the new and sterner legislation on serfdom (1649), and the growing wealth of the great merchants had all helped to change the structure of that level of society. The governing ideology had

7 *Moscow, Kremlin, Cathedral of the Annunciation: icon of the Virgin, from the Deesis by Theophanes the Greek, 1405*

two contradictory aspects: on the one hand there was the attempt to throw off the authority of the church, on the other there was the conservativism that used the forms of secular art solely as a means of enriching ecclesiastical splendour. Art and architecture reached out for the vivid and the realistic, reflecting the riveting spectacle of the world, but had to submit at the same time to the regulations issued by the imperial Arsenal in the Moscow Kremlin, in which the office for the supervision of masonry architecture had been subsumed.

With the spread of commerce, manufacturing and the distribution of goods, the middle classes had gained an appreciably stronger position in economic and political life. The churches built for their members symbolize their growing power and the high standards that they now set themselves in domestic comfort and decorative display: the craft and trade guilds of the suburbs were satisfied with a single narrow nave, usually with a shallow vaulted ceiling needing no pillars, but they liked exteriors to be attractive, and covered with elaborate decorative detail (Church of the Nativity of the Virgin, Moscow-Putinki, 1649–52; St Nicholas, Moscow-Khamovniki, 1679–82). The Moscow patricians and the mercantile family of the Stroganovs, the 'Russian Fuggers', favoured small, roomy hall-churches (Holy Trinity, Moscow-Nikitniki, 1634; the 'Stroganov' church in Gorky, started in 1697). The merchants of Yaroslavl, on the other hand, preferred large, cuboid buildings with four pillars and elaborately decorated with tiles and frescos, in which the eastern pair of pillars often merged into the wall between the apses (Church of the Prophet Elijah, 1647–50; St John Chrysostom, Korovniki, 1649–54). Other towns on the Upper Volga followed this lead.

All the varieties abandoned the austerities of earlier times and the mass of the building was relieved by ornamentation of the façades, openings let into the walls and the style of roof. The five-dome structure became the norm (above a pyramid of blind gables in Moscow) but the four subsidiary domes are 'blind', in that they are not open downwards into the interior, and are placed there purely for their decorative effect. The sprawl of ancillary structures is characteristic: chapels and galleries are added to the church building proper on its north and south sides, and the trapeznaya extends on the west side, a long, low vestibule used for services in winter, with a tall, tent-roofed bell-tower either directly in front of it again, or added at one side. The various kinds of roofing given to staircases and their landings enhance the fairy-tale elaboration of the silhouette. The polychrome fabric, often painted as well as naturally coloured, with carved white limestone against red bricks, and friezes of coloured tiles, increases the successive, painterly effect even more. A comparable baroque style developed in court architecture too, as the outcome of the course taken by ornamentation in Moscow and culminating at the end of the seventeenth century in the 'Moscow Baroque', named after Prince Lev Kirillovich Naryshkin.

Churches of the 'Moscow Baroque'

Patriarch Nikon's reforms around the mid-century, an attempt to return to the sober, monumental grandeur of the Cathedral of the Assumption in Moscow, were unable to halt the dynamic surge of the decorative style as his own buildings show (Church of the Twelve Apostles in the Moscow Kremlin, 1653–56). But they did bring about a more disciplined order and logic in the complex plans of new buildings and in the articulation of their façades. Additions that had no organic or properly motivated relationship to the main building disappeared, as did constricted spaces and low vaults. The churches of the 'Moscow Baroque' benefit from the regulations imposed by the patriarch: the ground-plan is integrated, the form symmetrical, the spatial structure light and well-balanced; the overall form of the exterior is still pyramidal but constructed in a completely new fashion, and the application of decorative structural elements, while lavish, is both plastic and well-differentiated (and assimilates West European elements that penetrated Russia via the Ukraine and Belo-Russia). The 'Naryshkin style' is not only seen in the buildings commissioned by the prince himself (Church of the Virgin of the Intercession, Moscow-Fili, *c*1693), but it also influenced monastery and refectory churches (in the Monastery of the Holy Trinity and St Sergius, Zagorsk, and the New Convent of the Virgin in Moscow) and patrician churches (Church of the Resurrection, Moscow-Kadashi, 1687–1713). Soviet art historians designate it the culmination and the conclusion of early Russian architecture. Its elegant, ceremonial character is already secular in tone. It marks the end of the transitional style of the seventeenth century and the beginning of the modern era, in which the domination of the church finally had to yield to the strength of the secular culture.

The Main Types of the Wooden Church

The essential factors that conditioned the transmutation of the Byzantine domed cruciform church in early Russian architecture stemmed from the country's indigenous timber architecture. Wood was the normal building material used in medieval Russia, masonry the exception which almost vanished from use again, in the two centuries following the Tartar invasion, except in the region of Novgorod and Pskov. Wood was the cheapest and most convenient material, not only for the huts of peasants and houses of ordinary townspeople, but also for palaces and churches. On the earliest known plan of Moscow, drawn by Herberstein 1517–26, the few masonry buildings in the Kremlin are far outnumbered by the wooden buildings.

The ratio changed in church architecture when it was felt necessary to embody the idea of the theocratic state. Stone and brick, at once more expensive and more durable, made it possible to create a more imposing, monumental effect, and to construct interiors capable of holding larger congregations. From the very first masonry architecture in Russia was influenced in innumerable ways by wooden architecture. When Kievan Rus adopted various structural forms and building techniques from the Byzantine empire in the late tenth and early eleventh centuries, following the conversion to Christianity, the aesthetic ideal of the entire people had already been formed by their own style of building with logs. It is simple, clear, comprehensible and yet at the same time it is picturesque, decorative and imaginative. It was the source of the extraordinary ease with which the domed cruciform plan was assimilated in early Russian architecture: both have their genetic origin in the central square, to which both add relatively independent spatial units (cells). Both emphasize the vertical central axis. The central dome or tower always soars above, and draws towards itself, the elements that surround it.

The North Russian Peasant House

The ancestral cell from which all wooden architecture in Eastern Europe is descended is the north Russian log-built peasant house, the izba. Its influence spread into Scandinavia in one direction, though impeded by the prevalence of stave-building until the middle of the fourteenth century, and far into the southern parts of Russia in the other direction, fanning out in a series of provincial variants. The walls are made of beams joined in various ways to form rectangular 'frames' and laid horizontally above each other. Windows and doors were cut out later. The structure was surmounted by a pitched roof or a tent roof, formed by piling square or octagonal 'frames' pyramidally on top of each other. Regardless of the shape of the roof, beams and planks were always laid horizontally; The tools were as simple as the material: the short axe was the main one, with the assistance of the scraper, the mallet, the chisel and a wooden wedge. The Russian carpenters used the axe to fell the trees, to shape the beams and to split them into planks; they even used the axe for the less intricate forms of decoration. The basic unit with four walls and a roof is already called a 'cell' (klet) in the eleventh-century sources. The peasant house consisted of three cells: the living room the izba in the narrower sense), which could be heated, was linked to a store room (also called a klet), which could also be used as a living room in summer, by a passage or hall (the seni). In order to be able to live above the level of the snow in winter, a second storey was built above the store room or the hall or both, which meant in turn that an exterior staircase had to be added, in order to reach the terem as this attic was called. Further cells were added horizontally and vertically as the need arose, and in this way the basic plan gradually developed and changed over the centuries.

40

Just as the tri-partite plan of the izba is repeated in the palaces of the Russian aristocracy, so it dominates the design of the Orthodox church, whose liturgical function also called for three different areas. In its simplest form it consists of three cells, arranged symmetrically: an area for the congregation in the centre, the sanctuary to the east and a vestibule (trapeznaya) to the west, which also served secular uses. The structure of the trapeznaya is similar to that of the summer living room of the izba: a bench runs along the inside wall, and the ceiling is supported by two carved and painted beams, which often rest on two pillars. This simple, modular type of building could be extended, like the peasant house, by the addition of any number of similar cells.

Development followed a course from the simple to the complex, from an integrated to an open structure, from the linear and simultaneous to the painterly and successive, affected to a significant degree by the particular laws of construction with logs. The progression of the types begins at the same point as this development, and pursues a parallel course, though always simplifying through abstraction, generalizing through systematization. The very material is one reason why this history must be presented in a summarized form: its perishability means that only a small number of wooden churches still exists. The most important of them are in remote regions of northern Russia, and the majority date from the seventeenth or eighteenth centuries. Survivals from the sixteenth or possibly the fifteenth century are very few indeed. But there are enough to make deductions about the stylistic traits of earlier buildings by analogy and with judicious reference to the written and iconographic sources at the same time. A complex, much-articulated structure is not in itself an indication of date, but rather of the means placed at the builders' disposal.

We shall concentrate on four main types, all of which are in evidence at a relatively early date: the simple three-celled plan, the octagonal tower with a tent roof (pyramidal roof), the 'twenty-walled' cruciform building with arms of equal length, and the type with a large number of domes. There is of course an abundance of transitional and mixed forms. The pyramidal structure of the first Cathedral of St Sophia in Novgorod, built of oak in 989 with thirteen domes, was already a model for the stone cathedral of the same name in Kiev. Tent-roof churches are mentioned and illustrated in eleventh and twelfth-century manuscripts. A Novgorod icon of the early fourteenth century depicts the Presentation in the Temple under three pyramidal roofs. The famous legend of Ustyug refers to a wooden cathedral built in 1492, which was 'round in the old fashion, with twenty walls': that is, an octagonal central structure supporting a tower and surrounded by four additional square structures for the sanctuary and vestibules; it was popular usage to describe octagonal and polygonal log frames in general as 'round', and to add the eight walls of the central octagon to the sum of the three exterior walls of each of the four additional cells. There is usually very little to distinguish those buildings which are known to be later in date from earlier ones. The basic types of wooden churches were probably

8 *Moscow, Kremlin, Cathedral of the Assumption, 1475–79, by Aristotle Fioravanti. Interior, north side, looking east: frescos 1642–44; icons, mainly 14th–17th centuries; bronze chandeliers, 17th and 19th centuries*

fully developed by the twelfth century and retained, though with some modification arising from contemporary influences, throughout succeeding centuries.

The relative constancy of the social, technical and aesthetic conditions led to formal consonance and homogeneity of development, though this must be understood with reservations. The important, ideologically inspired, stylistic change in monumental masonry architecture did not have a direct influence on wooden architecture, but merely suggested certain formal combinations, especially in the seventeenth century. The way of life and the attitude towards existence in the peasant communities were totally traditional and relatively uniform. It is true that the external phenomena of economic and non-economic dependency in Russia changed several times in the Middle Ages, but the feudal social structure as such did not change. It determined in the last resort the lives even of the family and village communities which were able to preserve an independent existence in northern Russia. The proverbial conservatism of these communities was intensified at a later date by the influx and influence of the Old Believers, who withdrew to that part of the country after the schism of the mid seventeenth century in the attempt to escape the oppression of the central authority and the official church.

Peasants, the poorer classes of town dwellers and monks always lived in wooden buildings, simply for economic reasons. They accommodated not only the traditionalists, the raskolniki, but also sects and heretical movements (or such as did not, like the Novgorod strigolniki, pray 'looking from the earth to heaven', make their confessions pantheistically to 'Mother Earth' and renounce church buildings altogether). In the fifteenth and sixteenth centuries wooden architecture reflected the warfare between the two monastic movements. The followers of Joseph of Volokolamsk, on the one hand, supported the partnership of church and state, stiffening the coenobitic ideal of the monasteries endowed by princes with theocratic theories, and advocating the causes of the strictly regimented 'religious state' and of monastic ownership of property on a feudal basis, but they were opposed on all these counts by the 'nonselfseeking' (Skit monks) in the small hermitages of northern Russia. Their ideological leader, Nil Sorsky (1433–1508), took as his model the anchorites of the Near East, who supported themselves by their own manual labour and lived of their own 'free will' in poverty and the strictest asceticism. In view of Sorsky's powerful polemics against architectural and liturgical ostentation, the simple three-cell church was adopted in the 'Skit' monasteries. The 'Josephites' preferred the more complex types, when they did not actually build in stone, for they held the wealth of the church to be the wealth of God.

Once the methods of log construction had led as far as the complex many-domed structure, the technical and aesthetic conditions they imposed were hardly subjected to any fundamental changes. Development followed a clear and consistent course: the ground-plan of the central cell grew from a square to an octagon, the beam frames rose higher and accumulated, the roof was given a steeper slope to alleviate the outward pressure of its component parts, and the walls of the central cell were buttressed for the same reason by additional cells, usually square units of the same size as the square contained within the central octagon. The trend towards vertical, painterly structures gathered force, so that there was a relaxation of the tectonic severity natural to log construction. The style was influenced in a positive fashion by the nature of the building material – the natural length of the beams limited the width of the walls and led to the addition of the square and rectangular cells – and by the method of construction, which had to take the thrust of the tower into account. The development process is revealed most clearly by the various kinds of roof, the number and arrangement of the cells and domes, and the accumulation of the variously shaped structural entities. The central area was originally open to the

43

9 Zagorsk, Monastery of the Holy Trinity and St Sergius, Church of the Holy Ghost, 1476–77: view from the west

apex of the tent, although the eye was unable to penetrate so far in the darkness. A diffuse light spread from this source. Not until the seventeenth century was the room separated from the tower by a canopy-like ceiling called a 'sky'.

44 The oldest surviving wooden building is an example of the simple type of three-cell church: the Church of the Raising of Lazarus from the monastery at Murom, built around 1390. The eighteenth-century Chapel of the Archangel Michael from Lelik-Ozero and the seventeenth-century Church of St Nicholas from Tukhola belong to the same type, but possess some complex formal details. The basement storey, which was sometimes used for storage, not only made the construction of an exterior flight, or double flight, of steps necessary, but also gave rise to galleries surrounding the building and relieving the vestibule of its secular functions.

Such a building with its succession of steep pitched roofs is the typological origin from which developed in the seventeenth century the type represented by St John the Evangelist on the River Ishna, near Rostov (1689). The central cell takes the form of a rectangular box placed on a narrow end, and supports a tower constructed of two octagonal stages, the higher smaller than the lower, and topped by an onion dome. But the type of octagonal ('circular') tent-roof church goes back much earlier, with documentary evidence dating from the eleventh and twelfth centuries. Eight walls enclose an area three times as great as can be encompassed by four walls of the same width. The tri-partite plan remains the same, but the broader base provided by the central octagon permits the vertical, pillar-like construction with the lofty pyramidal roof. A variant that developed late in the sixteenth century under the influence of masonry buildings is the type of the 'octagon on a square': the octagonal structure and tent roof are supported on a square base, the actual central cell. The Church of the Assumption from Kuritsko (1595) and the Church of the Assumption in Kondopoga (1774) are two examples of the type.

Integration gave way to a painterly, dynamic relaxation in the next stage of development, the many-domed church. This is the most complex of the types of wooden church building, but the old St Sophia in Novgorod shows that it is not chronologically the last. It is the expression of an unusual wealth of forms by the use of a wide variety of architectural means. The genetic reason for this could well have been a matter of structural necessity: the pillar-shaped central cell had to be buttressed. One method of doing this was by adding an extensive vestibule and a large sanctuary to the west and east of the load-bearing substructure, or else by adding to it symmetrically on all four sides, which provided the opportunity for inventive and original roof formations.

An example of the latest type of wooden church to develop, in which the east-west axis is stressed as well as the vertical line, is the Church of the Virgin of the Intercession on Kizhi (1764). This represents the plan of 'octagon on square', but its roof has a shallow, rather than a steep, slope, with eight surfaces to support the drums of its nine domes. The chronologically earlier type, which is nonetheless the last stage in the developmental process, is represented by the Church of the Transfiguration on Kizhi (1714). It is the outstanding example of what an artistically original form could be erected on the 'twenty-wall' groundplan, a pyramid rising in five tiers, surmounted by twenty-two domes. It unites the traditional type with the painterly formal language of the seventeenth century that was the outcome of increasing secularization.

Functional form and artistic form are inseparably united in all the types of wooden church building. The practical solution is also beautiful in appearance. The forms and stylistic variations are influenced by construction techniques, even such apparently decorative elements as the onion domes, the bochki (little barrels), the ornamental gable friezes, the prichelini (carved fillets on plank roofs), all contribute to an efficient system of draining water from the roof. The aesthetic impression is due above all to the simple, obvious proportional balance (often resting on the angle of inclination of the roof ridges, which is determined by the outward thrust of its components), the rhythm of the large and small forms, and the decorative finish of the outline. The carpenters used basic measurements in the ratio of 1 : 1 or 1 : 2, or where appropriate they took the diagonal of a rectangle, or intuitively (without a fixed plan) they used the Golden Section. The arrangement of forms, especially of the roof, the stairways, the windows and the galleries, shows a rhythmic recurrence in itself, regardless of whether the preferred effect is symmetry or asymmetry. The external outlines of the building are designed to be seen from a sufficient distance for the eye not to rest on each part in turn but to take in the whole as a single subject within its context of woods, meadows and lakes. Ornamental carving, which may be sparing or lavish according to the local custom and available resources, covers the gables, the door and window surrounds and the covered exterior staircases. The carvers used geometrical motifs such as six-pointed stars or spiral rosettes, as well as stylized animal figures, probably relics of Scytho-sarmatic iconography. The decoration never gets the upper hand even in the painterly style of the seventeenth and eighteenth centuries, and so never detracts from the overall impression.

The Exchanges Between Masonry and Wooden Architecture

From the very first there was a lively and complex interchange of influences between building in stone and brick and building in wood in early Russian architecture, without there being any question of wholesale transference of forms from one medium to the other. The differences in material and constructional technique were enough in themselves to ensure that each medium had its own individual architectonic language, though this was in turn modified by the terms of the overall artistic system. The laws governing building in wood resulted in its relatively independent development until the seventeenth century. It was not until the onset of the process of secularization that the successive and painterly stylistic variations it introduced led to both kinds of building moving in the same direction.

The actual stylistic change took place in masonry architecture. By means of the domed cruciform plan, the official church and the Orthodox liturgy and symbolism took log construction into their service, from groundplan to tent roof. Even so, masonry buildings continued to receive new impulses from wooden architecture and to learn from it. 'The more significant wooden architecture became from the thirteenth to the sixteenth century, the greater its influence on masonry architecture. From the fourteenth and fifteenth centuries onwards, characteristics occur in the masonry buildings of Novgorod, Pskov and Moscow which unmistakably demonstrate the influence of wooden architecture, weak and indirect to begin with, but becoming stronger. That influence is particularly noticeable in the masonry tent-roof churches, bell-towers and defensive towers in the sixteenth and seventeenth centuries, in masonry houses of the seventeenth century and masonry churches constructed in graduated tiers in the late seventeenth century.' (P. N. Maximov and N. N. Voronin, *Istoriya russkogo iskusstva.*)

The modification varies in degree and kind from one stylistic period to another. But its beginnings can already be discerned in Kievan Rus. The Byzantine type of the domed cruciform church was transformed from the very start by the innate Russian preference for tall, many-domed, pyramidal massing, by the accumulated experience of centuries of timber construction. The Cathedral of St Sophia in Kiev is a clear example, in the extent of its deviation from the Byzantine model. The Byzantine architects employed in the building of St Sophia, like other foreign architects at later dates, had to arrive at a compromise with the native labour force. Russian architects and the Russian donors of buildings always understood how to transmute any kind of style to fit in with their indigenous traditions. There is moreover the remarkable phenomenon that has occurred again and again in Russian history: the further the foreign visitors travelled from their homeland, the more firmly a sense of place and time, a consciousness of history and nationality and the Russian culture took possession of them.

It would be outside the scope of this book to try to describe all the forms which modified building in stone and brick in one way or another or to explain the complicated process of permeation, for which in any case hardly any of the source material has survived. We can only mention a few examples in a summary fashion and with reservations: the tent roof with eight faces probably derives from the wooden towers built as fortifications. Watch-towers and gate-towers were often equipped with a peal of bells and had a chapel under the roof as well. Such towers were invariably to be found as part of a fortified kremlin or monastery surrounded by palisades. The masonry type of combined church and bell-tower that emerged in Moscow in the fourteenth century derives from them: for instance, the church and bell-tower of Ivan the Great in the Moscow Kremlin (1505–08), St George in Kolomenskoye and St John the Baptist in the Monastery of the Saviour and St Euthymios in Suzdal (both early sixteenth century); the Church of the Holy Ghost in the Monastery of the Holy Trinity and St Sergius in Zagorsk (1476–77) is also related to this type. The tent roof suddenly appeared fully fledged in stone architecture in the middle of the sixteenth century.

In Kolomenskoye the tent-roof church became the monumental symbol of the idea of the Muscovite state, but it was introduced in the simple, intimate shape of a refectory church – the Church of the Assumption in the Monastery of the Saviour and St Euthymios, Suzdal, c1525. If one wanted to describe the reforms of Ivan IV as a 'monasticization', it would be possible to make some interesting comparisons on the basis of their reception in architecture. In the seventeenth century the type was used again as a monastic church, but the tent roof was modified to conform to the successive, painterly style (Church of the Assumption, Uglich, 1628), until it was totally transformed into a nonfunctional, grandiloquent ornament. For instance, the Church of the Nativity of the Virgin in Moscow-Putinki (1649–52) has three ornately decorated tent roofs, but they simply form a massive construction intended to catch the eye. The tent roof retained its structural, monumental effect only on free-standing masonry bell-towers, where it greatly enhanced the resonance of the bells, and the arches and openings necessary for the passage of the sound were added to the other decorative motifs. The tower with a tent roof is also the source of the stepped, pyramidal shape of the many-domed masonry churches, a composition strongly suggested by its structure. The influence of wooden architecture is in any case very obvious in the roof: there is the evidence of surfaces adapted to the irregularity caused by the additive cells or overriding it (as in the cases where three apses are covered by a single lean-to or pitched roof), the generous overhang of the eaves (as when the main cornice has a stepped profile, without active or passive members), and the outlining of the shapes of vaults and gables by the straight lines of the roof (examples in Novgorod).

After the roofing, it was the additive grouping of extra cells derived from the izba that had the strongest effect on the composition of ecclesiastical buildings in stone and brick: in the course of stylistic development churches acquired ever more accretions below and round about the nucleus, and as this happened the arrangement of exterior galleries and vestibules was obliged to be either, by the requirements of the domed cruciform plan, more symmetrical and linear, or, in keeping with the style of secular wooden buildings, more asymmetrical and painterly. The technique of log construction involves emphasizing the corners and the vertical articulation of a building (with fillets over the joints or vertical lines of log ends, where the cells meet) and this led to comparable effects in brick-built structures, though without any tectonic basis: attention was drawn by decorative means to pilasters and lesenes, fabricated when there were no corresponding interior members, to create an appearance similar to that of wooden buildings. The ornamental surrounds (nalichniki) of doors, windows and areas of wall surface probably had a forerunner in framed windows. Woodcarving was a cornucopia of decorative ideas: cornices, friezes, consoles, notching, bands of plaited or twisted rope, bosses, chain-links, 'melons' (bulges on the shafts of columns), elements of these kinds, repeated over and over for their decorative effect, constantly occur on masonry buildings.

There is some dispute as to the origin of the bochka ('little barrel'): a form of roofing in the shape of half a cylinder with the upper, curved edge raised to a point. Some authorities (such as H. Weidhaas) derive it from a type of roof where straw thatch was laid on purlins and rafters, that had undergone a refinement due to climatic factors. M. A. Ilin, P. N. Maximov and V. V. Kostochkin, on the other hand, believe that the bochka may be a result of the influence of masonry architecture upon wooden buildings, and derives from the round gables of the domed cruciform church. They also explain the octagonal drum of wooden churches as a reproduction of the round, masonry drums; the angular apses of wooden churches derive from the semi-circular apses of masonry ones, the tiers of kokoshniki from corbelled vaults, the overlapping, pointed shingles from roof tiles. When Nikon decreed that tent roofs should have four additional domes and an 'onion' at the apex, they were simply placed round the edge as decorative elements. Transferred to wood, with the passage of time these forms acquired original characteristics of their own and later exercised an influence back on to masonry architecture. I. E. Grabar and F. F. Gornostayev established that the 'octagon on a square' plan of the wooden tower-churches was another borrowing from stone and did not occur before the mid seventeenth century. Thus the only original aspect of the piling-up of alternate octagons and cubes in wooden towers is the gradation of size, not the principle. In all the developmental processes and stylistic peculiarities of the two architectural media, every instance of either influencing the other took place in a context of centralization and of the desire to add rectangular cells. Within this context formal changes corresponded to terms imposed 'from above' and 'from below'.

Liturgy and Architectonic Form

The domed cruciform church fulfils its true function in the Orthodox church service. The style of the architecture is instinct with the power to bind a congregation together and the form of the service governs the organization of the building's interior. There is not only a 'holy time' and a 'holy action' prescribed for the sacraments, but a 'holy place' as well. The tri-partite division of the building is characteristic, corresponding to the three levels in the church hierarchy: the sanctuary (bema) for the clergy, the body of the church, the nave and aisles (naos) for the communicant members of the congregation, and the vestibule or narthex (trapeznaya) for all those not admitted to full communion. The spatial division between the clergy and the lay congregation was given greater emphasis in Russia by the development of the altar screen, originally quite low, into the high iconostasis, while the barrier placed before the catechumens and various classes of penitents is often no more than a line of arches, though it is sometimes a solid wall. There is a caesura in the service at the point just before the mystery of the eucharist, when the priest calls out three times to the catechumens to leave the body of the church. After the conversion to Christianity there was hardly any division in Russia, except in the missionary areas, between the catechumens, who were mostly adults, and the baptized members of the congregation. The division has been retained in services to the present day, but has increasingly been regarded as symbolic. The vestibule served for baptisms and for burials, penitents were admitted to it, and the faithful gathered there to pray during midnight services. Many of them had often come a long distance and they could rest there. The vestibule often had another, secular function, especially in the churches of villages and small country towns: it was the place of assembly for such secular occasions as courts of justice, tax collection, governmental proclamations and the like. The iconographic programme generally indicates the functions for which it was principally used.

The sanctuary is also generally in three parts, with three openings in the iconostasis. The middle opening, the Royal or Paradise Door, leads to the altar, the 'Holy of Holies', called in Russian the 'throne' (prestol). Behind the door on the north side stands the prothesis with the altar of preparation or offerings (zhertvennik), where the sacraments are prepared, and behind the south door is the diakonikon (riznitsa), which serves as sacristy and vestry and the place for keeping articles needed in services, books and vestments, though in the large cathedrals this function may be spread into other rooms as well. The priests and deacons open, pass through and close the doors in a precisely ordained sequence.

Visual Climaxes of the Liturgy

The visual climaxes of the liturgy are what are called the Little and the Great Entry. In the Little Entry during the catechumens' liturgy, the deacon carries the gospel book in front of the priest as they walk from the altar, through the prothesis door to the middle of the nave and back through the Royal Door, to symbolize the appearance of Christ among his congregation. In the Great Entry during the liturgy for the baptized, the priest and deacon carry the sacraments, which have not yet been consecrated, over the same route from the altar of offerings to the main altar, while the Hymn of the Cherubim is solemnly sung, the action representing Christ's Passion and his triumph over death. The Royal Door is opened a number of times from behind and in front to symbolize various things: the creation of the world, Christ's enthronement, his birth, the removal of the stone from his tomb, the Resurrection. In Easter Week it remains open throughout the whole service. Closed, it represents the expulsion from Paradise.

The meaning of all liturgical actions lies in the repeated, 'continuing' representation of the story of divine salvation. The sequence is systematically ordered, with a daily cycle of nine services, a weekly cycle with set days of commemoration and an annual cycle with movable and immovable feasts. The hymns and texts are drawn from the rich, image-filled worlds of the Old and New Testaments, which are seen to be closely interrelated as 'Prophecy' and 'Fulfilment' of each other. As the clergy move about the cruciform church they are representing God's movements through the cosmos and the history of mankind. Their procession takes in the body of the church (which is also divided into three aisles), where the men were generally placed on the right, the women on the left and the aristocracy in the galleries above. This part of the building may be imposing and spacious, as in the princely cathedrals, or intimate and confined, as in the refectory churches and the churches built by townspeople, and in their palaces by princes for their own use. The processional way and the social symbolism governing its setting were subject, in Rus as in the Byzantine empire, to variations depending on whether the final voice came 'from above' or 'from below'.

Changes in the Liturgy

The three eleventh-century cathedrals dedicated to Holy Wisdom by their princely donors adopted the five-aisle version of the domed cruciform plan, originated in Constantinople under the influence of the 'Great Church', but after it had been reshaped by the Oriental school. Apart from the 'sacred stage' and the 'auditorium' opening on to it on three sides (three arms of the 'cross' and the two west corners), it also contains an 'ambulatory'. This is used in the Great Censing, when the priests walk round the walls, encircling the congregation and swinging their censers. This occurs three times, at the beginning and in the middle of the catechumens' liturgy and before the Great Entry. The central mysteries were performed in a circling movement between the sanctuary and the dais occupied by the priest reading the service (the ambo, the precursor of the pulpit), which stood beneath the apex of the dome in the middle of the 'stage'. The fusion of forms that had originated at the court and in the capital on the one hand and among the monks of the Near East on the other was initiated in the liturgy of the imperial church. Since the sixth century, this had fostered simultaneously two forms of service, both regulated by church law. The first is linked with the name of St John Chrysostom and with the 'Great Church', the Hagia Sophia, and derives from the liturgy of Constantinople. It already incorporated hourly prayers, which played an even more important role in the second form of liturgy, which was named after the monastic father, St Basil the Great, and was based on the practices of the Cappadocian monasteries. In spite of the growing influence of the monks the Basilian liturgy was restricted to ten days in the year after the Iconoclastic Controversy, since it took too long. The Constantinopolitan order of service spread throughout the Byzantine empire in a manner similar to the spread of the Roman liturgy in the West. For certain fast days a third form of service was introduced, that of the 'Presanctified Gifts' (celebration of communion using the reserved sacrament).

In Russia, too, monastic practices had a decisive influence on the shaping and further development of the liturgy. Although the Russian Orthodox church was formally a part of the Byzantine imperial church until 1448, it already showed a marked independence in the Kievan period. The seed-bed and nursery of patriotic ideas was the Monastery of the Caves in Kiev, which was founded by a Russian monk named Antoni, who had taken vows on Mount Athos. To give independence a solid theological foundation the monastery urged the canonization of Russian saints (Boris and Gleb, Feodosy Pechersky, Olga, Vladimir) and the introduction of Russian feasts (the translation of the relics of Nicholas Chudotvorets, the Protection and Intercession of the Virgin). Boris and Gleb in particular, and later the Virgin of the Veil, became the patron saints of national unity, with numerous churches dedicated to them. The first Russian-born metropolitan of Kiev, Hilarion, formerly a monk of the Monastery of the Caves, who held office for a short time (1051–54) with the support of Yaroslav the Wise, wrote his *Discourse on Law and Grace* with the purpose of giving his newly baptized compatriots a sense of their equality, as a nation, to any other. The legend that St Andrew the Apostle himself had made a missionary journey to Russia was born in the twelfth century. It appears in the Chronicle of Nestor, written *c*1113 by a monk of the Kiev Monastery of the Caves, which openly opposed the political ambitions of the Byzantine empire and championed the Russian dynasty.

Close ties always existed between Russian monks and the common people, and the forms of their services similarly had a popular appeal. This led as early as the eleventh century to the court liturgy being replaced by the monastic service form of Theodore of Studion (died 826). He was the author of a monastic rule which the Monastery of the Caves adopted in the version written down by Patriarch Alexios (1025–43), and the devotions it contained made their way – as previously in the Old Church – into simple parish services. By contrast with the cathedrals, there was a lively interchange between the liturgical forms of the monastic and secular churches. The daily cycle was composed of the hourly prayers which had become the customary practice in the monastic communities after the Iconoclastic Controversy. The 'holy sections' in which the priest enacts symbolically the events of Holy Writ, are fully consistent with a religious attitude in which the faithful have a direct, personal relationship with God, but which also strengthens the sense of community. The form of the responses (ektenya) is characteristic of this attitude. The content of the prayers, theologically the direct answer to God's call, embraces the whole of existence. We have no wish to parade that cliché the 'Russian Soul', but there is no denying that the piety of the Russian people is permeated with a profound humanism, which gives a human face to the unapproachable, ineffable God of the Byzantines, overcomes the sense of distance engendered by ceremonial, and puts the Orthodox ethic of brotherly love into practice. Thus the liturgy acquired a totally different symbolic meaning in Russia from that it had among the Greeks. At the same time the Church Slavonic language based on the translations of Cyril and Methodius was introduced in services, sermons, religious instruction and hagiographic literature.

A similar process can be observed in architecture. Along with the rule of Theodore of Studion, the simple type of domed cruciform church with only three aisles, the plan prevalent in the Christian Near East, became the norm in Rus. As N. Brunov has shown, it perpetuates something of the form of the Mesopotamian 'broad' church, in which the congregation occupied the transepts from north to south and the main dome was placed further to the east, directly over the middle of the altar steps. The processional way did not follow a virtually circular path, as it did in the building with five aisles, but ran along the altar screen, before which the congregation were lined up in parallel rows. It is therefore usual to speak of this area as a place where worshippers lingered for meditation. Similarly, in the churches of early Russia, the ordering of the interior modified the unremittingly centripetal, cyclic tendency in favour of a frontal, static treatment of the space, seeking some breadth, but without abandoning the visual focusing on the 'holy centre'. A section was cut, so to speak, in the circling movement, with the litugical structure of the iconostasis as the cutting plane. The ambo was moved to the middle of the altar steps, in front of the Royal Door, so that when the clergy came out through the door they appeared directly beneath the apex of the principal dome, in the centre of the light flooding down from it. The optical character of the 'sacred drama' was retained, but the 'stage' was moved to either side of the iconostasis, which both drew the eye to itself and led it on through the three doors. The two centres of worship that the Hagia Sophia had, that is the sanctuary and the ambo, were fused into a single unit. Insofar as early Russian churches adopted the domed cruciform plan with three aisles, movement was set up in two directions: on the one hand the processional way ran along the iconostasis, beneath the main dome from north to south and back, across the line of vision; on the other the congregation's frontal positioning and view in the transept formed by the crossing and the north and south arms of the cross forced their gaze to move into the sanctuary, where it fell upon the actual movement of the clergy going in and out. The oscillation of all these movements combined resulted in a cross which was encircled and centralized by the form of the dome.

As with the forms of service, early Russian architecture owed more to Oriental than to Constantinopolitan influences. Theatrical features were, however, retained in the liturgy, although with some substantial changes. They were clearly developed in the mystery plays—the Three Children in the Burning Fiery Furnace, the Washing of the Feet, the Ride on the Donkey, the Nativity play—which were performed on specific feast-days in the great cathedrals under the direction of a high-ranking priest until the seventeenth century. The survival of the Constantinopolitan liturgy was bound up with the claim of the Russian ruling house to the legacy of the Byzantine theocracy. In architecture it led for one thing to the retention of the use of the ambo (originally the nucleus of the 'sacred stage'), which N. Brunov has traced up to the seventeenth century, and

10 *Moscow, Church of the Ascension, Kolomenskoye, 1530–32: view from the north-east*

for another to the spatial unity reflecting the political. It made it possible for the processional way to take more of a circular path once again and created a suitable 'stage' for the mystery plays in front of the iconostasis. This trend reached its culmination in the Cathedral of the Assumption in the Moscow Kremlin, which is planned on the lines of a hall church. The ecclesiastical reforms resulting from Nikon's Byzantine renaissance helped to spread the type throughout the whole country, while the process of secularization that Nikon had hoped to prevent reached the same goal by a different path: the hall church developed from the pillar-less type of palace church and restored the 'stage', only this time due to the profane influence of baroque spatial conceptions. In court and middle-class baroque alike, people wanted to see and be seen. The kremlin in Rostov and the Church of the Holy Trinity at Nikitniki both provide examples. Meanwhile, however, the 'ambulatory' principle inherent in the five-aisle version of the domed cruciform plan did not disappear altogether in Russia, but is evident in the horseshoe arrangement of the tribunes in the great cathedrals.

The legacy of the broad churches of the Middle East was expressed in various different ways. In the four-pillar type the restriction of the tribune to the west end created a transept in front of the iconostasis, while the space above and below the tribune was extended to north and south (twelfth-century court churches in Vladimir-Suzdal, city churches in Novgorod, Cathedral of the Annunciation in the Moscow Kremlin). In the seventeenth century, in monastery refectories and in the Posad, the type of broad church emerged which had no pillars, a vaulted ceiling and no tribune whatever (Church of the Assumption in the New Convent of the Virgin, Moscow, 1685–87; St Nicholas, Moscow-Khamovniki, 1679–82). Broadening the interior in this way is always the expression of a devotional attitude and it occurs not only in secular churches but also in the intimate court churches which served the personal needs of the royal family. The positioning of portals at the north and south, which was usual in early Russian churches, extended the length of the processional way in that direction, and emphasized both the transverse movement and the 'ambulatory' principle, moving it outside, so to speak, if the west portal is also taken into consideration.

The move towards the spatial concentration and rigid ordering of the church interior was begun in the late fourteenth century, when the Muscovite all-Russian policy, with the support of the coenobitic monks, met with its first major successes: another order of service gained ground, a revival of the Jerusalemite liturgy, which involved yet another re-shaping of the architectonic traditions. Barrel vaulting was replaced by corbelled vaulting. South Slav, and particularly Serbian influences came into play in liturgy, literature and architecture. It is hardly possible today to gain a clear impression of the exact order of a service in the early Russian church; the more so because the Jerusalemite order merged with the Studite form. It is known, however, that the monasteries in the vicinity of Moscow were the first to adopt the new architectural forms along with the new liturgical forms: witness the cathedral of the St Savva monastery in Zvenigorod (c1404), which is related to the Cathedral of the Assumption in the city, the cathedral in the Monastery of the Holy Trinity and St Sergius, and the cathedral in the Andronikov Monastery of the Saviour. It is also known that the new service form was considerably more ceremonious than the old. The pre-eminence that the Muscovite Great Princes gained in their organization and unification of the Russian lands was gradually exalted into a caesaropapism, which required new forms of ceremonial and royal ostentation. There were two divergent trends in Russian society: on the one hand the struggle for national unity and inde-

11 *Moscow, Monastery of the Don, Old Cathedral of the Icon of the Virgin of the Don, 1591–93. Refectory and bell-tower (left), 1678–79, seen from the south-west*

pendence was being waged by people and rulers together, on the other the barriers resulting from the feudal and monarchic social order were being strengthened.

As the iconostasis took on monumental proportions it separated the sanctuary from the nave, the holy mysteries from the believers, and as in the Byzantine church the renewal of dramatic and aesthetic aspects of the liturgy was linked with a certain classifying of the congregation. At the same time, however, this was compensated for, under popular monastic influences, by fidelity to the practice of communal prayer, and this in turn gained in importance from the increased intercessional function of the iconostasis and the spatial emphasis given to the naos. The liturgy experienced further alteration in its form, though not its content, at various periods. One cause of change, was the 'dual faith', the survival of expressive, pagan rituals among the people, which led to the practice known as mnogoglasie ('many voices'). A single service was divided into several parts, which were read simultaneously in different places inside the church without any kind of inter-relationship between them. Mnogoglasie had a perfectly proper liturgical purpose: the nine services that had to be held each day followed each other so quickly that it had often been necessary to cut them, but in this form they could be read in full. The spread of the expressive form in the fifteenth, and above all in the seventeenth century, met with some opposition in the sixteenth. The Cathedral of the Virgin of the Intercession on Red Square, built in the reign of Ivan IV, which fuses nine separate churches into a single cellular complex, may represent an architectural compromise: each of the services could be held complete and unabridged in the separate parts of the same building. Under Ivan IV the Ride on the Donkey on Palm Sunday even joined the cathedral to the Cathedral of the Assumption in the Kremlin in a single processional way.

The Church as Icon

The theology of religious pictures which was systematized by the venerators of icons while the Iconoclastic Controversy was still in progress still holds good in the Russian Orthodox church today. It relates essentially to icon painting, but also has analogous application to the programmatic decoration of church interiors. The basic principles developed by John of Damascus, the patriarchs Germanos and Nikephoros, and Theodore of Studion, are based on two traditions: the first, the christological dogma of God's having become man, and therefore, by implication, capable of pictorial representation, and the other the Neoplatonist concept of the similarity between the image and the prototype consisting not in physical substance but in essence, in hypostasis. Consequently the manufacture and veneration of pictures, especially pictures of Christ, were elevated to unassailable dogmatic duties. If the image had a part in the essence of the divinity or sanctity of the prototype, it must receive the veneration due to the prototype itself, but it also followed that similar virtue emanated from it, raising the worshippers to immediate contemplation of the divine. In order to prevent any possibility of confusing the image with the prototype, drastic rules were laid down: the painted representations of the persons of God and the saints were to remain strictly two-dimensional and to be exact copies of the canonic schemata, and three-dimensional figures were completely banned from the interior of the church. These regulations had a decisive influence on the style of Middle Byzantine art and thus on its influence on the art of Kievan Rus. While Charlemagne expressly stated in the *Liber Carolini* that pictures ought 'to serve as ornaments in churches, and as reminders of events', but should in no way be objects of either adoration or veneration, in the reign of Ivan IV the Synod of a Hundred Chapters (1551) affirmed once again the validity of the ancient precepts and the religious symbolism.

'The Image of the Holy Church of God'

In the iconographic theology of the Orthodox church, the actual building of a church is also an icon, 'a window on eternity'. It is supposed to be an image of the mystical body of Christ, the house of God, visited by his actual presence, the meeting place of the heavenly church and of the earthly church, the congregation of the faithful with the clergy at their head. The gospel of salvation, as medieval Christians experienced it in the divine order of the universe and in divine service, was also the theme of architectonic symbolism. The symbolism was restricted essentially to the interior of the church building by the Greek church, but the popular piety and theology of the Russians led to its application to exteriors as well, which enjoyed the same religious veneration as the painted images of the saints. N. Brunov has made this the basis of a comparison with the primitive origins of architecture, when building first went beyond the limitations of pure utility with the placing of a 'mark' for religious reasons. In Orthodox ritual the building is consecrated by a bishop or other high-ranking clergyman as 'the image of the Holy church of God'. Since Christ is physically present in the church in the eucharist, the building contains, according to Simeon of Salonika, not only the Tree of Life, but the Life itself.

Even the consecrated foundation stone is regarded as a symbol of the Saviour. Names are taken from saints or the great church feasts. Dedications to the Resurrection are very common. The great popularity of the cult of the Virgin is reflected in the large number of churches named after the feast of the Dormition (Russian: Uspeniye; Greek: Koimesis; Latin: Dormitio; corresponding to the Roman Catholic feast of the Assumption of the Virgin: *assumptio animae et corporis,* celebrated on 15 August. We have chosen to use the form which is more familiar in the West, just as we use the form of John the Evangelist, known to the Russians as the Theologian: Bogoslov.) The alignment of the building is a matter of literal 'orientation', towards the east, towards the appearance of light, parousia, and the direction of Paradise. This is the rule throughout all Christendom, but absolute validity has never been claimed for it. There were already exceptions in local practice in the early church, and they are to be found in early Christian Russia as well. Many of the churches in Yaroslavl were oriented towards the River Volga. 'Some say that it is right to bow before icons and holy churches when they are aligned towards the east, but that if they are not aligned towards the east, you should not bow . . . But if you see a tsar or a prince, you bow before him not only towards the east but however the position happens to be. But if you bow even to a tsar or a prince towards the west, the north or the south, how much more ought you to bow to the image of the heavenly tsar . . . or the divine church.' Thus wrote Joseph of Volokolamsk, the ideologue of Muscovite theocracy.

The division of the domed cruciform church horizontally into three parts is derived from Old Testament precedents, from the Mosaic tabernacle and the Temple of Solomon. Simeon of Salonika regards it as a reference to the Trinity and to the three ranks of angels. The relationship of the sanctuary and the nave he interprets as an image of the two natures of Christ, the divine and the human ('of which the one is invisible, but the other visible'). He sees the vestibule as a symbol of the untransfigured, sinful world. The *Topographia Christiana* (535–47) of Cosmas Indicopleustes, the Alexandrian merchant who became a monk, influenced not only Christian concepts of the universe for a thousand years, but also architectonic symbolism. Like Noah's Ark and the Ark of the Covenant, a church building had to be rectangular like the earth, enclosed by four walls in the directions of the four quarters of the earth, and vaulted by the dome of heaven. Paradise lay at the east end, darkness at the west. The apocalyptic connotations are less well known. The cuboid mass topped by a dome can be related directly to the description of the Heavenly Jerusalem in the twenty-first chapter of Revelation: 'And the city lieth foursquare . . . The length and the breadth and the height of it are equal.' L. Kitschelt has shown that the long early Christian basilica, sometimes interpreted as a representation of the Heavenly Zion, is in no way comparable to the Heavenly City described in

Revelation, but is rather to be understood as an epitome of the city concept of late antiquity. The centralized domed cruciform plan yields a better opportunity of comparison, even when, as is the case with the Cathedral of the Virgin of the Intercession in Moscow (St Basil's Cathedral), the biblical symbolism is integrated with the secular symbolism of the contemporary Russian idea of the city.

Symbolism of the Interior and the Domes

As the image of the cosmos, the interior embodies the descent of the heavenly to earth, both horizontally and vertically. The symbolism of the structural members is heightened by the meaning of the paintings on them. The columns or pillars correspond to the supports of the church: angels and saints. The main dome, repeating the message of the altar canopy, symbolizes the heavenly abode of God. Like the keystone in a Gothic ribbed vault it points the way to Christ. The main dome is the focal point for the arrangement of the chandeliers, as the heavenly spheres and the orbits of the planets; and the wall-lights, as images of the stars. The altar steps (solea) in front of the iconostasis, on the right and left of which the church choir takes up its position, signify the fire which, according to St Paul (1 Corinthians 3 : 12–15), 'shall try every man's work'. The ambo symbolizes 'the stone, that was rolled away from the tomb of Christ, for there, representing the form of the angel, the priests and deacons preach the divine gospel' (Simeon of Salonika). This was the spot in the Hagia Sophia where the emperors were crowned. In the place of Paradise, the sanctuary reserved to the priests, the rectangular altar stands on the base line of the semicircular apse, as the throne of Christ, made present in the bloodless sacrifice. Corresponding to the separate stages in the course of the liturgy, the prothesis and bema—often in alternation—symbolize the locations of the events of the gospel, such as the stable in Bethlehem, Golgotha, the garden of the Resurrection and Mount Tabor where the Transfiguration took place. The processional cross and the seven-branched candlestick, the symbol of the Church, stand behind the altar, and behind them, directly against the wall of the apse, is the episcopal *cathedra*, or the stall of another high-ranking cleric, between the benches of the presbyters. The baptismal font often stands in the vestibule, aptly in view of its liturgical role. As the place of death and judgment the vestibule may also hold funerary monuments.

The number of the domes has its part in the symbolic importance that Russian Orthodoxy attached to the church exterior. Twelve smaller domes surrounding the main one signify Christ and the apostles, nine domes the nine choirs of angels, five domes Christ and the four evangelists and three domes the Trinity. One dome symbolizes the one God as head of the church. Since the plurality of domes is a peculiarity of Russian church architecture it was carried over into the construction of tent-roof churches. All the domes carry a cross, usually with the slanting beam across the bottom arm, and often a second cross-beam. A crescent moon at the foot of the cross is a sign of the victory over the Tartars. The dome itself symbolizes the effort of the church on earth to reach up to the heavenly Church, like a tongue of flame leaping up from a lamp.

The Function of the Tribune

The place closest to the symbol of the vault of heaven, and the best lit, was reserved for the ruler: the tribune. The Russian princes took over the Byzantine symbolism. They sat with their families and courtiers, enthroned in divinely ordained majesty in the upper storey of the church, which was connected directly to the palace, or else was accessible by separate staircases. They were able to receive the eucharist in the tribune, separately from the other worshippers, and to perform certain ceremonials: state receptions, council

12 *Rostov, Kremlin, Gate-church of the Resurrection, c. 1670: view from the south*
13 *(overleaf) Pskov, Kremlin. View over the River Pskova, showing the north-western fortifications and the Cathedral of the Holy Trinity, flat tower (foreground) and Kutekrom tower, 15th–17th centuries*

meetings and feasts took place in the aura of ecclesiastical splendour. While the ruling class enjoyed the bright, 'heavenly' light, the ordinary people had to stand beneath the low vaults in 'earthly' twilight. The lighting played a social role. In the princely cathedrals dating from before the Tartar invasions, the staircase-towers often flank the gallery like a rampart, compelling comparisons with the westwork of Western Europe. In both cases the structure symbolizes the temporal authority, in Russia in 'symphony' with, in the West in opposition to, the spiritual power. The baroque 'imperial box' for the lord or the patrician who endowed the church was a late emanation of the theocratic principle which was, however, expressed in a quite different fashion in the Cathedral of the Assumption in Moscow at the actual time of Moscow's rise to the central authority of the whole of Russia: here the nascent imperial power, as part of the campaign for the independence and unity of the realm, had the church built without a tribune, to demonstrate the oneness, the inseparability of the congregation (denied again, however, in the erection of the vast iconostasis). It is characteristic that the Russian word 'sobor', translated as 'cathedral', also means 'council' or 'assembly'. The interior of the church was meant to be the place where the whole people gathered together, with the tsar and the boyars at their head, before the throne of God.

The west tribune was given a different function by the burgesses of Novgorod in the thirteenth century. A new pendent to the sanctuary was built in the form of the little 'chapel-offices', reminiscent of the guild chapels in the churches of the Hanseatic towns. The donors used them to conclude commercial transactions, to receive foreigners and to entertain guests. The mystery of the sacrament was united under one roof with the symbol of middle-class commercial aptitude and economic power. The increased use of parts of churches as warehouses and storage rooms was connected with this process of mingling the sacred with the mundane. The petty bourgeois communities of the Moscow suburban quarters (Posad), from the late fifteenth century onwards, went so far as to build small stone churches with the secondary purpose of providing a safe place for keeping their valuables, which were constantly in danger of destruction by fire in their wooden houses. On the one hand earthly prosperity was given a religious justification, and efficiency in one's secular calling equated with a religious calling, on the other hand it was a manifestation of the urge to protect the normal course of natural phenomena and of human life against the influence of the Evil One, an urge that was not only eminently practical but also deeply rooted in survivals of pagan magic. The piety of the Russian people was characterized by active fraternal charity, and by the sensitive exercise of love and humility; but also by a hard-headed realism, that had grown out of the peasant's dependence on the elements for his sheer physical survival, and was densely permeated with superstition. The church building venerated as a 'monument' was also regarded as a symbol of human security.

The Iconographic Programme and the Spatial Structure

The spatial structure of the middle Byzantine domed cruciform church provided the ideal background for displaying the Orthodox iconographic programme. Early Russian art adopted both, though it laid the emphasis on the exterior of the building. The interior of St Sophia in Kiev is a good general example. The mosaics and mural paintings symbolize, in the same way as the icons, the liturgy and the structure of the building, the appear-

14 *Island of Kizhi, Lake Onega; Church of the Virgin of the Intercession, 1764: the domes seen from the bell-tower*

ance of Christ and the heavenly church in the midst of the earthly congregation, and the spread of Christendom. The scheme of decoration covers the whole interior and is arranged according to a very precise plan. There is hardly a corner where the congregation do not feel the watchful gaze of a saint on them.

The hierarchic principles of the iconographic programme follow the hierarchic spatial structure, both vertically and horizontally. The vertical arrangement corresponds on the one hand to the symbolism of Cosmas Indicopleustes' *Topographia Christiana,* and on the other to the Areopagite metaphysics of light. The most important and the largest paintings are placed in the highest and lightest zone, in the roof of the dome and in the apse. At lower levels, the closer the painted surface is to the ground, the more the heavenly motifs are superseded by earthly ones, the space darkens and the panels get smaller and more closely packed. The horizontal arrangement, following the liturgy and Christian cosmology, has an east-west directional flow, observing the hierarchy of the various areas of the interior. Since the pictures have to be strictly two-dimensional and avoid any illusion of perspective depth, the figures do not act behind the picture plane but in front of it, across the interior of the church. The architectonic space, with its multifarious forms, its vaults, spandrels, niches, wall-surfaces, itself becomes the pictorial space. In St Sophia in Kiev, for instance, the two pillars of the triumphal arch are used in the iconographic programme to depict the Annunciation, to portray the paired figures of the Archangel and the Virgin. The space is not painted illusionistically behind them, but is real space, between the figures and in front of them, depending on the direction of the onlooker's gaze. This is what Otto Demus means by the 'spatial icon', which draws the congregation of the faithful into itself optically and physically.

Vertically the iconographic programme starts in the apex of the main dome, the highest and lightest place of honour, with the Pantocrator, Christ as the ruler and judge of the universe. The congregation is constantly exposed to his penetrating gaze and is at the same time strictly separated from him by the intervening light that falls through the windows of the drum. The 'head', however, is never without his 'body' and therefore, in direct reference to the Incarnation, a large figure of the Mother of God, 'Orans' with outstretched arms, 'Hodigitria' with the Child on her left arm, or enthroned with the Child, his hand raised to bless, on her lap, appears in the semi-dome, the concha, of the apse, behind and above the altar. She stands before God as representative of the church on earth, to answer for the sins of the world. An inscription above the mosaic in St Sophia in Kiev refers to her intercessionary role: 'In her is God; she cannot falter. God stands by her from day to day.' The Pantocrator is surrounded by the four archangels, his servants and instruments, which proclaim him and his rule 'standing on the four corners of the earth' (Revelation 7 : 1), for which reason they are portrayed above the four crossing pillars. The prophets and apostles, the Old Testament heralds of the Parousia and the New Testament emissaries of Christ, are arrayed between the windows of the drum, sometimes accompanied by the patriarchs Abraham, Isaac and Jacob, while the pendentives, which form the transition from the dome of heaven to the crossing of earth, are occupied by the four evangelists, whose divinely inspired gospels, directed to the four corners of the earth, join this world to the world hereafter. The ceiling vaults and the upper part of the walls carry a cycle depicting the most significant scenes from the life of Christ, and other important festivals in the church calendar, including the Nativity of the Virgin, the Annunciation and the Assumption. The lowest zone of the niches, arches, pillars and the north and south walls serves for portrayals of the choirs of saints and biblical events, of decreasing importance from east to west. Within the limits of the prescribed hierarchy, this zone offers the greatest freedom of thematic choice.

The east end, the area about the altar, where the mystery of salvation actually takes place, governs the horizontal programme. Both liturgically and symbolically, God is located here and in the main dome. The iconography in the sanctuary refers to the birth, crucifixion, burial and resurrection of Christ. He is shown, above the Virgin in the main apse, usually in a Deesis group or as High Priest, together with the Descent of the Holy Ghost. Lower down, the Last Supper is depicted, in direct allusion to the sacrament celebrated at the altar, with the apostles taking the bread on the left side and the wine on the right. Lower still there is a line of figures, the church fathers, archdeacons, the great liturgists and the con-celebrants in the sacrament. The wall of the prothesis, the starting point of the Great Entry in the service, often bears an appropriate allegory, such as 'Hospitality'. The diakonikon has the Three Children in the Fiery Furnace. The decoration of the sanctuary also includes a Hetoimasia ('preparation of the throne') in reference to Christ's sacrificial death and the Second Coming.

The nave (naos), centred on the open area of the crossing beneath the dome, which symbolizes the visible heaven at the apex and the earth at ground level, has a direct and close relationship with the bema. Its iconographic programme of saints and biblical events is essentially vertical in its arrangement. The pillars or columns bear the figures of hierarchs, martyrs, ascetics and soldier-saints. The west end of the church, the west wall of the nave or the vestibule (narthex), is given over to the Last Judgment, the Passion, the Assumption of the Virgin or the better-known martyrdoms, according to liturgical function and symbolism. On the wall above the main entrance into the nave from the vestibule there appears either the figure of Christ with the gospels open in his hand, as Acheiropoietos, with the Virgin and John the Baptist, or the Madonna and Child. The remaining wall surfaces bear the figures of holy women and hymnographers, and illustrations of the Old Testament, ecumenical councils, hymns and the Book of Revelation.

In the course of the development of late Byzantine art, and even more so in that of Russian art, this programme was varied and expanded on Christological, Mariological, hagiographical or historical lines, without infringing its fundamental significance. Favourite subjects included the Russian saints and their legends, national church feasts such as the Protection and Intercession of the Virgin, provincial Russian variants of the types of the Virgin and the associated legends, local princes and metropolitans, national events. The donors wanted to assist the propagation of church dogmas, which had become more complex in their interpretation, and of theocratic ideas. There was a parallel to the *Biblia pauperum* in the selection of scenes from the Old Testament with typological equivalents from the New. Notable changes in iconography on these lines took place in the reign of Ivan IV and in the seventeenth century. In the first period it served the didactic and authoritarian purposes of the centralized theocratic government, and in the second it resulted in the secularization of the subject matter, in spite of the measures prescribed by Patriarch Nikon. Mural painting in the towns along the Volga, especially Yaroslavl, and also in Moscow, made use of the engravings in the Piscator Bible, which was well known in Russia in the seventeenth century, and even introduced genre and history scenes in the nave. True fresco (with a paint made of pigments mixed with water, applied to fresh, moist plaster) was rare in the seventeenth century. It was much more common to combine it with the fresco-secco technique. Early Russian fresco painting usually involved two or three layers, the bottom a compound of brick dust and plant fibres. The single layer of white plaster only came into use in the fourteenth century, and was first used in the Moscow region. The binding agents and pigments were oil, honey, wax, yolk of egg, lime, coloured minerals, soot and kaolin paste.

The
Iconostasis   The purpose of the iconostasis, the liturgical structure on the border between 'earthly' and 'heavenly' existence, is to reveal, through the pictures on it, the unseen mystical

event that is taking place behind it. It separates the congregation from the 'Holy of Holies', the nave from the sanctuary, and simultaneously connects them by its three doors. Under the influences of the ceremonial of the Jerusalemite liturgy and the expansion of the scope of theological iconography, the iconostasis in the Russian church grew steadily taller, even reaching the ceiling vault on occasion; as it did so it concealed or severely limited the view of the paintings on the east wall and to a certain extent even came to take the place of the altar in the eyes of the lay congregation. It had developed from the altar screen which was already a feature of early Christian churches. To begin with, in Byzantine churches, icons of Christ, the archangels, prophets and apostles were placed along the top beam (architrave). At a later stage the centre was taken up with a Deesis, that is, a picture of Christ enthroned between the interceding figures of the Virgin and John the Baptist, and in the eleventh century a second tier of icons, depicting the months and feast-days, was arranged below the Deesis. On the appropriate occasions in the church year, each icon was taken from its place and exhibited on a lectern for veneration.

The idea of intercession, which played a leading role in Byzantine theology, seized on Russian art at a time when the country was starting to unite and to free itself from Tartar oppression, in the late fourteenth and early fifteenth centuries. The depiction of the communion of saints uniting in prayers on behalf of mankind was also understood as a summons to the Russian people to unite in the common struggle for freedom. An additional factor was the role played by the Virgin as 'the hope of the despairing', as the first in this saintly communion; the worship of the Virgin, influenced by pagan traditions, became an important popular cult, and she herself the most important intercessor for the forgiveness of sins. Early forms of iconostasis, often with wholly arbitrary groupings of icons, can be traced back to the beginning of the thirteenth century in Russia, but it was not until *c*1400 that the arrangement was developed according to fixed principles, centring on the Deesis.

The Deesis, which is already found in the Cathedral of St Sophia in Kiev, in the form of three mosaic medallions in the semi-dome of the main apse, and enjoyed great popularity in the icon and mural painting of Vladimir-Suzdalia, developed into the dominant iconographic theme. By gradual stages it fell into three individual parts, joined up with rows of other saints and then, during the thirteenth and fourteenth centuries, flanked by another tier of feast-day icons and later by tiers of prophets and Old Testament patriarchs. The most important iconostasis, surviving in large measure in its original position, is that in the Cathedral of the Annunciation in the Kremlin in Moscow, which was created in 1405 under the direction of Theophanes the Greek, Master Prokhor of Gorodets and Andrey Rublev. V. N. Lazarev has described it as the classic Russian type, to be regarded as the starting point of the whole of the subsequent development. The iconostasis is often fixed on the front of a massive stone screen, a characteristic which has been established in numerous church buildings of the Moscow region in the fifteenth and sixteenth centuries, and which probably goes back to an Oriental influence, by way of the local style of Ryazan. But as a rule the stone surface was dispensed with. The uprights of the frame were secured directly to the east crossing pillars. The fully developed, 'classic' Russian form consists of five or six 'rows', 'tiers' or 'storeys' (Yarus) and is often crowned by a cross.

The path of revelation runs from top to bottom. The top tier comprises the Old Testament patriarchs, Adam, Jacob, Moses, Isaac, Abraham and others, and there is usually an icon of the God of Sabaoth, the Saviour or the Trinity in the middle of the row. The next row is of prophets, usually flanking a central 'Madonna of the Sign'. The prophets, of whom often only the head and trunk are depicted, hold open scrolls with prophecies of Christ's coming as Redeemer. Beneath these two tiers of Old Testament themes comes the tier of feast-day icons: in addition to Easter, represented by the Women at the Tomb or by Christ's Descent into Hell (Anastasis), there are usually six feasts relating to the life

Iconostasis   (Cathedral of the Annunciation in the Kremlin, Moscow)

A *Tier of patriarchs, with the God of Sabaoth in the middle*

B *Tier of prophets, with the Virgin Hodigitria enthroned in the middle (16th century)*

C *Feast-day tier: 1 Annunciation 2 Nativity 3 Presentation in the Temple (Purification of the Virgin) 4 Instruction (Mid-Pentecost) 5 Baptism of Christ 6 Transfiguration 7 Raising of Lazarus 8 Entry into Jerusalem 9 Last Supper 10 Crucifixion 11 Deposition 12 Christ's Descent into Hell (Anastasis) 13 Ascension 14 Descent of the Holy Ghost 15 Assumption of the Virgin*

D *Deesis tier: 1 St Basil the Great 2 St Peter 3 Archangel Michael 4 the Virgin 5 Enthroned Christ 6 St John the Baptist 7 Archangel Gabriel 8 St Paul 9 St John Chrysostom (tiers C and D 1405)*

E *Icons of the months (18th century)*

F *Veneration tier: 1 Virgin of Tikhvin (16th century) 2 Archangel Uriel, on the door to the prothesis (18th century) 3 Enthroned Saviour (17th century) 4 Virgin Hodigitria (16th century) with medallions of women of the Old Testament (18th century) 5 Royal or Paradise Door, with panels depicting the Annunciation and the evangelists 6 Enthroned Saviour (1337) 7 Annunciation of Ustyug (17th-century copy) 8 John the Baptist, the Apostle Peter, Alexis 'the Man of God' (1683) 9 Archangel Raphael on the door to the diakonikon (18th century) 10 Saviour of Smolensk (16th century)*

of Christ, the Nativity, the Baptism, the Presentation in the Temple (Candlemas, or the Purification of the Virgin), the Triumphal Entry into Jerusalem, the Ascension and the Transfiguration; these alternate with four feasts of the Virgin: her Nativity, Offering (Introduction in the Temple), the Annunciation and the Assumption; the tier is completed with representations of Pentecost and the Raising of the Cross. Pentecost is depicted either by the Old Testament Trinity as 'Hospitality' (Philoxenia), the visit of the three angels to Abraham and Sarah in the grove of Mamre, or else through the Descent of the Holy Ghost. The feast of the Raising of the Cross commemorates the discovery of the True Cross by the Empress Helena in Jerusalem in 326. In the case of an exceptionally large iconostasis, as in the Cathedral of the Annunciation in the Moscow Kremlin, this tier has additional icons of Christ's life: the Crucifixion and Burial, the Last Supper, the Raising of Lazarus and the Instruction (Mid-Pentecost). The Russian feast of the Protection and Intercession of the Virgin (Pokrov) is also frequently depicted. The tier beneath the feast-day icons, the second tier from the bottom, is the Deesis row, with icons of large figures, often more than life size. The central figure of this, and of the whole screen, placed immediately above the Royal Door, is Christ enthroned, with the Virgin to the left and John the Baptist to the right. Both are bowing towards the Son of God, their bodies forsaking the frontal stance by a quarter of a turn. In spite of the association in general terms with the Last Judgment, Christ does not appear as the stern Judge, the Pantocrator, but as the benevolent Redeemer and Saviour. The other figures in the row, all in attitudes of supplication, are, on the left, the Archangel Michael, St Peter the Apostle and St Basil the Great, and on the right, the Archangel Gabriel, St Paul the Apostle and St John Chrysostom; St Demetrius of Salonika, St Gregory of Nicaea and St John the Evangelist are often also added to the left, and St George, St Nicholas the Miracle-Worker and St Andrew the Apostle on the right.

The Deesis is the determining factor in the selection and arrangement of the entire programme of icons. The earthly congregation at prayer experiences the manifestation of the presence of the 'heavenly church' making supplications on their behalf. The part of the screen below the Deesis tier is also arranged schematically. There is sometimes an intermediate row of small icons of the months or apostles, saints and martyrs. The bottom row, embracing the three doors, is called the Veneration tier, because worshippers are able to reach the icons and pay them direct homage by kissing them, bowing and making the sign of the cross before them. The rules are less stringent in this tier and local preferences are indulged to a certain extent, but a prescribed order is still discernible: on the right of the Royal Door there is an icon either of the Saviour or of the church's patronal feast or saint, and on the left there is an icon of the Virgin and Child. The centre of significance in this tier is the actual main entrance to the sanctuary, which the priests only go through at certain prescribed moments in the service. It is at this point, on the altar steps (solea), that the Communion of Believers takes place, and for that reason the Eucharist, the institution of the sacrament in the Last Supper, is usually depicted above the doorway. The panels of the Royal Door itself, the symbol of entry into the Kingdom of God, usually bear the four evangelists, or occasionally early fathers of the church, and another Annunciation in the top pair. The liturgists St Basil the Great and St John Chrysostom appear again on the door posts. The two other doors, the left-hand leading into the prothesis and the right-hand into the diakonikon, are usually adorned with the Archangels Michael and Gabriel, the leaders of the heavenly host, or with archdeacons, who take over the role of the angels in services.

The iconostasis in early Russian churches took over all the themes of the programme of murals systematically—the patriarchs, prophets and apostles from the dome, the evangelists from the pendentives, the feast-days from the vaults and walls, the Deesis and the Eucharist from the main apse—it even pre-empted the spiritual significance of the arrangement of the paintings within the interior, if it was large and tall enough and monumental in execution. That happened especially in Moscow and its vicinity under the rule of the Great Princes, where the dimensions of the icons and of the screens themselves grew in proportion with the larger churches that were being built from the fifteenth century onwards. The tendency of the iconostasis to dominate the church was intensified in the seventeenth century by the introduction of grandiose, ornately decorated and gilded wooden frames, the high relief carving on which demanded as much attention in its own right as the paintings. Examples are to be found in the Cathedral of the Virgin of Smolensk in the New Convent of the Virgin in Moscow, and in the Church of the Prophet Elijah in Yaroslavl.

Symbol of God — the House of the People

Early Russian architecture, like icon painting, belonged in equal measure to the whole Russian people, who took an active part in the victories and the defeats, in the development and the retrenchment of the state as *Imperium Christianum,* even though the upper classes, jealous of their authority and privileges, constantly attempted to exploit art as an expression of their dominant position. N. N. Voronin has stressed the homogeneity of the stylistic development, which never experienced any division into two opposing cultures along class lines in spite of the changes and vicissitudes in the historical circumstances, in spite of the differences of social roles and motivations. Architectural forms eventually came to renounce altogether the optical illusionism in interiors, the geometric regularity in construction, and above all the incommensurability of proportions, which were integral to middle Byzantine architecture. The dimensions virtually ceased to crush the vitality of a building any more. What happened essentially was that a preference that had its origins in folk art prevailed, a preference for organic structures.

Konrad Onasch has traced a 'progressive humanization of the aesthetic principles' of icon painting. Even in so early a work as the Icon of the Virgin of the Monastery of Caves (*c*1299) the depiction of the two abbots Antoni and Feodosy is almost portrait-like. There are elements of a realistic style in one of the earliest literary monuments of Kievan Rus, the Paterikon of the Monastery of Caves. Architecture, too, developed anthropomorphically, according to the scale of the human exchange with nature and of social existence. Increasing significance accrued to physical forms that were relatable to human forms, that could be interpreted and transcended in anthropomorphic terms. The gentle Redeemer who took humanity upon himself was more sympathetic to the spirit of Russian piety than the sublime, unapproachable God of the Byzantine church, and the religious disputations of scholars were also alien. Similarly, super-sophisticated aestheticism was as foreign to the three-dimensional structural principles of Russian architects as abstract mathematical concepts. Groundplans, elevations and constructional details were only sketched out (as 'patterns'), a store of practical experience was handed down from generation to generation, but there was no precise working-out of numerical proportions.

Ultimately the specific character and significance of the Russian church derives from the humanistic ideal of 'sobornost', the Orthodox community of brotherly love, which is closely connected with the traditions of the peasant community (mir). The liking for liturgical ceremonial, attended by a congregation that stood (though seldom still for long), was merely an expressive intensification of the feeling that approached God humbly but without intermediaries in a spirit that was basically one of tenderness (umileniye), and to which neither detached rationalism nor the theocratic blending of piety with fear had anything to say. In the eyes of the common people the wealth and splendour of courts were not merely a burden laid upon their own existence but also entailed the risk of separation from God through pride. This attitude to life and to faith was incisively expressed by Nikolai Leskov in his story *On the Edge of the World.* 'It was not in Byzantine splendour, surrounded by incense, that we found him; it is only with us that he is the true God, who is everywhere with us, simple and familiar, who comes to us without incense, like a gentle breath of cool air beneath the benches of the bath-house, and nestles on our bosoms like a dove.'

God was to be made human and the purpose of prayer was to forge the link between heaven and earth, to be a 'personal assurance of the actual presence of the Kingdom of God and the Saints' (E. Benz), to be love in action and the means of strengthening the communion of believers. A church building, like an icon, was intended to help to bring about union with God on earth and therefore needed to embody parallels between heaven and earth. It had to be an image of the mystical body of Christ and of human forms and of the expression of which they were capable. The much-praised instinct of Russian architects for proportion, rhythm, outline and decoration derives ultimately from the traditional schemata of simple peasant structures and processes, and of naive, pantheistic surrender to the forces of nature, by which a pre-Christian, rustic sense of community was evoked.

The piety of the people was permeated with a sense of closeness to nature which interpreted Christian rebirth quite literally as the beautifying of the earth and the transfiguration of human life. A church building had a double significance, as an embodiment of the meaning of Easter and as part of the world of nature, a beautiful organic growth, willed by God, blending harmoniously into the landscape or into its monastic or urban surroundings—one of the characteristics of early Russian architecture is the easy relationship between groups of buildings. The anthropomorphic attitude is reflected in the terminology: the dome is called the 'head' or 'forehead', the drum the 'neck', the vaulting or rounded gable at the top of a wall the 'shoulder', the sectional vaulting below the drum the 'bosom'. Other expressions allude to dress or objects in everyday life: 'onion', 'poppy' and 'helmet' for various shapes of dome, 'kokoshnik', a women's hairstyle, for the ogee-ended gable, 'belt' for the horizontal frieze on a façade, 'melon' and 'girka' (a small weight) for decorative elements.

Russian architecture freed itself from the restraints of Byzantine models in the same way as icon painting, humanizing the religious and aesthetic norms. The sacred 'monument', was not crystalline but anthropomorphic. Even the site, the careful choice of which is described in numerous chronicles and saints' lives, had to be appropriate to human requirements: whether the upper classes' desire for an imposing grandeur, or the approachable humility beloved of the common people. In the Middle Ages, the people did not only assemble inside the churches for services, but outside in the open air as well in large numbers, watching the 'holy action' through the open doors. They wanted to feel 'at home' inside and outside the church. Just as they worshipped the creator in the natural creation, so they honoured the church building, regarding both as equally animate. Art was in fact a fundamental instinct of their own nature: a 'milestone of God', bearing witness to the human capacity for self-realization. As the Russians put their energy and imagination into their buildings, they unfurled and developed their own selves, transformed uncanny and menacing forces into familiar ones, and in the world made by their own hands they could contemplate and experience something that was nobler, more worthy and more beautiful than the circumstances in which they lived.

HUBERT FAENSEN

PLATES

Kiev and Vladimir-Suzdal – Rus before the Tartar Invasions

The City-States of Novgorod and Pskov

Moscow, the Centre of a Unified Empire

The Period of Transition: the Seventeenth Century

Typology of the Wooden Churches

Kiev and Vladimir-Suzdal—Rus before the Tartar Invasions

[15–33] *Kiev, Cathedral of St Sophia, 1037–61*   **16, 17** *East aspect, showing original masonry*   **18** *Mosaic in the central dome,*
mid 11th century: the Evangelist Mark

[15–33] Kiev, Cathedral of St Sophia, 1037–61 **19, 20** *Mosaics on the pillars of the triumphal arch, mid 11th century:*
the Annunciation: the Archangel Gabriel and the Virgin **21** *West corner of the south tribune, showing clustered column*

[15–33] *Kiev, Cathedral of St Sophia,*
1037–61   **22** *The inner north gallery, looking*
towards the tomb of Grand Duke Yaroslav
the Wise   **23** *Marble sarcophagus of Yaroslav*
the Wise, with relief decoration, 1125

[15–33] Kiev, Cathedral of St Sophia, 1037–61
24 Mosaic in the main apse, detail from the north side: the Eucharist   **25** Encrusted cross, mid 11th century, on the rear wall of the clergy stalls on the north side of the main apse   **26** Mosaic on the south pillar of the triumphal arch, mid 11th century: medallion depicting the Martyr Lisimachus   **27** Mosaics from the row of bishops in the south part of the main apse, mid 11th century: St John Chrysostom and Gregory of Nicaea

[34–36] Kiev, Demetrius
Monastery, c. 1062, later
St Michael's Monastery 'with
the golden roofs': works now in
the museum of the Cathedral
of St Sophia **34, 35** St George
of Cappadocia and St Theodore
Stratilates, left and right ends
of a relief in red schist, c. 1062
36 St Stephen mosaic, c. 1113

37 *Kiev, Church of the Saviour, Berestovo, early 12th century: partial view of the north front*
38 *Kiev, Monastery of the Caves, Gate-church of the Holy Trinity, 1106–08, with baroque facing c. 1700: view from the east*

[39–41] Chernigov, Cathedral of the Transfiguration,
c. 1036   **39** West side, upper part of the north-west tower,
and south-west tower, 18th century   **40** Detail of the
north-west tower   **41** The south arcade, seen from the nave

[46, 47] *Chernigov, the Pyatnitsa Church in the market-place, second half of the 12th century* **46** *View from the south-east*
47 *Detail of the west front*

48 *Bogolyubovo, Palace of Andrey Bogolyubsky: the north staircase-tower with bridge to the tribune of the Court Church, 1158–65, seen from the north-east*

49 *Vladimir, Golden Gate, 1164, east side; above the gate the Church of the Miracle of the Veil, 15th–17th centuries*

50 *Pereslavl-Zalessky, Cathedral of the Transfiguration, 1152–57: view from the south-west*

[51–55] *Bogolyubovo, Church of the Virgin of the Intercession, on the River Nerl, 1165*   **54** *Interior of the dome*   **55** *View from the north-west*

[56–63] *Vladimir, Cathedral of St Demetrius, 1194–97*   **56** *View from the north-east*   **57** *Central division of the south front*
58 *(overleaf) Reliefs in the pediment of the central division of the west front: King David or Solomon with animals*   **59** *(overleaf,*
right) Reliefs on the west front: saints, and the dove symbolizing the Holy Ghost, framed by columns of the blind arcade

[56–63] *Vladimir, Cathedral of St Demetrius, 1194–97* **60** *Sculptures on the archivolts of the west portal* **61** *Friezes and blind arcades on the apses* **62** *Relief carving of a lion on a springer in the interior*

[56–63] *Vladimir, Cathedral of St Demetrius, 1194–97* **63** *Reliefs on the central division of the west front: animals, horsemen and plants*

[64–66] *Vladimir, Cathedral of the Assumption, 1185–89 (first building 1158–60)* **64** *View from the north-east*

[64–66] *Vladimir, Cathedral of the Assumption, 1185–89 (first building 1158–60)*   **65** *Blind arcades on the south front*
66 *View of the west and south fronts*

[67–69] *Suzdal, Kremlin, Cathedral of the Nativity of the Virgin 1222–25/1528–30* **67** *South aspect* **68, 69** *Damascened panels, c. 1227–37: (from the south door) the three youths in the fiery furnace, and Lot receiving the angels; (from the west door) the Crucifixion*

[70–79] *Yuryev-Polsky, Cathedral of St George, 1230–34/1471* **70** *View from the south-east* **71** *South front* **72** *Detail of the relief frieze on the south front: masks of warriors and lions*

[70–79] *Yuryev-Polsky, Cathedral of St George, 1230–34/1471*   **73** *Capital in the south-west corner: masks and figures of saints*   **74** *Relief over the north portal: St George with escutcheon*

[70–79] *Yuryev-Polsky, Cathedral of St George, 1230–34/1471* **75, 77** *Blind arcades with figures of saints, on the north-west corner* **76** *Relief over the south portal: the Virgin of the Sign* **78** *Relief on the south front: one of the Seven Sleepers of Ephesus*

[80–86, 88] *Novgorod, Kremlin, Cathedral of St Sophia, 1045–52* **80** *View from the west*

[91, 92] *Novgorod, Monastery of St Anthony,*
Cathedral of the Nativity of the Virgin, 1117–19
91 *Interior, showing the main dome and west gallery*
92 *East front and north-west staircase-tower*
93 *Novgorod, Court of Yaroslav, Cathedral*
of St Nicholas, 1113–36, north-east aspect; behind,
on the left, the Church of St Procopius, 1529

94 *Novgorod, Yuryev Monastery, Cathedral of St George, 1119–30, by Master Peter: view from the south-west*
[95–98] *Novgorod, Church of the Saviour, Nereditsa, 1198* **95** *Frescos in the main apse, 1199: St James and St Phocas*

[95–98] *Novgorod, Church of the Saviour, Nereditsa,*
1198 **96** *View from the south-east*   **97** *(below)*
View of the church across the River Nereditsa
98 *Fresco in the north burial-chamber of the main*
apse, 1199: Bishop Peter of Alexandria

[99–100] *Novgorod, Paraskeva-Pyatnitsa Church in the market-place, 1207/14th and 16th centuries* **99** *Detail of the west portal* **100** *View from the north-west*

[101–103] *Staraya Ladoga, Church of St George, second half of the 12th century*
101 *Mural painting in the drum, c. 1180: prophet* **102** *Apses and north front*
103 *Mural painting, c. 1180: St George slaying the dragon*

104 *Novgorod, Church of the Annunciation, near Arkazh, 1179/17th century: the east front seen from across Lake Myachin*
105 *Novgorod, Church of the Nativity of the Virgin (in the former Monastery of the Nativity of the Virgin) 'at the place of Perun',*
1221: view from the south

[106, 108–111] Novgorod, Church of St Theodore Stratilates, 1360–61   **106** *(top, left) View from the south-west, bell-tower and extension, 17th century*   **108** *Fresco by Theophanes the Greek (?) in the drum, second half of the 14th century: head of a prophet (Ezekiel?)*   **107** *(bottom, left) Novgorod, Church of St Nicholas, Lipna, 1292: view from the south-east*

[106, 108–111] Novgorod, Church of St Theodore Stratilates, 1360–61 **109** *Fresco by Theophanes the Greek (?) in the drum,
second half of the 14th century: archangel* **110** *View from the north-east; bell-tower, 17th century*

[106, 108–111] *Novgorod, Church of St Theodore Stratilates, 1360–61* **111** *Decoration on the west front and drum*
[112–114] *Novgorod, Church of the Transfiguration, in the Street of Elijah, 1374* **112** *View from the south-east*

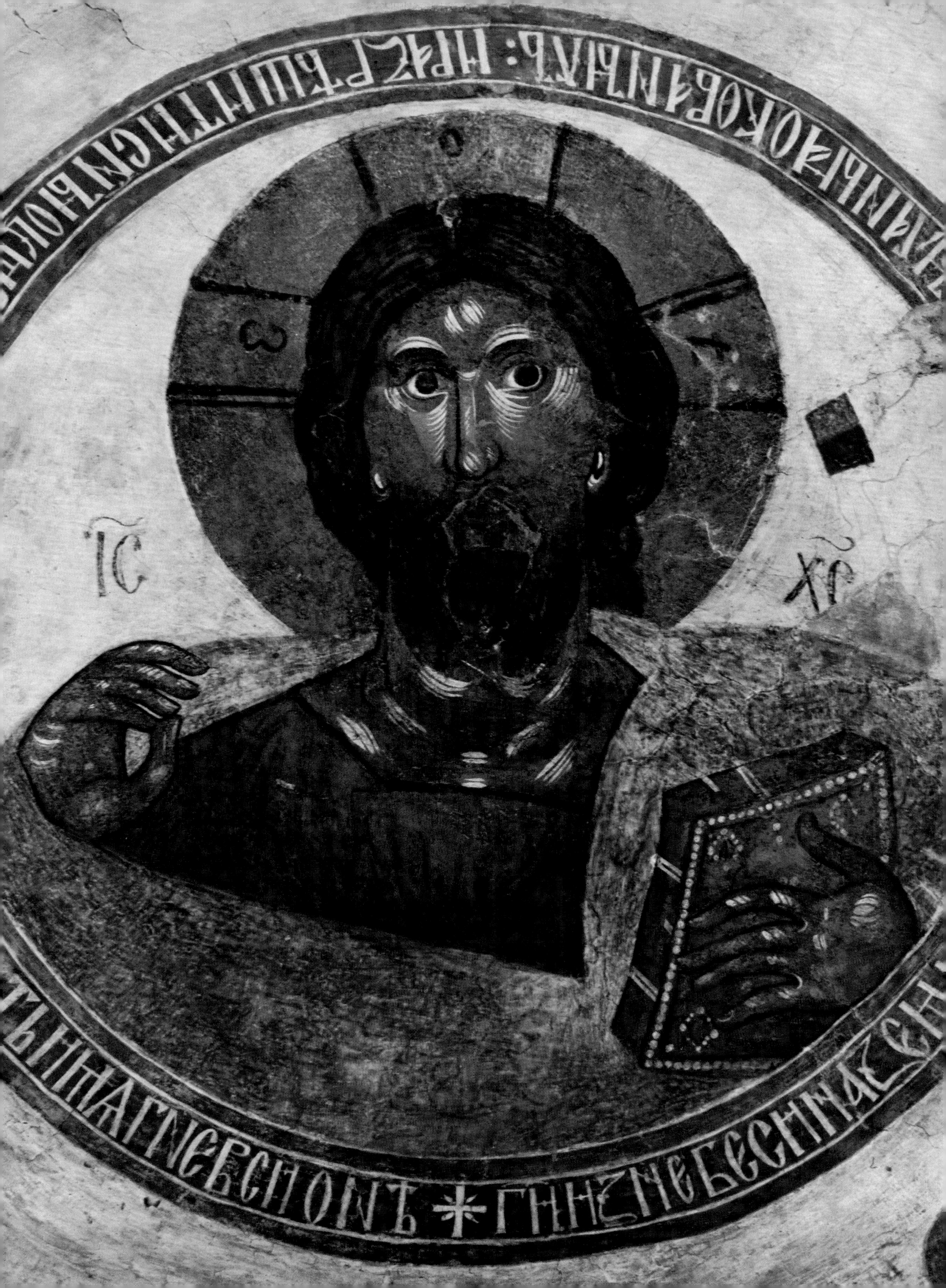
IC
XC

115 *(top, left) Novgorod, Church of the Annunciation on the Commerce Side (right), 1362/16th century; bell-tower,
17th century; and (left) Church of the Archangel Michael, 1300–02/1454/1812; from the south-east*
116 *Novgorod, Church of St Demetrius of Salonika, 1381–83/1463, and bell-tower, 1691; from the north-east*
117 *Novgorod, Church of St John the Evangelist, Vitko, 1383–84: view from the south-east*

120 *Novgorod, Court of Yaroslav. View from the east, showing the Church of St Procopius (left), 1529; and the Church of the Women Carrying Anointing Oil (right), 1510* **121** *Novgorod, Monastery of the Holy Ghost, Church of the Holy Trinity, 1557: view of the south domes*

[122–127] *Pskov, Mirozh Monastery, Cathedral of the Transfiguration, 1156*   **124** *Fresco in the south arm, mid 12th century: the Nativity*   **125** *The south arm seen from the nave*

[122–127] *Pskov, Mirozh Monastery, Cathedral of the Transfiguration, 1156: frescos, mid 12th century* **126** *Scene from the apocryphal Childhood of the Virgin, in the south-west chapel* **127** *Two Apostles (?), in the south arm*

[128, 129] *Pskov, Monastery of St John, Cathedral of St John the Baptist, c. 1240* **128** *View from the south, showing bell-gable and extensions, 15th–16th centuries* **129** *Detail of the bell-gable*

133 *Pskov, Church of St Basil 'on the Hill', 1413, roofing and chapels 17th and 19th centuries: view from the north-east*
134 *Pskov, Church of St Nicholas by the Wall, 15th–16th centuries: east front*

135 *Pskov, Church of the Epiphany, Zapskovye, 1496: view from the west*
136 *Pskov, Church of St Clement, Zaveliche, 16th century: view of south chapel, roofing and dome, 18th century, from the north-east*

137 *Pskov, Thunder tower on the town wall, 1525*
138 *Pskov, Church of the Assumption 'by the ferry': bell-gable, 1521*

140 *Pskov, Church of SS Peter and Paul 'on the river-bank', 1540; east front*

[139, 141] Pskov, Old Church of the Ascension, 16th century   **139** View from the north-east; bell-tower, 17th century
141 Brick ornamentation on the drum

[142, 143] *Pskov, Church of St Nicholas 'on the Dry Land', 1535–37*   **142** *View from the north-east*   **143** *South-east burial chapel and part of the east front*

144 *Pskov, Church of the Ascension, Stadishche, 1532; extensions and bell-gable, 17th century: view from the south-west*
145 *Pskov, Church of the Virgin of the Intercession and of the Nativity of the Virgin 'at the Breach', 16th century: west front*
146 *Pskov, town wall, tower of the Virgin of the Intercession, first half of the 16th century*

147 *Izborsk, Temnushka tower, 14th century*
[148–154] *Pechory, Pskov Monastery of the Caves*   **148** *Western fortifications with tower of the upper grating (foreground) and Tararigin tower, mid 16th century*

[148–154] *Pechory, Pskov Monastery of the Caves*   **149** *Bell-gable of the St Nicholas Gate-church, 1581*
150 *Representation of the Pskov Monastery of the Caves and the Virgin, icon in the St Nicholas Gate-church, 16th century (?)*
151 *St Nicholas Gate-church, 1565: view from the south-west*

155 *Zvenigorod, Cathedral of the Assumption 'in the little town', 1399: east front*

[156–158] Zagorsk, Monastery of the Holy Trinity and St Sergius, Cathedral of the Trinity, 1422–23 **156** *Frieze on the north front* **157** *View from the north* **158** *(right) The Cathedral and Nikon Chapel, 1548: view from the east*

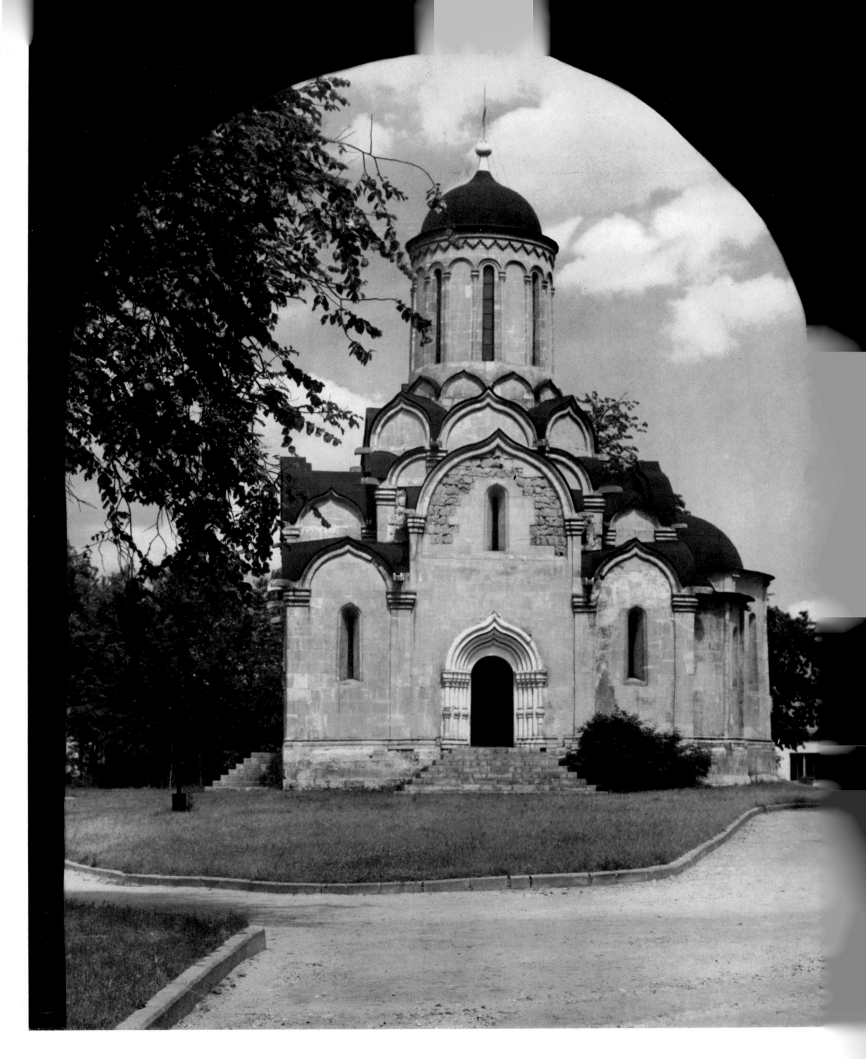

[159–161] *Moscow, Andronikov Monastery of the Saviour, founded 1360*   **159** *View of the western fortifications,*
17th century; the refectory (left), 1496–1508; and (behind) the Church of the Archangel Michael, 1691–1739
160, 161 *Cathedral of the Saviour, 1422–23, south portal and (above) the south front seen through the gate in the monastery wall*

[162–171] *Moscow, Kremlin, Cathedral of the Assumption, 1475–79* **169** *The 'Monomakh Throne', praying-desk of Tsar Ivan IV, carved in wood, 1551* **170, 171** *Reliefs on the sides of the 'Monomakh Throne': (above) Council of the Boyars; (below) Battles of Vladimir Monomakh, Duke of Kiev; scenes from the legend of the granting of the imperial insignia to Vladimir Monomakh by the Byzantine Emperor Constantine Monomakhos*

[172, 173] *Moscow, Kremlin, the bell-tower 'Ivan the Great', 1505–1624*   **172** *The belfry and tower seen from the north-west*
173 *East side: left, tower by Bon Fryasin, 1505–08, with upper storey and dome, 1600; belfry in the middle by Petrok Maly,*
1532–39 (1543); on the right, the 'Filaret' extension with tent roof, 1624

[174, 175] *Moscow, the Kremlin* **174** *Gate of the Saviour, 1491; upper part, 1625* **175** *Gate of the Holy Trinity, 1495; upper part, 1685*

[176–190] *Moscow, Kremlin, Cathedral of the Annunciation, 1484–89* **182** *The iconostasis seen from the tribune;*
on the north-west pillar (left), fresco by Feodosy, c. 1508: the Miracle of the Archangel Michael at Khonae **183** *Detail of*
the feast-day tier of the iconostasis: icon by Andrey Rublev, c. 1405, depicting the Nativity

[176–190] *Moscow, Kremlin, Cathedral of the Annunciation, 1484–89*   **184** *Fresco on the north-west pillar, c. 1508:*
Duke Alexander Nevsky and Grand Duke Ivan Kalita   **185** *The south-east corner, in front of the iconostasis; on the south-west*
pillar (right) St George and St Demetrius, fresco, c. 1508; floor-slabs of polished jasper, 16th century

[176–190] Moscow, Kremlin, Cathedral of the Annunciation, 1484–89 **186** Fresco on the vault in the south-west corner below the tribune, early 16th century: Christ as Horseman, scene from the Apocalypse **187** Fresco by Feodosy on the vault in the north-west corner below the tribune, c. 1508: the Forty Martyrs of Sebaste **188** Portal from the north gallery; stone-carving, mid 16th century; copper-panelled door, 15th or 16th century (?)

[176–190] *Moscow, Kremlin, Cathedral of the Annunciation, 1484–89* **189** *Panel from the door of the north gallery, 15th or 16th century(?): Sibyl and Christ (Queen of Sheba and Solomon)* **190** *Frescos on the vault of the west gallery, mid 16th century: the Tree of Jesse, portraits on medallions of Christ's ancestors, philosophers of ancient Greece, and Dukes of Moscow*

191 *Moscow, Kremlin, Faceted Palace (Granovitaya Palata), 1487–91, by Marco Ruffo and Pietro Antonio Solario*
192 *Moscow, Kremlin, Church of the Miracle of the Veil, 1484–86: view from the south-east*

[193–199] *Moscow, Kremlin, Cathedral of the Archangel Michael, 1505–08, by Alovisio Novo* **193** *View from the north-west*
194 *Interior of the nave, showing (foreground) the tombs of Grand Dukes of Moscow and Tsars, and (beyond) the tomb*
of Tsarevich Dmitry (right); fresco Andrey Bogolyubsky on the south-east pillar, c. 1660; the stone baldachin, 1628;
and the 19th-century iconostasis with icons of 15th–17th centuries; gilt chandeliers, 17th century

[193–199] *Moscow, Kremlin, Cathedral of the Archangel Michael, 1505–08* **195, 196** *West portal, and detail of sculpture*

[193–199] Moscow, Kremlin, Cathedral of the
Archangel Michael, 1505–08, frescos, 1652–66
197, 198 The Miraculous Draught of Fishes,
and angels, in the prothesis   **199** Duke
Alexander Nevsky, on the south-west pillar

200 *Kirillov, Therapontos Monastery, Cathedral of the Nativity of the Virgin, late 15th century: detail of the west front*
[201–204] *Vladimir, Convent of the Duchesses, Cathedral of the Assumption, early 16th century; mural paintings 1647–48*
201 *The prophet Daniel and an angel, detail from the Last Judgment, fresco on the west wall* **202** *View from the south-east;
corner building, 19th century* **203** *(overleaf) Russian prince, fresco on the north-west pillar* **204** *(overleaf, right) Pantocrator,
fresco in the dome*

[205–208] *Moscow, New Convent of the Virgin, Cathedral of the Icon of Our Lady of Smolensk, 1524–25* **205** *View from the north-west, showing (left background) the bell-tower, 1689–90* **206** *Altar ciborium, 1653* **207** *(overleaf) View from the south-east* **208** *(overleaf, right) Iconostasis, 1683–85, with icons of the 16th–17th centuries; mural paintings, late 16th century; holy water font (in the centre), 1685*

[209–210] *Suzdal, Convent of the Virgin of the Intercession* **209** *View over the River Kamenka to the fortifications, 16th–18th centuries; in the middle of the group of buildings, the Cathedral of the Virgin of the Intercession, 1518, and refectory, 1551* **210** *Holy Gate with Church of the Annunciation, c. 1518: view from the south-west*

211 *Rostov, Cathedral of the Assumption, early 16th century: view from the north-west; bell-gable (right), 1682–87*

[212, 213] *Suzdal, Monastery of the Saviour and St Euthymius, founded 1352* **212** *Gate-church of the Annunciation, early 16th century: north front* **213** *Bell-tower, tower on the left,* **and** *Church of the Birth of John the Baptist, early 16th century; bell-gable (right), 16th to 17th centuries*

[222, 223] *Yaroslavl, Monastery of the Saviour, Church of the Transfiguration, 1506–16* **222** *View from the east* **223** *Fresco in the south apse, 1563–64: The Lord God of Sabaoth*

[224, 225] *Zagorsk, Monastery of the Holy Trinity and St Sergius, founded 1340* **224** *View from the south-east: fortifications 16th to 17th centuries; (above, from left to right) refectory, 1686–92; bell-tower, 1741–70; Cathedral of the Assumption, Pyatnitsa tower, 1640; Gate-church of St John the Baptist, 1693–99; Red tower with Holy Gate, 16th–19th centuries; (left foreground) Paraskeva Pyatnitsa Church, 1547; and Pyatnitsky well-chapel, 17th–18th centuries* **225** *Cathedral of the Assumption, 1559–85, seen from the north-east*

226 *Moscow, Monastery of the Don: view from the south, showing the Old Cathedral of the Icon of the Virgin of the Don, 1591–93/1678–79, and (in the background) the New Cathedral, 1684–93*

227 *Moscow, Church of Triphon, Naprudnoye, late 15th century, south front*

228 *Moscow, Church of the Conception of St Anne 'in the corner', 1478–83; view from the south-east; in the background, the Rossiya Hotel*

229 *Rostov, Church of the Blessed Isidore, 1566: view from the south-east*

The Period of Transition: the Seventeenth Century

Typology of the Wooden Churches

230 *Moscow, Church of the Nativity of the Virgin, Putinki, 1649–52: tent roofs and domes*

[231–237] *Moscow, Church of the Holy Trinity, Nikitniki, 1634: mural paintings, 1652–53* **231** *Fresco on the south wall of the nave: the Crucifixion* **232** *Fresco on the north wall of the nave: the Parable of the Mote and the Beam*

259 *Moscow, Church of St Nicholas, Khamovniki, 1679–82: south front*
260 *Moscow, Church of St Nicholas, Bersenevka, 1656: view from the south-east*
261 *Moscow, Church of the Resurrection, Kadashi (suburb of the coopers), 1687–1713: view of the upper structure*
[262, 263] *(overleaf) Moscow, Church of the Assumption, Gonchari (suburb of the potters), 1654–1702* 262 *View of the domes; relief modelling of the Evangelist Matthew on tiles on the drum of the south chapel, 17th century* 263 *View from the north-west*

[271–276] *Yaroslavl, Church of St John
the Baptist, Tolchkovo, 1671–87* **271** *The
west gallery; frescos 1694–95* **272** *View
from the south-east* **273** *The south-east
domes*

[271–276] *Yaroslavl, Church of St John the Baptist, Tolchkovo, 1671–87; frescos 1694–95*   **274** *Part of the nave, north side*
275 *Miraculous appearance of the Icon of Our Lady of Tolga, in the north gallery*   **276** *Eschatological scene, on the vault of the west gallery*

[277,278] *Yaroslavl, Church of the Epiphany, 1684–93* **277** *Tiled decoration on the south gallery* **278** *View from the south-east*

[286–290] *Moscow, New Convent of the Virgin, founded 1524* **286** *Church of the Assumption, and refectory, 1685–87: view from the south-east* **287** *The Lopukhin Palace, 1687–89* **288** *View of the fortifications on the north-west, showing (from left to right) Gate-church of the Transfiguration, Lopukhin tower, bell-tower, Naprud tower, and the domes of the Cathedral of Our Lady of Smolensk, 16th–17th centuries*

291 *Moscow, Church of the Virgin of the Intercession, Fili, 1693: view from the north-west*
292 *Moscow, Upper Monastery of St Peter, founded 1380: Church of Peter the Metropolitan (right), 1690; Gate-church and bell-tower, 1694*

293 Moscow, Andronikov Monastery of the Saviour, Church of the Archangel Michael, 1691–1739: view from the south-east
294 Moscow, Monastery of the Don, New Cathedral of the Icon of the Virgin of the Don, 1684–93: view from the west

312 *Island of Kizhi, Lake Onega. Church of the Virgin of the Intercession (left), 1764, and the Church of the Transfiguration of the Saviour, 1714 with the surrounding wall, from the north-east*
[313–315] Island of Kizhi, Lake Onega, Church of the Virgin of the Intercession, 1764
313 *Corner construction*   **314** *Decoration on the exterior stairs leading to the gallery*
315 *Iconostasis, 17th–18th centuries*

[316–319] *Island of Kizhi, Church of the Transfiguration, 1714*   **316** *View of the domes and Lake Onega*   **317** *View of the interior; iconostasis, 18th century*   **318** *Twin staircase leading to the gallery*   **319** *(overleaf) View from the south-east*

COMMENTARY

Kiev and Vladimir-Suzdal–Rus before the Tartar Invasions

1, 2, 15–33, 320–324   Kiev Киев

Cathedral of St Sophia, 1037–61
Собор Софии
Sobor Sofii

The Cathedral of St Sophia in Kiev has seen many vicissitudes in its long existence. The chronicles record the laying of its foundation stone in 1037 and its consecration in 1039. Founded by Yaroslav the Wise to be the principal shrine of the burgeoning state of Kievan Rus, it suffered extensive damage in the invasion by the hordes of Batu Khan. It was not used for services for long periods at a time between the thirteenth and sixteenth centuries and fell increasingly into a state of disrepair. Reconstruction began in the first half of the seventeenth century, at the enlightened instigation of the Metropolitan Peter Mogila (1632–47) and in the early stages of the Ukrainian people's struggle to liberate themselves from the foreign yoke. But it was not until the War of Liberation (1648–54) was over and the Ukraine was reunited with Russia that concentrated attention could be paid to the work of rebuilding the cathedral. A substantial grant from the Russian state treasury in 1685, at the decree of Tsars Ivan and Peter, enabled the work to be finished by 1707. The exterior of the building was fashioned according to the aesthetic taste of the late seventeenth century, which

A. Novitsky's reconstruction of St Sophia as it was c 1100

was responsible for the alterations to the domes and for the attic storeys, gables and stucco decoration characteristic of the Ukrainian Baroque, for the window surrounds, which are typical of the Moscow School of the seventeenth century, and for covering all wall surfaces uniformly with a coat of white

plaster. The exterior lobbies on the north and south sides, which were originally open, were walled in and an extra storey and a dome were added to each, with the additional support of squat buttresses. The interior was also decorated in conformity with the spirit of the age.

Scholarly interest in St Sophia was awakened early. The research of I. V. Morgilevsky was particularly productive. Between 1920 and 1939 he investigated the fabric of the building, and succeeded in laying bare some of the original masonry, tracing the connections between different stages in the construction, and uncovering fragments of the old decoration of the interior. His work was the basis of the first scholarly reconstruction of the original state of the building, and of the chronology of the accretions to it. The interesting alternative reconstructions by N. I. Brunov, A. I. Nekrasov, A. Novitsky and K. Konant place less reliance on Morgilevsky's research and draw on analogies from Byzantine buildings. M. K. Karger devoted great energy and attention to the study of St Sophia. He began his work in 1939–41 and resumed it after the war. From 1950 to 1954 M. I. Kresalny, assisted by Y. S. Aseyev and V. Volkov, investigated the façades, especially at the north end, and the roofing of the domes and galleries. In spite of all this attention some questions still remain to be answered before the cathedral can be reconstructed in its entirety.

The nucleus, the oldest part of the building, consists of a domed cruciform church with five aisles, twelve pillars and five apses, the central one being enclosed by five sides of a regular dodecagon. The middle aisle and the transepts are clearly distinguished from the other aisles, being twice the width ($24\frac{1}{2}$ feet) and having barrel vaulting. There are galleries on the north, west and south sides, with arcades that were originally open. The area of the individual bays in the side aisles and galleries is one quarter of the area of the crossing. The exterior faithfully reveals the groundplan. The crossing rises high above the rest of the building, surmounted by the principal dome which rests on a tall drum with twelve windows. The roofs of the two inner side aisles are at a level a little below the drum and support four somewhat smaller domes. The roofs of the two outer aisles are yet lower. There are eight more domes, smaller still, two at the west end and one at the east end of each of the outer aisles, and one at the west end of each of the inner side-aisles. The drums were originally polygonal. The exterior arcades at ground level were originally only one storey high and had flat roofs forming terraces called gulbishche. The central apse rises to the height of the roof of the middle aisle, while the side apses are lower, corresponding to the lower roofs of the other aisles. In a manner corresponding to the visual differentiation by height of the galleries, the aisles and the domes, there is a graduation of the distances to which the apses project, the central one coming out the furthest. No Byzantine domed cruciform church has either such a large number of domes or the pyramidal composition, which must be due to the influence of wooden architecture and became the distinguishing characteristic of all early Russian churches. The gradual rise, step by step, of the units of the church towards its centre, is still the dominant feature of St Sophia's distinctive outline (pls 16, 17).

Soon after the original building was completed, around 1100, an upper storey was added to the exterior galleries, and new, wider, arcaded lobbies built on outside them. Towers were built at both corners of the west front — the south rather later than the north — containing staircases giving accress to the tribunes. These were domed, adding two to the pyramidal arrangement of the thirteen over the aisles. To take the thrust of the vaulting, flying buttresses in the form of a quarter of a circle were constructed — long before their appearance in Gothic architecture — which were then incorporated in the later lobbies. They were discovered in the investigation of the fabric.

The facades of the cathedral were not originally covered with plaster. Some of the original masonry has been exposed, on the apses (pls 16, 17) and elsewhere, revealing the builders' technique. The lower part of the wall consists of irregular courses of rubble and quarry stone. The irregularities were levelled by flat bricks embedded in a layer of mortar of almost the same thickness, made of lime and brick fragments. The layers of mortar were ground down, so that the façades presented the appearance of alternating stripes of red brick and pink mortar, through which the stone could be seen. The stones gradually become smaller towards the top of the wall and brick increasingly predominates. The weaker pillars, arches, vaults and domes were constructed exclusively of carefully fired bricks.

The horizontal articulation of the wall in pink and red stripes proved to have limitations as a means of decoration. Monotony was warded against by double recessed niches of various sizes, surmounted by round arches, arranged in rows along the galleries and framing the windows. A saw-tooth frieze (porebrik) was used on the arches.

The cathedral has been found to have narrow, strip foundations of quarry stone, reaching to a depth of 2 feet 6 inches below the galleries and of 4 feet 8 inches below the apses, and 4 feet 11 inches wide. The stones in the foundations of the interior walls were laid without any kind of binding agent, but are topped by a layer of strong cement 2 to 3 inches thick. The foundations of the outer walls are held with a mortar of lime and brick fragments. Two-thirds of the vaulting of the main dome was accom-

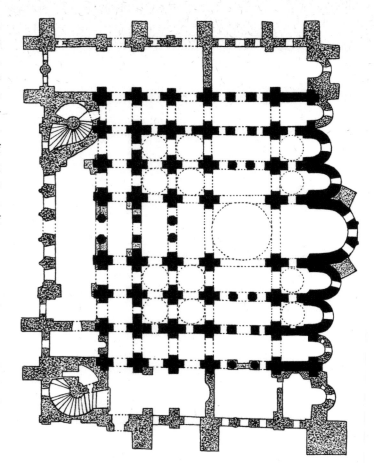

plished without the wooden framework necessary in the construction of an arch or vault: a kind of false vault was built by corbelling one row of bricks upon another, gradually closing in on the centre. The top third was executed with the aid of a wooden framework (centering) and planking. This segment of the dome forms a constructional peculiarity which became typical of early Russian architecture and was known as a skufya (skullcap). The twelve smaller domes were constructed by the same methods. They were all coated with mortar on the outside and covered with specially made brick tiles, curved to follow the curve of the dome. Another layer of mortar was spread on the tiles over which the final casing of lead was laid.

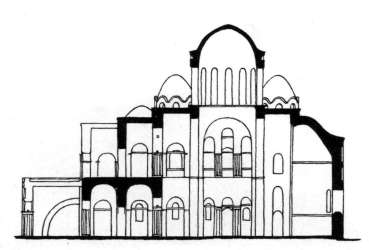

The crossing and its four great round arches dominate the interior of the cathedral (pl. 1), almost reducing all the other additive elements to seeming equality. The apex of the main dome is 95 feet above the floor. The two pillars of the Triumph Arch merge with the partition walls of the inner apses, so that the sanctuary is divided into three parts, opening on to the crossing and the north and south transepts. The ceiling of the sanctuary is as high as that of the transepts. There was originally only a low screen, probably of marble, separating the area of the main apse from the crossing. The cruciform central area composed of the middle aisle, the transepts and crossing and the main apse is hedged in by darker spatial cells, above which are built well-lit, broad, spacious tribunes. The arms of the central cross terminate in two storeys of arcades, each of three arches (pl. 30). The pillars of these arcades are octagonal at ground level, but at the upper storey they are basically square, with respond-like three-quarter shafts on the four sides. The arcade has not survived at the west end, but the foundations of the pillars have been excavated. All the other pillars are cruciform in section and support transverse arches, and there are corresponding pilasters on the walls. The imposts are relatively low. The various spatial cells of the transepts, side aisles and the narthex, defined by pillars, pilasters and transverse arches, have barrel-vaulted roofs. Where there is a dome, pendentives effect the change from the square groundplan of the bay to the circle of the drum.

The vast tribunes in the side aisles and at the west end—built for use by the Great Prince, his family and attendants and probably linked to the palace by bridges off the stair towers originally—receive their light directly from the drums of the domes and the windows in the upper storey, while the ground floor used by the ordinary congregation remains in semi-darkness. The parapets under the triple arcades and arches giving on to the central part of the church are made of slabs of schist carved in shallow relief (pl. 30). There are curious areas at the west end of the two side tribunes, each with a clustered pillar in the centre which supports the transverse arches below four domes (pl. 21).

The decoration of the interior of the cathedral is unusually rich and varied and displays striking artistic taste. The combination of frescos and – extraordinarily well preserved – mosaics in a single, unified iconographic programme is new, and may well have been instigated by Yaroslav and his spiritual counsellors. The two techniques were not customarily used in combination in the Byzantine empire. The use, additionally, of polished and cut gemstones, reliefs, majolica and incrustation is also of unsurpassed skill. There is an encrusted cross made of square and triangular pieces of marble set into the wall behind the clergy stalls on the north side of the main apse (pl. 25). The metropolitan's throne, or cathedra, in the middle has also been preserved (pl. 322).

Yaroslav the Wise's white marble sarcophagus, with its low-relief carvings of crosses, cypress branches, rosettes and other symbolic motifs, gives the impression of early Christian work, but it was probably made by Byzantine craftsmen who upheld archaic traditions (pl. 23).

The mosaics are arranged according to the middle Byzantine iconographic programme, starting with the Pantocrator in the main dome: Christ is depicted in a medallion, a half-figure with a stern, solemn gaze, his right hand raised in blessing while his left holds the closed book of the law, which shall be opened on the Day of Judgment. He appears as teacher and as apocalyptic judge, uniting the first and second person of the Trinity (pl. 2). Only one of the four archangels immediately surrounding the medallion, dressed in rich, beaded robes, is the original. The others were restored by oil-painting in the late nineteenth century, as were the majority of the figures of the twelve apostles ranged between the windows of the tall drum: only the upper part of St Paul is the original mosaic (pl. 320). A fragment of the ornamental frieze above the windows also survives. Of the four medallions above the apexes of the crossing arches, two escaped destruction: Christ as High Priest to the east, and the Virgin to the west. The pendentives below the main dome carry the evangelists, of whom St Mark survives complete (pl. 18), St John in part and St Matthew and St Luke only fragmentarily. Thirty half-figures of the Martyrs of Sebaste were represented in medallions on the soffits of the south, north and east crossing arches (ten on each), of which fifteen have survived (pl. 26). The remaining ten on the west arch were executed in fresco. There is an Annunciation

on the Triumph Arch, though the figures are separated: the Gabriel on the north-east crossing pillar relates to the Virgin on the south-east, who carries the spindle traditional in the Eastern Church (pls 19, 20). Each of the figures makes its effect independently. The angelic herald of the Saviour's birth steps above the concha, which is itself occupied by an 18-feet-high figure of the Virgin Orans, which dominates the central area (pl. 15). The inscription reads: 'In her is God, she cannot falter. God is with her from one day to the next.' In allusion to this and because of the popular belief that this wall was the only one left unharmed when the Mongols sacked Kiev, the figure is also known as the 'Virgin of the indestructible wall.' The spiritual expression of the oval face adds emphasis to the exalted attitude in which she prays to the Pantocrator in the dome for forgiveness of the sins of mankind. She is wearing a dark blue dress under a violet mantle striped with gold, and has a white kerchief embroidered in gold and purple in her girdle. Depending on the angle from which she is viewed, the figure stands out against the golden background haloed by a glowing flame, or in a gently shimmering light. The middle zone of the main apse, below the Orans, is filled with a representation of the Eucharist (pls 24, 324). Christ is depicted twice, performing the priest's office on both sides of the altar which stands beneath a ciborium, distributing the bread on the left and the wine on the right. On each side an angel stands behind him as deacon, with a rhipidion (eucharistic fan) in the hand, and the apostles approach in line, advancing the left or right foot alternately. The line on the left is led by St Peter (pl. 24) and that on the right by St Paul (pl. 324). The High Priest Aaron, the Old Testament precursor of Christ's priesthood, is depicted at the same level on the inner side of the north-east crossing pillar. Below the Eucharist, at the level of the apse windows, there is a row of mosaics which are among the most interesting in the cathedral: known as the Row of Bishops it consists of the figures of eight of the early Christian fathers and two archdeacons, though only the upper parts survive in their original state. The group on the right (south), and especially the figure of St John Chrysostom (pl. 27), is particularly fascinating, in spite of the conventional treatment, for the individual psychological expression. The gaunt, nervous face tellingly evokes the rigorous preacher of asceticism, the fanatical moralist. Apart from the figures there are fragmentary remains of mosaic ornaments in several places, on the soffits of windows and arches, connecting members and the like. In order to preserve the particular compositional and colouristic character of the original state the mosaics were never reworked and were only thoroughly secured and cleaned during the major restoration of 1952–54. They glow today with their pristine radiance in the light that they were originally intended to receive, strength-

ened by the reflecting capacity of the curved surfaces in which they are set. In spite of the rich colour scale and the large number of nuances of each colour – V. N. Lazarev counted 117 different shades – the overall chromatic effect is restrained. It is achieved with relatively large pieces of mosaic in shades of greyish-violet, dark and light blue, green and harsh yellow, in compositions that stand out impressively from the gleaming gold backgrounds and are intended to be viewed from some distance. The figures, executed in an integral linearity and apparently floating in space, in frontal, statuesque poses, are among the oldest and most valuable works of Christian art.

There is no total agreement on their place in the history of art. The view that the mosaics are without exception the work of masters from various workshops of the Constantinople School is not shared by V. N. Lazarev. He believes that the work was done by a team, led by a major Greek artist who had been trained in Constantinople, but including mosaicists from various provinces of the empire and from Russia. The archaic manner of the Eucharist and the Pantocrator certainly points to an Oriental influence, while the Row of Bishops suggests the hand of a refined, individual artist with a polish acquired in the capital city, probably the team leader himself. Lazarev is inclined to the view that the mosaics in the central area were already completed by 1046, the others not later than 1067. In that case they come between the mosaics of Hosios Lukas in Greece (early eleventh century) with which they are sometimes compared, and those of Vatopedi on Mount Athos.

The frescos in St Sophia are the work of a mixed Byzantine-Russian studio. Those in the central area can all be dated in the eleventh century, and some others, for instance in the chapels and lobbies, in the twelfth. They have not survived in such good condition as the mosaics, and were subjected, in the nineteenth century, to barbarous over-painting in oils, which had to be carefully removed again during the restoration work that began in 1936 and went on into the 1950s. There were originally sixteen cycles illustrating the gospels on the ceiling vaults and the upper zones of the walls, but only eight survive in a fragmentary condition. The portraits of Yaroslav the Wise's family in the central aisle deserve particular interest, in spite of the ravages of time. The women are arrayed on the south wall, the men on the north, while the Great Prince himself, the cathedral's founder, with a model of the building in his hands, was depicted with his wife Irina (Ingigerda) on the west wall, which was demolished.

The murals in the side apses have disappeared save for a few fragments. They depicted the saints to whom the chapels were dedicated: St George, Yaroslav's Christian name-saint, in the outer north chapel (pl. 33), the Archangel Michael, the patron of the prince's sovereignty, in the outer south chapel *(pl. 321),* and St Paul in the inner south chapel.

The inner south apse still has a cycle of the life of St Joachim and St Anne, the Virgin's parents, which includes the Visitation *(pl. 32)*: the Virgin goes to visit Elizabeth, the elderly wife of Zacharias, whose pregnancy is a sign foretelling the Messiah. There is a relaxation of the severity and awe surrounding the Queen of Heaven in favour of a human grace and dignity, which is especially apparent in the representation of the affectionate embrace of the two women and their blessed condition. A girl is watching the meeting from the house.

Relief carvings from the tribune balustrades

The walls, pilasters and pillars are covered with full-length figures or head-and-shoulder portrayals of prophets, high priests, martyrs and holy women *(pls 28, 31),* with the male figures placed near the sanctuary, while the women are relegated to the side areas and the west end of the cathedral. The frescos in the galleries intended for the use of the Great Prince and his retinue depict the Eucharist, with related scenes from the Old and New Testaments: Hospitality (the Old Testament Trinity), the Sacrifice of Isaac, and the Three Children in the Fiery Furnace. The walls of the two towers containing the spiral staircases by which the galleries were reached, are decorated with scenes of the Hippodrome in Constantinople and life in the Kievan court: gladiatorial games, wrestling, dancing, tumblers and musicians, hunting *(pl. 29)*. Just as the westwork of Romanesque cathedrals became a symbol of the secular power, so the Great Prince's autocratic rule was intended to be expressed allegorically in the west towers of St Sophia. The triumph accorded to the Byzantine emperor

in the Hippodrome was supposed to reflect also on the ruler of Rus, who considered himself the emperor's equal.

The carved wooden iconostasis dates from 1731–34 and is in the Ukrainian Baroque style. The columns are decorated with wreaths of roses instead of the usual vines.

It can be said in summary that Yaroslav the Wise's intention of erecting a central public building in the capital of Kievan Rus that should celebrate the liberation from 'heathen darkness', the authority embodied in his own person, and the might and independence of his realm through the symbol of 'divine wisdom', was given an unforgettable expression by the architects and artists who created St Sophia.

34–36, 325   Kiev Киев

Demetrius Monastery, later St Michael's Monastery 'with the golden roofs', !1th–12th centuries

Дмитриевский монастырь, позже Михайловский Златоверхий монастырь

Dmitriyevsky monastyr, pozzhe Mikhaylovsky Zlatoverkhy monastyr

Virtually nothing is known of the history of the Demetrius Monastery in Kiev. It was founded by the son of Yaroslav the Wise, Prince Izyaslav Yaroslavovich, in honour of his baptismal name-saint, was also known as the Monastery of the Fathers, and is mentioned in connection with other events after 1051. It obviously acquired the name of St Michael's Monastery 'with the golden roofs' after the later cathedral of that name, but why and when this occurred has not been recorded. The earliest reference to St Michael's Monastery in chronicles dates from the fourteenth century. In a document of 1523 King Sigismund I of Poland instructed the military governor of Kiev, Andrey Nemirovich, to hand over St Michael's Cathedral to Abbot Makary on condition that he restore St Michael's Monastery and found a community. Two of the monastery's churches, St Demetrius (*c*1062) and St Peter (*c*1087), were destroyed in the second half of the thirteenth century when Batu Khan's hordes took the city, and were not rebuilt. Archaeological explorations of the eighteenth and nineteenth centuries produced virtually no information about their appearance. St Michael's Cathedral, built *c*1108 and restored in the Ukrainian Baroque style, survived until the 1930s. Its original groundplan was a three-aisled rectangle, with six pillars, three apses and a vestibule at the west end. There is an exemplary reconstruction by Y. Aseyev. M. K. Karger excavated the whole site in the 1950s and laid the foundations of further research.

The Orthodox church's rejection of three-dimensional sculpture accorded well with Russian folk art's liking for shallow relief, fostered by wood-carving, the influence of which can also be seen in the rectangular slab of red schist carved with the figures of St George of Cappadocia *(pl. 34)* and St Theodore Stratilates *(pl. 35)*. Notwithstanding the influence of Byzantine reliefs of equestrian subjects in the composition, there is no mistaking the impact of popular, primitive modes: the surface appears flat, with almost no rounding of the forms, and the folds of the cloaks, the horses' manes and tails are delineated with the help of incised lines that run parallel to the outlines. The warrior saints are depicted realistically in contemporary armour, riding towards each other, and each plunging his lance into a serpent, the symbol of evil. The companion piece to this carving is a piece of schist with Nestor killing the gladiator Lius, and Demetrius of Salonika. It is likely that these reliefs, dating from c1062, were originally intended for the baptistery of the Church of St Demetrius, as heraldic emblems in honour of Yaroslav the Wise and his son Izyaslav. They were later moved to St Michael's Cathedral and are now preserved in the museum of St Sophia.

St Michael's Cathedral was famous in its day for its frescos and mosaics, but regrettably very few of them have survived into the twentieth century. As Paul of Aleppo noted in the seventeenth century, the iconographic programme was very similar to that in the sanctuary of St Sophia in Kiev, but recalled even more strongly that in the Cathedral of the Assumption in the Monastery of Caves. When the building was demolished the mosaics of St Stephen from the Row of Bishops *(pl. 36)* and of the Eucharist *(pl. 325)* were removed to the museum of St Sophia, and the mosaic of St Demetrius of Salonika to the Tretyakov Gallery in Moscow. These mosaics are ascribed to what is known as the Second Kiev School, which had its inception with the building and decoration of the Cathedral of the Assumption in the Monastery of Caves (1073–78), and are dated c1113. The pieces of mosaic, of various sizes and shapes and a great variety of chromatic and tonal nuances, are fitted very closely together, to give figures that are both refined in execution and psychologically subtle. While the dominant features of the Stephen are still the clearly defined outline and the austere expression of repose, the effect of the Eucharist – especially when compared to the archaism of the same composition in St Sophia – is outwardly less inhibited and inwardly more animated. What V. N. Lazarev calls its 'calligraphic beauty' leads to an illusionistic effect of greater lightness and relaxation. The mosaics are probably the work of the artists who were summoned from Constantinople to decorate the Cathedral of the Assumption in the Monastery of Caves and who became monks there. Traces of a workshop where mosaic pieces were prepared were found in 1951 within the bounds of the Monastery of Caves.

37, 326 Kiev Киев

Church of the Saviour, Berestovo, early 12th century
Церковь Спаса на Берестове
Tserkov Spasa na Berestove

The church belongs to the Monastery of the Saviour, a princely foundation, which is first mentioned in a document of 1072. The exact date of the building is not known. It many have been built at the behest of Vladimir Monomakh at the beginning of the twelfth century near a grove of birches or elm trees (beryosa: birch; berest: elm). That dating is based on the brick masonry of a technique typical of that period, in which courses of projecting flat bricks alternate with courses of inset bricks which are covered by a thick layer of mortar. The church is mentioned a number of times in twelfth-century chronicles in connection with the interment of members of the royal family: Euthymia, the daughter of Vladimir Monomakh, was buried there in 1138, Prince Yury Dolgoruky in 1158, and Yury's son Prince Gleb in 1173. A. Kalnofoisky wrote in the early seventeenth century, in the text accompanying a plan of Kiev: 'the walls are hardly still standing at the present time, the rubble covers the ground.' The plan has a drawing of the ruins of a large stone church, but a cross on it appears to indicate that it was still used by worshippers. In the work of restoration undertaken by the Metropolitan Peter Mogila in 1640–42 the old walls were cleared of rubble and new ones were built, on a cruciform groundplan of the Ukrainian type.

Between 1909 and 1913 P. P. Pokryshkin examined the Church of the Saviour with the intention of discovering what parts were left of the twelfth-century fabric and restoring them. Excavation revealed the original groundplan: three aisles with six pillars and three apses. The narthex at the west end is unusual in that it is wider than the body of the building, so that it projects on both sides. At its south end it incorporates a tower with a spiral staircase to the gallery. The north end of the narthex was probably intended to be the baptistery, but later accommodated the burial vault which was originally in a chapel that adjoined the church at the south-east corner. Excavations showed that there were porches at the north, south and west entrances, giving rise to the form of a cross, but they may have been added later than the beginning of the twelfth century.

The west end survives to about two-thirds of its original height *(pl. 326),* so it is possible to form some idea of the church's appearance. The façades were divided into three by shallow lesenes and terminated in rounded gables (zakomari). A brick meander frieze ran round the building at the level of the springing line of the gables, and is still clearly visible on the north wall *(pl. 37)*. The surfaces of the walls were decorated with double-recessed niches and ornamental crosses. The roof was probably 'wavy'.

The west porch had a trefoil vault, traces of which can still be discerned on the walls. The form is not usual in Byzantine, Western European or Oriental architecture, so was probably an original Russian invention. It consists of a semi-circular arch flanked by two quadrants, the apexes of which are level with its imposts. This form of vault was not fully developed until the later part of the twelfth century, and then in Novgorod. The all-brick masonry of the church at Berestovo differs from the opus mixtum (a mixture of brick and stone) generally used in Kiev in the tenth and eleventh centuries. The façades were striped in two colours, due to the mortar covering alternate rows of bricks. The mixture of the mortar included fragments of broken brick and the layers were much thicker than the courses of flat bricks *(pl. 37)*.

The painted decoration of the Church of the Saviour at Berestovo was done by Greek artists from Athens in 1542–44. The murals include a portrait of the most important Ukrainian ecclesiastic of the seventeenth century: Metropolitan Peter Mogila. The bell-tower on the west side was built in 1814.

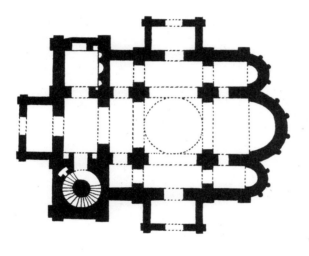

38, 327   Kiev   Киев

Gate-church of the Holy Trinity in the Monastery of the Caves, 1106–08

Троицкая надвратная церковь Печерской Лавры

Troitskaya nadvratnaya tserkov Pecherskoy Lavry

The Monastery of Caves was not founded by the Great Prince or a boyar, but by the hermits who dug out their cells in the slopes above the bank of the Dnepr. One of the earliest was probably Hilarion who took on the office of preacher and confessor at the court of Yaroslav in the 1030s and was metropolitan of Kiev for a short time from 1051. But the actual founder is acknowledged to be Antoni (died 1073), a monk who took vows on Mount Athos and who came to Hilarion's cave around the middle of the century after many years of wandering. He

Longitudinal section

settled and gathered other hermits about himself. Before withdrawing again into solitude he named one of them abbot: Theodosius (died 1074), under whom the monastery started to build above ground, adopted a strict regimen according to the Rule of Theodore of Studion, made itself the cultural centre of Kievan Rus and became the nursery of early Russian nationalism. The caves came increasingly to be used as subterranean burial chambers. The first Russian chronicler Nestor and the first Russian painter Alimpi, both monks of the Monastery of the Caves, are supposed to be buried there. The community lived according to standards of moderate asceticism and practical works. When Nikon 'the Great' was elected abbot in 1077–78 the Cathedral of the Assumption (1073–78) was being built; donated by Prince Svyatoslav Yaroslavovich, it was the prototype of a simpler, more austere type of monastic church. It introduced the Second Kiev School and provided new guide-lines which governed the further development of the domed cruciform plan in all the Russian territories in the twelfth century. It combined traditional and innovatory, Russian and Oriental stylistic elements. It had a clearly defined three-aisle plan with six pillars, three polygonal apses, a horseshoe-shaped tribune, a separate narthex and one dome. It is believed that there was a difference in height between the intersecting barrel vaults and the vaults above the corner cells. There was no staircase-tower. The cathedral was destroyed during the Second World War.

The Gate-church of the Holy Trinity was built 1106–08 by Prince Svyatoslav of Chernigov, who lived in the monastery under the name of Nikolai Svyatosha. It is not hard to reconstruct its original form in spite of its Baroque rebuilding *(pl. 38)*. It originally stood over the three archways which formed the main entrance to the monastery. It is almost square and has four cruciform pillars and three apsidal niches let into the east wall, which are not discernible from the outside. It is surmounted by a dome on an octagonal drum. Lesenes divide the façades into three parts, of which the middle one is wider and higher than the others, and the walls originally terminated in rounded gables (zakomari). The south wall is the only one to have survived in approximately its original state *(pl. 327)*. Although the gable has been altered and given a Baroque ornamentation the structure still reveals characteristics of early twelfth-century architecture: the double recessing of the blind arches and windows, the row of niches, the width of the lesenes and the overall block character. The fabric of the church is the oldest kind used in Kiev, the opus mixtum. The apsidal vaults were fashioned from golosniki of an elongated oval shape.

The gate-church received structural alterations in the eighteenth century. A large structure to hold the main staircase was built on to the north wall. The appearance of all the façades, except the south, was changed by plaster and painted decorations in the Ukrainian Baroque style. The 'mob-cap' dome typical of the style was built at the same period. The paintings on the east wall date from c1900.

39-41 Chernigov Чернигов

Cathedral of the Transfiguration, c1036

Спасо-Преображенский собор

Spaso-Preobrazhensky sobor

The building was started by order of Prince Mstislav Vladimirovich (1024–36) who was buried in it before it was completed. His brother Yaroslav the Wise continued the work for, as the chronicler said, at the time of Mstislav's funeral the walls were no higher than a man standing on a horse. The cathedral's fate was similar to that of many others of Kievan Rus. After the capture of Chernigov by Batu Khan in 1239 it fell into a semi-ruinous state. In 1611 it suffered under the onslaught of the Poles. After restoration in 1675 it was spared until severely damaged by a fire in 1750. It was considerably rebuilt between 1770 and 1799. In the interior the north and south tribunes were demolished. The whole of the decoration was given a classical slant, including the new wooden iconostasis. The exterior was plastered, the old north tower was given an extra storey and a conical roof, and a south tower was built to match, probably on the site of the baptistery. These eighteenth-century additions considerably detract from the original formal clarity of the building (*pl. 39*).

The groundplan is that of a domed basilica: a rectangle with an east-west longitudinal axis, measuring $92\frac{1}{2}$ by $62\frac{1}{2}$ feet, with eight pillars, three aisles and three apses. The crossing and main dome above it are moved westwards to the centre of the nave, and separated from the side aisles by arcaded screens, while the east arm of the cross together with the two domed corner cells form a transept which includes the solea. The apses are brought forward as far as the eastern pair of pillars. As was usual in eleventh-century architecture, a two-storey narthex was built at the west end, the upper storey of which was connected to the side tribunes. Access to this was provided by the spiral staircase in the sturdy round tower on the north-west corner. The reposeful, massive structure is crowned by five domes. The walls, decorated by lesenes and double-recessed niches, terminated in rounded gables (zakomari), the outlines of which were followed by the corresponding sections of the roof. The roof rested directly on the vaults. The arms of the central cross of the building are considerably higher than the corner cells – an early instance of what was to become characteristic of Russian architecture. The walls are built in the mixture of stone and brick common

in the eleventh century, giving rise to the characteristic stripes in two colours, clearly recognizable where the old masonry has been uncovered on the north-west tower (*pl. 40*). The arrangement of the narrow windows and niches typical of the period, and the meander frieze made of bricks can also be observed there.

Small burial chapels for members of the prince's family were built on to the cathedral at its eastern corners before the end of the eleventh century.

The upper storey in the narthex rests on a vaulted ceiling, but the tribunes in the two side-aisles were constructed on a platform of wooden beams which was later demolished. They gave on to the central area beneath the dome through triple arcades of stone, supported by two marble pillars at ground level (*pl. 41*). These pillars are now faced with bricks. The parapets of the tribunes consist of slabs of schist, carved in low relief, like those in St Sophia in Kiev. A number of fragments of eleventh-century frescos have been discovered on the interior walls, including a head of St Thecla (on one of the arches supporting the drum of the north-west dome). Excavations have uncovered fragments of the beautiful floor too, which was made of schist with coloured inlay. Some scholars have suggested that the west arm of the central aisle also originally contained a gallery and that the west arcade was later removed.

The Cathedral of the Transfiguration reflects the general trends in masonry architecture that had already made their appearance in Kiev. A provincial undercurrent is revealed, however, in the ways in which it differs: the massive effect of its overall appearance, the thicker walls and smaller window openings, the integrated simplicity of its groundplan and finally the basilical aspects of its interior arrangement. Its scheme is similar to that of the Desyatinnaya in Kiev.

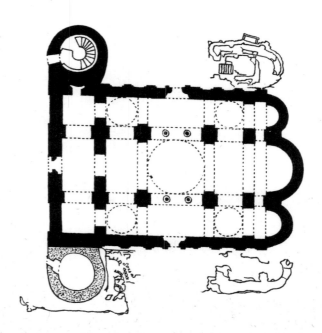

Cathedral of SS Boris and Gleb, 12th century
Борисоглебский собор
Borisoglebsky sobor

Cathedral of the Assumption in the Yeletsky Monastery, mid-twelfth century
Успенский собор Елецкого монастыря
Uspensky sobor Yeletskogo monastyrya

The Cathedral of SS Boris and Gleb was built between 1097 and 1123, in the reign of Prince David Svyatoslavovich, plundered by the hordes of Batu Khan in 1239, but restored in the second half of the thirteenth century. It suffered badly again in the Polish campaign of 1611. After it had been converted to the use of a Roman Catholic Dominican convent in 1628, it was restored to the Orthodox Church in 1649. Extensive renovations were made in 1659, including the construction of a small rotunda before the west front. Further alterations were made between 1790 and 1805, and in 1857 the old apses were demolished in order to extend the aisles. The cathedral was severely damaged again in the Second World War. N. V. Kholostenko discovered that the old, twelfth-century kernel of the building had survived and was capable of restoration. Even the foundations of the demolished apses were uncovered. Restoration began in 1948 and was completed in 1955.

The groundplan is a dumpy rectangle on an east-west axis with six pillars, three aisles, three apses and a narthex, arranged in the usual scheme of a domed cruciform church. The original building was at one time surrounded by exterior galleries, the foundations of which were uncovered in excavation. The stairs leading up to the interior tribunes are not in an adjacent tower but built in the thickness of the wall in the north-west corner. The fronts are articulated by lesenes, with thick demi-shafts built against them *(pl. 43)*. The limestone capitals are decorated with relief carvings of pairs of animals, such as griffins and panthers, plant motifs and strap-work *(pl. 44)*. The roofing, following the outline of the rounded gables and revealing the extra height of the arms of the cross centring on the single, wide dome, corresponds to the common, undulating form of vaulting (pozakomarem in the Russian expression). The apses, the middle one of which is articulated by vertical lesenes, reach the full height of the wall *(pl. 42)*. The narrow, high windows and the sparing use of relatively small double-recessed niches are characteristic of the apses and of the cathedral as a whole. The springing line of each of the round gables and the main cornice of the apses are marked by a frieze of round arches, which also runs round the base of the dome, at the top of the drum. The triple recessing of the portal is an innovation, not found in the Kievan buildings of the eleventh century. The cathedral was built of flat bricks with thick layers of a lime and brick mortar. The masons put their marks on the exposed faces of the bricks.

The Yeletsky Monastery was founded by Prince Svyatoslav Yaroslavovich in the year 1060, but there were clearly no masonry buildings at first. The Cathedral of the Assumption was not built until the middle, or even the second half of the twelfth century. Sacked by the Tartars in 1239, it remained in a semi-ruinous state until 1500. After further depradations in the war with Poland, it was given to the Uniat communion, but returned to the Orthodox Church in 1649. Restoration work in 1679 gave it the appearance which it retains essentially to the present day. The façades and domes were altered or rebuilt in the style of the Ukrainian Baroque and most of the windows were widened. A narrow, one-storey annex was built on to the south side *(pl. 328)*.

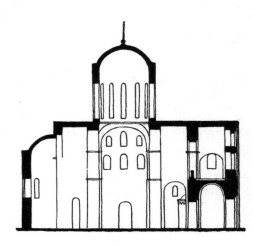

The groundplan is similar to that of SS Boris and Gleb, with the same three aisles, three apses and six pillars. The narthex is, however, separated from the nave by a wall and has a small baptistery at its south

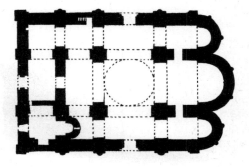

end, the apse of which projects into the south aisle *(pl. 45)*. The building had originally only one dome, and the subsidiary domes were built in the seventeenth century. In the twelfth century the roof was covered with lead, which lay directly on the vaulting, following its undulations. The fronts are articulated with lesenes, with superimposed demishafts. There was a ceramic frieze of a round-arch motif at the level of the springing line of the round gables (zakomari), corresponding to the base of the vaults, the same motif which still decorates the apse of the baptistery. The groin vaulting beneath the tribunes in the two west corners of the interior represents a structural innovation in twelfth-century architecture. The stairs are set in the north wall. The layers of mortar in the all-brick fabric have become so narrow that the façades, which were originally not plastered, must have looked like modern brick walling.

Austere, simple, clearly articulated, sparingly decorated, without structural additions, the Cathedral of the Assumption in Chernigov had all the characteristics of the new style which had originated in the cathedral of the same name in the Monastery of the Caves in Kiev.

Fragments of twelfth-century frescos have been found in the interior.

46, 47 Chernigov   Чернигов

Pyatnitsa Church, second half of the 12th century

Пятницкая церковь

Pyatnitskaya tserkov

The Pyatnitsa Church was part of a nunnery which appears to have been founded by Prince Ryurik Rostislavovich in the twelfth century. There are no surviving written sources about its early history. The nunnery was secularized in 1786. All its buildings were demolished in 1805, with the exception of the church which still stands. Up to the Second World War the original building was concealed by plaster, ornamentation and structural additions dating from 1750 and 1818-20.

After receiving considerable damage during the war, the building was investigated between 1943 and 1945 by P. D. Baranovsky, who made some extremely important discoveries about it. He advanced the possibility that the architect may have been Peter Miloneg, to whom the church at Ovruch and an immense feat of structural engineering, the stone support wall and quay at the Vydubitsky Monastery in Kiev, are also attributed, dated 1199. Since the Pyatnitsa was an original and unique monument of Kievan Russian architecture of the twelfth century it was reconstructed in its original form. It belongs to the simple one-dome, four-pillar type which evolved in small Russian monasteries in the second half of the twelfth century, to meet the modest requirements of their inmates. The groundplan is the usual rectangle with three aisles with apses, three entrances and stairs to the west tribune in the west wall. The transept is the same width as the middle aisle. The two together occupy very nearly the whole space and form an exact square at the crossing in the centre of

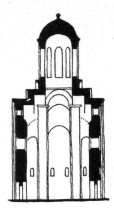

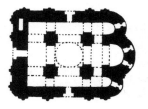

the building, while the pillars are very close to the exterior walls, making the side aisles very narrow.

The exterior appearance, especially the construction of the dome, is significantly different from all earlier church buildings. The fact that the crossing arches are one step higher than the vaults over the four arms of the cross, which are already high in themselves, while the rounded arches on the outside walls are a step lower than the vaults, gives a pyramidal, dynamic roof form. The quadrant vaults over the corner areas of the building lead up to the base of the barrel vaults and so create the basis of the upward drive of the interior and the trefoil top of the façades. The vertical movement is emphasized still more by the slender proportions and angular ornamentation (*pl. 47*). The church is built in bare, unplastered brick and its decoration includes a number of original forms which have no precedents in earlier Kievan buildings. Some of the motifs show the influence of folk embroidery and woodcarving. The facades are divided into three by pilasters, with clusters of long thin columns, like responds, against them. The decoration of the middle division of the walls is particularly elaborate: over each of the round-arched recessed doorways in the north, south and west walls there is a hood-mould, semi-circular in section, with a small niche above it. There is another niche above that, which comes to a sharp arrow-point, and is flanked by two windows, and these three elements rest on a frieze; on the west wall it comprises two bands of saw-tooth with a zigzag band (begunets) in between (*pl. 47*), while the north and south walls have a narrower frieze with one band in a simplified meander pattern. At the level of the quadrant vaults at the top of the two outer divisions of the wall, the middle division has a row of five small niches. A narrow begunets band lies between them and the round arch of the gable, which has three windows on the north and south sides and one on the west. The walls of the tall apses are divided by slender engaged columns which reach up to become the pillars in the row of simple niches at the top of the wall. The niches rest on a broad band of an unusual lattice pattern, all in brick (*pl. 46*).

The Russian adaptation of the domed cruciform plan received bold new expression in the Pyatnitsa Church. It was influenced by the native wood architecture, where specifically the form of the roof, mounting stepwise to the dome in a series of bochki, had developed. The corbelled vaulting in the interior was the masonry equivalent of the wooden constructional method, and also made vaulting without pillars possible. The new type of small, four-pillar church with a painterly vitality was born of the popular ideal of architectural beauty: a leavening of the usual cube of masonry by vertical and centripetal forces. Similar trends existed in Smolensk, Polotsk and Pskov. They show that even before the Tartar invasion, while the separate principalities had their own schools of architecture, certain forms common to all Russian building, and symptomatic of the future, were already evolving, embodying the ideal of the unification of the Russian people in the teeth of feudal divisions. The Tale of Igor's Campaign provides an analogy in contemporary literature. The unusual, dynamic resolution of the upper part of the structure was widely followed in the limestone buildings of fourteenth and fifteenth-century Muscovy.

329   Vladimir-Volynsky

Владимир- Волынский

Cathedral of the Assumption, *c*1160/19th century

Успенский собор   *Uspensky sobor*

Vladimir-Volynsky, the capital of the Volynsky principality and one of the first Russian dioceses, was an important cultural and artistic centre in the twelfth and thirteenth centuries. A local school of architecture flourished at the same period, whose work resembled the Kiev and Chernigov Schools in construction and composition. Prince Mstislav ordered the building of the Cathedral of the Assumption in 1160. Its plan is related to that of the cathedral of the same name in the Kiev Monastery of the Caves. It has no staircase tower, nor any other kind of structures built on outside the basic nucleus of the simpler type of domed cruciform church with three aisles and six pillars, and a single dome, resting on a drum with windows. Its exterior resembles the Cathedral of SS Boris and Gleb in Chernigov. The walls terminate in rounded gables (zakomari) and are articulated by engaged columns. The corners are accentuated by lesenes. A frieze of a round-arch motif runs round at the level of the springing line of the vault. The brick ornamentation on the gables also appears on the capitals of the columns and lesenes. The windows are arranged in rows, horizontally and vertically, and are typically tall and narrow, and recessed. As a result of the nineteenth-century restoration of the cathedral, nothing of its original interior decorational scheme survives.

330, 331   Galich   Галич

Church of Panteleymon, early 13th century

Церковь Пантелеймона

Tserkov Panteleymona

The old city of Galich, which gave its name to the province of Galicia, has vanished. It lay on the hills beside the Lukva, a tributary of the Dnestr. During the twelfth and thirteenth centuries, as the second-biggest town in the country, it became the political and cultural centre of a powerful, independent principality. The invading Mongols and Tartars

Corinthian capital and impost from a portal

destroyed Galich and its monumental architectural complexes, of which there were more than thirty according to documentary sources. Archaeologists have carried out a large-scale investigation of the site. Numerous churches have been excavated but nothing is left of them except remnants of foundations and the plinths of walls, which give little idea of their original styles and make reconstruction extremely difficult. One building that survived, however, was the Church of Panteleymon built by Prince Daniel Romanovich (1228–64), probably in a monastery on the edge of the town (now in the village of Shevchenkovo), which was rededicated as the Catholic Church of St Stanislas in the sixteenth century, and considerably altered. The lower parts of the walls, the two portals and the decoration of the apses are all that survive of the thirteenth-century building.

The church was built on a square plan (length and breadth 52 feet 6 inches), with four pillars, one dome and three apses. The interior had an affinity to the simple, four-pillar, Russian churches of the twelfth century, but it departed from the type in the Romanesque elements in its exterior. German architects whom the prince invited to his lands with other colonists, in the hope of gaining western allies against the Tartars, may have been responsible for them.

The Romanesque is most clearly in evidence in the blind arcading on the three apses, which was renovated in the eighteenth century, and which is supported by columns with semi-circular shafts, gemmaceous capitals and Attic bases, in the form of the windows and in the two ornate portals (on the west and south sides), set in recesses with columnar mouldings. Unlike the Dnepr region and Volynia, Galician builders did not use brick but the local varieties of limestone. The walls are faced with carefully cut ashlar stones, with a hollow interior filled with rubble, quarry stone and lime. There is a precision in the various measurements of the plan and details of the church which is most unusual in early Russian architecture.

332   Grodno   Гродно

Church of SS Boris and Gleb at Kolozh, second half of the twelfth century

Борисоглебская Коложская церковь

Borisoglebskaya Kolozhskaya tserkov

The Church of SS Boris and Gleb, which survives only in a severely dilapidated condition, was built on the steep banks of the Neman in Kolozh, a suburb of the ancient city of Grodno, in the extreme north of Volynia. Erosion of the banks by the river caused a landslip in the mid nineteenth century, which brought down the whole of the south wall of the church and half of the west. The dome and the vaulting had already collapsed before that. The groundplan shows the church had three aisles, three apses and one dome, although some hold the view that there were three domes originally. There are two octagonal pillars directly in front of the walls separating the apses, while the vaults were supported on six columns. This must have given the interior a

spacious, hall-like character. The tribunes were probably high, narrow, wooden balconies, stretching the full length of the sides as far as the sanctuary. There were stairs in the south-west corner and in the outer walls of the side apses. The transept and central aisle, intersecting beneath the dome, are almost identical in width. All the other areas are narrower.

In spite of its relatively small size (43 feet by 82 feet), the church used to present an imposing appearance. The treatment of the façades is especially effective. They are articulated by shallow lesenes, projecting in three steps (or two, on the corners of the west wall), and decorated with stone and majolica inlay (pl. 332). The original window surrounds have not survived. The stones used for the inlay are pieces of polished granite and gneiss in shades of red, greyish-green, pink, olive and brown. The pieces of majolica, in the shapes of crosses, flowers and rhomboids, arranged asymmetrically in relation to the main articulation of the façades, display a high standard of artistic taste. The floor was also made of polychrome ceramic tiles. Behind carefully laid faces of fired bricks, which were not plastered, the walls are filled with broken brick and flint. The architectonic details were constructed with moulded bricks in various shapes. The mortar layers are generally the same thickness as the bricks. The lime cement includes fragments of chaff, brick and charcoal. Golosniki were let into the upper part of the walls, opening on to the interior, to improve the resonance.

333   Polotsk   Полоцк

Cathedral of St Sophia, 1044–66

Софийский собор

Sofysky sobor

In the eleventh and twelfth centuries Polotsk was the capital of a wealthy principality whose territory stretched as far as the Gulf of Riga and which even threatened to rival Kiev and Novgorod. The prince's

palace lay outside the city boundaries and his power was severely circumscribed by the Veche (popular assembly). In the thirteenth century the principality became a dependancy of Smolensk. The oldest building in the town of Polotsk is the Cathedral of St Sophia, built soon after St Sophia in Kiev, in association with far-reaching political plans. It underwent substantial alterations in the seventeenth and eighteenth centuries: the domes were demolished, the walls made higher and the altar moved further to the east. In its present form the cathedral is more like a Romanesque basilica with Baroque ornamentation inside and out. Only the lower parts of the walls and the apses remain of the original fabric.

The plan of the original building was almost a square, with five longitudinal aisles, intersecting with five transverse aisles. The crossing was in the centre of the square, where the axes of symmetry intersected. A further peculiarity of the cathedral is that it has not five but three apses, placed in accordance with tradition at the east end, but there are three more corresponding apses, placed symmetrically at the west end. The west group, which recalls the duplicate choirs of Romanesque churches, is separated from the body of the church by a wall. It may in fact be a later addition. There were no staircase towers or exterior galleries. According to old manuscript sources the cathedral had 'over seven tops'. It can be supposed that there were five domes surmounting the bulk of the building, and two more on the central east and west apses. Tribunes ran round the interior on three sides and the ends of the central transverse aisle were screened off by arcades on octagonal supports. The walls were constructed of flat bricks, in courses alternately exposed and covered with a mortar of lime and broken brick. The apses are polygonal and decorated with the typical double-recessed niches, the articulation of the façades is simple and severe. Although the cathedral has not yet been sufficiently examined archaeologically, the existing evidence suggests that it is a simplified variant of the pattern of St Sophia in Kiev, but already possessing elements of an independent local style, that of the centrally-planned domed cruciform churches usual in the twelfth century in Polotsk and Smolensk.

334   Polotsk   Полоцк

Cathedral of the Saviour in the Monastery of the Saviour and St Euphrosyne, 1128–56

Спасский собор Спасо-Ефросиниева монастыря

Spassky sobor Spaso-Yefrosiniyeva monastyrya

The Cathedral of the Saviour in the Monastery of the Saviour and St Euphrosyne, which lies on the edge of the town, was built between 1128 and 1156 by the

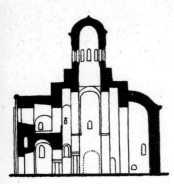

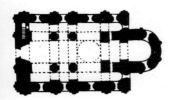

order of the Princess Euphrosyne, who was later canonised by the Russian Church. The architect was the Polotsk monk John, who had previously worked on the Belchitsky Monastery. His building was a popular, pyramidal adaptation of the cuboid, domed cruciform type, though the original form can hardly be discerned from the cathedral's present-day appearance. In order to give the building as a whole a stepped, upward movement, the walls had to be very thick and buttressed by lesenes with demi-shafts against them, and the six interior pillars had to be particularly strong. As a result, since the building is relatively small, the space is almost crushed by its mass.

The movement in the interior develops in two directions. On entering by the west door, the longitudinal axis dominates as in a basilica. In the sequence of the bays, squares alternate with narrow rectangles. One peculiarity is the way in which the two west pairs of the octagonal pillars are brought very close to each other, so that the low vestibule appears to be an extension of the middle aisle. It is extended at the east end by the distance that the stilted semi-circular apse projects and by the joining of the east pair of pillars to the inner walls of the side apses. The church lacks the usual north and south doors. The passage-like side aisles are another peculiar feature, being narrower than the massive pillars. Since the arches between the pillars and the walls start at a lower level than the vaults, the cell-like divisions of the interior are very noticeable. The side apses are contained within the thick east wall and the relationship between them is lost. The second directional flow is to be experienced in the crossing: the height of the drum, the effect of the crossing arches having a span greater than the intersecting arms, the enlarging of the area by the eight smaller rectangles (including the side apses) that surround it, create the typically Russian, successive vertical thrust.

The façades are divided by lesenes with engaged columns. An additional ornament, originally, was provided by projecting mouldings over the windows, which were coated wholly or partly by a lime mortar coloured reddish-brown by an admixture of fragmented brick. But the dominant characteristic of the exterior was the impression of a pyramidal tower. The building dispensed with the wavy roof usual at the time, and rose in steps. The two-storey structure with a round gable at the west end, and the prominent central apse at the east end formed the first step. The second was formed by the round gables of the main structure, three on each front. Over them lay a square pedestal, decorated with shallow, blind trefoil arches, which necessitated the maximum strength in all the supporting members and raised the slender drum of the dome a step higher. There is no Byzantine or Romanesque church constructed in this manner. The projection at the west end contains the low narthex and a tribune, approached by a

stair in the thickness of the north part of the west wall. In its two corners, behind partition walls, are the chapels where St Euphrosyne led her life of asceticism.

Both the external fabric and the interior, which were considerably altered during the nineteenth century, are in need of restoration.

335   Smolensk   Смоленск

Church of the Archangel Michael (Svirskaya), 1191–94

Церковь Михаила архангела (Свирская)

Tserkov Mikhaila arkhangela (Svirskaya)

Thanks to its position on the main intersection of the Varangers' route to the Black Sea from the Baltic along the waterways, at the watershed of the Dnepr and Volga and the rivers of the Lake Ilmen basin, Smolensk developed as an important centre of trade

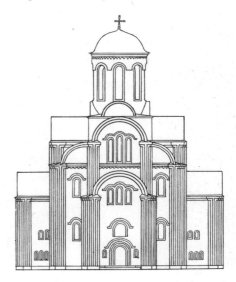

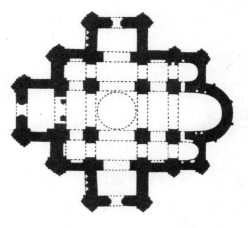

and crafts, with a social structure resembling Novgorod's. The prince, who attained independence in the middle of the twelfth century, during the process of feudal decentralization, had an energetic rival for power in the Veche, the citizens' assembly. His palace stood on a hill on one side of the Dnepr, while the quarters of the merchants and craftsmen lay on the other side, protected by a natural barrier of marsh and streams.

Prince David Rostislavovich had the Church of the Archangel Michael built in his palace by local builders between 1191 and 1194. It has much in common structurally with the Cathedral of the Saviour in Polotsk, but differs in the even more pronounced symmetry, verticality and centrality of its composition. It has three aisles and three apses stretching well to the east of the crossing. Only the central apse is high and projects in a semicircle, while the low side apses terminate in straight walls. The east pair of the six pillars almost join on to the apse walls. The crossing, below the dome, is well to the centre of the building and is defined by the two remaining pairs of pillars, and the cruciform plan of the whole is unusually clear. Vestibules with broad openings on to the body of the building are added to all three of the north, west and south arms. There is clearly a relationship between the quadrant vaults over the corner cells and the barrel vaults over the apses, and the exterior appearance. But since the whole of the upper part was rebuilt in the nineteenth century and has not yet been sufficiently investigated, it can only be spoken of tentatively. The façades were divided in three vertically and terminated in zakomari, forming a trefoil arch. It is possible that, like the Cathedral of the Saviour in Polotsk, the drum rested on a pedestal with trefoil blind arches. The central core of the building rose above the lower vestibules and apses. The compound pilasters with illusory demi-shafts, and the hood-moulds over the portals and windows are characteristic features of the decoration. The church was built in the common fashion with flat bricks laid in courses alternately exposed and set deeper in the thickness of the wall, beneath a layer of mortar.

The typically Russian upward impulse of the forms is evident not only on the exterior of the 'Svirskaya' but inside as well. An unbroken vertical movement dominates the exterior, emphasized by the powerful upsurge of the pilasters. The interior climbs in symmetrical steps: from the side apses and the vestibules in the centre of the other three walls, which are equal in height, to the roof of the main apse and the central cross, and on up to the dome on its slender drum. The total effect is more spacious, higher and lighter than in the Cathedral of the Saviour in Polotsk. The original decoration of the interior has not survived.

336 Suzdal Суздаль

Church of SS Boris and Gleb in Kideksha, 1152
Церковь Бориса и Глеба в Кидекше
Tserkov Borisa i Gleba v Kidekshe

Like Andrey in Bogolyubovo, Yury Dolgoruky before him built his palace in Kideksha, a place not far from where the Kamenka flows into the Nerl, and of strategic value for the protection of the waterway which was important to the city of Suzdal. According to legend, it was also the 'encampment' of the 'holy princes' Boris and Gleb, when they were travelling from Rostov and Murom to Kiev. The choice of site thus had ideological value as well: the association with the first Russian saints, the two patrons of national unity, enhanced the prestige of the princes of Suzdal in the struggle for pre-eminence.

SS Boris and Gleb was built of limestone in 1152 to be the palace church. It is one of the two oldest monuments of Vladimir-Suzdalian hewn stone architecture, though it is nothing like so well preserved as the other, the Cathedral of the Transfiguration in Pereslavl-Zalessky. After the Tartar onslaught it had to be repaired for the first time in 1239, but then deteriorated again and was rebuilt in the sixteenth and seventeenth centuries in a form that bore no relationship to its original appearance. The building is an example of the common mid twelfth-century plan of a domed cruciform church with four pillars, one dome, three semi-circular, projecting apses and a tribune over one-third of the area of the church at the west end. The simplicity of the groundplan is reflected in the modesty of the exterior: shallow lesenes divide the façades into three sections with round gables and no form of decoration except the string-course and the windows, which were originally narrow. The spacing of the lesenes corresponds to that of the pillars inside. The narthex dates from the nineteenth century. Arched tombs were constructed beneath the tribune for members of the royal family; among those who lie there are Yury's son, Boris Yuryevich, and his wife. The frescos discovered in 1947 probably date from the 1180s, and may have been commissioned by Vsevolod III in memory of his mother. The impression given by the church in its original form was of a simple cuboid mass. Its massive proportions and heavy, sparing ornament create a sense of obstinate, oppressive power.

48, 337 Bogolyubovo Боголюбово

The palace of Andrey Bogolyubsky, 1158–65
Резиденция Андрея Боголюбского
Rezidentsiya Andreya Bogolyubskogo

On a site to the east of his capital of Vladimir, not far from where the Nerl flows into the Klyazma, Andrey, the prince of Vladimir-Suzdalian Rus, had himself a palace built, between 1158 and 1165, from which he received his surname and where he was assassinated by rebellious vassals in 1174: Bogolyubovo. His all-Russian policies required him to keep great state, at great expense. He needed a magnificent palace to house the numerous ambassadors,

guests and merchants he received. The account of his death, which also describes his palace, compares the fortified complex to Vyshgorod, the palace of the Great Princess Olga, near Kiev. It comprised the palace itself, two stone churches (the Nativity of the Virgin and St Leonti) and separate buildings for domestic purposes. The palace was surrounded by earth ramparts, and a stone bastion on the south slope. A new town grew up around it but after being sacked by the Tartars in 1238 it lost its importance and gradually sank back to the level of an ordinary village. The ruins of the royal palace were converted into a monastery during the thirteenth century in honour of the icon of the Virgin of Bogolyubovo. Prince Andrey was canonized in 1702, which made the monastery a popular pilgrimage centre. It became wealthy and began to bring the old buildings into line with the new ones, or to replace them. The old palace church, which was connected to the palace, collapsed during an attempt to widen its windows, and the present Baroque building was erected on its site in 1751.

Archaeologists began to investigate the palace at Bogolyubovo in the middle of the nineteenth century, but it was not until 1934–38 that it could be reconstructed in its essentials, after the systematic excavation directed by N. N. Voronin and much painstaking historical work. The work was resumed in the 1950s.

Section of the north tower

There survive of the twelfth-century complex only the north tower of the palace, two storeys high with a staircase and a small chamber, the bridge leading across to the palace church, the Nativity of the Virgin, and the foundation walls of the church itself *(pl. 48)*.

The tower is almost square in plan. The entrance on the east side leads to a narrow spiral staircase, whose steps are fixed to the central pillar. The stairs are roofed by a vaulted ceiling that climbs with them and the lower part is lit by four narrow windows, similar to arrow slits. A triple-arched window in the east wall gives the chamber in the upper storey a magnificent view towards the meadows beside the river and the Nerl Church in the distance. The room has a groin-vaulted ceiling which has been altered, however, probably while the tent-roofed belfry above was being built in the seventeenth century. The bricked-up doorway, which used to lead to the bridge connecting the tower to the palace, can be seen from the outside in the north wall. The bridge on the south side was almost exactly like that on the north. It connected the tower to the tribune inside the church, so that the prince could go straight to a service from the upper rooms in his palace. Both the bridges took the form of little chambers lit by small rectangular windows, with barrel-vaulted ceilings and with a door at each end, placed above lofty, open archways at ground level, with a groin vault. The exteriors of the tower and the bridge correspond in every respect to the style which developed in the middle of the twelfth century in Vladimir-Suzdalian Rus, and was also that of the palace and the church.

All the buildings were of white limestone. Their west fronts were articulated horizontally by a blind arcade with little columns and a saw-tooth frieze *(pl. 337)*, the same as can still be seen on both storeys of the tower, on the upper providing a connection to the decoration on the bridge, and running round to the north and east sides on the lower *(pl. 48)*. The corners of the tower are accented by lesenes, but the edges are encased by three-quarter shafts with crocket capitals. The zakomari surmounting the facades probably remained in position until the third storey was built in the seventeenth century, when the present semi-circular blind gables were constructed, and the original roof was either a simple four-sided tent, or an octagonal tent supported on columns. The triple-arched Romanesque window on the east side, with its two stumpy columns and their powerful-looking bases and capitals, is a particularly interesting feature from an architectural point of view. Andrey employed architects from Western Europe, but his adoption of Romanesque forms was also a gesture of his independence of the Byzantine canon. The bridge is also decorated by a blind arcade, but the columns here do not rest on carved consoles, as they do on the walls of the tower, but on a horizontal splay in the wall. The decorational zone is interrupted asymmetrically by two windows.

The court church of the Nativity of the Virgin, which collapsed in the eighteenth century, has been carefully investigated. It formed the central point of the whole palace complex. Andrey decked it with magnificent icons and frescos, jewels and inlay, valuable ornaments and utensils. According to the chronicle, he liked to take guests into the gallery in order to amaze them by the splendour and wealth displayed. The surviving parts of the original building – the foundations, parts of the north wall and the sculptures – make reconstruction possible. Its composition, distribution of space and mass and the decorational scheme display a close formal affinity to churches of a somewhat later date which have one dome and four columns: the Church of the Virgin of the Intercession on the Nerl and St Demetrius in Vladimir. The church at Bogolyubovo was unusual in that the four interior supports were not pillars but columns with Attic bases and gigantic, gilded leaf capitals.

The carvings at Bogolyubovo are earlier than the outstanding sculpture in other buildings of Andrey and Vsevolod III. There are examples of all the known motifs, for instance women's heads and lion masks, in a style that has strong Romanesque traits but also demonstrates an original local interpretation. G. K. Wagner believes that at least eight sculptors were involved. N. N. Voronin's excavations and G. K. Wagner's studies have also made it possible to make a reliable reconstruction of the 'holy tent', dating from about 1165, a tent-like canopy or ciborium supported by eight columns above a basin of white limestone, which served either as a cantharus or a holy-water vessel. According to legend, Prince Andrey took presents out of the basin to give to the builders of his palace. It stood outside the court church, at the south-west corner, on the spot where there is now a seventeenth-century chapel with four pear-shaped pillars *(pl. 337)*. Equally interesting is the discovery of the position of the 'Madonna Column' (analogous to the column outside Würzburg Cathedral), where the icon of the Virgin of Bogolyubovo is supposed to have appeared to Prince Andrey.

49   Vladimir   Владимир

Golden Gate, 1164

Золотые ворота

Zolotye vorota

This white limestone gate-tower, which includes the Gate-church of the Miracle of the Virgin's Veil, was built by Prince Andrey Bogolyubsky in 1164 as part of the fortifications surrounding his capital of Vladimir. It was modelled on the Golden Gate in Kiev, which in turn was based on the prototype in Constantinople. The name comes from the copper mountings and gold paint on the oak panels of the doors, from the gilded roof and the gilded dome of the church. The gate led into the prince's quarter of the city from the west and has survived in a substantially altered form. The chronicles refer to more than one major restoration: by the well-known Moscow architect Vasily Yermolin in 1469, and in 1641 by Antip Konstantinov, another Muscovite, whose estimate has survived. The scale of the work on both occasions is unknown. It would appear that the gate-church got into a serious condition, as a chronicler reports in 1691 that it had been 'rebuilt anew'. The last changes to the Golden Gate were made between 1785 and 1810, after the removal of the earth ramparts that reached right up to the walls of the gate and the demolition of the old church and vaulting. At the same time the corners were given extra support by buttresses in the form of round turrets, a staircase was built on the south side to give access to the new church, and a house was built on the north side.

Since the level of the ground has risen by about five feet, the Golden Gate originally looked taller and more slender than it does now. All that survives of the original structure are the two massive parallel walls, made of ashlar blocks of white limestone, which form an 'outer skin' for a filling of quarry stone and strong cement. The passage through was roofed by a barrel vault of tuff, supported by six transverse arches, resting on pairs of pilasters. The arches were 46 feet high at their crown. A strainer arch was constructed halfway up the third pair of pilasters within which the doors were hung. The wrought-iron brackets which held the hinges and the grooves made to take the thick bolts can still be seen. There are deep, square sockets in the pilasters below five of the arches, which held the ends of the dressed timbers which served both as braces and as joists supporting the planks of a wooden platform. This platform, built at the height of the strainer arch and occupying the full width of the passage, had a parapet and embrasures, from which defenders could fire arrows and pour boiling oil or water. The platform was reached from the first landing on a roofed-in staircase in the south wall. A second flight of stairs led up to a broader defensive platform, at about the level of the present-day windows, which extended a

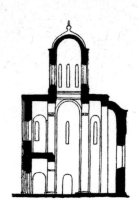

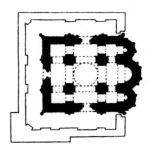

height, buoyancy and light and successfully avoids any sense of constriction, The narrow span of the barrel vaults between the pillars and the walls and the movement upwards out of the apses intensify the illusion of height. The imposts between the pillars and the arches are carved in the form of pairs of lions crouching face to face, representing the vanquished principle of evil.

The Church of the Virgin of the Intercession has overcome the heaviness of the churches in Kideksha *(pl. 336)* and Pereslavl-Zalessky *(pl. 50)* and its height is slightly greater than its length, which is accentuated by the formal elegance and the predominantly vertical articulation. It transmits an impression of soaring weightlessness, complete formal harmony, a painterly concord with the landscape of meadows and rivers that surrounds it, and evokes – like a willow tree beside a quiet lake – a peaceful, contemplative mood. Reflected in the waters of the Nerl and the Klyazma, the church is one of the most enchanting monuments of early Russian architecture.

The perfection of the constructional system, which is integrated with the architectonic forms, deserves attention. The pilasters and engaged columns, and the corresponding members on the inside walls form a skeleton of supports with the four pillars. Linked by arches above, these elements create a stable structure, capable of resisting pressure, fleshed out by the walls, which are thicker towards their base, and the roof. The building material is ashlar-cut limestone.

The archaeological excavations conducted by N. N. Voronin in 1954 and 1955 brought numerous lost parts of the building to light and so made fundamental corrections to concepts of its original form. It was part of a monastery. There is still a door in the south wall *(pl. 51)*, which gave access to the tribune from a former staircase or bridge. The limestone foundations of an open gallery were discovered, running round the north, west and south sides of the church. This was built of magnificently cut blocks of white stone (between $15\frac{1}{4}$ and $16\frac{1}{2}$ inches high), and probably enclosed the staircase in the southwest corner. It was also found that the site selected by Prince Andrey at the former confluence of the Nerl and the Klyazma was flooded to a depth of ten feet in the spring, and therefore had to be strengthened by an artificial hill of firmly packed alluvial soil, which enclosed the church's foundations, which reach to a depth of $17\frac{1}{2}$ feet. The foundations are of quarry stone, on which the stone blocks of the base of the walls and pillars were laid and banked up with earth on either side. Steps led up to the artificial hill from the water, and it was covered with flagstones. The discovery of the foundations of the gallery unleashed a violent scholarly controversy. The argument that the appearance of the church is complete and whole without a loggia and needs no such

addition, is refuted by the south Russian traditions of the eleventh and twelfth centuries. The Desyatinnaya and St Sophia in Kiev, SS Boris and Gleb in Chernigov and St Sophia in Novgorod all possessed exterior galleries. The feature disappeared from Russian architecture at the beginning of the thirteenth century, to be sure, but it was revived in the fifteenth.

The sparingly applied relief decoration on the Nerl church has been examined by numerous scholars (S. Stroganov, N. P. Kondakov, B. A. Rybakov, V. N. Lazarev, M. V. Alpatov, N. N. Voronin) who have produced several varying interpretations. One of the most recent studies is by G. K. Wagner, who does not rule out a Russification of the Romanesque but establishes that the decoration is not so much a variant of Romanesque style as a consciously new creation, appropriate to the sovereignty of Vladimir-Suzdal. He suggests that the principal sculptor came from Galich. The carvings on the upper panels of the north, south and west walls evoke the solemn, elevated mood of the Book of Psalms. The central group on each wall is up in the middle gable: King David, sitting on a throne, with his harp in his left hand and raising his right hand in blessing, while pairs of birds and lions that have lost their predatory character gather around him and are listening to the Psalmist *(pl. 52)*. The groups relate to the 98th, 148th and 150th Psalms, which were exceptionally popular in the Middle Ages for their poetic praise of God as the creator of the natural world. As a prophet of the Virgin, David has a direct significance for the church, and as popular hero, conqueror of the Philistines, founder of the state, monarch and singer of God's praise he is a prototype of Andrey Bogolyubsky. Beneath the central group there is a frieze of three female heads with plaited hair: symbols of the Virgin and of the proverbial maternity of the earth and of the people. Finally on each side of the window at the level of the springing line there is another lion crouching with his front paws crossed, his tail between his rear legs and chained by a ring to a branching tree. The significance of this figure is to be found in the *Physiologus*, the early medieval bestiary which was probably the most widespread book after the Bible between the seventh and thirteenth centuries. The lion's 'second nature' is described thus: 'When he is asleep in his cave, his eyes are watchful.' It is therefore not by chance that there are two lions over each of the doors: they represent the 'never-sleeping watchmen' that guard against the entry of hostile forces. The predators in the two flanking zakomari, on the other hand, ravening griffins with lambs (or perhaps young fallow deer) in their claws, obviously embody the principle of evil, which takes part in the hymn of praise to the Creator against its will. They are also interpretable as symbols of war (G. K. Wagner). There are two female masks below the griffins. The consoles supporting the small columns in the blind arcades are carved in the forms of the heads of women and bearded men, chimeras, lions, porcine snouts, griffins, birds and bulls. There is also one snow-leopard. In G. K. Wagner's view these figures express the idea of the divine protection afforded to mankind, and of the defence of peace. In their naive immediacy and simple dignity they contain many elements of folk art.

56-63, 338, 339 Vladimir   Владимир

Cathedral of St Demetrius, 1194–97

Дмитриевский собор

Dmitriyevsky sobor

Prince Vsevolod III, called the Mighty Thicket on account of his numerous progeny, built a church in the middle of his new palace between 1194 and 1197, and dedicated it to his patron saint, Demetrius of Salonika. It conforms to the simple domed cruciform plan and has one dome, four pillars, three aisles, a west gallery, three apses, round gables (zakomari) on the façades and a roof covering laid directly on to the vaulting. Its length from east to west is a little more than its breadth (49 feet by 53 feet, not including the apses). The walls are divided vertically into three, the middle division being wider and higher than the others. The articulating members are stepped lesenes with engaged three-quarter columns, and clearly reveal the structural principle. There are also three clearly differentiated horizontal zones: the lowest zone of blank masonry, broken only by the door-ways, and at the west end by two windows; the middle zone of blind arcades with little columns supported by consoles carved with figures; and the top zone, interrupted by the windows and carpeted with relief carvings. The horizontal lines of the carvings conform to the separate courses of the hewn limestone masonry *(pl. 57)*.

The Cathedral of St Demetrius is very similar architectonically to the Church of the Virgin of the Intercession on the Nerl, but its architects were not ordinary copyists. The proportions are more squat, the form closer to a cube. The west façade, for instance, is 50 feet 10 inches wide and 54 feet high. The apses are again in the form of massive half-cylinders *(pl. 56)*. Similarly it is the horizontal articulation, not the vertical, that is dominant in the decorational scheme: the blind arcades are fashioned as if they were reliefs in strip form, so that the little pillars do not so much exert an upward, supporting force, as hang downwards like heavy tassles. The large drum rising above a small square pedestal strengthens the impression of solemn repose, sublimity and harmony, and accentuates the uncompromisingly central character of the building, without which it would seem too heavy.

As V. I. Kazarinova has shown, the dimensions and forms are precisely scaled to the actual weight. The leitmotiv of the three-quarter column is treated according to the functions it has to fulfil: slender on the drum, thicker on the blind arcades, at its most massive on the portals and façades. In every case the proportions and diameter decrease from the bottom to the top. The arches make a second leitmotiv: above the portals they are not precise semi-circles but rise very slightly higher, almost as if drawn by hand (their radii at the springing line are between $40\frac{1}{2}$ and $41\frac{1}{3}$ inches, and at the apex are $49\frac{1}{3}$ inches), while on the blind arcades they are pronounced horseshoes, and on the round gables ellipses, with a vertical principal axis. The upper zone of the walls is intersected by tall, narrow windows in deep, stepped recesses *(pl. 57)*. The three portals differ in size and in decoration. The west portal is the largest and the whole frame of the arch is covered with a complicated pattern of plants, fabulous beasts and bands of strap-work *(pl. 60)*. The outermost archivolts of the south and north portals are plain, while the forms of the carving on the other archivolts are cruder.

The cathedral now stands alone, but in the twelfth century it was surrounded by the other buildings of the princely palace. There were still two round towers placed symmetrically at the north-west and south-west corners in the middle of the nineteenth century. In all probability they contained staircases by means of which the royal family were able to reach the west tribune. There were originally exterior galleries on the north and south sides, reaching to the height of the blind arcades, similar to the ones that have been discovered round the Church of the Virgin of the Intercession on the Nerl. That is probably the reason why the whole of the lower part of the cathedral walls is free of sculptural ornament. Regrettably all these exterior elements were demolished between 1837 and 1839, without adequate investigation or archaeological documentation, in the belief that they were more recent additions.

The work of the stone-masons displays a sensitive awareness of the effects of daylight. The carvings on the north front, which are reached by sunlight only early on summer mornings, were brought out in sharper relief and the intersections were executed at a more acute angle than in any of the other carvings. In general the height of the figures gradually increases as they rise up the wall, to allow for the viewpoint from which they are normally seen. The misconceived restoration work of the mid nineteenth century, which saw the demolition of actual sections of the building, was also responsible for the banal reconstructions of some of the carvings (figures of saints and columns on the blind arcades and some of the animal figures) and the arbitrary replacement of numerous stones.

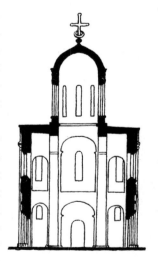

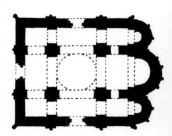

*Relief carvings on the east division of the north front
Reconstruction by G. K. Wagner*

The relief carvings covering more than half of the total wall surfaces represent an apotheosis of the sovereign power, as indeed the building itself does. They are not confined only to the plane surfaces, but spread over the little columns of the blind arcades, the archivolts of the doorways, the apses and the fields between the windows in the drum.

Every zone and every façade has an individual theme, which is part of an overall, unified iconographic programme, invoking the sovereignty of God to sanction the divine nature of earthly sovereignty. This basic theme is presented in various aspects: the idea of creation, praise, the medieval concept of the universe, the glorification of nature, references to the *Instruction* of Vladimir Monomakh, the *Song from the Book of Doves* (Cosmic Hymn), the *Tale of Igor* and the *Physiologus,* and an unending imaginative play on material from Slav and heathen traditions. The world and all its living creatures appear in forms that are friendly, playfully naive and popular – in contrast to the stylized abstraction and severity of middle Byzantine religious art, and the awe-inspiring, apotropaic character of Western European figurations. On all three fronts the central figure in the middle gable is a biblical king seated on a throne and receiving the honour

due to him as the founder or the upholder of an independent, united realm: David or his son Solomon, with a scroll in the left hand and the right raised in a gesture of exhortation, surrounded by angels, saints, fabulous creatures and animals *(pl. 58)*. As with the Nerl Church, Psalm 148 offers a gloss. But the essential point seems to be that by his might and wisdom the sovereign orders the world, which thrives under him. Subsidiary motifs, like Alexander of Macedon's ascent into heaven in the eastern gable of the south front *(pl. 339)*, and the portrait of Vsevolod III with his son Vladimir-Dmitry on his lap in the east gable of the north front *(pl. 56)*, also relate to and interpret the overall theme. The glorification of Vsevolod, the idea of unity under his rule, the prayer for heavenly assistance, were not the concerns only of the prince and his court in those troubled times of feudal disintegration, but were also expressions of the longing of the common people for a well-ordered and peaceful world.

The iconographic interpretation and the arrangement of the reliefs have exercised scholars for many years. V. Dobrokhotov, N. Chayev, N. P. Kondakov, D. V. Aynalov, N. V. Malitsky, L. A. Matsulevich, B. A. Rybakov, V. N. Lazarev and N. N. Voronin have all made important contributions. The most recent study is that of G. K. Wagner, which establishes four main groups: anthropomorphic carvings, human figures in conjunction with zoomorphic motifs, zoomorphic carvings and teratological motifs. By reconstructing the entire decorative scheme, including those lines of it destroyed by time and restoration, Wagner arrives at the following conclusion, so far as the subject matter is concerned: the complete sequence of blind arcades was a spectacular Deesis, devoted to the Christian martyrs on the north front, the apostles – with Christ, the Virgin and John the Baptist in the centre – on the west front, and the patron saints of the royal family on the south side (the south doors were known as 'royal'). Unfortunately only the figures in the west division of the north front survive in this original form, the centre of the west front is now occupied by a Trinity: the Holy Ghost in the form of a Dove, Christ in the mitre of a high priest on his left, God the Father on the right, and two of the evangelists on each side *(pl. 59)*.

The representation of trees, birds, lions and other animals at the feet, and above the heads, of the saints can be interpreted as symbolizing life in Paradise. This Paradise is above all else the one that existed in the popular imagination: a picture of the beauty of the earth itself. Ten or eleven lines of the zones above the blind arcades, about to the level of the springing line of the round gables, present life in a varying pattern of lions, panthers, deer, birds, griffins, centaurs, basilisks, sirens and plants, and present it as a condition of constant flux between strife and reconciliation *(pl. 57)*. The figures of St Theodore Stratilates and St George can be seen in the middle division of the west front (pl. 63, bottom), both represented on horseback as holy warriors, bringing order to the world. St Boris and St Gleb appear in the same place on the south front (pl. 57). They were regarded as the patrons of the Russian princes in secular matters. The actual gables, as already described, were given over to the wisdom that belonged to the office of ruler, while the drum was decorated with traditional symbols and figures of the heavenly church.

It would appear that a large group of some 45 to 50 masons were engaged on the stone carving, including both Russians and South Slavs. It is possible to distinguish between separate styles and techniques and even between the work of individual artists. There is unmistakable evidence of Oriental, Byzantine, Armenian and West European-Romanesque influences, but they are no more than components of the style which is fundamentally Slavo-Russian and helped to solve what were specifically and historically Russian problems. It transmutes elements from embroidery and woodcarving. Popular influence is especially evident in the large number of animal motifs, while the small number of saints in the blind arcades are determined by the ecclesiastical canon (pl. 59).

The interior of St Demetrius is dominated by the brightly lit crossing, which reaches upwards to the dome, framed by beautifully constructed arches. The tribune was built at the west end, as was the usual practice in the more intimate court churches. The pairs of lions carved on the springers are the principal survivals of the sculptural decoration (pl. 62). In the twelfth century the walls and vaulted ceiling were covered with frescos of which only fragments survive beneath the tribune. There is a scene from the Last Judgment on the middle bay of the vault: the twelve apostles seated on thrones, with angles in free poses behind them, and the heavenly hosts arrayed opposite them. The faces are astonishing in their spiritualized beauty, individuality of expression, psychological depth and a certain elegiac mood. Paradise is depicted on the vault of the little bay in the south corner. As well as the enthroned Virgin, an angel and the patriarchs Abraham, Isaac and Jacob can be discerned (Abraham's Bosom). The procession of the righteous into Paradise is led

by St Peter (pl. 338), while two angels playing trumpets bring up the rear. The style reveals the hand of a Russian artist, while the painting in the middle bay is the work of a Greek.

64-66, 340-343   Vladimir   Владимир

Cathedral of the Assumption, 1158-60/1185-89
Успенский собор
Uspensky sobor

Andrey Bogolyubsky's claim to overlordship of Russia, to the political inheritance of St Vladimir, found expression in the largest building to be erected in his capital in the twelfth century: the limestone Cathedral of the Assumption. It was intended to represent the strength of the regime, the regard in which it was held and – as a new episcopal see to which Andrey also planned to move the metropolitanate – the struggle for ecclesiastical independence and liberation from Byzantine tutelage. Thanks to its position on the slope of a hill it still dominates the town and the surrounding countryside. It was founded in 1158 and completed in 1160, the fresco decoration and equipping with valuable liturgical utensils following in 1161. However when the entire city was engulfed by a great fire in 1185 the cathedral was among the victims of the flames and had to be virtually rebuilt.

The surviving old parts that were incorporated in the new building permit us to reconstruct the original. With its three aisles, three apses, six pillars, west tribune and one dome, the building was akin to the cathedral of the Monastery of the Caves in Kiev in its architectonic scheme. The west front was flanked by two staircase towers. The fragment of a wall with a blind arcade, a window and frescos has survived in the north aisle. Apart from that, stones with low relief carving have been found by excavation and in the facing of the old walls. During the rebuilding from 1185 to 1189, under Andrey's successor and brother Vsevolod III, the apses of the first church were demolished and the walls between the pilasters were removed, to make a more roomy sanctuary, which projected much further than before (pl. 64), and to create an arcade which opened on its other

320	321	322	323
324		325	
326	327	328	329
330		331	332

[320–324] Kiev, Cathedral of St Sophia, 1037–61; mosaics and frescos, 11th century   320 Mosaic in the drum: the Apostle Paul   321 Fresco in the Chapel of the Archangel Michael: St Laurence   322 The throne of the Metropolitan in the main apse, detail   323 Upper storey of the west gallery   324 Mosaic in the main apse: Eucharist, detail of the south side   325 Kiev, Monastery of St Michael 'with the golden roofs': detail of mosaic depicting the Eucharist, c. 1113   326 Kiev, Church of the Saviour, Berestovo, early 12th century: west front   327 Kiev, Monastery of the Caves, Gate-church of the Holy Trinity, 1106–08: south front   328 Chernigov, Yeletsky Monastery, Cathedral of the Assumption, mid 12th century: south front   329 Vladimir-Volynsky, Cathedral of the Assumption, c. 1160/19th century: east front   330, 331 Galich, Panteleymon Church, early 13th century: blind arcades in the main apse, and view from the north-east   332 Grodno, Church of SS Boris and Gleb at Kolozh, second half of the 12th century: view from the north-east

350

and the entry of the righteous into Paradise, led by Peter and Paul, on the north side. The two Russian artists place a more human, milder interpretation on the stern Byzantine model of retribution and reward, so that the faces of the apostles express gentleness and benevolence. V. N. Lazarev and Y. A. Lebedeva regard the Vladimir frescos as marking the beginning of Rublev's second, mature period. The present, pompous Baroque iconostasis (1773-74) replaces the original icons painted by Rublev. Fortunately they were sold to the village church in Vasilyevsky where they remained from the eighteenth century until 1922, when they were removed to Moscow for restoration. They are now in the Tretyakov Gallery in Moscow and the Russian Museum in Leningrad.

The massive Cathedral of the Assumption has an important place in the history of Russian architecture as the model for numerous urban churches. When Ivan III sent for the Italian architect Aristotle Fioravanti in 1475 to build the Cathedral of the Assumption in the Kremlin in Moscow, he instructed him to study and to imitate the forms of the Vladimir School. The young, aspiring imperial power, eager to make a reality of national unity, consciously evoked the traditions of Vladimir-Suzdal. The claim of legitimacy was supported by a revival of the pre-Mongolian tradition, of which the old cathedral was an important and valuable exemplar.

5, 67-69, 344   Suzdal   Суздаль

Cathedral of the Nativity of the Virgin, 1222-25/ 1528-30

Рождественский собор

Rozhdestvensky sobor

The cathedral in the old centre of Suzdal, near the prince's palace and belonging to the kremlin complex, has been rebuilt several times in the course of its history, which is now nearly nine centuries old, so its form has undergone fundamental changes. The first building was erected under Vladimir Monomakh between 1101 and 1120, the second under Yury Vsevolodovich between 1222 and 1225. The alterations of the sixteenth century and the period between 1682 and 1750, which gave the cathedral its present shape, assimilated the contemporary styles into the traditional scheme. The result is a cube, the walls articulated vertically by lesenes and horizontally by the thirteenth-century blind arcading, and terminating in round gables (zakomari). The lesenes support the main cornice, which intersects the zakomari at the springing line. The old interior gallery was torn down at the end of the seventeenth century and a high, narrow window let into each division of the wall above the arcades. A roof with four faces was built in 1750, which was removed in the recent restoration, and the five onion domes date

from the same year. Further additions were constructed on the north and west sides of the cathedral in the eighteenth and nineteenth centuries. The restoration of 1954–55 gave particular priority to revealing the thirteenth-century base of the building and removed a dirty covering of plaster. The octagonal bell-tower in the kremlin was built in 1635, the Archbishop's Palace (now the museum) between 1682 and 1707.

The most recent archaeological studies by A. Varganov and N. N. Voronin provided the basis for the reconstruction of the cathedral. Nothing of the original building of 1101–20 could be found except the foundations, which are of rubble and a mortar of lime mixed with broken brick. They are 5 feet 7 inches wide and reach to a depth of 23 inches. The walls were constructed in the same way as the Church of the Saviour at Berestovo in Kiev. The flat bricks used here, called plinfy, are between 1 and $1\frac{1}{2}$ inches thick with face measurements of $7\frac{1}{2}$ by $9\frac{1}{2}$ inches, $9\frac{1}{2}$ by $9\frac{3}{4}$ inches, $9\frac{1}{2}$ by $8\frac{7}{8}$ inches and $9\frac{1}{2}$ by $14\frac{1}{4}$ inches, and they were made in wooden moulds in a brickworks on the banks of the Kamenka and in the kremlin itself. They are sometimes bent and bear the impression of fingers. The surfaces of the walls were prepared very carefully: rows of exposed bricks alternated with layers of smooth pink mortar $2\frac{1}{3}$ inches thick. The building had three aisles, six cruciform pillars, three semi-circular apses and a narthex at the west end, separated from the body of the church by a wall. The architects were probably from Kiev, and took the 'Great Church' of the Kiev Monastery of the Caves (1073–78) as their model, but the evidence of the excavations indicates that the Suzdal church was considerably smaller.

As has already been mentioned, the regions of Rostov, Suzdal and Vladimir began to develop their own artistic styles and concepts in the twelfth century, beginning with the cathedral in Pereslavl-Zalessky (1152), but the development was interrupted by the Tartar invasions of 1237–38. The Cathedral of the Nativity of the Virgin, in its form of 1222–25, was one of the last buildings in this line of development. The chronicler reports that at the beginning of the thirteenth century the old domed cruciform church of Vladimir Monomakh was becoming tumbledown, and it may well also have been the case that it was no longer acceptable to the new, more luxurious taste. It was demolished in 1222 by order of Prince Yury Vsevolodovich. The masonry of the old walls must have proved perfectly sound, since large sections of wall were found, not broken up, in the excavations. The foundations of the new cathedral were laid without regard to the old foundations, at a slight angle to them, placing the new axis somewhat to the north of the old. The new building took three years to erect (1223–25) and according to the chronicler it was 'more beautiful than the first'. The Bishop of Vladimir, Simon, a famous writer of the day and one of the authors of the collection of legends of the saints issued by the Monastery of the Caves in Kiev, was also involved in the building and performed the service of consecration in September 1225. The new church fell victim to an inexplicable disaster in 1445. All that the chronicler can say is that the coffins of the high-ranking clergy buried in the church began to burn, and that the upper part of the building collapsed the next day. No attempt was made to repair it, and it remained in a semi-ruinous condition until 1528. Between then and 1530, on the orders of Tsar Vasily III, the top half of the walls, that is, as far as the blind arcading, was demolished and rebuilt in brick. As a result the early thirteenth-century building can only be reconstructed on the basis of the painstaking investigations made by Varganov and Voronin. It was a domed cruciform church, built of roughly hewn slabs of porous tuff, with the decorative elements in limestone. It had a massive tribune at the west end, six pillars, three apses and three square vestibules which turn the rectangular groundplan into a cross; the two on the north and south sides used to open directly into the transepts.

The present-day appearance of the building corresponds to the generous proportions of the old plan. The north and south fronts are divided by shallow, smooth lesenes into four unequal sections which do not correspond to the positions of the three pairs of pillars inside. The lesenes therefore have no structural function, and are themselves intersected by a band of ornament (pls. 67, 344). The exterior is dominated by the decorational principle. The west front is divided into three, with the middle division wider and higher than the other two. The horizontal ornamentation consists of a blind arcade and a saw-tooth frieze. Unlike the majority of twelfth-century churches, the short cylindrical shafts of the columns do not rest on consoles but on cuboid bases, which in turn rest on a ledge set in the wall. The capitals and shafts seem heavy, the bases are decorated with low relief carvings of plant and animal motifs. All the decorative elements, even the saw-tooth frieze, are covered with a low-relief ornament of a plant motif, which plainly owes something to woodcarving. To judge by remaining fragments, the old windows were aligned on the axis of each of the divisions of the walls, above and below the blind arcade, with surrounds like the one that Varganov discovered in the south division of the west front. This consisted of little columns on each side of the embrasure, the carved capitals of which supported a little arch constructed of bricks and a thick layer of lime mortar, and constitutes a curious repetition of the blind arcading. It is possible that the (now reconstructed) ogee-shaped zakomari that surmount each of the divisions of the walls, formed by drawing the semicircle up to a little point, were used for the first time

in Suzdal. The cathedral's three domes were an innovation in the region. The main dome was over the crossing, and the two smaller ones were placed either above the eastern corners to light the enlarged sanctuary or at the west corners to light the tribune, which was not reserved for the prince and his family alone, but used also by wealthy merchants.

The sculptural decoration of the cathedral has been preserved on the portals and blind arcades on the west and south sides, though not all of what is there is original. The south front faced towards the old city and was given the most elaborate decoration for that reason. The carvings were the work of the best stone-masons. The predominant motif in the shallow, lacy ornamentation is a kind of palmette. The lesenes are interrupted by a shallow frieze of strap-work, and there used to be lion masks above it at the corners (pl. 344). The bead pattern appears for the first time in Russian art, on the columns on the façades, together with the strap-work. The female masks and animal motifs repeat the earlier examples in Vladimir, but make a more attractive and decorative effect. It is likely that the upper parts of the walls, which were demolished, were also decorated elaborately with stone-carvings.

The inside of the cathedral had cruciform pillars and a massive tribune in the western part, larger than the one in Vladimir's original building, reaching as far east as the second pair of pillars, that is, to the crossing. The stairs leading to it were in the north wall of the west vestibule, which originally had two storeys until the upper one was demolished at the end of the seventeenth century. The later entrance and the arch over it are still discernible in the west wall, from the outside, above the new roof of the remaining one storey of the vestibule. The size and layout of the tribune, which was not connected in

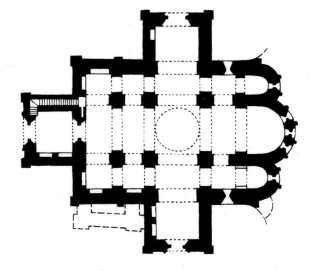

any way to the palace, indicate that it was intended primarily for the patricians from the city. The part of the church beneath it served as a burial vault. Arched tombs were set in the lower zones of the walls for the princes and bishops. Sarcophagi stood against the pillars. The constriction of the space to the west of

responded to the lower part, between ground level and the blind arcade. Another peculiarity was the two-storey construction of the west vestibule. The upper floor opened on to the church like a balcony and assumed the function of the tribune in other churches. The little room was lit by a window with three arches, supported on little columns, akin formally to the Romanesque window in the staircase-tower at Bogolyubovo. The third special feature was the lavish sculptural decoration, covering the entire area of the façades from top to bottom like a tapestry and spreading over the structural members as well (pl. 71). Even the capitals of the pilasters on the corners are adorned with the masks of women and warriors (pl. 73). There survive some 440 of these reliefs, carved in white limestone, including human figures modelled in such high relief that they are two-thirds of the way to being free-standing statues. The combination of high and low relief, as these figures merge directly into the linear, filigree pattern of plant motifs, was both an artistic and a technical innovation. St George's has every right to its description as the Russian Chartres.

The original arrangement of the carvings has been lost, but it has been reconstructed as follows by G. K. Wagner. The pedestal below the drum bore Christ as Emmanuel, his hands raised in blessing, and angels, corresponding to the idea of the 'upper heaven' in the *Topographia Christiana* of Cosmas Indicopleustes. The gables depicted the Transfiguration on the west front, the Crucifixion on the north front and the Resurrection on the south. The Seven Sleepers of Ephesus (pl. 78) and perhaps the Ascension were grouped with the Transfiguration, and the Three Children in the Burning Fiery Furnace and Daniel in the Lions' Den with the Crucifixion, for iconographic reasons. The Resurrection was grouped with Alexander of Macedon's ascent to heaven, surrounded by poetic symbols of the forces of nature – griffins, dragons, lions and the like – and perhaps also a representation of the Virgin of Intercession and Protection. This zone corresponded to the 'lower heaven' of Cosmas Indicopleustes. The theme of the Church on Earth is worked out on the wall below the capitals, including in the blind arcades. The central composition here is a Virgin of the Orans type in the gable of the west vestibule, surrounded by soldier saints – St George, St Demetrius, St Theodore Tiron and St Theodore Stratilates – the patrons of the princes of Vladimir. The line of these saints is continued on the north and south fronts by Old Testament kings and prophets, including David and Solomon. Below them there is a row of saints and miracle-workers, such as Boris and Gleb, Panteleymon, Cosmas and Damian. There must have been a Deesis in the gable over the doorway of the

west vestibule when it still had its upper storey, since the idea of intercession is continued for the whole length of the blind arcades in frontal representations of archangels, apostles, martyrs and warrior saints. The north-west corner, which survives from the original structure, has the figure of Demetrius of Salonika between Christian martyrs (pls. 75, 77). The gable of the north vestibule contained a portrait of Prince Svyatoslav above a representation of St George whose shield bears a rampant panther, the badge of the Vladimir dynasty (pl. 74). On either side of the portal, a little above the capitals, two friendly lions kept watch. The Virgin of the Sign (Znameniye) was depicted over the entrance of the south vestibule (pl. 76). Additionally, there were archangels, cherubim and seraphim all round the walls. The whole of the lower zone was intended to portray the Paradise of the earth in flower. The walls are completely covered with carvings of fabulous trees, plants, birds, animals and imaginary beasts. Stylistic analysis has made it possible to distinguish the hands of ten sculptors. One of them signed the right relief of the Saviour on the north vestibule with the name 'Baku' which might be Bakun, a very common Russian name at the time. It appears that the same artist executed the portrait of Prince Svyatoslav, the masks of warriors on the capitals and other carvings. There are Romanesque traits in Bakun's work, which suggest that he was a native of the southern part of Galicia-Volynia.

The carvings on St George's Cathedral are not merely a local phenomenon. An all-Russian style is developed in them, which is also organically connected with the art of the rest of the world in that it transmutes and creates something fresh from its Romanesque and Byzantine elements and anticipates features of the nascent Gothic style. It makes an effect of costly enamel-work. These carvings rightly suggest the end of the Romanesque style with its zoomorphic symbolism and the beginning of a new style which avails itself of the abundance of human circumstances. F. Halle emphasizes that 'a whole world separates these young, strong, but stylized figures from the degenerate figures of St Demetrius' Cathedral'. It is significant that the St George carvings prefer Christ as Emmanuel to the Pantocrator, and emphasize the youth rather than the military qualities of the angels and the warrior saints. None of the reliefs depict a bloody conflict. Even the masks of animals lack a monstrous air. The strong Russian character of the faces and the influx of motifs from folk art are striking. A new artistic conception of human beings and of the world was in the process of forming, livelier, more intimate and painterly, even thought the ecclesiastical requirements dominated the iconography.

The City-States of Novgorod and Pskov

3, 80-86, 88, 345   Novgorod   Новгород

Cathedral of St Sophia in the Kremlin, 1045–52
Собор Софии в Кремле
Sobor Sofii v Kremle

The chronicle relates that a cathedral dedicated to 'divine wisdom' was built of oak at the end of the tenth century (989) – 'commanding attention' and having 'thirteen tops' – which stood for sixty years and then burnt down. The foundation stone of a new building was in fact laid in the kremlin four years before the old one was destroyed. A new cathedral of St Sophia was built at the command of Prince Vladimir, the son of Yaroslav the Wise, under Bishop Luke, between 1045 and 1052, only eight years later than its model and namesake in Kiev. Originally serving as the chief cathedral of the principality, it was taken over in the 1130s by the administration of the new aristocratic republic founded by the boyars and the merchant class of the city. The prince, his function reduced to military commander, had to move to Gorodishche, where the Yuryev Monastery was founded. The kremlin, on the Sophia Side of the river, became the residence of the chief ecclesiastical authority, an archbishop from 1165, who also enjoyed the rank of head of government as well. The archbishop was *ex officio* president for life of the 'Council of Lords', and was thus the representative of the popular assembly (the Veche) in dealings with other states, and after the deposition of the prince he played the most important role in politics. 'Where St Sophia is, there also is Novgorod', the chronicle states, referring to the cathedral's symbolic significance for the trading metropolis and the whole territory of the 'Lord Great Novgorod', which stretched far into the north of Russia.

In its nine centuries of existence the cathedral has experienced numerous alterations. Apart from the fact that the chronicle does not mention them all,

the additions and alterations made shortly after the original building was completed can no longer be distinguished. The reconstruction of the original plan and structural details is therefore an extremely complex problem, which has occupied scholars for years. The discussion is forever being rekindled by new written sources coming to light or by discoveries made in the course of restoration work. The nucleus of the church is a domed cruciform church with five aisles and twelve pillars, but only three apses. The central cross is emphasized by the width of the middle aisle and the transepts. The imposing dome over the crossing, closely encircled by the four smaller domes over the angles of the arms of the cross, is balanced by the broad main apse, which is flanked by two narrow apses at the ends of the inner side aisles, while the outer aisles originally terminated at the east in straight walls. A tower surmounted by a dome, in the south-west corner, houses a broad staircase leading up to the west tribune, but this may have been a slightly later addition. The domes are all helmet-shaped.

From the outside, the original nucleus can be discerned by its greater height. Its walls are divided by lesenes into sections that terminate in semi-circular or triangular gables. On the west front, the round gable-end of the middle aisle is succeeded to the north by, first, a triangular gable and then another round one *(pl. 345)*. On both the north and south fronts the division of the wall immediately to the west of the transept has a triangular gable, while the roof of the east division simply comes down to the top of the wall, in accordance with the half barrel vault (a quarter of a circle in section) over that corner of the building; these two features give the fronts a unique outline *(pl. 3)*. The gables of the outer divisions of the east walls are of course quadrants. The pair of domes at the east end are brought to the very edge and rise directly up from the east wall on rectangular pedestals. The galleries that surround the

345	346	347
348	349	350	351
352	353	354
355	356	357	358

345 *Novgorod, Kremlin, Cathedral of St Sophia, 1045–52, view of the surrounding district, including Volkhov and Lake Ilmen, beyond the roof of the Cathedral, seen from the Euthymios clock-tower, 1443*   **346** *Novgorod, Kremlin, 15th–17th centuries: view looking along the wall towards the Kokuy tower, and the tower and Church of the Virgin of the Intercession*
[**347, 348**] *Novgorod, Monastery of St Anthony, Cathedral of the Nativity of the Virgin, 1117–19*   **347** *View from the south-west*
348 *Fresco depicting the head of a bishop, 1125*
[**349, 350**] *Novgorod, Yaroslav Court, Cathedral of St Nicholas, 1113–36*   **349** *View from the south-east*   **350** *Fresco, first quarter of the 12th century: Job's wife, detail of Job's sufferings*
[**351, 352**] *Novgorod, Yuryev Monastery, Cathedral of St George, 1119–30, by Master Peter*   **351** *View of the main dome and west end seen from the altar*   **352** *View from the north-east, with domed staircase-tower in the north-west corner*
[**353, 354**] *Novgorod, Church of the Annunciation, near Arkazh, 1179/17th century*   **353** *View from the south-east*
354 *Fresco, late 12th century: head of a young water-carrier*   **355, 356** *Novgorod, Church of the Transfiguration, in the Street of Elijah, 1374: frescos by Theophanes the Greek between the windows of the drum, 1378: Melchizedek and Abel*
[**357, 358**] *Novgorod, Church of the Nativity, in the cemetery, 1381–82*   **357** *Fresco on the north wall, c. 1390: the Assumption, detail*   **358** *View from the east*

nucleus of the church on the north, west and south sides at ground level were originally only one storey high and supported flying buttresses. Their bays were roofed by barrel vaults with the longitudinal axis at right angles to the cathedral walls. They were not walled but the cruciform pillars bearing the roof formed simple, round-arched arcades on both the inner and outer sides. The date of their construction is not known, but it is likely that they were built at the same time as the aisles. Their arches were walled in before the end of the eleventh century, creating the south vestibule, later named after Archbishop Marturi of Novgorod, which served as a burial vault for boyars and clerics. At the end of the eleventh century, or the beginning of the twelfth, an upper storey was built on, which was still not as high as the nucleus of the building. The façades of the galleries, which retain their two storeys to the present day, are slightly out of step with the articulation of the nucleus on the north and south fronts, but repeat the pattern of lesenes and gables, though the latter are all rounded, not triangular *(pls 3, 80, 345)*. They have lean-to roofs at both ends. At the end of the fifteenth century the little Chapel of the Nativity of the Virgin was built on to the east wall of the south gallery, and a similar addition was made to the north gallery for the sake of symmetry. The additions of later centuries were matters of detail (such as the seventeenth-century portal and window on the west front) rather than fundamental alterations. The restoration at the end of the nineteenth century was corrected when the Soviet Department for the Care of Monuments repaired the damage inflicted in the Second World War, which was particularly severe in the upper part of the building. The studies of 1945–60 produced the information that the walls were constructed of large, irregular, rough-hewn stones. The lime mortar, coloured pink by the addition of finely broken brick, followed the outlines of the stones, thus drawing attention to their irregularities. The walls were not plastered, but the result was not the same as the 'striped' masonry of Kievan architecture. Instead, the combination of the large stones and the pink mortar must have had the effect of a huge, arbitrary mosaic, contained within the framework of the lesenes and gables, and in which the arched surrounds of the windows and doors, made of dressed bricks, must have stood out sharply.

The interior is divided in two horizontally: the low vaults under the tribunes create a gloomy lower storey outside the central cross, divided into numerous cells, while the central area, composed of the lofty crossing and the barrel-vaulted arms of the cross, and the upper floor of the tribunes themselves, are flooded with light. The arms of the cross terminate in arcades of two arches each on both floors *(pl. 85)*. The arches are all of equal thickness. The twelve pillars between the aisles are cruciform, those of the arcades square. Examination of the interior has shown that the original floor – probably of majo-

363

359	360	361
362		363
364	365	366	367
368		369

359 *Novgorod, Church of St Vlasi, in the Volos Street, 1407: view from the north-east*   360 *Novgorod, Church of the Twelve Apostles 'by the gorge', 1455: view from the north-east*   361 *Novgorod, Zverin Monastery, Church of St Simeon, 1467: east front*   362 *Novgorod, Church of St John the Baptist 'on the rock', 1453: view from the south*   363 *Novgorod, Church of the Assumption, in the market-place, 1458: view from the north-west*   364 *Novgorod, Monastery of St Anthony, Church of the Purification of the Virgin, and refectory, 1535–37: view from the south-east*   365 *Novgorod, Church of SS Boris and Gleb, Plotniki, 1536: north front*   366 *Novgorod, Monastery of the Holy Ghost, Church of the Holy Trinity, 1557: view from the east*   367 *Pskov, Snetogorsky Monastery, Cathedral of the Nativity of the Virgin, 1310–11: east front*   368 *Pskov, Church of the Assumption 'by the ferry', with bell-gable 1521: view from the south-east*   369 *Pskov, Church of St Anastasia, Kuznetsi, 1539: east front*

lica slabs – lay about 4 feet 3 inches lower than the present level, that the decorational scheme included ceramic mosaics, and that part of the walls and arches were faced with alternate layers of bricks and smooth plaster – a technique known as Byzantine masonry.

In spite of the many alterations made to the interior in nine hundred years it still conjures up an impression of severity and sublimity. The decoration was simpler than in Kiev: there were none of the large mosaic figures, marble inlay or schist reliefs. The iconographic programme consisted chiefly of the mural paintings executed in the middle of the twelfth century, probably by artists from Constantinople, which have survived only in a few fragments. The present paintings date from the late nineteenth century. Although they do not claim to be ideal, the interior would seem rather cold without them. Around 1108, or possibly already before 1100, at all events before the artists from Constantinople arrived, a picture of the Byzantine Emperor Constantine and his mother Helena was painted *al secco* (not in true fresco) on the south side of the pillar in the Marturi vestibule *(pl. 86)*. The flat style, the absence of any kind of modelling, and the very careful delineation, as well as the Slav features of Helena, give the impression of a work by a local artist. The characters and the orthography of the inscription that used to be on the painting suggested that he was actually a native of Novgorod. The chronicle records that the full painted decoration was done around 1144. The prophets in the central drum and the four high priests above the arches of the doors between the central apse and the side apses must be ascribed to that period. Unfortunately the shell that shattered the main dome in 1941, during the Second World War, also destroyed the fresco of the Pantocrator. Fragments of frescos were found on the bottom zone of the walls during excavations: the remains of a Deesis in the Marturi vestibule, and several heads of men wearing princes' caps. The walls above the clergy seats in the main apse are faced with large mosaic plaques, on which a little arch and columns frame a field with flowers, crosses and human figures. The iconostases in front of the main altar and in the little Chapel of the Nativity of the Virgin date from the second half of the sixteenth century and include some masterly icons of the Moscow School.

The decorative stone crosses inlaid in the walls are an unusual feature. The large cross with low-relief carvings in the west wall was executed in the second half of the fourteenth century in fulfilment of a vow by Archbishop Alexey. In order to emphasize the ends of the arms of the cross, which are shaped like battle-axes, it was hewn from a piece of limestone with an oval top edge, in oval curves. The reliefs on it depict five church feasts, of which the Crucifixion, in the centre, is the best *(pl. 88)*. The crucified Saviour, with the S-curve of the body, is in perfect harmony with the figures of Mary and John as they incline towards him. The group is characterized by restrained gestures, sweeping lines and a naive treatment of the forms that disregards details.

The west portal contains the famous pair of bronze doors, 11 feet 10 inches high and 7 feet 10 inches wide, known as the Korsun (Kherson) Door. In spite

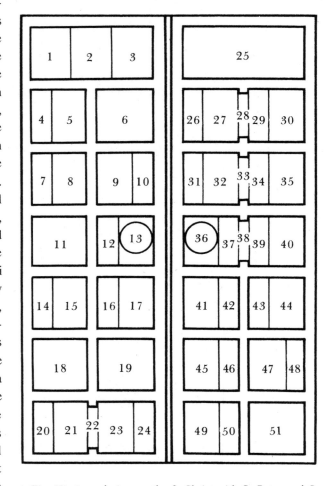

1 *The Virgin and six apostles* 2 *Christ with St Peter and St Paul (traditio legis)* 3 *Six apostles* 4 *Christ's baptism* 5 *The Annunciation* 6 *The Nativity* 7 *A beardless layman with a book* 8, 9 *Adoration of the Three Kings, on the right: the Virgin and Child* 10 *Rachel weeping for her children* 11 *The Presentation in the Temple* 12 *A deacon with a censer* 13 *Lion's head with the door-handle and five human heads in its jaws, Russian inscription: Hell consuming sinners* 14 *The Visitation* 15 *The Flight into Egypt* 16 *A deacon with a book* 17 *Bishop Alexander of Płock between two deacons* 18 *The assumption of Elijah* 19 *Two knights standing on dead adversaries (the Triumph of Virtue over Vice)* 20 *Bronze-founder Riquin* 21 *The Fall of Man* 22 *Russian addition: Master Avram* 23 *The Creation of Eve* 24 *Bronze-founder Waismuth* 25 *Maiestas Domini (Christ in the mandorla with angels and the symbols of the evangelists)* 26 *Man holding out a garment* 27 *Entry into Jerusalem* 28 *A knight fighting a beast (Victory of Good over Evil)* 29 *Man with a scroll* 30 *Inhabitants of Jerusalem awaiting Christ at the city gates (belongs with 27)* 31 *Man with a dog* 32 *Christ taken prisoner* 33 *Knight over a figure standing on its head (Victory of Good over Evil)* 34 *Man with a snake* 35 *Christ in prison or Peter being released by an angel* 36 *Lion's head with the door-handle and a man's head in its jaws* 37 *King with a sword* 38 *Knight fighting a beast (Victory of Good over Evil)* 39 *Herod* 40 *Flagellation* 41 *Crucifixion* 42 *Nicodemus* 43 *Russian addition: figure in women's clothing* 44 *Women bearing anointing oil at the tomb* 45 *Harrowing of Hell* 46 *(Arch)-bishop Wichmann of Magdeburg* 47 *The Ascension* 48 *Man with a sword* 49 *Three knights (St Maurice and companions?)* 50 *Massacre of the Innocents (belongs with 37)* 51 *Russian addition: a centaur with a bow*

364

making them an annex to the Archbishop's Palace, where the Council of Lords met on the St Sophia Side.

These historical vicissitudes are reflected in the structure of the cathedral. Its original architectonic form was abandoned and it acquired the character of a large city church. It lost the four drums, surmounted by domes, from its four corners, the tops of the walls were straightened out to terminate in a horizontal line, and the wavy roof that had followed the lines of the round gables was exchanged for a roof with four inclined faces, a vestibule was added on the north side, and vaults were erected inside the building to create two storeys. From the groundplan it appears that St Nicholas originally belonged to the type of the domed cruciform church with three aisles, six pillars, a tribune at the west end, five domes and three apses. Unlike its contemporaries, the Cathedral of the Nativity of the Virgin in the Monastery of St Anthony, and St George in the Yuryev Monastery, it has no staircase-tower. The walls are so thick that a spiral staircase could be built in the wall in the southwest corner.

In spite of the alterations the building is still impressive. The broad lesenes project boldly from the façades, and continue in energetic lines into the semicircular arches of the original gables, thereby indicating the construction of the interior (pl. 349). The massive apses, standing very close together, rise to the level of the roof (pl. 93). The irregularity of the masonry creates a play of light and shadow all over the blank walls. The fabric is the usual Novgorod mixture of rubble and alternate courses of brick. Architecturally, the cathedral shows a strong dependence on the schools of southern Russia, especially on the cathedral of the Kiev Monastery of the Caves, expressed both in layout and in decoration, for instance, in the niches that articulate the walls of the apses (pl. 93). In spite of its monumental character the cathedral displays numerous painterly traits, such as the slight irregularity in the form of the semi-circles of the arches, the absence of strictly symmetrical articulation, and the plasticity of the walls (pl. 349). The cathedral was decorated with frescos at the time when it was built, of which there have survived a depiction of the sufferings of Job in the south-west corner of the ground floor (pl. 350), fragments of the row of bishops in the sanctuary and ornamental motifs in the window embrasures. In style they are close to Kievan mural paintings of the eleventh and early twelfth centuries. The most notable of the fragments, which has a Russian inscription, is the picture of Job's wife, standing in silent emotion in front of her suffering but steadfast husband, holding a rod with a small pot hanging from it. The slight inclination of the head, the long oval of the face and the gentle modelling are the expressions of a realistic artistic conception, free of any abstract symbolism.

94, 351, 352 Novgorod Новгород

Cathedral of St George in the Yuryev Monastery, 1119–30
Георгиевский собор Юрьева монастыря
Georgievsky sobor Yuryeva monastyrya

369

The Yuryev Monastery was built by order of Prince Vsevolod Mstislavovich, on the left bank of the Volkhov opposite the new palace at Gorodishche, about a mile and a half from the kremlin, during the abbacy of Kiriak. The traditional date of the monastery's foundation is 1030, but the earliest documentary mention of it occurs in 1119 in connection with its first stone building, the Cathedral of St George built by Master Peter, and the second largest building in the city, after St Sophia.

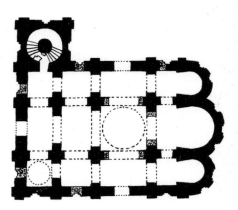

In plan it is an oblong, on an east-west longitudinal axis, divided into three aisles by six cruciform pillars. It has three apses at the east end and three asymmetrically placed domes. It makes an integrated, monolithic impression. Its massive, imposing composition recalls the cathedral in the Monastery of St Anthony. Like that, it has a staircase-tower in the north-west corner, although in this case the tower is square in plan (pl. 352). Its west front combines organically with the west front of the main building, so that the two units are preceived as a unified, massive whole. This unity is emphasized by the care taken to relate the windows and niches of the two parts to each other. All the fronts, except the east, are articulated by powerful lesenes (pl. 94), which duly record the structure of the building, corresponding to the positions of the pillars and the width of the aisles and transepts, and running without interruption into the arches of the round gables. There is no horizontal articulation of the exterior. The three tiers of windows and niches might have performed that function, but their elongated forms and their positioning precisely one above the other tend rather to create a vertical movement.

The monumentality created by the strictness of its proportions, the clarity of its articulation and the simplicity of its forms, makes the cathedral one of the most outstanding and perfect buildings of the early twelfth century. It represents the style of the first period of building in stone in Novgorod, which still displayed a certain dependency on south Russian and western models in many of its characteristics. It was much altered in the nineteenth century, but the restoration of 1933–36 cleared away all the modern additions and alterations. The narrow, arched windows and the characteristic double-recessed niches in the walls of the apses, the tower and the other fronts were restored to their original shape. Three round-arched portals with concentric mouldings were also uncovered. The principle of using niches to decorate the façades goes back to the traditions of Kiev, but in Novgorod the shape of the recesses and the arrangement are simpler.

The interior makes a powerful impression because of its unusual height *(pl. 351)*. From floor level the distance between the pillars seems very small, and the height of the vaults very great. The princes, the chief citizens and the boyars were interred here. One of them, Dmitry Miroshkinich, who was assassinated by rebellious citizens in 1209, was buried with chains and a sword at his feet. The traditional tribune was built at the west end, but it in no way detracts from the verticality and the general abundance of light.

The walls and ceiling vaults were repainted in the nineteenth century in imitation of the original abstract and conventional frescos. A few fragments of a strap-work motif survive in the embrasures of the windows. At the top of the staircase-tower, between the windows in the drum, some figures of church fathers and saints have been preserved, characterized by dry, linear modelling and the reddish-brown colouring of their faces. Head-and-shoulders portrayals of a Virgin Hodigitria and a Pantocrator have also been uncovered. The frescos are stylistically close to Kievan murals of the twelfth century, though they were probably the work of Novgorod artists.

95-98   Novgorod   Новгород

Church of the Saviour, Nereditsa, 1198

Церковь Спаса на Нередице

Tserkov Spasa na Nereditse

There was a recession in the building activities of the princes of Novgorod immediately after the completion of St George's Cathedral, since the revolution in the city imposed considerable restrictions on their power. The last building to be instigated by one of the princes came in the second half of the century, at the beginning of a new and independent period in the development of architecture in Novgorod, when it had freed itself of the imitation of south Russian and Western models. This was the Church of the Saviour, which was built on the orders of Prince Yaroslav Vladimirovich on a hill beside the Nereditsa, not far from his palace at Gorodishche *(pl. 97)*. The construction occupied three and a half months in the

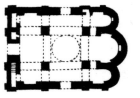

summer of 1198. Not long afterwards it formed part of the court monastery, whose ideological function was to support the claims of the princes. There is no further information in the historical sources. The monastery began to decline in the sixteenth century but struggled on through the seventeenth and eighteenth, until it was finally dissolved in 1764. The old Church of the Saviour was affiliated to the city churches in Gorodishche. Services were held in it only once a year, on the feast of the Transfiguration (6 August), and it was therefore spared any significant alterations, and the frescos in the interior, dating from 1199, were preserved in pristine condition until the Second World War. The church was destroyed by shell-fire between 1941 and 1943. It could not be rebuilt until 1955–58. The important and comprehensive programme of murals was lost beyond repair, except for the equivalent of fifteen per cent of the original area.

By comparison with the monumental structures built by earlier princes of Novgorod, the Church of the Saviour seems small and modest. It belongs to the cuboid type and is almost square in plan, with four widely spaced square pillars, three apses and a tribune at the west end constructed of timbers. The stairs are set in a slit in the thickness of the west wall. There is a chapel in each corner of the tribune, so that only the middle section opens on to the church, like a balcony, but it affords a view of the entire interior. The Church of the Saviour lacks the formal and linear precision of the princely cathedrals, which are all of a high technical and architectural standard. The fabric of the walls, composed of grey and dark red limestone, interspersed with layers of bricks and the usual pinkish mortar, coloured by fragments of crushed brick, is thick and coarse, but its uneven, irregular surfaces, and the rounded corners create the impression of a painterly plasticity. Its exterior appearance is of a cube surmounted by a large dome on a powerful drum, which is pierced by windows. Lesenes, running on into the semi-circular gables without interruption, divide all the walls into three sections, which are all of very different widths on the north and south walls. The windows, placed one above the other in the vertical axis of each division of the walls, have no symmetrical relationship to each other. On the north and south walls they are arranged in the form of a cross around the pair placed halfway up the wall of the middle division, the base of the cross being provided by the doors in each wall, which have straight lintels below shallow, semi-circular niches. Each of the gables is braced by an oak beam at the level of the springing line. The roofs were covered with lead, laid directly on to the vaults. The middle apse reaches up into the semi-circle of the gable, while the symmetrically flanking side apses do not project so far, and are little more than half as high *(pl. 96)*. The exterior walls are not decorated in any way. The only ornamentation is on the drum, where instead of a cornice there is a frieze of the typical Novgorod type, a row of round arches outlined in porebrik.

The Church on the Nereditsa illustrates the development that had been taking place since the middle of the twelfth century in the architecture of Novgorod, away from the grandiose type of ceremonial cathedrals towards the simple, intimate congregational churches, but at the same time it preserves the monumental traditions, using the same architectonic means, only on a smaller scale. It stands midway between the conservative style of the churches built under princely auspices, and the more modern trend preferred by citizen patrons.

The frescos, painted in 1199, were among the outstanding monuments of early Russian art. They were the best preserved and the largest group of medieval murals in Europe, and their condition made it possible to comprehend the decorative iconographic programme as a whole, without the need to rely on any kind of conjectural reconstruction. They covered every part of the building. The Ascension was depicted in the dome: the Saviour was seated on a rainbow, borne upwards by six angels. The drum contained an upper tier of the apostles, and then the prophets between the windows. The Forty Martyrs of Sebaste were painted in medallions on the supporting arches. The evangelists appeared in the pendentives, and the archangels and cherubim in the lunettes and the east bay of the ceiling. The apse was occupied by a Virgin Orans with a medallion of Christ on her breast. Holy men and women approached her from both sides in procession, led by St Boris and St Gleb. Below that there was a frieze of three eucharistic scenes, the Tier of Bishops, and a Deesis composed of Christ as High Priest with John the Baptist, Martha in place of Mary (in allusion to Prince Yaroslav's wife), and other saints. The walls of the prothesis were decorated with a Virgin Orans, holy fathers and scenes from the life of St Joachim and St Anne, and the diakonikon with scenes from the life of John the Baptist and holy women. The paintings on the north and south walls depicted events from the Old and New Testaments as well as military saints, martyrs and venerable princes. In the arched tomb in the south wall Prince Yaroslav is shown presenting the model of a church to Christ. The west wall was covered with an impressive Judgment, with all imaginable torments of Hell.

The frescos in the middle apse are the best preserved, particularly the figures of St James, St Phocas and St Gregory in the Bishops' Tier, and Bishop Peter of Alexandria in the (burial?) niche to the right of the Deesis. Scholars (V. K. Myassoyedov, M. I. Artamov, V. N. Lazarev and M. K. Karger) distinguish ten different artists' styles. The paintings reproduced in this book (pls 95, 98) display a graphic manner. For all the vitality of the figures and individuality of characterization there is a rigidity in the movements and gestures. The artist emphasized the linear outline, placed his highlights by means of delicate, chalky brush-strokes, made the faces on the small heads appear flat-featured and the details almost ornamental. The frescos all lacked aristocratic elegance and refinement. Their outstanding characteristic was a stern, energetic and popular realism; they were evidently painted by local artists and conformed both to the canonical requirements of the ecclesiastical authorities and to the wishes of the princely founder.

99, 100   Novgorod   Новгород

Paraskeva-Pyatnitsa Church in the market-place, 1207/14th and 16th centuries

Церковь Параскевы Пятницы на Торгу

Tserkov Paraskevy Pyatnitsy na Torgu

From the middle of the twelfth century architecture in Novgorod was stamped by the requirements and tastes of its citizens. After the uprising of 1136, which transferred government from the prince to an oligarchy of boyars, large numbers of the inhabitants, by then some 20,000, took a direct part in the city's cultural life. This change is reflected in the very size of the new buildings. In contrast to the monumental princely cathedrals with six pillars, smaller, simpler, more intimate parish churches with four pillars were erected, which met the more modest needs of the new founders. As well as the educated, wealthy patrons from the upper class, an ever-increasing role was played by the associations of merchants and craftsmen and other urban communities, such as the strictly organized districts of streets, 'hundreds' and 'fifths'. The oldest monument of the new style in Novgorod itself is the Church of the Annunciation at Arkazh (1179), although St George's in Staraya Ladoga appears to have been built before it.

The Paraskeva-Pyatnitsa Church was built in 1207 by the wealthy and influential merchants who ran Novgorod's overseas trade, on the market-place on the Commerce Side, not far from the quays on the Volkhov. It was named after the saint who is the iconographic embodiment of Good Friday, the patroness of housekeeping in the popular imagination, and particularly of trade in Novgorod – Friday was the day of fairs and markets. The church belongs in general terms to the type that predominated from the middle of the twelfth century, the simple cube with one dome, but, as M. K. Karger established beyond doubt, it occupies a special position in that new constructional and artistic techniques were put to use in it. It survived to the twentieth century only in a much altered condition, and it was not until the archaeological investigation and partial restoration of 1960 that the opportunity arose of returning it to its original form. Its history includes the record of numerous destructive fires; that of 1342 caused the roof to fall in. The entire upper part of the building, including the vaulting and the disproportionately small dome, was rebuilt in the fourteenth century in the contemporary style, the roof with eight sloping faces was constructed in the sixteenth century, and the little windowless drum and cupola supporting a cross was placed on top of the helmet-shaped dome in the eighteenth century.

The church is almost square in plan, only slightly longer on the east-west axis, but the wide middle apse and the massively projecting vestibules on the north, west and south sides turn the oblong into a pronounced cross shape. The outward form of the building has lost much of its expressive force as a result of the alterations to the vaulting and the roof, but it should be envisaged as a harmoniously proportioned cube, with a dome erected on a low pedestal. The façades did not end in the usual round gables (zakomari) but in the trefoil outline corresponding to the shape of the roof: barrel vaults over the arms of the central cross, quadrant vaults over the corner cells. The semi-circular middle apse is flanked by two smaller apses that are rectangular on the outside. The barrel-vaulted vestibules are lower than the nucleus of the building, relaxing the regularity of the cube and creating an impression of rising by stages (pl. 100). Further ornamentation comes from the broad, clustered pilasters, which project in three steps and a central demi-shaft (pl. 99), the small windows, the large, triple-recessed blind niches and the portals. The local masons developed an unusual fabric for the walls: courses of limestone alternate with irregular courses of square, flat bricks, held by a mortar of lime and brick-dust. Free of either plaster or whitewash, the natural colours of the masonry create a strikingly polychrome effect (pl. 100).

The interior, which had been severely deformed by a ceiling inserted at two levels, has been restored. Its character is governed by the accent on the crossing beneath the dome, the round supports and the traditional semi-circular outline of the main altar and the prothesis. The circular form of the prothesis is disguised on the outside by being encased by straight walls that meet at a right angle, but the diakonikon is rectangular both inside and out. There is no tribune, and its function is performed by the vestibules, which are two-storeyed and open on to the body of the church through broad arches. There is one staircase leading to the upper storey of the vestibules, built in the thickness of the wall at the north-west corner, and the three are connected at the level of the upper floor by a passage in the thickness of the wall. The original decoration has not survived, but fragments that have been found indicate that the floor was covered with slabs of limestone that shaded from dark red to violet.

The Paraskeva-Pyatnitsa Church represents a recurrence of architectonic peculiarities that we have already met in the Pyatnitsa Church in Chernigov and St Michael's (Svirskaya) in Smolensk: a pyramidal structure, a harmonious, balanced relationship between the height of the vestibules and the height of the body of the church, the trefoil profile of the fronts and the dynamic clustered pilasters. Churches of a similar composition are to be found in Pskov, Polotsk, Grodno, Putivla and other towns. The following stylistic period of Novgorod architecture adopted and transformed many of these early thirteenth-century elements, and creatively adapted them to the artistic taste of the time.

101-103 Staraya Ladoga Старая Ладога

Church of St George, second half of the 12th century

Церковь Георгия

Tserkov Georgiya

The church is a well-preserved and typical example of Novgorod architecture in the second half of the twelfth century. It is almost square in plan, with four interior pillars and three apses at the east end. The walls are divided by lesenes into three sections that terminate in round gables (zakomari). The different widths of the divisions of the fronts, with the east division narrower than the other two, places the dome somewhat to the east of centre, giving rise to a slight asymmetry which, like the arbitrary placing of the windows, characterizes the building (pl. 102). There is a tribune inside the church at the west end, the corners of which are occupied by separate chapels, linked by a wooden passage. The stairs are let into the west wall.

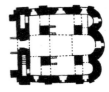

Tribune level

The frescos resemble those in the church at Arkazh stylistically, so they can be dated in the 1180s. Although they were greatly harmed by the clumsy restorations of 1780 and 1849, they are probably the most valuable monument of Russian mural painting from the pre-Tartar period, now that the paintings in the Church of the Saviour on the Nereditsa have been lost. They were cleaned and repaired comprehensively and expertly in 1927 and 1933. It is therefore relatively easy to reconstruct the original programme. The paintings consist of the Eucharist and the Tier of Bishops in the middle apse, Christ ascending into heaven, surrounded by eight angels, and the Virgin and twelve apostles in the dome, eight prophets between the windows of the drum, the Archangel Gabriel in the prothesis, the Archangel Michael and some of the legends about him in the diakonikon, the Last Judgment on the west wall, and gospel scenes, martyrs, bishops and saints on the other walls. They have survived in greatly varying conditions. Their style is uniform, and they are all obviously the work of a single artist, with a delicate, graphic technique best exemplified in the linear differentiation of garment folds, faces and, especially, hair (pl. 101). St George overcoming the dragon is

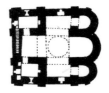

Ground level

also an imposing composition, by reason of the strong emphasis on the outlines, the formal grace, the naive, folk conception of knightly splendour, the instinct for colour and the brilliance of the chromatic range *(pl. 103)*.

104, 353, 354 Novgorod Новгород

Church of the Annunciation near Arkazh (Myachino), 1179/17th century

Церковь Благовещения близ Аркажи (на Мячине)

Tserkov Blagoveshcheniya bliz Arkazhi (na Myachine)

Earlier writing has referred to this church as the Church of the Annunciation near Arkazh, but the village did not exist, or no longer existed, at the time when the church was built. It has therefore come to be identified in recent years by Lake Myachino, which lies to its east. It is the oldest surviving example of the new stylistic period that Novgorod architecture embarked on in the middle of the twelfth century, characterized by simplicity of structure and modesty of composition. There is a legend connected with its construction in 1179: the builders are said to have used up all their resources, but were rescued by a horse which appeared from nowhere with a bag of gold and a bag of silver attached to its saddle.

The church has an oblong plan, only a little longer from east to west than its breadth. It has four rectangular pillars and three apses. Broad, prominent lesenes divide the outside walls into three sections, which originally terminated in round gables. In accordance with tradition, the middle division in each wall is the widest, the east division the narrowest *(pl. 353)*. This system of articulation, which developed at the end of the twelfth century and the beginning of the thirteenth, is exclusive to the churches of Novgorod. The roof of the church caved in in the sixteenth century and was replaced by one with eight inclined faces. The drum was decorated with bands of pentagonal indentations and a pattern of little triangles formed by bricks. The wooden shingles covering the dome date from the restoration in the fifties. In the seventeenth century the old, narrow window niches were widened and the new windows placed in surrounds typical of the Moscow style of the second half of that century: pilasters built of specially moulded bricks, and a shallow pediment with a stone at its apex.

The church was painted throughout in 1189. The diakonikon is decorated with scenes from the life of John the Baptist, the prothesis with scenes from the life of the Virgin. The soffits of the arches between the main apse and the side apses bear the figures of warriors and saints. There must have been

a Tier of Bishops in the main apse. Although the frescos, uncovered in 1930 and 1937, suffered severely in the last war, they still command attention by their colours, which are bright and saturated although the artist's palette was extremely limited, and the graphic, linear style which stresses the outlines. The highlights are usually applied in sharp lines. The team of artists, probably local men from Novgorod itself, must have included one, however, who was a master of modelling in soft, painterly forms, as the head of the young, realistically conceived watercarrier shows *(pl. 354)*. The frescos spared in the war were restored again in 1946–48.

105 Novgorod Новгород

Church of the Nativity of the Virgin 'at the place of Perun', 1221

Церковь Рождества Богородицы на Перыни
Tserkov Rozhdestva Bogoroditsy na Peryni

The church stands in a clump of fir trees on a low hill beside the River Volkhov, to the south of Novgorod, at the point where the river leaves Lake Ilmen. Excavating archaeologists have discovered a heathen shrine of the early Slavs here, a low, round building which contained a wooden image of the god Perun. When the Slavs were converted to Christianity under St Vladimir, the first bishop of Novgorod, Joachim, had the statue thrown into the Volkhov, and a wooden church dedicated to the Nativity of the Virgin built nearby. In 995 he founded a monastery in association with the church. The church then came to be known popularly as the 'Perun Church'. The masonry church on the site today was not built before 1221, was substantially altered during its history, and restored to its original form in 1962. It represents an important stage in the development of the Novgorod style from the thirteenth to the fifteenth century, when the 'classic' plan with one dome, four pillars and walls with the trefoil outline was evolving. It was built of large blocks of the local limestone and alternate layers of thin brick tiles, with a mortar of lime and broken brick.

The groundplan is almost square, and the four pillars are placed so far apart that the middle aisle is almost two and a half times as wide as the side aisles. The two west pillars are octagonal in section, which is rare in the architecture of Novgorod. There was a tribune at the west end. The interior does not make an impression of great size, but it does seem proportionately very high. There is no vertical articulation of the exterior walls. The lesenes at the corners turn without a break into a double-recessed cornice that follows the curves of the top of the vaulting, forming a trefoil gable out of two quadrants, surmounted and linked by a semi-circle. The gable itself is outlined by a narrow band of porebrik. The west, north and

105

south walls are pierced by windows at three levels, arranged symmetrically on an axis formed by the perpendicular dropped from the centre of the gable: one central window at the top of the wall, two close together in the middle, and two placed well apart, close to the lesenes, near the foot. A simple door with a straight lintel, placed on the vertical axis, leads into the church. A frieze of round arches in low relief encircles the drum beneath the low, hemi-spherical dome. The one apse is very low and small. The extreme paucity of decorative elements is compensated for by perfect proportions. The walls are slightly inclined inwards and get progressively thinner towards the top, and similarly the window niches become taller and narrower, the further they are from the ground. The resemblance to the later Church of St Nicholas on Lipna, and the simple plan of which St Nicholas is the standard example, is unmistakable: a plastic construction which develops on a vertical axis, as the human body does.

4, 107 Novgorod Новгород

Church of St Nicholas on Lipna, 1292

Церковь Николы на Липне

Tserkov Nikoly na Lipne

St Nicholas on Lipna is one of the five surviving Russian buildings of the thirteenth century. Although the region of Novgorod was not conquered by the Tartar hordes of Batu Khan, there was a marked recession in the development of masonry architecture in the region and especially in the city itself. But the situation changed fundamentally again in the last decade of the century, as Novgorod began a new period of economic, political and cultural expansion. St Nicholas, originally the church of a monastery, lies five miles to the south of the city, on a little marshy island not far from where the River Msta flows into Lake Ilmen (*pl. 107*). The monastery was probably founded in the twelfth century when, according to legend, the icon of Nicholas Mirlikisky, painted on a round plaque, floated to Novgorod from Kiev (cf. K. Onasch, *Ikonen,* p. 349). The citizens are supposed to have fished it out of the water at this spot and placed it in the Cathedral of St Nicholas on the Court of Yaroslav. The chroniclers record that the building was erected in 1292 under Prince Andrey, Archbishop Kliment and Mayor (Posadnik) Andrey Klimovich. There are no further historical records. The monastery, a poor one at best, gradually declined and was first restored by order of Tsar Michael Romanov between 1641 and 1645, then finally dissolved in 1764. Apart from the Church of St Nicholas, all the buildings were pulled down during the course of the eighteenth century. The church itself was much altered: the interior was divided into two storeys by a vaulted ceiling,

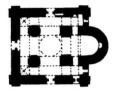

the corners were built higher, a new roof with four inclined faces was constructed, some of the old windows were bricked up, and new ones placed elsewhere, and lastly a vestibule and a tall bell-tower were built on to the west front. The building was seriously damaged by shell-fire during the last war, but it has been carefully examined since then and has been restored to its old form.

The form of St Nicholas is a rather tall cube, its sides approximately 34 feet long. It has four pillars, one dome on a large drum, and one small apse at the east end, reaching only to half the height of the wall. It was built of rough hewn Volkhov stone with alternating layers of long bricks from a height of 16 feet, and the window openings and niches on the façades, the vaults, the drum, and the cornice and arch frieze outlining the tops of the walls are all constructed of the bricks alone. The mortar used was a mixture of lime and sand. The masonry gave the walls an irregular, uneven surface which needed frequent plastering, but its plasticity makes a painterly effect. The composition is similar to that of the Perun Church. The walls terminate in trefoil arches and have no vertical articulation other than the lesenes at each corner, and the windows are placed at three levels: on the south wall, there is one at the top, four in the middle and one at the foot, near the east corner. The three doors are set simply into the walls without any articulation. A small round-arched niche, intended perhaps for an icon or a fresco, appears in the wall just above the arch of the doorway. The round-arch frieze that follows the trefoil outline of the tops of the walls and runs round the base of the dome, and the hood moulds decorated in porebrik over the windows in the drum, are interesting features.

The interior of the church was decorated with frescos as soon as the building was completed, that is approximately between 1292 and 1294. They are reminiscent of the period before the Mongol invasions, and the artist may well have been the one who painted the local icon of St Nicholas: Alexey Petrov. This icon, which is now in the Novgorod Museum, is the earliest Russian panel painting to be signed and dated (cf. K. Onasch, *Ikonen,* p. 351). Obviously the cosmopolitan trading city was the most likely kind of place for the medieval tradition of anonymity to be abandoned. The frescos were overpainted in distemper in 1877, restored in 1930 and again from 1946 onwards, following the damage they incurred during the war, but they now survive only as a few fragments.

The Church of St Nicholas on Lipna is an important link in the evolutionary chain of the Novgorod style from the thirteenth to the fourteenth and fifteenth centuries. The artistic and structural techniques link it with earlier buildings. The vaults over the two west corners are the only parts to which there are no analogies. (The Swedish art historian

It has an almost square groundplan, four pillars, a west tribune and one apse. The exterior presents the usual appearance with its one dome and the eight inclined faces of the roof, determined by the triangular gables of the four fronts. The eyecatching ornamentation on the drum and façades, a kind of lace or smocking pattern in bricks, is created by alternate bands of porebrik and begunets. Porebrik is made by laying bricks, on end or on their side, at an angle so that one edge is flush with the plane of the wall (with a notched effect, like the edge of a saw). In begunets, the bricks are laid in a zigzag line, with their sides flush to the plane, creating triangular gaps between them with the apexes pointing alternately upwards and downwards. Compared with other fourteenth-century buildings, St Demetrius of Salonika evinces a certain squatness in its proportions which robs its external appearance of sublimity and grandeur. In the form it received in the rebuilding of 1463, it is the last important structure in the Novgorod style, which came gradually but inexorably under the influence of Moscow in the sixteenth century, and lost its independence and originality.

117 Novgorod Новгород

Church of St John the Evangelist, Vitko, 1383–84

Церковь Иоанна Богослова на Витке

Tserkov Ioanna Bogoslova na Vitke

This church, built in 1383–84 and also known by the name of Radokovitsi (Commerce Side), is a typical example of the classic Novgorod style of the second half of the fourteenth century and the early fifteenth, in a group that also includes St Theodore Stratilates, the Church of the Transfiguration in the Street of Elijah, and SS Peter and Paul in Kozhevniki. Almost square in plan, it has four pillars, one apse, one dome and a form that is slightly elongated, harmoniously proportioned and small in its dimensions. Narrow lesenes divide the walls into three sections, the middle one higher than the others. The symmetry is unusual in Novgorod. The church originally had a roof that followed the trefoil outline of the gables, but it was later replaced by eight inclined faces over triangular gables The ornamental forms on the middle division of the south front reveal the influence of the Church of the Transfiguration in the Street of Elijah. The portal is set into the thickness of the wall, in a graduated recess some of whose gradations are semi-cylindrical, not squared. Above it there is a row of three windows and two interspersed niches, surmounted by a hood mould, trefoil in form and decorated with porebrik. The outline repeats the original form of the roof. The minimal decoration contrasts well with the blank surfaces of the outer divisions of the wall and of the apse, and

the contrast emphasizes the plastic beauty of the building. The low west vestibule was built in the seventeenth century. The decoration of the interior has been lost. There is one unusual feature not found in other contemporary churches: the chapels in the corners of the tribune, completely partitioned off by massive walls, served as storerooms. The drum was constructed of clay golosniki. As usual in Novgorod, bricks were used only to make the masonry courses level, in the parts of the structure that have arched outlines, and in the decorative elements. The bricks used are smaller than those found in any other Novgorod churches of the same period, and are thus in keeping with the smaller size of the whole building.

118 Novgorod Новгород

Church of SS Peter and Paul in Kozhevniki, 1406

Церковь Петра и Павла в Кожевниках

Tserkov Petra i Pavla v Kozhevnikakh

This church on the St Sophia Side, in the Novgorod style of the second half of the fourteenth century and the early fifteenth, is the only one which was not covered with plaster when it was restored in the 1950s, and on which wooden shingles were used for the roof and the dome. As a result the architectonic and structural elements are particularly easy to discern, revealing it as a striking work of architecture. It stands on the banks of the Volkhov, with its apse pointing towards the river, presenting a painterly silhouette to ships approaching from the Baltic, while the south front has been treated as the principal façade to greet people approaching from the city. In the sixteenth century a floor of wooden beams was constructed in the church at the level of the tribune, to create storerooms underneath. At the same time

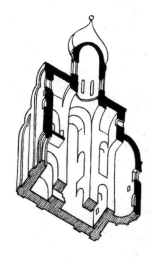

the trefoil roof was replaced by one with eight inclined faces, some of the windows were turned into doors while others were widened and yet other new ones were made. The restorers attempted to reproduce the original form.

The shape of the shingled roof, very similar to a bochka, and the variety of the masonry are immediately obvious. The walls of Novgorod churches of the fourteenth and fifteenth centuries were built of roughly hewn, local quarry stone, creating a natural polychrome fabric that contrasted with the red bricks of which the drum, the vaults, the lesenes, the ornaments and the surrounds of the doors and windows were constructed. It is also possible that, as N. Brunov believes, the fabric was coated with a lime plaster, producing a contrast reminiscent of the traditional dress of the people of Novgorod—made of handwoven white cloth with red stripes.

The church has an almost square groundplan, four pillars, a stone staircase in the south-west corner leading up to the tribune, one apse and one dome. It is the traditional slightly tall cube. The walls are divided unequally into three by lesenes. In keeping with its function as the front most exposed to view, the south front is the most ornately decorated, with stone crosses in relief, niches of various shapes, rosettes and friezes made of bricks laid diagonally, a very clearly outlined portal and so on. Nearly all the ornamental forms are borrowed from the elegant ornamentation on the façades of the Church of the Transfiguration. As well as the by now familiar frieze of round arches and a band of begunets, the drum is decorated with a single course of projecting bricks above a band of porebrik, which together run all round it at the level of the imposts of the arches of the windows, rising over each window to outline the arch. This ornament continued to be used on drums until the eighteenth century. The interior of the church has not been preserved.

359 Novgorod Новгород

Church of St Vlasi, in the Volos Street, 1407

Церковь Власия на Волосовой улице

Tserkov Vlasiya na Volosovoy ulitse

A wooden church dedicated to St Vlasi (St Blaise) was built on the St Sophia Side very soon after the adoption of Christianity, on the site previously holy to the heathen god Volos, whose function as protector of cattle was transferred in the popular belief to St Vlasi. The stone church that now stands there was built in 1407, severely damaged in the last war and restored between 1956 and 1961 after a very thorough examination of the surviving parts; the parts which had been destroyed (vaults, drum, dome) were reconstructed in their old forms. The church is almost square in plan and has four pillars and one apse. Its exterior appearance is that of a near-cube with trefoil roof and one dome. The composition and the decoration of the façades conform in every respect to the Novgorod style developed in the second half of the fourteenth century. The recessed doorway

with parabolic archivolts is characteristic, as is the much simpler grouping of the windows and niches on the middle division of the wall, by comparison with the Church of the Transfiguration and SS Peter and Paul. The concha and the dome were not built of the usual brick but of stone slabs.

119 Novgorod Новгород

Church of St John the Compassionate in Myachino, 1422

Церковь Иоанна Милостивого на Мячине

Tserkov Ioanna Milostivogo na Myachine

The Novgorod chroniclers refer to the building of about forty new churches between 1407 and 1422. Even so, St John the Compassionate (1422) on the St Sophia Side is the only one of them to survive. Unfortunately it underwent substantial alterations in the seventeenth century, when the roof and uppermost parts, the four pillars and a room built on to the north side were demolished. These circumstances have hindered the formation of a more precise conception of the development of the Novgorod style in the first half of the fifteenth century. The monuments from the second half of the century and from the sixteenth show that it must have undergone an important change in that period. The present-day appearance of the church is low, with squat proportions, an eight-faced roof with a shallow slope, and a broad apse. There are analogies to the façades and decorative elements in buildings of the second half of the century, but these are simpler. Excavation has shown that the structure on the north side had no apse and that it was roofed by a kind of four-celled domical vault, which rested on a pillar in the centre of the room—a novel construction in Novgorod. In spite of the substantial alteration made to its proportions, an eight-faced roof with a shallow slope, wide double arch of the bell-gable over the west wall, the church attracts attention for its archaism, and as the only specimen of the extensive programme of church-building in Novgorod in the first quarter of the fifteenth century it is extremely important.

360 Novgorod Новгород

Church of the Twelve Apostles 'by the gorge', 1455

Церковь Двенадцати апостолов на Пропастях

Tserkov Dvenadtsati apostolov na Propastyakh

The earliest mention of the original wooden building dates from 1230, in the context of a mass grave prepared nearby for the victims of an epidemic. It is likely that it was built as a memorial in a single day. The existing miniature church on the St Sophia Side,

Carrying Anointing Oil, on the Court of Yaroslav on the Commerce Side, in 1529. Like the earlier church it is built of brick and has three storeys, the lowest below the level of the ground. The form is a cube, in the old Novgorod style, and the façades are divided into three by thick lesenes. While the middle divisions terminate in ogee niches, the lower, outer pair on each front finish in ornamental quadrant arches. These are contained within triangular gables, which determine the shape of the eight-faced pitched roof. There are three tall, unarticulated apses on the east side. The dome rests on a slender drum, which has four rectangular slits for windows. The horizontal divisions of the interior are reflected only in the arrangement of the niches and doors in the middle divisions of the north and south fronts. An exterior wooden staircase leads to the entrance in the north front. A relatively low vestibule was built on to the west front, articulated by broad lesenes at its corners. Its north and south end walls terminate in ogee arches. A frieze of ogee arches also decorates the drum.

The new influence of Muscovite architecture and the strong local traditions meet in St Procopius. The Novgorod style of the late fourteenth century is present in the superbly judged proportions, the massive walls with the deep shadows of the window openings and the soft modelling of the surfaces, the triangular gables and the pitched roof. At the same time the Moscow style makes a tentative appearance in the three apses and the ogee arches.

364   Novgorod   Новгород

Church of the Purification of the Virgin and Refectory, in St Anthony's Monastery, 1535–37
Церковь Сретения с трапезной в Антониевом монастыре
Tserkov Sreteniya s trapeznoy v Antoniyevom monastyre

The Church of the Purification of the Virgin and the refectory that adjoins it to the west were built in the old Monastery of St Anthony on the Commerce Side in 1535–37. The church was built without pillars and without an apse, and the ceiling took the form of a steep domical vault surmounted by a dome. The refectory is an extensive room with a vaulted ceiling supported by a central pillar. The church has a slender, harmoniously proportioned form, but its roof was constructed with eight inclined faces, not the traditional trefoil form. The articulation of the façades by lesenes also no longer has any structural foundation but simply serves a linear, decorative end. The recessed ogee arches at the tops of the outer divisions of the walls, and the ogee niches which appear even on the lesenes, have an extraordinarily

enlivening effect. In their late phase the Novgorod traditions were already strongly influenced by Moscow architecture – the horizontal cylindrical mouldings are another instance. Unfortunately the façades have been robbed of their original expressive force by the addition of new windows. The Church of the Purification of the Virgin served as the model for numerous refectory-churches in the sixteenth century, for instance the one in the Khutynsky Monastery.

365   Novgorod   Новгород

Church of SS Boris and Gleb in Plotniki, 1536
Церковь Бориса и Глеба в Плотниках
Tserkov Borisa i Gleba v Plotnikakh

SS Boris and Gleb was built in 1536 in the Plotnitsk 'End' (quarter) on the Commerce Side, on the site of an older, tumble-down church which had to be demolished entirely. According to the chronicles it was completed in five months, by twenty-eight 'great' master-builders from Novgorod, who received fifty-three roubles for their work. The bill was paid by the residents of Zapolskoy and Konyukhovoy Streets, with the help of merchants from Novgorod and Moscow.

The structure represents a harmonious intermingling of Novgorod and Moscow traditions. The brick-built church has an almost square plan and four pillars. The apse resembling the old Novgorod forms at the east end is wider than the middle division of the east wall and not so high as the springing line of the gable, which gives it a massive, thick-set appearance. Lesenes divide the walls into three sections, each terminating in an ogee gable. The form of the roof and the five domes are in the style of Moscow churches. The only decoration is the frieze of shallow, double-recessed pentagonal niches encircling the drums and the apse at the level of the cornice.

121, 366   Novgorod   Новгород

Church of the Holy Trinity in the Monastery of the Holy Ghost, 1557
Церковь Троицы Духова монастыря
Tserkov Troitsy Dukhova monastyrya

The Monastery of the Holy Ghost on the St Sophia Side was founded in the twelfth century. Its first stone building, the Church of the Holy Ghost, was erected in 1357 but has not survived. The architecturally more interesting Church of the Holy Trinity of 1557 belongs to the type of monastic refectory-church which originated in Moscow, and in Novgorod is associated with Archbishop Makary (1526–42). Makary, later metropolitan of Moscow and

All Russia (1542–63), was an adherent of Joseph of Volokolamsk in ecclesiastical politics, and therefore pursued the conversion of the hermitages into coenobitic monasteries as energetically as he supported the concept of 'Moscow, the third Rome'. Consequently the Church of the Holy Trinity bears virtually no relationship to the Novgorod style of the fourteenth and fifteenth centuries. It is a two-storey building, entirely of brick without plaster coating, with five domes and three apses. The wooden shingles on the roof, the domes and the apses were carefully restored in the 1950s. The refectory is an extensive, two-storey building adjoining the church to the west. The main structure is a tall building surmounted by five domes. The six decorative triangular gables running along the top of each wall, and the octagonal pedestals adorned with two tiers of similar gables that support the drums and domes, give the roof a unique and original form. The effect is unusually painterly and the system was not repeated in other churches. The articulation of the façades in three divisions by means of compound pilasters (lesenes on the apses), which run on up to form ogee gables or blind gables, is purely decorative. These vertical lines are intersected horizontally by friezes. The upper parts of the façades, however, have a system of articulation of their own, which is independent of the pilasters. Although details of the decoration stem from the Novgorod tradition, the friezes of pentagonal niches on the drums, the apses and the walls, the ogee niches on the pilasters, the whole character of the building, all bespeak the dominating influence that Moscow exercised over the architecture of Novgorod in the sixteenth century. The upper storey where services were held has no pillars and is roofed by a domical vault. The surviving churches which resemble the church in the Monastery of the Holy Ghost most closely are St Nikita in Moscow Street (1555–57) and St Varlaam in the Khutynsky Monastery (1551).

122-127   Pskov   Псков

Cathedral of the Transfiguration in the Mirozh Monastery, 1156
Спасо-Преображенский собор Мирожского монастыря
Spaso-Preobrazhensky sobor Mirozhskogo monastyrya

Up to the middle of the fourteenth century Pskov belonged to 'Great Novgorod', and was therefore able to offer the products of its flourishing craft workshops on an international market, and to share the prosperity of the larger city. Novgorod, too, was the channel whereby the influences of Kiev and Asia Minor were transmitted that are discernible in the early architectural monuments of Pskov. The first

bishop of the independent republic, Nifont (1130–56), a convinced Graecophile and perhaps actually a Greek, founded a series of monasteries and churches in the Novgorod region, including the Mirozh Monastery (before 1153) and its cathedral (completed 1156).

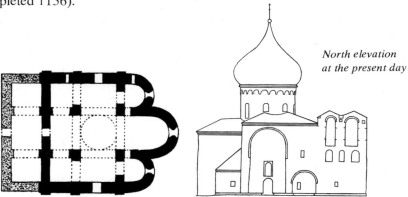

North elevation at the present day

The cathedral, the oldest church in Pskov, has a special place in the history of early Russian architecture: the two west corner cells and the two side apses at the east end *(pl. 122)* were originally built only half as high as the vaults of the nave and transept, so that the cruciform plan was clearly distinguishable from the outside. It also dominates the groundplan and the interior. The high nave runs on into the equally high central apse, while the low side apses open directly on to the high arms of the transept. Either the west corner cells were separate chapels with small doors opening into the nave, which would have been unusual, or there were no more than arches between them and the nave and transept as there are today and as was the usual practice *(pl. 125)*. The dome rises above the crossing on the broad drum which has narrow windows and an exterior frieze of round arches at the base of the dome. The façades are without articulation of any kind, even the usual lesenes. The fabric consists of slabs of the local limestone and thin bricks, called plinfy, used in two typically Kievan techniques: the opus mixtum and the striped masonry with brick courses alternately exposed and inset behind thick plaster. Soon, before the end of the twelfth century, the west corners were built up to the same height as the nave and covered with barrel vaults, necessitating a roof that followed the form of the round gables. The roof was altered a number of times subsequently and its present form dates from 1902. The west vestibule and the bell-gable were built at the end of the sixteenth century and the beginning of the seventeenth.

The cathedral of the Mirozh Monastery, which has been the subject of a special study by V. G. Alferova, is related to the architecture of Kherson (Korsun) and the Byzantine provinces of Asia Minor. This characteristic obviously owes something to the personal taste of Bishop Nifont. But after the raising of the west corner cells the cathedral became the model for the four-pillar churches of the fifteenth and sixteenth centuries in Pskov.

The frescos decorating the Cathedral of the Transfiguration are the oldest in Pskov, and date from the mid-twelfth century. The exact date is not known, but they appear to have been executed immediately, or very soon, after the completion of the building work: In iconography and arrangement they revert completely to the middle Byzantine system, another reflection of Nifont's sympathies. The frescos were touched up in the sixteenth century, whitewashed and actually plastered over in the early nineteenth century, cleaned in 1889 but again, in 1897, crudely travestied by Suzdal icon painters. The task of cleaning them systematically, embarked upon in 1926, continues to the present day.

The frescos that have been cleaned already prove to be in a relatively good state of preservation, and the sixteenth-century overpainting to be not very extensive in its effects. The Deesis in the concha of the main apse was evidently influenced by Asia Minor and Oriental models. Below it there are the traditional Eucharist and Tier of Bishops, lined up in two rows in this case. The Transfiguration is depicted on the east bay of the roof, and the pillars of the Triumph Arch bear an Annunciation and figures of Christ and his Mother seated on thrones. The evangelists occupy the pendentives, with two acheiropoites between them, and Christ Emmanuel, Mary and an archangel with a staff on the abutments of the transverse arches. Holy men from the Old Testament appear on the soffits of the arches and sixteen prophets on the piers between the windows. The dome contains an Ascension. The frescos on the walls and ceiling vaults are arranged as separate friezes and depict episodes from the Gospels. There are no upright divisions, so each scene runs on horizontally into the next. The most noteworthy are the paintings of the Nativity *(pls. 124, 125),* Christ appearing to the disciples on the Sea of Gennesaret *(pl. 125),* the Presentation in the Temple *(pl. 125),* the Baptism of Christ and the Assumption of the Virgin. The lower zones are filled with figures of stylites *(pl. 123),* martyrs, warriors and other saints. The apostles are also depicted *(pl. 127).* An apocryphal cycle in the southwest corner is devoted to the childhood of the Virgin *(pl. 126).* The west wall is given over entirely to the Last Judgment. The prothesis and the diakonikon are decorated with scenes from the life of John the Baptist, exploits of the Archangel Michael and pictures related to the liturgy and the eucharist.

The style of the frescos differs from that of other Novgorod wall paintings, placing even stronger value on line and plane. Figures and faces are heavily outlined and forms within the figures, such as the folds of garments, are treated purely graphically. There is hardly any modelling worthy of the name. Even so emotional expression does not disapear beneath serene abstraction, but is portrayed in calm, epic terms. Nothing is known about the executants. V. N. Lazarev believes that neither Byzantine nor Novgorod artists were responsible, while M. K. Karger has traced connections with the classic products of the Byzantine School in the figures and the composition. N. V. Malitsky, M. I. Artamonov and M. N. Soboleva have also devoted attention to the Pskov frescos, but many questions of fundamental importance still remain to be answered.

128, 129 Pskov Псков

Cathedral of St John the Baptist in the Nunnery of St John, *c*1240

Собор Иоанна Предтечи Ивановского монастыря

Sobor Ioanna Predtechi Ivanovskogo monastyrya

The Nunnery of St John was a princely foundation, one of the oldest in Pskov, and the women of the royal family were also buried there. The earliest written reference to it comes in documents of 1243, in connection with a 'miraculous' icon which lay beneath the sarcophagus of the wife of Prince Yaroslav Vladimirovich. The pronounced stylistic affinity that the cathedral has to the twelfth-century churches built by princes in Novgorod has led some scholars to date it, too, in the late twelfth century.

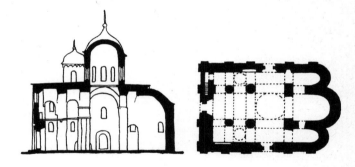

It is a simple, monumental building, following the domed cruciform plan, with three aisles, six pillars and three apses which occupy the entire height and width of the east wall. The exterior vertical articulation of the other walls follows the Novgorod tradition, with four divisions in the north and south fronts and three in the west. The double-recessed lesenes run on directly into the round gables (zakomari) *(pl. 128).* The form of the cross, already emphasized in the groundplan, is expressed spatially by the greater breadth and height of the middle aisle and transept. The solid drum, pierced by wide windows, rises above the crossing, supporting the low dome which has a frieze of round arches round its base. The plan and structure of the cathedral are thus very similar to those of the churches in Novgorod built by Master Peter, except for the lack of a staircase-tower. Two smaller domes were raised over the north-west and south-west corners, which were also encircled by round-arch friezes at the top of the drum. In order to save space, the bottom part of the interior pillars were rounded, which was to become a characteristic of Pskov architecture. It is likely that there was a tribune, which would have been well-lit, at the west end.

The bell-gable of two arches above the south wall *(pl. 129)* was probably built in the fifteenth century. The almost total absence of decorative elements is remarkable. We should also note that the proportions of the building have changed considerably: it has come to appear much more squat than it was at the time of its construction because of the rise in the level of the ground. It was built of local Permian limestone and alternate courses of brick. The masonry was given a pinkish covering with a plaster of lime and broken brick. The cathedral was severely damaged during the Second World War, and has been only partly restored (1948–50). The extension on the west side dates from the seventeenth century. The interior is in need of thorough scholarly examination.

130, 131, 367   Pskov   Псков

Cathedral of the Nativity of the Virgin in the Snetogorsky Monastery, 1310–11

Собор Рождества Богородицы Снетогорского монастрыря

Sobor Rozhdestva Bogoroditsy Snetogorskogo monastyrya

Only three buildings have survived of the monastery, erected on the banks of the Velikaya in the thirteenth century: the Cathedral of the Nativity of the Virgin (1310–11), the refectory and Church of St Nicholas (1518), and the Church of the Ascension and its bell-tower (early eighteenth century). The cathedral was built at a time when the construction of churches took very much a second place to that of fortresses. In the second half of the thirteenth century and the first half of the fourteenth, the chronicles record the building of no more than two other churches which have not survived, but which may have been the small, four-pillar structures whose foundations have recently been discovered in excavations in the old 'Dovmontov' quarter. The desperate struggle against the Germans and Lithuanians demanded that energies had to be concentrated on the fortification of the city.

The original form of the Cathedral of the Nativity of the Virgin was a repetition of the composition of the cathedral in the Mirozh Monastery after its corner cells had been built higher. A vestibule was added to the west side in the fifteenth century, which was altered again later and joined to the old nucleus of the building by broad arches. Another extension was added to the vestibule in the seventeenth century and an open exterior staircase with rich tile decoration was built. At the end of the seventeenth century a hipped roof with four faces was built and

the drum was raised by means of a band of ornamentation carved in the local Permian limestone: a frieze of small round arches in low relief at cornice-level, below that the typical triple row of begunets, and at the bottom a shallow frieze of large ogee arches *(pl. 367)*. The result was to lend the drum more slender proportions. The west vestibule was altered yet again in the eighteenth century, apparently in order to make possible the rebuilding of the stone tribune which had been demolished once. The cathedral is a relatively small building with four pillars, one dome and three apses at the east end. The fact that the side apses are very low, as in the cathedral of the Mirozh Monastery *(pl. 367)*, effectively adds to the height of the transept. It can be assumed that the three divisions of the west wall were, originally all the same height, but that the western divisions of the north and south walls did not terminate in round gables. The basis of this hypothesis is that the western cells were roofed with shallow barrel vaults with east-west longitudinal axes. The interior is dominated by the form of the central cross, which is separated from the corner cells and the sides of the vestibule by low, wide arches. The continuation of the height of the middle aisle without a break into the west vestibule creates a basilical, west-east movement, which is accentuated by the longitudinal axis of the barrel vault *(pl. 131)*.

The frescos were painted in 1313. They were covered by whitewash, probably in the eighteenth century, and fragments in the main apse, the prothesis and the tribune were rediscovered by chance in 1910. The systematic cleaning begun in 1928–29 and resumed in 1948–49 has yet to be completed. At present the following compositions have been uncovered: the Last Judgment, the Assumption of the Virgin, the Annunciation, the Purification of the Virgin, the Flight into Egypt, the Baptism of Christ, the Raising of Lazarus, the Crucifixion, the Deposition, the Harrowing of Hell, the Women carrying Anointing Oil, the Descent of the Holy Ghost *(pl. 130)*, scenes from the lives of St Joachim and St Anne and the Virgin, and rows of saints. The Snetogorsky frescos depart from the canonical scheme in some points of iconography and also include some new subjects taken from apocryphal books. For

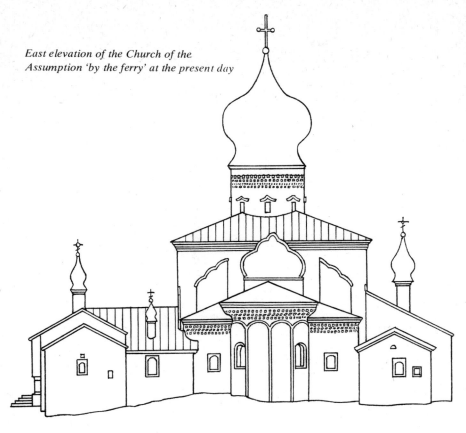

East elevation of the Church of the Assumption 'by the ferry' at the present day

height of the walls was reduced in the corners and a roof with sixteen faces constructed, producing a form analogous to the church at Meletovo. The higher arms of the central cross were given normal pitched roofs, and the lower corner cells inverted ones. In the interior the ceiling follows the forms of the roof, rising gradually from the corners in beautifully shaped vaults. The wooden tribune at the west end has chapels in its corners and the middle section is like a balcony. The stairs up to it are in the west wall. The present proportions of the building are nothing like its original ones, since the level of the ground has risen considerably.

142, 143   Pskov   Псков

Church of St Nicholas 'on the dry land', 1535–37
Церковь Николы со Усохи
Tserkov Nikoly so Usokhi

The church, built on a site obtained by draining a piece of marshy ground, belongs to the type of small churches built by the ordinary citizens of Pskov, characterized by their four pillars, three apses, one dome and cruciform, eight-faced roof. A chapel was added on the north side, which repeats the form of the central nucleus in miniature (sixteenth century). The bell-gable of two arches was probably not built before the seventeenth century and is placed above the middle division of the north front *(pl. 142)*. In the sixteenth century a small, low chapel was built over a tomb in a shallow angle against the south apse, equipped with the characteristic short, thick Pskov supports, carrying the arch over the entrance and the wide arched openings in the long walls, and with a pitched roof and a small, slender dome *(pl. 143)*. The exterior staircase built at the west end in the seventeenth century connects the exterior galleries. Like the other Pskov churches of the fifteenth and sixteenth centuries, it is built of irregular slabs of the local grey, porous, Permian limestone, used not only for the walls and lesenes but also for indentations and friezes of recessed round arches. The characteristically soft and plastic treatment of the forms is due to the nature of the stone, which, however, has been covered by a thick layer of plaster since the seventeenth century because of its propensity for weathering.

St Nicholas was severely damaged during the last war. Now restored to its original form (1948, 1964–66), it is an excellent example of its period. Its cruciform roof, the walls and all the articulating elements, and the ornamentation on the drum and the apses were all renovated. The central dome was covered with green glazed tiles. The rise in the level of the ground gives a distorted impression of the proportions. The original interior has not been preserved.

are generally found. The bell-tower was built in the seventeenth century. Its arches rest on what are known as Pskov supports, but its tent roof and its composition – an octagon on a cube – derive from Moscow models.

The church was restored in 1957 and 1963-64. The wooden shingles on the dome and the wooden roof date from then, and the multifoil blind arches in the gables and the original dimensions and forms of the doors and windows were restored.

140   Pskov   Псков

Church of SS Peter and Paul 'on the river-bank', 1540
Церковь Петра и Павла с Буя
Tserkov Petra i Pavla s Buya

The composition and decoration of the church are typical of Pskov in the sixteenth century. It has an almost square plan, four pillars, three apses and one dome, and the original roof was eight-faced and cruciform, above triangular gables. It also followed tradition with its two side chapels and the gallery surrounding the central nucleus, with a vestibule at the west end. Alterations were made to the building in 1610, 1713 and 1810. The cross on the onion dome and its covering with sheet-iron appear to date from the seventeenth century. There is an ornamental relief incised in the pieces of metal. In 1810 the north and south chapels and the bell-gable were demolished, the ornamentation on the drum broken off and an exterior staircase built in front of the west vestibule. In the restoration work of 1962, the

Church of the Resurrection at Stadishche, 1532
Церковь Воскресения со Стадища
Tserkov Voskreseniya so Stadishcha

392 The Nunnery of the Resurrection at Stadishche (named after a piece of grazing land) is mentioned in documents for the first time in 1458. The present church dates from 1532. In the seventeenth century north and south chapels and a west vestibule and porch were added; the west wall of the vestibule extends upwards in a three-arched bell-gable. In the eighteenth century the cruciform eight-faced roof was replaced by a hipped four-faced one, in a process that involved the removal of the apex of the gable over the middle division of each wall and the raising of the outer divisions. The church belongs to the type of those built by the citizens, with four pillars, three apses and one dome. The lesenes dividing the walls into three are double-recessed and run on into the multifoil blind arches. The characteristic ornamentation in the local limestone is to be seen on the drum and apses, four adjoining bands made up of square and triangular indentations and stepped round arches. The four supports of the bell-gable have cuboid pedestals, a form typical of the seventeenth century. The two short thick pillars on either side of the porch are also frequently to be found on contemporary houses in Pskov.

145 Pskov Псков

Church of the Virgin of the Intercession and of the Nativity of the Virgin 'at the breach', 16th century
Церковь Покрова и Церковь Рождества от Пролома
Tserkov Pokrova i Tserkov Rozhdestva ot Proloma

The Church of the Virgin of the Intercession 'in the corner' or 'at the breach' belonged to the Convent of the Virgin of the Intercession which used to stand on the site. The convent is first mentioned in documents in 1456 in connection with the building of wooden defences for this part of the town (Okolny), which was destroyed by fire in 1544. Evidently it, and the church, were soon rebuilt, as in 1581 the records mention the building of an additional, adjoining church, the Nativity of the Virgin, in commemoration of the siege of Pskov by King Stephen Batory of Poland. It is not clear whether the twofold church served a convent of both male and female inmates. It was substantially altered during the eighteenth and nineteenth centuries, but restored to its sixteenth-century form in 1955–63 after thorough scholarly examination.

The building is a rare example of a double church. Two exactly similar buildings, without pillars and

each having a pitched roof and a dome, are separated by a single wall. The roof of the low narthex in front of the common west wall repeats the outline of the two obtuse-angled gables. There is a similar repetition in the two little pitched roofs over the two-arched bell-gable in the middle of the west front. The whitewashed masonry of irregular slabs of porous Permian limestone creates a plastic, modelled effect. The doors, windows and niches, and the shadows thrown by the overhanging roof and gutters are the only means whereby the severity of the architecture is relieved. As usual in Pskov, the characteristic begunets frieze is found on the drums. The domes are covered with green glazed tiles (the original domes had not survived, so they were reconstructed by analogy with other Pskov domes).

146 Pskov Псков

Tower of the Virgin of the Intercession, in the city wall, first half of the 16th century
Покровская башня
Pokrovskaya bashnya

With its five storeys, the Tower of the Virgin of the Intercession is one of the most impressive structures in the complicated and carefully planned defences of Pskov, which surrounded the ever-growing city in four rings (cf. *pls 13, 137, 295*). It stands, broad and powerful, on the bank of the Velikaya. It is 78 feet in diameter and there are 36 firing embrasures in its walls. There is a sally-port in the wall beside it. In the restoration carried out 1955-63, the upper part of the tower was rebuilt, with the tent roof, all the staircases, and the wooden floors between each storey. The double church of the Convent of the Virgin of the Intercession has a compositional relationship to the tower, and may have been part of the defences of the sally-port, standing outside it on a slight rise. These relationships, as well as the sections of the wall along which soldiers could patrol, adjoining the tower, illustrate the characteristics of the defensive architecture of Pskov in the sixteenth century.

369 Pskov Псков

Church of St Anastasia, Kuznetsi, 1539
Церковь Анастасии в Кузнецах
Tserkov Anastasii v Kuznetsakh

The first Church of St Anastasia was built in wood in 1488, and rebuilt in stone at the beginning of the sixteenth century. It is described as a stone building in the reports of the fire in 1539. It is typical of the churches built by citizens of Pskov in the sixteenth century, with an almost square groundplan, four pillars supporting the one dome, three apses added at the east end and two symmetrically placed chapels on the north and south sides. The structure is also true to form: the walls divided into three by lesenes, and with trefoil arches outlined in the gables. As well as the usual frieze of begunets, the main apse is also decorated with a blind arcade of slender cylindrical shafts. During the eighteenth and nineteenth centuries the eight-faced roof was replaced by a four-faced one, the decoration removed from the drum, and the dome given a new shape. Large, rectangular windows were also inserted and a new bell-tower built at the west end.

147   Izborsk   Изборск

Temnushka tower, 14th century

Башня Темнушка

Bashnya Temnushka

Izborsk is one of the oldest fortified towns in Russia and a western outpost of the Pskov region. According to the Russian chroniclers it was the stronghold of the Varangian leader, Truvor. The prehistoric settlement of Truvorovo was nearby, and remnants of its defensive wall and ditch still exist. In 1303 the fortress was moved to its present position, because the natural contours of the ground lent themselves more readily to defence. Originally it was built of wooden palisades and had only one stone tower, the Lukovka tower, which still exists. Its ground-plan is simple and compact. In 1330, under Shelog, the head of the government of Pskov, it was replaced by a strong stone castle. The fortifications were strengthened again at the end of the fourteenth century, since the onus of defending the town against the aggression of the German and Lithuanian feudal lords was increasingly laid on the townspeople themselves after Pskov had gained its independence in 1348. Thicker walls and five new towers were built, including the Temnushka tower, whose name suggests that it may also have been used as a prison. It looks thickset and ponderous, was divided into several storeys by wooden floors connected by ladders, projects well forward at the angle of the walls and served as a bastion on the side that lay most open to attack. In the fifteenth century, the walls, built of the local Permian limestone with a lime mortar, were strengthened even more and the towers were all built higher at the same time. In the background in plate 147, to the right, the domes of St Nicholas (14th, 17th and 19th centuries) can be seen.

1 *Gate-church of St Nicholas* 2 *Refectory* 3 *Sacristy and Library* 4 *Principal bell-gable* 5 *Churches of the Assumption and the Virgin of the Intercession* 6 *Holy gate* 7 *Prison Tower* 8 *Tailovsky Tower* 9 *Tower of the upper grating* 10 *Tararygin Tower* 11 *Izborsk Gate-tower* 12 *Tower of the Annunciation* 13 *Tower of the lower grating* 14 *Nicholas Tower*

Towers of the Pskov Monastery of the Caves, 15th-18th centuries

Псково-Печерская Лавра, Башни

Pskovo-Pecherskaya Lavra, Bashni

The origins of the Monastery of the Caves are shrouded in obscurity, and its recorded history begins in 1470. It is a powerful fortress, thrown across a romantic, thickly wooded little valley. It was built by the inhabitants of Pskov at their western frontier as a defence against the German and Lithuanian knights, and played a strategic military role once more in the struggle led by the central power of Muscovy. At the beginning of the Livonian War (1558–83) which Ivan IV waged against the Livonian Order and which extended to include Poland-Lithuania and Sweden, the fortifications of the monastery were strengthened by Abbot Kornily, a member of a Pskov patrician family, educated in the Mirozh Monastery and later murdered by the tsar. The monastery distinguished itself by its heroic defence against the siege laid to it by the Polish king, Stephen Batory, Peter the Great also saw fit to construct new ramparts and ditches and six bastions. It was only with the Peace of Nystad (Finland), which put an end to the Northern War and brought Russia substantial territorial gains in the Baltic region, that the monastery lost its strategic significance and the monks could pursue a normal life.

The walls surrounding the monastery form a seven-sided figure, making a rough circle for part of its circumference *(pl. 150)*. Within them, the most important buildings were grouped along an axis. The walls and towers, built in the middle of the sixteenth century in the style of the fortifications

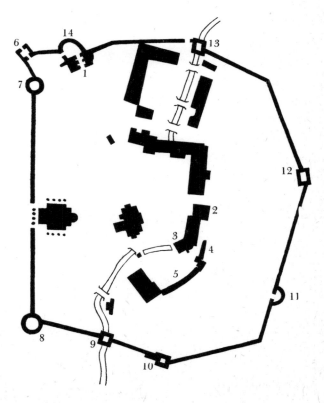

of Pskov, have survived. The western section, with the tower of the Upper Grating and the Tararygin tower *(pl. 148),* both restored in the 1960s, is particularly forbidding and massive in appearance. The monumental tower of the Upper Grating straddling a stream, is square in plan and has six storeys with a large number of slits for firing through and a tent roof with a lookout platform. The Tararygin tower beyond it is simpler in appearance. The tops of the roofed walls, following the contour of the slopes between the towers, rise in steps, with a rectangular slit in each step. The other sections of the outer wall are less impressive. They have been considerably renovated and given a coat of plaster, smoothed with the aid of a level, which has robbed them of the charm of authenticity.

The Holy Gate was constructed in a square tower, which was converted into a church in the eighteenth century *(pl. 154).* It now has a hipped roof, above which rises an octagonal drum supporting a 'mob-cap' dome in the Ukrainian Baroque style. The gallery running round the tower below the eaves was built at the beginning of the twentieth century, and the platform for patrolling guards was restored in the 1960s. The icon above the gate is a modern copy of the Virgin of Vladimir (Vladimirskaya).

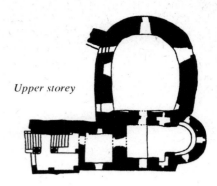
Upper storey

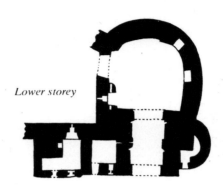
Lower storey

149, 151   Pechory   Печоры

Gate-church of St Nicholas in the Pskov Monastery of the Caves, 1565

Надвратная Никольская церковь
Псково-Печерской Лавры

Nadvratnaya Nikolskaya tserkov Pskovo-Pecherskoy Lavry

Most of the buildings in the monastery have lost their original appearance. One exception is the Gate-church of St Nicholas the Miracle-Worker, over the entrance to the lower courtyard, which is an impressive example of Pskov architecture of the sixteenth century. The dichotomy between monastic seclusion and military fortification that dominates the entire monastery seems to be concentrated in it. Built by order of Abbot Kornily in 1565, after the work on the walls had been finished, it was originally directly incorporated in the defences round the main gate *(pl. 150).* It belongs to the small, pillar-less type with a square groundplan and corbelled vaults. The semi-circular apse adjoins the curved outline of the Nicholas tower. The south front is decorated by three shallow, narrow niches, rounded at the top, and above them two wider, semi-circular niches. The drum over the (later modified) hipped roof bears the typical ornamentation of small round arches and a triple band of begunets. On the west side, the exterior staircase with the thick Pskov supports and

the tall bell-gable with pitched roofs over its two arches form an imposing group *(pl. 149).* They were constructed in 1581. The decoration of the church's interior includes an icon commending the Monastery of the Caves, known since time immemorial as the 'House of the most pure Mother of God', to the protection of the Virgin *(pl. 150).* The icon probably comes from the studio set up by Kornily, is an important guide to the reconstruction of the monastery, and shows very clearly how the wooden domestic buildings were grouped round the stone churches in the sixteenth and seventeenth centuries.

152, 153   Pechory   Печоры

Churches of the Pskov Monastery of the Caves, 15th–19th centuries

Псково-Печерская Лавра, Церкви

Pskovo—Pecherskaya Lavra, Tserkvi

The Pskov Monastery of the Caves plays as significant a role in north-western Russia as the Monastery of the Holy Trinity and St Sergius in the Moscow region. Its authentic history begins in 1470, when the Moscow priest Ioann settled in one of the caves, took monastic vows and the name of Jonah. He himself helped to build the Church of the Caves, which was dedicated to the Assumption of the Virgin in 1473. It was completely refurbished in the eighteenth century, in the Ukrainian Baroque style. The church houses the relics of St Kornily. According to the ancient chronicle, the abbot was beheaded at the gate of the monastery by Ivan IV in a fit of rage. The tsar was as quickly overcome by repentance for his deed, and himself carried the body into the church. The metropolitanate declared the death a martyrdom. The little eighteenth-century iconostasis in the church, covered with luxuriant baroque carvings and reaching right up to the vault, has medallion-icons in the lunette, and an icon of Kornily to the right of the Royal Door and one of the Virgin of Vladimir to the left *(pl. 153)*. The Church of the Assumption occupies only the lower floor of the building, which stands up against the slope of the hill where the monks dug their caves, while the upper floor holds the Church of the Virgin of the Intercession. The ostentatious eighteenth-century decoration of the façade has been considerably modified in recent years.

The two churches *(pl. 152, right)* stand next to the seventeenth-century sacristy *(left)* on the monastery's lower plateau, adjoining which there is an exterior staircase of the Pskov type, with two flights of steps and the familiar thick columnar supports. It is from the staircase that the ringers pull the bell-ropes. The peal is famous over a wide area for its beautiful sound.

The bells are hung in the characteristic Pskov gable surmounting a wall. The essential structure was built in 1523, but additions were made to it in the eighteenth and nineteenth centuries: the extra arch with a slender dome built above the original arcade to hold another bell, and the tent-roofed casing for the clock. The high, smooth wall with its seven squat, irregularly spaced supports and their square-cut capitals, forms the central point of the ensemble of monastery buildings. At the base of the wall is the entrance to the caves, whose principal function in more recent centuries was that of burial vaults for the monks.

The architecture of the Pskov Monastery of the Caves has not yet been adequately examined. There is a possibility that little-known details remain to be found of the fragmentary frescos on the exterior walls of the buildings. These were, however, so thickly overpainted in the twentieth century that it is at present impossible to make a proper assessment of their artistic quality.

Moscow, the Centre of a Unified Empire

155, 370   Zvenigorod   Звенигород

Cathedral of the Assumption 'in the little town', 1399

Успенский собор «на Городке»

Uspensky sobor 'na Gorodke'

After the principality of Moscow had assumed the political and cultural leadership of Russia in the middle of the fourteenth century, with the backing of the church, and Dmitry Donskoi had administered to the Golden Horde its first decisive defeat at Kulikovo in 1380, architecture in stone and brick was able to advance again, though at first only slowly, out of the stagnation into which it had been forced during the years of Mongol rule. Some half-hearted initiatives were made under Ivan Kalita, but the first building activity on any sort of large scale began in the time of Dmitry Donskoi and Vasily I. In order to strengthen the idea of national rebirth, the churches of the fourteenth and early fifteenth centuries looked back to the architecture of twelfth-century Vladimir-Suzdal: the type preferred was thus that with four pillars, one dome and three apses, executed in ashlar-cut white limestone, but the shape of the roof was modified in a way that we have already observed on the Pyatnitsa Church in Chernigov. Yury Dmitriyevich, prince of Zvenigorod and Galicia, the second son of Dmitry Donskoi, rivalled Great Prince Vasily I and the metropolitan as a builder of churches. At the age of fifteen he took up his residence in the city that was his share of the feudal patrimony,

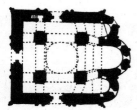

and where he lived until 1425. He paid for two stone churches with the booty he brought home from his campaign against the Volga Bulgars. In 1399, in his palace outside Zvenigorod, he built the Cathedral of the Assumption, a building in ashlar-cut limestone, almost square in plan, with four pillars and three apses, and a few years later (*c*1404) he built the cathedral in the Storoshevsky Monastery of St Savva on similar lines.

The court church 'in the little town' is almost a cube in shape, surmounted by a dome and drum on a tall octagonal pedestal. The proportions are well-balanced and harmonious. Narrow pilasters with slender engaged columns against them, and clustered columns at the corners of the building, divide the walls into three equal sections, each of which has an ogee gable. This was the start of the ogee arch's domination of Russian architecture. The three apses, which originally all had long windows, are almost the full height of the cube and are likewise decorated by engaged columns. The horizontal articulation draws attention to the base of the walls, and they are divided into two zones by a triple frieze round the three sides, which also appears at the cornices of the apses and of the drum. The lower zone of the middle division of the north, south and west walls contains a doorway in an ogee-arched recess whose slanting sides are lined by five columns on each side. The windows in the upper zone are surrounded by a simple, cylindrical moulding. The small rose window in the west wall lights the stairs up to the west gallery, which are set in the thickness of the wall.

One can sense the influence of St Demetrius in Vladimir in the cathedral, but there are some important differences: the simpler shape, the less elaborate decoration and the less soaring proportions. The Muscovite architects were beginning to work out their own schema. In particular, the pilasters on the façades have lost any structural justification. They have no relation to the interior construction and no connection with the pillars, which are spaced well apart and to the east. The blind arcading has been replaced by the low relief ornamentation of the triple frieze, whose motifs recall the carved decoration of an izba. Apart from the capitals of the columns on the façades and in the doorways, there is no three-dimensional ornamentation. The hipped roof that now covers the cathedral dates only from the seventeenth century. Originally the upper part of the building was pyramidally constructed, with a rising series of gables. There are three possible reasons for this, all of which may have contributed: the deliberate resumption of the pre-Mongol, specifically Russian tradition, the process of transition to the system of vaulting with corbelled arches, and its more practical suitability to the Russian climate, since rain-water drained more efficiently from this complicated roof-form than from the wavy roof. It is believed that originally blind gables, aligned to the diagonals of the building, rose at the corners, above the ogee gables of the walls, and that above them there were kokoshniki, at the eight corners of the pedestal. The pedestal conceals the corbelled arches, which are now part of the vaulting, since the individual arches were strengthened and levelled in the 1830s. The pyramidal roof was typical of Muscovite architecture in the late fourteenth and early fifteenth centuries.

Yury Dmitriyevich sent for the artist-monk Andrey Rublev to paint the interior of the cathedral. Only a few fragments of the frescos survive, and their condition is so poor that precise dating and attribution is extremely difficult. Y. A. Lebedeva does not dispute that other artists were engaged besides Rublev, but sees no serious reason for attributing the survivals to the master himself, while V. N. Lazarev sees the first signs of an independent style in them. Rublev's contribution to the iconostasis is equally disputed. It is likely that three icons of the Deesis are his work, but only two, the Zvenigorod Saviour and the Archangel Michael (cf. Onasch, *Ikonen,* pls. 94 and 97), can be attributed to him with full scholarly authorization. In view of the prince's close connections with the Monastery of the Holy Trinity and St Sergius and the probability that the artists came from its icon studio, V. N. Lazarev dates the murals and panel paintings *c*1400, when Rublev is believed to have been active in the studio. Y. A. Lebedeva suggests the period 1417–20, which lies between Rublev's work in the Cathedral of the Assumption in Vladimir and his frescos

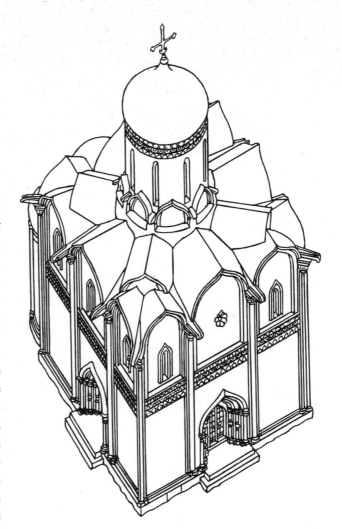

and icons in the Cathedral of the Trinity in the Monastery of the Holy Trinity and St Sergius, because it was not until then that the prince would have been able to refill his coffers by his conquest of the region of the Northern Dvina and Zavoloch.

156-158   Zagorsk   Загорск

Cathedral of the Trinity in the Monastery of the Holy Trinity and St Sergius, 1422–23

Троицкий собор Троице-Сергиевой Лавры

Troitsky sobor Troitse-Sergiyevoy Lavry

The hermitage founded *c*1340 in the forest to the north-east of Moscow by Sergius of Radonezh (1314–92) and his brother developed quickly into an important monastic community whose reforming zeal made it the starting-point for missionary and colonisatory expansion in northern Russia. By the end of the fourteenth century it already had thirteen daughter-houses. Its spiritual

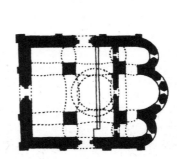

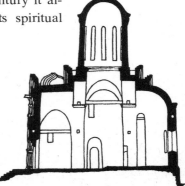

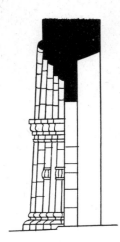

Columns lining the architrave of a doorway.

and ideological atmosphere was doubtless well represented by the teaching of Nil Sorsky in the fifteenth century. The monks were equally opposed to state regimentation of public and private life and to the increasing worldly wealth of the church, in so far as it interfered with the cure of souls, but at the same time they supported the Muscovite princes in the struggle for national independence. Sergius himself had condemned the fratricidal conflicts engendered by feudalism, and the spiritual support and blessing he had given to Dmitry Donskoi before the battle of Kulikovo (1380) was remembered with gratitude. The ideal of Christian humility, moral strength and noble humanity confronts us in the icons of Andrey Rublev, who was trained in the icon studio of the monastery and is believed to have returned there to work in his old age.

Sergius' godson, Prince Yury of Zvenigorod, paid for the monastery's principal cathedral, which was erected over the saint's tomb in 1422–23, in the abbacy of his successor and pupil Nikon. The schema of the cathedral resembles that of the Cathedral of the Assumption in Yury's palace. The groundplans and basic decoration of the two churches are very similar, but there are important differences in the structural composition and the proportions. The balance and harmony of the court church are replaced by a monastic simplicity and severity. The Cathedral of the Trinity looks robust and thickset, is relatively small, has four pillars, three apses and one dome, and is built of massive, ashlar-cut blocks of the white Moscow limestone. The north and south walls are divided vertically by pilasters into three sections, the middle one of which is appreciably larger. The divisions terminate in ogee arches outlined by mouldings, which accentuate the broad, niche-like graduation of the walls and the irregularity of the lines. The ogee arches appear again on the east side, above the three apses, which noticeably taper towards the top *(pl. 158)*. The windows are narrow slits and lack a decorative surround. In order to light the area in front of the altar, the interior pillars and with them the drum—unlike the cathedral at Zvenigorod—are displaced towards the east. The horizontal articulation is by means of a relief frieze, delicately carved from the limestone, consisting of three bands of intertwined leaf, tendril and cross motifs, which is also seen on the apses and the dome *(pl. 156)*. A notable feature of the construction of the vaulting is the marked graduation of the arches: the height increases at the point where the barrel vaults intersect without the radius being changed at all. Seen from outside, however, the roof lacks the complexity of the Cathedral of the Assumption 'in the little town'; there is only one tier of blind gables placed diagonally above the ogee gables of the façades, and the pedestal below the drum is a plain square. As in other, contemporary, Muscovite buildings, the doors are set in deep, graduated recesses,

with ogee archivolts and 'melon' bulges on the shafts of the columns. The interior, where there was never a tribune, makes an impression of spaciousness, and bears no relationship to the articulation of the exterior. The character of the building is essentially a blend of the monumental and the massive, accentuated by the slight centripetal inclination of the walls and pilasters, as well as by the great size and sublimity of the dome. The masses seem to grow organically.

In 1548 the Nikon Chapel was built alongside the south front of the cathedral. The arcading on the apses, with its cylindrical shafts reaching right down to the ground, the vertical trend of the proportions, the narrow drum and aspiring onion dome, all produce a more slender and delicately knit impression. The Serapion Palace was built beside the Nikon Chapel in the 1560s, and the west vestibule of the cathedral dates from the end of the century.

The Life of Nikon by the Serbian monk Pachomius tells us that the abbot, inspired by the desire to see the cathedral's interior painted before his death, sent for Andrey Rublev and Daniel Chorny, who carried out the commission with assistants in a fairly short time ('they wanted to complete it quickly'). Since Nikon died some time between 1428 and 1430, the frescos can be dated 1427–28. Unfortunately they have not survived. They were either overpainted in 1635 and several times subsequently, or else were stripped from the walls with the plaster then and there. Three tiers of the iconostasis are contemporary with the frescos: the Deesis and the tiers of feast days and prophets. By no means all the icons are directly associable with the school of Rublev, and in any case it is difficult to distinguish between the work of the master and his pupils. The question of attribution has therefore called forth a wide variety of differing opinions. The icons of the Apostle Paul and of the Baptism of Christ are indisputedly by Rublev himself. The famous Trinity, based on the iconography of the Old Testament type of hospitality (cf. Onasch, *Ikonen*, pls 98–101), not only exemplifies the special individual character of Rublev's art, but also embodies the typical early Russian artistic ideal of the beauty of mankind and the world. Rublev painted it between 1411 and 1423: V. N. Lazarev dates it in 1411, the year in which a wooden church was erected above the tomb of Sergius of Radonezh and dedicated to the Trinity. Y. A. Lebedeva believes that it was intended for the stone cathedral, and was therefore painted in 1422 or 1423. Whatever the date, it was commissioned by Nikon 'in honour of Father Sergius', and was at first placed on the saint's tomb; the earliest reference to it as a local icon, placed as such on the right of the Royal Door, is in the seventeenth century. The Synod of a Hundred Chapters (1551) recommended it to artists as a 'classic' model for them to imitate. It is now an exhibit in the State Tretyakov Gallery in Moscow.

Andronikov Monastery of the Saviour, 15th–17th centuries

Cathedral of the Saviour, 1422–23

Refectory, 1496–1508

Спас-Андроников монастырь

Спасский собор

Трапезная

Spas-Andronikov monastyr

Spassky sobor

Trapeznaya

The Andronikov Monastery of the Saviour was founded in 1360. Its first masonry buildings date from the early part of the fifteenth century. As it now stands it consists of the Cathedral of the Saviour (1422–23), the refectory (1496–1508), the Church of the Archangel Michael (1691–1739), the Prior's House (late seventeenth century), the monastic cells (eighteenth and nineteenth century), and the walls and towers (seventeenth and eighteenth centuries).

The Cathedral of the Saviour, built under Abbot Alexander (1418–27) and the elderly Andrey Rublev, is an example of the early Moscow School of architecture of the late fourteenth and early fifteenth centuries, of which some fifteen monuments survive. It is typical in the pyramidal composition of its upper part, deriving from the construction of the vaulting, and in its use of blocks of white limestone, presenting smooth faces between 12 and 16 inches high, for the walls. The four pillars, three apses and one dome are an acknowledgement of the legacy of Vladimir-Suzdal, but the vaulting and therefore the form of the roof derive from the traditions of Chernigov and Smolensk and of Novgorod and Pskov. The corner cells of the building are so low that while the ogee gables in which their sections of the walls terminate form one tier, the gables of the arms of the central cross form a separate, second tier. A third tier conceals the transverse arches, higher than the roofs of the arms, which support the drum, and that in turn is encircled by a fourth tier of purely decorational gables *(pl. 161)*. In order to establish the connection between the low corner cells, quadrant gables were constructed, which give the walls a graduated, trefoil outline. This roof form meant that the walls had to be divided into three by flat pilasters corresponding to the lesenes inside the church, and was also responsible for the symmetrical arrangement of the narrow window openings and the absence of any horizontal articulation, apart from the pronounced socle, with its 'Attic' moulding. The decoration of the cathedral, including the three doorways, is typical of the architecture of Moscow in the fifteenth century. The doorways, placed above the socle and approached by short flights of steps, are flanked by three pairs

of columns with 'melons' and bead moulding halfway up the shafts, cube capitals and 'Attic' bases, and two pairs of quarter-pillars with the same type of base and capital, between the columns. Above these supports is an ogee arch with analogous five-fold moulding *(pl. 160)*. The decoration of the drum was influenced by the twelfth-century Vladimir style. In spite of the building's small dimensions, the dynamic upward movement of forms which dominates the exterior is repeated inside. The room gives an impression of great height, augmented by the contrast between the well-lit area below the soaring dome and the darkness of the low corner cells. There are diagonal corbelled arches between those that mark the intersection of the barrel vaults. The centripetal system of short, superimposed arches provides the primary articulation of the interior, so that the cube vanishes altogether. The whole upper part of the building collapsed in 1812. It was rebuilt without any regard to its original construction. It was not until 1961 that it was restored in its old form under the direction of L. A. David; many of the original blocks of stone which had been used in the earlier rebuilding were used yet again.

Soon after the building work was finished, the walls and ceilings were decorated with paintings by Andrey Rublev, Daniel Chorny and assistants, but only fragments of ornamental plant motifs have survived in the window soffits. The Serbian monk Pachomius draws on the accounts of contemporaries to relate many affecting details of the death of the two artist-monks, who were close friends and are supposed to have died very soon after they had completed the decoration of the cathedral. Joseph of Volokolamsk and seventeenth-century sources confirm that Rublev died in the Andronikov Monastery and was therefore buried there, but the grave has not as yet been identified. The Rublev Museum of Early Russian Art has been set up in memory of the outstanding master of icon painting in the place where he did his last work.

The two-storey refectory (1496–1508) is a well-preserved specimen of early architecture in Moscow *(pl. 159)*. It is square in plan and continues a trend already found in Kiev and Novgorod, where the influence of wooden architecture was felt, in that it has a room in the upper storey whose ceiling consists of four bays of vaulting supported by a square central pillar. The west wall is articulated by a lesene corresponding to the position of the central pillar and by two corner lesenes, and these two divisions each include, in the upper storey, a window set in a rectangular niche. A building containing domestic offices, with an upper storey dating from the seventeenth century, adjoins the refectory on the north side, and the combined west fronts of the two buildings are actually part of the fortifications. Below the overhang of the four-faced tent roof there runs a pronounced cornice decorated with saw-tooth,

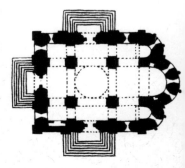

zigzag and wedge-shaped motifs, which in part recall the ornamentation of the Vladimir School, and which are also used on the drum of the Cathedral of the Saviour. The cornice dates from the seventeenth century and is continued along the walls of the Tower-church of the Archangel Michael which adjoins the refectory to the east *(pl. 293)*.

8, 162-171 Moscow Москва

Cathedral of the Assumption in the Kremlin, 1475–79, by Aristotle Fioravanti
Успенский собор в Кремле
Архитектор Аристотель Фиораванти
Uspensky sobor v Kremle
Arkhitektor Aristotel Fioravanti

The Cathedral of the Assumption, standing in the centre of the Kremlin and therefore at the heart of the young capital city, was the chief shrine of all Russia. In it was housed the 'miraculous' icon of the Virgin of Vladimir, in it the tsars were crowned, in it the metropolitans, and later the patriarchs, were interred. It was in the cathedral that Ivan III tore up the Khan's proclamation of the Golden Horde's suzerainty over Russia. As Russia's nationhood was consolidated it became increasingly clear that only Muscovy was capable of uniting the separate territories, forming a strong state and liberating it from the Tartar yoke. After 'Tsargrad', the imperial city of Constantinople, had been taken by the Turks (1453), the Great Princes took their chance to declare themselves the guardians of Orthodox Christianity, and Moscow 'the third Rome', and thus to give their government a theocratic foundation. Apart from the actual walls and towers of the Kremlin, the cathedral is probably the most powerful masonry building of the late fifteenth century. Its predecessor of 1326, a relatively small limestone structure, was in a tumbledown condition by 1472, due to several fires and the effects of weathering: the cracked vaults were propped up with thick wooden beams, the walls threatened to collapse, and the Peter Chapel in the north-east corner did fall down. Ivan III and Metropolitan Filip I decided to build a new cathedral. The immediate motive could have been the subjugation of stubborn Novgorod for the first time (1471), the annexation of the lands of other principalities, and the first overtures of peace from the khan—a triumph that brought the Great Prince the title of tsar. As was customary at the time, the commission was put out to public tender and awarded to the contractor who offered the lowest charge: in this case to Ivan Krivtsov and a Myshkin (whose first name is not given in the records) who worked for Ivan Golova. The two drew up the plans for the new building on the model of the twelfth-century Ca-

thedral of the Assumption in Vladimir, on the tsar's instructions, but enlarged it in both length and breadth by about 10 feet. The chronicler records the beginning of the demolition of the old church, mentions that it was contained within the new walls, being smaller, and tells of the construction of a temporary wooden church on the spot where the altar was to be, in which the wedding of Ivan III and the Byzantine princess Sophia Paleologos was celebrated in 1472. The demolition of the old building was completed when the new walls had reached the height of a man. In May 1474 the new building, by then almost completed, suddenly collapsed: the north wall, which contained the stairs leading up to the tribune, part of the west wall and the tribune adjoining it and the vaults all fell down. It is hard to establish the true cause. The chronicle states that Moscow was shaken by a 'trus', an earthquake. Architects from Pskov, who were summoned as assessors at the public inquiry, praised the 'smoothness' of their colleagues' work, but found that the lime had been mixed too thinly with sand and that the bond of the masonry was not a good one. Interestingly enough, they refused the invitation to take on the work themselves. The Italian architect Fioravanti, who arrived a year after the accident, also considered the lime used in the mortar a poor binding material and the stone too soft. Evidently all these reasons and some constructional errors as well contributed to the architectural disaster.

It may well have been on the advice of his wife Sophia that Ivan next decided to seek help among the Venetians, making use of the ambassador Semyon Tolbusin, who was going on a diplomatic mission to the Doge in 1474. He was commissioned to find a competent architect and bring him back to Moscow. The Bolognese architect and engineer who was recommended to him in Venice, Rodolfo Fioravanti, agreed to take the job for a salary of ten roubles or two pounds of silver a month. Fioravanti, his son Andrea and his assistant Petruccio began their journey in January 1475, and reached the Russian capital at the end of March. After inspecting the ruin he rejected the idea of completing his predecessors' building, and persuaded Ivan III to pull it down altogether. The Muscovites were amazed at the speed with which the site was cleared: 'It was three years in the building, but demolished in a week.' Fioravanti ordered the building of a special brickworks to produce bricks baked to extreme hardness in the oven, and of a fairly large size ($11\frac{1}{2}$ x $4\frac{1}{2}$ x $2\frac{3}{4}$ inches). He was equally exacting in his prescription for the mortar, to ensure a high quality mix: the lime had to be like a thick paste to be handled with trowels, so that when it dried out towards the next morning it could not be scraped away even with a knife. Fioravanti started on the foundations in June 1475 'according to his own ideas, and not in the way the Moscow architects did it'. The chronicles of the period give detailed accounts of all his innovations, such as the mixed masonry of brick and limestone blocks, the four round pillars in the body of the church and the two square, brick pillars in the sanctuary, the thinness of the vaults and their wide span, the iron girders in the walls and the iron ties (instead of oak beams) between the pillars, the use of level and compasses. Fioravanti made no mystery of his craft, told anyone who was interested exactly what he was doing, and engaged the assistance of a large number of Muscovite builders and architects. He was nicknamed Aristotle in honour of his many-sided abilities. The foundations were finished by the autumn. Reaching throughout to a greater depth (*c*13 feet) than the preceding building, and resting on oak piles, they were constructed of quarry stone and slaked lime. The work was halted until the spring of 1476, since building was forbidden in winter by law. Fioravanti was ordered by Ivan to spend the time in Vladimir, studying the Cathedral of the Assumption and other twelfth-century buildings. It was necessary to the ambition of the young Muscovite state to legitimize itself by registering its adherence to pre-Mongol traditions. It demanded an unbroken development of the national architecture, so Fioravanti's work in Russia does not mark the beginning of an epigonal Renaissance but an original, creative continuation of the autochthonous tradition. From Vladimir he travelled to the White Sea and evidently visited the Kola Peninsula and the Solovetsky Islands. In the second year of construction the cathedral rose as high as the blind arcades, which are particularly reminiscent of the Vladimir-Suzdalian style with their Romanesque engaged columns. The basic structure was finished in 1477. The domes and the finishing of the interior took another two years. In 1477 Fioravanti accompanied Ivan III on his last campaign against Novgorod and designed the bridge across the Volkhov. The cathedral was finally consecrated on 15 August 1479 (Old Style).

At first sight the Kremlin's new cathedral appears to conform to the Great Prince's command that it should imitate the Assumption in Vladimir and employ forms we have already seen in the architecture of Vladimir-Suzdal and Moscow over the last three centuries. It has five domes, six pillars and five apses, but there are only three aisles. It has a rectangular groundplan with an east-west longitudinal axis. The three fronts of ashlar-cut white limestone, articulated primarily by pilasters and the blind arcading, terminate in round gables which govern the form of the roof, and each contains a doorway flanked by columns. The pilasters correspond to the position of the interior pillars. Nevertheless the cathedral has many new and original features. It was originally raised on a socle 10 feet 6 inches high, with flights of steps leading up to the entrances which are now partly below the flagstones

of the square since laid round the building. All the vertical divisions of the walls–four on the north and south fronts, three on the west–are equal in width, and their gables all rise to the same height. The blind arcades divide the building horizontally into two zones, the lower blank, interrupted only by the doorways (with the single exception of the east division of the south front, which has a window with an ornamental surround). Two narrow slit windows are placed precisely in the centre of each of the vertical divisions, the lower in the blind arcade, conforming exactly to the width and height of the other arches, and the other up in the gable (*pl. 164*).

The apses are relatively low and very much flattened on the outside. From the north and south sides they are concealed by massive projections at the ends of the walls, which look like broad corner pilasters. The two windows in ornamental surrounds in the lower zones of the two south apses date from the seventeenth century. The articulation is accentuated by windows and engaged columns of the same width. Between the top of the apses and the round gables of the east wall there are three large panels with wall paintings on them (*pl. 165*). The overall structure of the building shows that the architect was well acquainted with the domed cruciform plan but that his architectural conceptions rested on the classical basis of the Renaissance and its store of technical experience. He took the traditional semi-circle motif and used it consistently, on the portals, the blind arcades, the lunettes on the south front, the gables, the windows and the domes. But the cathedral lacks the plasticity, the impression

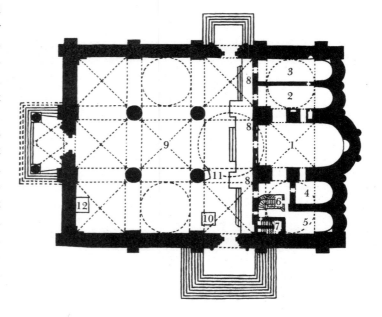

1 *Sanctuary* 2 *Prothesis* 3 *Chapel of SS Peter and Paul* 4 *Diakonikon, with the site formerly occupied by the Chapel of the Glorification (Pokhval) in front of it* 5 *Chapel of St Demetrius* 6 *Stairs up to the sacristy and library* 7 *Stairs to the Chapel of the Glorification (Pokhval) two storeys above* 8 *Iconostasis* 9 *Aisles* 10 *Monomakh Throne (prayer-desk of Ivan IV)* 11 *Prayer-desk of the patriarch* 12 *Bronze canopy (Holy Sepulchre)*

Blind arcading

of having been moulded, of its models in Vladimir-Suzdal. Instead it impresses by its application of geometrical laws, leading to a harmonious inter-relationship of the individual forms. The Golden Section was used to particularly good effect in marking out the groundplan and in the division of the façades. The ornamental restraint, the sym-metry and balance of the proportions, the simple, clear articulation, the structural integration, and above all the solidity of the domes give the Kremlin's principal cathedral the monumentality appropriate to the power of Muscovy.

M. V. Alpatov has demonstrated that the cath-edral makes the impression, not of growing organi-cally out of the ground, but of resting on it like a perfect crystal, and that Fioravanti put the prin-ciples of Renaissance architecture into practice, without translating its forms to Russian soil. The idea that it should be possible to experience and to measure religious and artistic concepts appealed to both the Italians and the Russians in the late fifteenth century, more as a historical and scientific concept to the former, more emotionally and immediately to the latter. The influence of early Renaissance modes – the classical orders of columns and pil-asters, the system of articulation – is already present in the Cathedral of the Archangel Michael, built some thirty years later. In this context, historians point out that the ideas of modern humanism were beginning to take effect in social, political and artistic conceptions in Russia at about that period, and also that heretical movements were again on the increase.

The south front of the Cathedral of the Assump-tion was always envisaged as the principal façade. It faces on to the main square of the Kremlin, the Square of the Cathedrals, while the palaces of the tsar and the metropolitan block the views of the north and west fronts. All the important church ceremonies were performed in front of the south side, and processions used the south portal, which was more ornately decorated and further adorned by richly coloured frescos *(pl. 162)*. Our Lady of Compassion is depicted in the lunette, princes of the church between the columns of the blind arcade, and archangels on either side of the doorway. The view of the cathedral from the south captures to the full the serenity and repose created by the monu-mentality of the formal concepts, and which are not diminished by the displacement of the five domes east of centre. The drums are placed close together, and the melodious outlines of the helmet-shaped domes help to emphasize the scale appropriate to the cathedral's importance. These five domes, which were intended to be yet another special symbol of the power and renown enjoyed by the Great Princes of Muscovy as rulers of all Russia, became one of the most influential motifs in Russian architecture, like the form of the building itself. Throughout the six-teenth and seventeenth centuries the Assumption

was copied in any number of monastic and urban churches. The Cathedrals of the Assumption in Rostov and in the Monastery of the Holy Trinity and St Sergius, St Sophia in Vologda, SS Boris and Gleb and Holy Trinity in Novgorod and many others were directly influenced by the cathedral in the Moscow Kremlin. Of the decorative forms, architects particularly liked the double arch with the pendant girka over the steps outside the west door. In the middle of the seventeenth century, when Patriarch Nikon was banning the octagonal church with tent roof, he still prescribed the austere sil-houette of the five-domed Cathedral of the As-sumption as the proper model.

The three aisles of the interior present a hall church as harmonious, unified and integrated as the exterior *(pl. 8)*. The unusual spaciousness made a great impression on contemporary beholders. The chronicle states: 'Of a truth, this church is very won-derful in its dignified serenity, height, lightness and in its fame and renown, such as there has never been in Russia before, except in the churches of Vladimir.' It differs in one respect from earlier cathedrals built by princes, in the lack of any kind of tribune. The tsar's seat, beneath a ciborium, stood immediately in front of the altar steps, thus conforming to the new national idea in being united with the con-gregation instead of raised above them. Another innovatory feature is that, of the six supports of the groin vaults and domes, the four in the aisles are circular in section (as in the court church at Bogo-lyubovo) and also – and this seems of the greatest importance – equidistant from each other. As a consequence, there is no special emphasis given to the central space beneath the main dome. The four slender, free-standing columns (originally with Corinthian capitals), which the chronicler compares to trees, do not restrict the view but clear it, opening up a broad and splendid hall. It was the place where the whole congregation, with the tsar and boyars at their head, assembled together before the throne of God. The two square pillars of the sanctuary are hidden by the iconostasis. If we remember that the iconostasis, which reaches right up to the ceiling, was not added until the seventeenth century, we can realize that the effect of the interior would originally have been even more grandiose. Fioravanti's method of constructing the vaults gives rise to yet a third peculiarity: since all the transverse arches between the pillars are equal, the drums should all have been of equal diameter. But as the early Russian tradition demanded that the central drum and dome should be larger than the others, Fioravanti increased their diameter by placing them on a round pedestal, which made it possible for the walls to describe a circle a little outside the inner one. The pedestal was made as light as possible by being hollow. In this way the central drum was larger than the others on the outside, while the distances between the supports remained constant on the inside of the building. Indeed, the total impression is that the exterior was intended to be a stone shell for the hall-like interior, serving no requirements but the spatial one.

Fioravanti employed every technique he knew to make the cathedral as durable as possible. Instead of wooden tie-beams he used iron ones with S-shaped braces at their ends which are visible on the outside walls. The ceilings were groin vaults constructed of only one thickness of bricks, while the walls were of great blocks of white quarry stone which permitted a sturdy bond. In spite of all these precautions, however, cracks started to appear in the vaults by the beginning of the seventeenth century, so the court architect, John Taler, inserted extra metal ties in the weakened places in 1626. Unfortunately the capitals were demolished in the process. The cathedral suffered virtually no other major alterations. In the second half of the seventeenth century two extra floors were constructed in the two south side apses, which are now accessible only by a separate staircase. The seventeenth-century staircase, repaired in the nineteenth, against the north wall of the outermost of the apses, leads to the first of the upper floors, the stairs against the south wall to the second floor date from the fifteenth century, and also lead up to the roof. The Chapel of the Glorification (Pokhval), originally positioned at the entrance to the sanctuary in the inner apse, was moved to the space immediately beneath the south-east dome, on the top floor and occupying the width of both apses. The middle floor was given over to a sacristy, above the inner apse, and a library, above the outer one. The diakonikon in the inner apse and the Chapel of St Demetrius in the outer apse were lit by small rectangular windows in their east walls and in the south wall of the chapel (the east division of the south wall); these windows have surrounds typical of the seventeenth century, with small columns carved to look like turnery. There is absolutely no foundation for the speculation of some scholars that Fioravanti took the Pokhval Chapel from the fourteenth-century cathedral, and that the windows were constructed by him in the fifteenth century. All the windows in the cathedral were widened in the eighteenth century, but restored to their old shape early in the twentieth. In the nineteenth, the floor was raised very slightly and the limestone flags replaced by square plates of cast iron. The bases of the portals were also altered a little and the facing of the socle and the walls replaced in part.

The iconostasis and the murals inside the cathedral were executed soon after it had been consecrated. The chronicle recounts that in 1481 'the icon-painter Dionysius, the priests Timofey, Yarets and Konya' received the commission to paint the Deesis, the feast-day tier and the prophets for 100 roubles. Dionysius, then about forty, was probably the oldest artist in the team. The work may have been commissioned by Ivan III's confessor and spiritual counsellor, Vassian, archbishop of Rostov, who, in an open letter of 1480 advocating war against the Tartar Khan Ahmed, had exhorted the Great Prince: 'Tsar, justify your title!' The paintings were a thank-offering for the victorious outcome of the battle on the Ugra. It is not clear whether the three tiers were painted for the iconostasis (which is the more likely) or for the stone altar screen. I. J. Danilowa thinks it possible that the altar screen was originally included in the compositional scheme of the iconostasis, as its substructure, so to speak, but ascribes the frescos to one of the other artists, not to Dionysius, on the strength of the surviving fragments of figures of saints. V. N. Lazarev dates the two rows of frescos on the altar screen earlier altogether, between 1479 and 1481, and assumes that the wooden iconostasis would then have concealed them. M. V. Alpatov dates them 1482 or 1514 to 1515. It is known for certain that all the walls were painted in fresco in 1514–15. These frescos survived to the seventeenth century, but were apparently in a very decayed condition when they were overpainted in 1642–44. Since the restorers were instructed to copy all the scenes and figures exactly, drawings were made of all the destroyed murals before the plaster was stripped from the walls, placed in sacks and dropped in the river. More than 150 painters from Moscow, Ustyug, Suzdal and Vladimir are supposed to have taken part in the restoration. The murals were restored several times in the eighteenth and nineteenth centuries, three times in oils, even. It was not until 1914 that the task of uncovering the original frescos was undertaken, a task resumed in the 1920s, in 1949 and 1950, and again recently. The plan is to remove all the paintings above the seventeenth-century layer, to replace the lost portions, to gild the backgrounds, and thus to recreate the impression of the artistic unity of the interior as a whole.

There are undoubted stylistic similarities between the old frescos of saints painted on the stone altar screen (which even Napoleon's troops treated with respect when they removed the iconostasis) and the surviving fragments of the late fifteenth and early sixteenth centuries in the apses. There is no united opinion on the attribution among the authorities. If Dionysius himself is not the author, his school was certainly involved. The Synaxis of the Virgin and Child (pl. 166), discovered on the north wall of the old Pokhval Chapel in the inner south apse, is particularly closely related to the master's style. Unfortunately the lower part of it was destroyed when the low vaults dividing the storeys were built in the seventeenth century. Basically it depicts the Adoration of the Magi. The Child is seated on the lap of the Virgin, who is enthroned and surrounded by an aureol. Two of the Magi are on the left, one bearing gifts in his hands which are

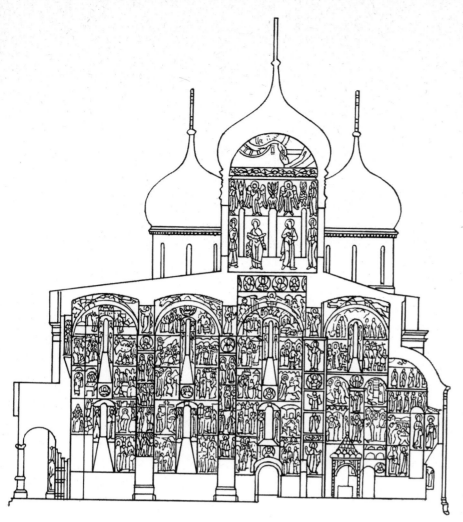

covered in liturgical fashion. Three angels are making obeisance in the background of jagged rocks. The painting is characterized by the slender figures, the refined facial features, the elegant gestures and the light, delicate colouring. The birth of John the Baptist is depicted on the south wall, and the Glorification of the Virgin, from which the chapel took its name, on the ceiling. The restoration work of the 1920s led to the discovery in the prothesis of a painting of the Three Children in the Burning Fiery Furnace, and of the Seven Sleepers of Ephesus and fragments of scenes from the life of St Paul in the Chapel of SS Peter and Paul, adjoining the prothesis on its north side. There is an unmistakable stylistic resemblance between these frescos and those in the Therapontos Monastery which Dionysius painted 1500–02, with his two sons and other assistants. The escape from the strait-jacket of the frontal stance, the elongated proportions of the elegant figures and small heads, the melodious, pliant curves, the soft, graceful lines, the confident 'direction', in the theatrical sense of the word, the animation of the scenes, the delicate shading from one to another of the harmonious combinations of pale blues, ochres, pale greens and pinks, the plastic use of light, the simultaneously ceremonial and dynamic atmosphere, the homiletic trait, all argue for an origin in a common school. While V. N. Lazarev also attributes the Forty Martyrs of Sebaste on the south wall of the Peter and Paul Chapel (pl. 167) to the same school, other experts ascribe it to a different studio, though

there is no dispute as to its dating at the very end of the fifteenth century or the beginning of the sixteenth. Only twenty-four of the figures are now to be seen; the rest appear to have been destroyed in 1819, when part of the wall was pulled down to make an archway over the tomb of Metropolitan Peter, who had commissioned the first church on the site. All the martyrs are individually characterized; they are depicted as complete figures, stripped to the waist, standing in two or three rows. Their dramatic gestures express the exhaustion and agony caused by the penetrating cold of the sea water in which they were left to freeze to death. The undulating horizontal lines, especially above the heads, create an impression of disquiet and tension. The musculature of the naked parts of the bodies is treated completely in accordance with the principles of Renaissance art, which paid great attention to scientific anatomy.

The records of the paintings done in the Cathedral of the Assumption from 1642 to 1644 include the names of a large number of icon painters employed by the tsar, Michael Romanov (died 1645): Bazhen Savin, Ivan and Boris Paisein, Sidor Pospeyev, Mark Matveyev and others (to an approximate total of 150 men), as well as the names of Ivan Murav, Vasily Ilin and Lyubim Ageyev, who specialized in the preliminary cartoons. They all worked in the state icon workshop, which later merged with the so-called Armoury, and grew in importance as the tsar's desire for ostentatious display grew. The workshop employed artists from all over Russia, and beyond. In the Cathedral of the Assumption they used the mineral colours usual at the time, pigments extracted from the local coloured clay and other minerals, mixed with water and bound with egg-yolk, vegetable size and other agents, and painted on surfaces of damp (fresco) or dry (secco) plaster, or more often in a technique combining the two.

Some of these artists, Lyubim Ageyev from Kostroma for example, are known for other great sequences of murals dating from the second half of the seventeenth century, for instance in the Monastery of St Cyril of Belozersk. The paintings in the Cathedral of the Assumption are devoted to the themes of the Glorification of the Virgin and of the most important Christian dogmas. Christ is depicted in the hemisphere of all five domes in monochrome representations marked by a linear simplification; in the central dome he appears as Pantocrator, and in the other four as Emmanuel, the God of Sabaoth, the Acheiropoïetos (pl. 168), and the Holy Child on his Mother's lap. Whole figures of the patriarchs, prophets and apostles are painted on the piers between the windows of the drums, the evangelists on the pendentives, and the feasts of the Church on the vaults of the aisles. The semi-circular east wall of the middle apse bears a huge painting of the Assumption of the Virgin and one of the liturgical procession, the Great Entry, the latter only rediscovered in

1960; while the Tier of Bishops is on the walls between the middle and adjacent apses. The pillars are divided horizontally into five zones, with whole figures of men and women canonized for their Christian witness in the early history of the Church (pl. 8). The west wall is taken up by a Last Judgment and some scenes from the life of the Virgin, and the north and south walls by a representation of the ecumenical councils and more scenes from the life of the Virgin and her parents. The Demetrius Chapel is decorated with cycles of the lives of St Demetrius and the prophet Elijah (1642-43).

In their present condition the murals do not make the impression of a unified programme or harmonious ensemble. They were overpainted on several occasions in the intervening centuries, and the attempt at restoration between 1914 and 1917 was bungled. It was only the research and restoration of 1960 and 1961 that at last succeeded in uncovering, beneath the eighteenth and nineteenth-century layers, the seventeenth-century paintings of the Great Entry in the sanctuary, Elijah's Assumption in the fiery chariot in the Demetrius Chapel, and figures of martyrs and saints on the north pair of pillars. Stylistically these paintings are very close to the sixteenth-century tradition. The human figures are solemn and ceremonial, with elongated proportions, thin, elegant limbs and small heads. Movement is represented as calm and fluid, and reveals the pains taken not to disturb the symmetry and balance of the pictorial construction.

The present five-tiered iconostasis, reaching as high as the ceiling, dates from 1652 and stands in front of a low, stone altar screen, decorated with frescos, which was built of a piece with the square, east pillars. It is likely that originally wooden tyabla, shelves, were fixed above it on consoles, on which the traditional tiers of icons, the Deesis, the feasts and the prophets, were displayed. The first, Dionysian iconostasis of the end of the fifteenth century was extended to a height of about 52 feet in 1652, and its four upper tiers furnished with icons that conform stylistically to the murals of the same period. In the mid nineteenth century the backgrounds of the icons were overlaid with silver mounts engraved in a manner imitating the old drawings, the icons themselves were overpainted and some even replaced altogether by paintings on canvas. At the end of the century the frame of the iconostasis received a chased, silver-gilt casing (pl. 8). The oldest and artistically most valuable icons are those in the bottom tier and in the shrines along the north and south walls. It is possible to see on plate 8, bottom left on the iconostasis, the icon 'Every creature rejoices at Thee', from the circle of Dionysius's pupils (late fifteenth century), and, bottom left behind the column, the 'Saviour with the angry look' (mid fourteenth century). The icon of St George is probably from Novgorod (twelfth century). Christ

'with golden hair' and the Archangel Michael (both first half of the thirteenth century) are probably from Vladimir-Suzdal and were brought to the Moscow cathedral at the same time as the Vladimir Virgin (now in the Tretyakov Gallery). The Assumption of the Virgin and the Apocalypse can be attributed to the Moscow School (both dating from the turn of the fifteenth to the sixteenth century), while the icon of Metropolitan Peter in a frame of sixteen scenes from his life is evidently by Dionysius himself. Most of these panels have been painstakingly restored by the Soviet Department for the Care of Monuments, while others still remain to be seen to. The full complement of unique monuments of Russian painting between the twelfth and seventeenth centuries is far from exhausted by those that have actually been mentioned here.

The applied arts, too, played a major role in the adornment of the Cathedral of the Assumption. The pair of doors at the south entrance are remarkable; made of iron, they are covered on the outside with sheets of copper on which there are twenty biblical scenes, damascened (opus inauratum chrysographia) on a dark ground. According to a Suzdal chronicle they were brought to Moscow in 1405— probably from the north portal of the Cathedral of the Nativity of the Virgin in Suzdal. Doubt is cast on this provenance, however, by the depiction of two Muscovite saints who were not canonized until the fifteenth century. A later dating is also supported by the inscriptions, which are in the Novgorod dialect, and by the representation of the Virgin according to the Novgorod model. It is nonetheless possible that if the doors were taken to Moscow at the end of the fifteenth century, they were restored and had additions made to them at that time.

In the immediate proximity of the south door there is a carved wooden prayer-desk, reserved for the use of the tsars, known as the Monomakh Throne, which was made in 1551 on the orders of Ivan IV (pl. 169). In form it resembles sixteenth-century ciboria raised over altars: a canopy constructed as a many-tiered tent roof with kokoshniki rests on the four columns of a rectangular pavilion, which is supported in turn by four recumbent lions also carved in wood. The bottom part of the pavilion is enclosed by panels on three sides and a low door on the fourth. The panels are carved in low relief with scenes from the legendary campaign of Vladimir Monomakh, prince of Kiev, in Thrace, and his receipt of the imperial insignia from the Byzantine emperor, Constantine Monomachos. The carvings were intended to express the Muscovite thesis of the direct descent of the tsars' power from Byzantium, and so they depict military trains and battles, the reception of emissaries, councils of princes and boyars, and the presentation of the famous 'Cap of Monomakh' and the coronation robe (pls. 170, 171). The armour and clothing, other objects and buildings are all sixteenth-century in style and Vladimir himself looks like Ivan IV. The wealth and ostentation, the rich, multiform, imaginative power of that age are combined in the elaborately turned columns, the plant ornaments on the tent roof, the overlapping ornamental gables, the carved flowers and the goblets filled with grapes, even in the ornamental inscriptions on the cornice and the panels of the door. The pinnacle of the roof is surmounted by the imperial double-headed eagle.

The patriarch's desk stands immediately in front of the south-east pillar, to the left of the Monomakh Throne. Made of white stone, it was set up there in the sixteenth century and may originally have been carved, but it was later covered with ornamental paintings in seventeenth-century style. The casework of bronze lattices, surmounted by a tent roof, in the south-west corner of the cathedral, dates from 1624. Its symbolism may be related to the medieval architectural concept of the Holy Sepulchre, since it was originally intended to house relics (a throne with what was believed to be a fragment of Christ's clothing). In 1913 the tomb of Patriarch Germogen, who died during the Polish Intervention in 1612, was placed in the shrine. The lattice is beautifully worked, in a pattern of branches that just touch each other, which used to be known as the 'cube pattern'. A bud and shoots is inserted into each cube cell, in such a way that the ornament simultaneously plays a structural role, strengthening the screen as a whole. The construction and decoration of the pillars, the meshes and the ornamental gables placed on the cornice display a particularly fertile imagination. The canopy is the work of the 'Master Coppersmith' Dmitry Sverchkov. Some paintings of Passion scenes, also dating from the seventeenth century, have been preserved on the underside of the tent roof. The twelve gilded bronze chandeliers are further valuable monuments of seventeenth-century craftsmanship (pl. 8). They vary in type, but they have one thing in common: their entwined tendrils are piled up in a pyramidal form, with the number of candle-holders in each tier steadily decreasing towards the apex. The main chandelier hanging in the middle aisle was cast from the silver that Cossacks took from the retreating Napoleonic troops who had stolen it in 1812. It was made in classical style from a design by Master Geldung. The tombs of the Russian metropolitans and patriarchs are placed around the walls of the cathedral, the last to have been buried here being Patriarch Adrian who died in 1698.

6, 174, 175   Moscow   Москва

Kremlin, 15th–17th centuries

Кремль

Kreml

The history of the Kremlin in Moscow starts in 1156. Nine years after the founding of the town the first wooden fortress was built on the Borovitsky hill, on the spit of land caused by the confluence of the Moskva and Neglinnaya rivers. Between 1326 and 1340, under Ivan Kalita, its extent was enlarged, the first stone churches were built within it, and new fortifications of oak palings were constructed. The unceasing confrontation with the Golden Horde, the principality's increasing power, and the final removal of the metropolitan's seat from Vladimir to Moscow, made it necessary for the citadel's limits to be extended once more, and for it to be enclosed within limestone walls and towers under Dmitry Donskoi in 1367 (or 1366 according to another source). It was characteristic that when this was done, the south wall was built at the bottom of the Borovitsky hill, along the shore of the Moskva, leaving the view of the increasing number of imposing stone buildings inside the wall unimpeded. There is still a clear view of the whole panorama (pl. 6), although the massive programme of rebuilding instigated by Ivan III governs the present-day appearance of things. In order to provide the new capital of the united Russian states with an emblem that would be known to all and that would also symbolize the new political concept, the Kremlin had to assume more monumental architectural forms. The overall unifying plan according to which the team of Italian and Russian architects set to work in 1485 will have been motivated by military, defensive, architectonic and not least by ideological considerations. Both Russian traditions and the topography of the site influenced the plan which is a rough triangle, dominated by the cathedrals in the centre. The new walls of red brick were built before the old ones, of limestone blocks, had been demolished, following the old outline with hardly any change, except for being slightly outside it. The total length of the brick walls is nearly $1\frac{1}{2}$ miles (7330 feet) and they enclose an area of 69 acres.

The rebuilding began on the south side, which had the greatest strategic importance, was pursued on the east side as far as Red Square, and finished c1516 under Ivan III's son, Vasily III, with the north-west side along the Neglinnaya, since the swamps on that side for one thing provided relatively good protection in themselves, and for another necessitated considerable hydro-technical engineering work. The towers were always built first in any section. The three corner towers and several others were equipped with wells to ensure water supplies in the case of prolonged siege. The slender stone tent roofs were added in the seventeenth century. The original appearance was governed by the tiers of defensive platforms for marksmen and artillery and by the wooden tent roofs with their lookout platforms. The towers project in front of the line of the

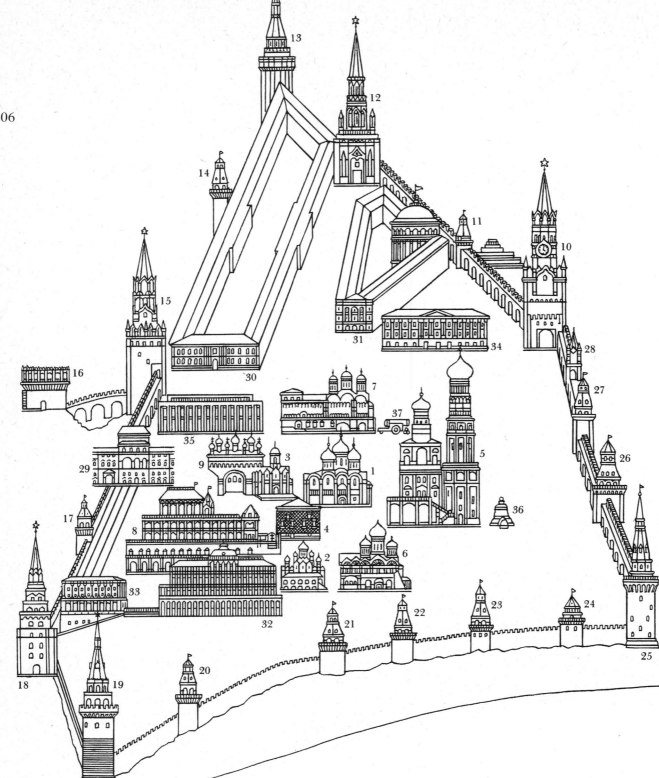

1 *Cathedral of the Assumption* 2 *Cathedral of the Annunciation* 3 *Church of the Miracle of the Virgin's Veil* 4 *Faceted Palace* 5 *Ivan the Great Bell-tower* 6 *Cathedral of the Archangel Michael* 7 *Church of the Twelve Apostles and Patriarch's Palace* 8 *Terem Palace* 9 *Terem Churches* 10 *Saviour (Frolov) Gate-tower* 11 *Senate Tower* 12 *St Nicholas Gate-tower* 13 *Arsenal (Sobakin) Tower* 14 *Middle Arsenal Tower* 15 *Trinity Gate-tower* 16 *Kutafya Watch-tower* 17 *Arms Tower* 18 *Borovitsky Gate-tower* 19 *Pump (Sviblov) Tower* 20 *Annunciation Tower* 21 *Secret Tower* 22 *First Nameless Tower* 23 *Second Nameless Tower* 24 *Petrov Tower* 25 *Beklemishevsky Tower* 26 *Constantine and Helena Gate-tower* 27 *Alarm Tower* 28 *Tsar Tower* 29 *Pleasure Palace* 30 *Arsenal* 31 *Offices of the Council of Ministers of the USSR* 32 *Great Kremlin Palace* 33 *Armoury* 34 *Kremlin Theatre* 35 *Congress Palace* 36 *Tsar-kolokol (giant bell)* 37 *Tsar-pushka (giant cannon)*

walls, so that they command not only the ground in front of them but also the face of the walls. The three corner towers—the Pump tower in the south-west, the Beklemishevsky in the south-east and the Arsenal in the north—are tall and round, to give a circular field of fire. The gate-towers giving on to the main streets, the market on Red Square and the quays on the Moskva, are also massive and powerful-looking.

They had heavy oak doors mounted in cast iron, and could be barred by iron portcullises. Other purely defensive towers were built between the corner towers and the gate-towers. The irregularity of the spaces between them was partly due to the range of the fire-arms available at the time of building, but also to architectonic considerations of their appearance as a group and as part of the urban landscape. From

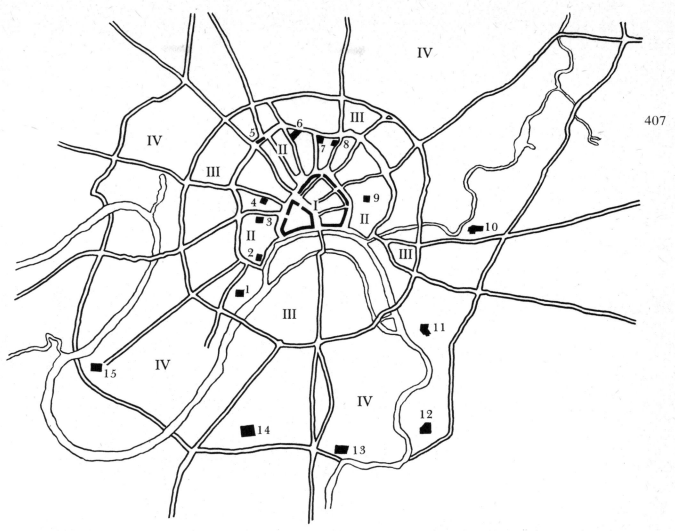

I *Kremlin and Basket Town (Kitai-Gorod)* II *White Town (Bely-Gorod)* III *Country or Wooden Town (Zemlyanoi-Gorod)* IV *Area of Moscow bounded by the Chamber-College vallum* *Northern defensive ring:* 1 *Monastery of the Conception* 2 *Alexey Monastery* 3 *Monastery of the Elevation of the Cross* 4 *Nikita Monastery* 5 *Passion Monastery* 6 *St Peter's Monastery* 7 *Nativity Monastery* 8 *Monastery of the Purification of the Virgin* 9 *St John's Monastery* *Southern defensive ring* 10 *Andronikov Monastery of the Saviour* 11 *New Monastery of the Saviour* 12 *Simon Monastery* 13 *Daniel Monastery* 14 *Don Monastery* 15 *New Convent of the Virgin*

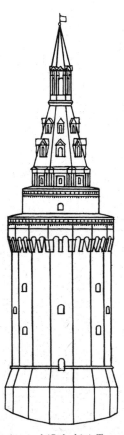

Arsenal (Sobakin) Tower

the south the eye of the spectator is skilfully directed to the most significant buildings, the Cathedral of the Assumption, the Royal Palace and the bell-tower *(pl. 6)*. At the same time, the layout did not neglect defence: the large number of angled turns in the wall and the concave curve of its line as a whole, as if following the bend of the Moskva, offered the best outlook over the immediate terrain and allowed defenders to take proper aim at any attacking force. By 1516, too, a new moat was completed, running along the east wall and connecting the Moskva and Neglinnaya, and so completing a protective triangle of water-courses around the Kremlin.

The work was under the direction of Fioravanti to begin with, followed at various times by other experienced architects summoned from the cities of northern Italy: Antonio Fryazin, Mark Fryazin (also called Marco Ruffo), Pietro Antonio Solario and Aleviz Fryazin the elder. Since the Tartars made their attacks most frequently from the south, and it is therefore likely that that wall was in the worst state of repair, the rebuilding began there. The first part to be built was the Secret (Tainitsky) Tower, (present height: 125 feet) 1485-86, probably by Antonio Fryazin, which projects especially far from the line

of the wall, and owes its name to the subterranean passage leading from it to the Moskva. The original tower has not survived, but was reconstructed in its original shape 1771–73. In 1930 the upper part of it was demolished and the passage through it walled up. It is on the extreme left of plate 6. In 1487 Mark Fryazin built the Beklemishevsky tower (present height: 152 feet) in the south-east corner, and the Sviblov tower in the south-west corner was built by Antonio Fryazin in 1488; this was renamed Pump tower in 1633, after the machinery in it for raising water (present height: 188 feet). The remaining towers in the south wall were all built *c*1490: the Annunciation tower, immediately to the east of the Pump tower (present height: 101 feet), and the three towers illustrated to the right of the Secret tower in plate 6, the First Nameless (Besymyanny) tower which used to hold the powder magazine (present height: 112 feet), the Second Nameless tower which has retained its present appearance since the seventeenth century (present height: 99 feet), and the Petrov tower (present height: 89 feet). On his arrival in Moscow in 1490, Pietro Antonio Solario was at once charged with the construction of a new tower to replace the old Borovitsky tower in the south-west corner (present height: 166 feet) and the section of wall linking it to the Sviblov tower. He gave the new tower, a gate-tower serving domestic purposes and containing the oldest gateway in the Kremlin, an unusual, staggered form, with three rectangular stages one above the other on a massive cuboid base. He also built the Constantine and Helena Gate-tower in the east wall in 1490 (present height: 115 feet), with a stone bridge across the moat. The bridge has been demolished, the moat filled and the gate walled up. In the present-day layout of the city the position seems an arbitrary choice for a gate, but in the fifteenth century it gave on to the so-called Great Street, which traversed the 'Kitai Gorod' (one of the districts of the city, see the commentary on plates 231–37), where the Rossiya Hotel now stands. Before his death in 1493, Solario built the principal entrance tower, the Frolov tower, later renamed the Saviour tower (Spasskaya bashnya) (1491); the St Nicholas Gate-tower (present height: 231 feet) beside the old Monastery of St Nicholas, with a drawbridge over the moat (1491); the Sobakin (later Arsenal) tower with thirteen-feet-thick walls (present height: 197 feet) (1492); and the wall as far as the Neglinnaya. For a time it seems that either there was no available master architect, or else the work on the south and east sections was finished. At all events, the chronicle does not refer again to the building of the walls until 1495, when '. . . the stone wall was built along the Neglinnaya, but not on the old foundations because the city was to be enlarged'. The Trinity Gate-tower was the very last to be built, after the windowless Middle Arsenal tower (present height: 128 feet), the Commandant tower next to the more recent Pleasure Palace (present height: 135 feet), and the Arms tower (present height: 107 feet). These were all built under the direction of Aleviz Fryazin.

The Kremlin's walls and towers were constructed in a well-fired red brick measuring 11.8 (12.2) x 5.5 (5.9) x 2.75 (3.5) inches. They weighed about $17\frac{1}{2}$ pounds each, which is why the builders called them two-handed. They were only used for the exterior surfaces of the walls, and the filling was white limestone, possibly the stone made available when the fourteenth-century walls were knocked down. The mortar was sand and lime, occasionally strengthened by an admixture of crumbled brick.

The height of the walls, not counting the merlons, varies between $16\frac{1}{2}$ and $62\frac{1}{2}$ feet, and their thickness between $11\frac{1}{2}$ and $21\frac{1}{2}$ feet. The parapet has 1,045 merlons of the swallow-tail form, that is, with forked tops, between $6\frac{1}{2}$ and $8\frac{1}{4}$ feet high and $25\frac{1}{4}$ and $27\frac{1}{2}$ inches thick. The coping consists of slabs of limestone with gutters for drainage. Every other merlon has a slit for a defender to fire through, or even two slits, one above the other, on sections of wall particularly vulnerable to attack. A broad platform stretches along the wall behind the battlements,

with a brick parapet on the inner side. At the foot of the wall, on the inside, there is a row of shallow niches with occasionally a deeper, higher one with a vaulted roof; the heavy artillery was fired from these, but the slits in the wall were bricked up in the nineteenth century. In order to allow the defenders to move about out of sight of the enemy and also to ensure the flow of munition supplies, a barrel-vaulted corridor ran beneath the top platform. It has been preserved in a good condition between the Constantine and Helena tower and the Alarm tower (present height: 125 feet), but in other sections it has been filled in with builders' waste and old stone cannon balls and then bricked up. The walls were accessible from the ground only by way of the Saviour tower, the Alarm tower, the Constantine and Helena tower, the Trinity tower, the Borovitsky tower, the Annunciation tower and the Petrov tower; none of the towers had entrances at ground level. In time of war wooden ladders were usually placed against the inner parapet, which had intermittent gaps in it to allow access (it was not until the eighteenth century that the gaps were partly filled in). Since it was common practice for a besieging force to dig tunnels towards a fortress, to blow up walls and towers, secret 'listening' passages were constructed as a precautionary countermeasure, reaching far out into the city.

The disposition of the defences was not significantly altered between the fifteenth century and the beginning of the seventeenth. In the summer and autumn of 1612 a fierce battle was waged in the War of the Polish Intervention, between the Poles defending themselves in the Kremlin, and the Russian popular army. The heroic deeds of Kusyma Minin and Dmitry Pozharsky, who took the citadel by storm through the Saviour Gate and the St Nicholas Gate, wrote a glorious page in the history of Russia, but a general overhaul of the defences was undertaken soon after. And although no substantial alterations were made to the arrangement of towers and walls, they acquired a totally new artistic character in their appearance. The painterly style of the seventeenth century made its influence felt. Numerous changes have been made to the fortifications since then. The long-drawn-out war against the Swedes, who even threatened Moscow itself in 1707, the so-called Trinity Fire in 1737, the Napoleonic occupation in September 1812 and the subsequent destruction of the principal towers by the French as they began to withdraw—all these events made substantial repairs necessary. There was in any case a considerable amount of rebuilding carried out in the second half of the eighteenth century and in the nineteenth, and although this principally concerned the palaces, all the other buildings were overhauled. The October Revolution ushered in a new era, in which the historical monuments of artistic value have been systematically surveyed and repaired, and the modern Congress Palace was built in 1961. The Kremlin now possesses twenty towers, four of them with gateways through them: the Saviour, St Nicholas, Trinity and Borovitsky towers.

The Frolov tower was the first to undergo a change to its original appearance, in the seventeenth century (pl. 174). In the Godunov plan dating from the early years of the century it is low, with a small turret, apparently of wood, beneath a four-faced tent roof surmounted by the imperial double-headed eagle. A bell hangs in the turret (which perhaps struck the hours); a wooden drawbridge lies across the moat towards Red Square; a battlemented, pentagonal bastion stands on each side of the gateway. Solario's original tower was only half the height of the present structure (221 feet). The square base of the tower has double walls, with passages and steps in the space between them. The entrance was always regarded as the 'holy' main gate of the Kremlin and its use was reserved for such special events as ecclesiastical processions and the reception of ambassadors. Even the tsar had to bare his head here. The door carries an impressive inscription in Latin and Russian: 'Ioann Vasilyevich, by God's grace Great Prince of Vladimir, Moscow, Novgorod, Tver, Pskov, Vyatka, Ugorsk, Perm, Bulgaria and others, and Ruler of all Russia, ordered this tower to be built in Year 30 of his reign, and Pietro Antoni Solari the Milanese made it in the Year 1491 since the Incarnation of Our Lord. Ch. M. P.' The English clockmaker Christopher Galloway and the Russian architect Bazhen Ogurtsov added the tower's upper storeys in 1625, to take the clock and its carillon. Their instructions were not only to accentuate the main entrance but also to alleviate the lack of proportion between the cathedrals in the Kremlin and especially the bell-tower, and the Cathedral of the Virgin of the Intercession on Red Square. The tower's new form was extraordinarily successful, uniting the buildings inside and outside the Kremlin walls in an organic ensemble. A tall, square stage rose above the old defensive platform, and a second, smaller stage above that, with the dials of the clock on its four faces. The faces of the lower, larger stage were covered with ornamental stonework originally: large, ogee-arched niches (for paintings or statues), and a balustrade in the form of an arcade, its columns and arches covered with reliefs and crowned with finials and figures of lions and bears. The stage with the clock-faces supports an octagon with three much-ornamented zones, the last of which with the arches for the carillon is roofed over by a tall tent roof. Galloway and Ogurtsov devised a beautiful and harmonious silhouette for the successive form as each merges into the next. The gradual, pyramidal rise, and the contrast between the blank walls and mass of the lowest section and the abundant ornament and slender verticality of the upper stages create a

highly attractive impression. The rugged old defensive tower was transformed in this way into an elegant, dignified building and began to serve the function of the city's principal clock tower. The upper part caught fire soon after it was completed, and was restored, but the same thing happened again on several occasions during the eighteenth and nineteenth centuries, so the clock had often to be repaired. The double eagle on the tip of the spire was replaced by the Red Star in 1935.

The Frolov tower was renamed Saviour tower in 1658 at the tsar's instigation. The new form it acquired at the beginning of the seventeenth century had a decisive structural and artistic influence on the other towers. With the exception of the St Nicholas tower, ornamental upper stages were constructed on all of them in the second half of the century, all terminating in sharp-pointed, elegant, octagonal, stone tent roofs. The ornamental elements in limestone make a painterly effect. The St Nicholas tower was rebuilt in the Neo-Gothic style in the early nineteenth century.

The Trinity Gate-tower built by Aleviz Fryazin in 1495 (pl. 175) was intended to command the northwest side of the Kremlin, towards the Neglinnaya. There is documentary evidence that it already had a clock by 1585. It was battlemented at the top. In 1685 it too was given several extra storeys with limestone ornamentation, a carillon (destroyed in the fire of 1812) and the tall tent roof, which displays stylistic elements of the Saviour tower in a modified form. Its deep cellars were used as dungeons. The Trinity Gate used to be the entrance to the Patriarch's Courtyard and the tsarina's apartments. The stone bridge of 1516, which led across to the former drawbridge of the Kutafya Watchtower on the other side of the Neglinnaya, survived to the end of the nineteenth century, but was rebuilt in 1901 in its original form. The present height of the tower, to the point of the star, is 262 feet on the side of the Alexander Gardens, and 227 feet on the Kremlin side.

Just as the Kremlin seen from outside harmonizes with the surrounding landscape—the buildings on the hill beside the Moskva dominate the environment far and wide—so, too, the disposition within its walls forms an organic whole. In the fifteenth and sixteenth centuries there were still simple residential quarters beside the numerous cathedrals and palaces, which were characterized by their irregular yet functional construction. The alleys wound about the wooden houses as if at random, creating a complicated, painterly street scene. The centre is still, as it has always been, Cathedral Square, and again, the churches round it are in an asymmetrical grouping. Their domes rise in two massive waves towards the vertical accent of the giant bell-tower 'Ivan the Great'. The scale of this tower set the standard for the development of the whole of the rest of the city, outside the Kremlin as well as in.

Ivan the Great bell-tower in the Kremlin,
1505–08/1532–43/1600/1624

410   Колокольня «Иван Великий» в Кремле

Kolokolnya 'Ivan Veliky' v Kremle

Recording the start of the construction of the new
bell-tower in the Kremlin in 1505, the chronicle
remarks that it is being built on the site of the old
church 'under bells'. The completion of the work is
noted in 1508 and the architect is named at the same
time—Bon Fryazin (Marco Bono). The old bell-
tower church from the time of Ivan Kalita (1329),
dedicated to St John Klimakos (Ivan Lestvichnik),
had its bells hung in the drum of the dome, so may
be regarded as having anticipated the new 'pillar-
church' to a certain extent. In fact the new church
had less in common with the type of church 'under
bells' (as represented by the Church of the Holy
Ghost in the Monastery of the Holy Trinity and
St Sergius) than with the pillar-shaped bell-tower
type (which distinguishes the Monastery of Joseph
of Volokolamsk and is also found in the Monastery
of the Saviour and St Euthymios in Suzdal). The
new bell-tower of 1505–08, called Ivan the Great,
consisted of two octagonal storeys, the upper
a little narrower than the lower, each with an arcaded
bell-chamber. In 1532 work began, under the direction of Petrok Maly (perhaps an Italian), on the
construction of a separate bell-gable of the Novgorod
type against the north wall of the tower, providing
the east side of Cathedral Square with a continuous
façade *(pl. 173)*. The base of the new building consists of four storeys, their fronts decorated with
Italian Renaissance elements, such as the window
surrounds, pilasters and the scallop niches. The
native Russian tradition reasserts itself in the upper
part, with its massive arches for the bells (one, the
Annunciation bell, weighed 15¾ tons) and dome and
tall drum, the base of which is elaborately decorated
with two bands of closely aligned engaged columns,
separated by a projecting cornice and surmounted by
triangular kokoshniki *(pl. 172)*. After Petrok Maly's
departure from Moscow in 1539, the building was
continued by Russian architects and completed in
1543. The third storey contained the Church of the
Ascension, and a monumental stone staircase leading up to it from Cathedral Square was built in 1552.

The bell-tower remained in its original shape for
nearly a hundred years. When Boris Godunov was
crowned tsar in 1600 he ordered 'the dome to be
made higher and gilded'. This order resulted in the
addition of the third octagonal storey and the round
drum—probably under the direction of the fortress
architect Fyodor Kon. The three-line inscription
immediately below the dome emphasizes the building's political significance. 'In accordance with the

will of the Holy Trinity, at the command of the
mighty lord, the Tsar and Great Prince Boris Fyo-
dorovich, Autocrat of all Russia, and of his son, the
orthodox mighty lord, Fyodor Borisovich, Tsarevich
and Prince of all Russia, this church was completed
and gilded in the second year of their reign.' The
accent in the compositional axis of the Kremlin, the
tower was now 266 feet high and gathered the surrounding churches and cathedrals together in a
harmonious ensemble; it had become both the most
impressive vertical feature in the entire city and as it
were the 'highest' symbol of the central political
power in Russia. It was also used as a watchtower,
commanding a view of up to twenty miles over the
surrounding countryside and its gilded dome shone
out to greet the traveller above all the other domes,
when still ten versts (six and a half miles) away, as
Paul of Aleppo vividly describes. Already in the first
half of the sixteenth century it was the last stage in
a chain of signals that involved a number of towers
and tower-churches to the south of Moscow and was
devised to give warning of attack by the Tartars.

The foundations of the tower, constructed of
ashlar-cut blocks of white limestone, take the form of
a blunt pyramid and reach to a depth of more than
33 feet below the ground. The socle, cornices and
other decorative members are also of limestone,
while the walls and vaulted ceilings are of brick. The
walls of the ground floor, where the Church of
St John Klimakos is found, are about 16 feet thick,
those of the floor above 8 feet, and of the top floor,
built in 1600, 3 feet. In order to sustain the whole of
the pillar's great height, interlocking iron bars
were incorporated in the masonry in an original
system. A staircase in the thickness of the wall leads
up to the first floor, where it is succeeded by a spiral
staircase in the south-west wall. From the top floor
an iron spiral staircase in the room leads up to the
drum which has narrow, blind windows. The dome
has an iron framework, covered with sheets of
copper, gilded and secured by screws.

The three octagonal storeys of the bell-tower rise
in separate stages, each narrower than the one
below *(pl. 173)*. Only the transition from the third
octagon to the circular drum is fluid and ornamented
by two tiers of kokoshniki, the lower ogee-shaped,
the upper triangular. The conical tapering of the two
lower stages not only helps to maintain their stability
but also increases the effect of verticality. The three-
fold repetition of the bell-arcades, each smaller than
the one below, and the decrease in size of the architectonic and decorative members the further they
are from the ground serve the same end. The system
of proportions governed by the Golden Section suggests the involvement of western architects, but it
had been known to Russian builders since the
twelfth century.

At present the tower is whitewashed, but Heinrich
Staden, a member of Ivan IV's bodyguard, men-

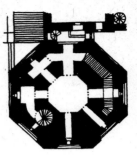

*First floor above ground
level*

tions in his description of Moscow in the second half of the sixteenth century that the building was red, which suggests that the brick fabric was probably not whitewashed then. The exterior articulation is plain, consisting of broad lesenes, shallow niches, ogee mouldings and cornices with round arches, saw-tooth and wedge-shaped ornaments (pl. 172). The walls are pierced in a few places by slit windows. Only the arcades and the bells hanging within them give a direct indication of the interior structure of the building. The majestic proportions and the laconic decoration correspond perfectly to the artistic simplicity and sublime grandeur of this pillar-shaped tower-church, which had a decisive influence on Russian architecture in the sixteenth and seventeenth centuries. The sculptural and structural elements combine to form a harmonious whole.

In 1624 the Russian architect Bazhen Ogurtsov added a new, rectangular bell-tower to the north of the bell-gable, on the instructions of Patriarch Filaret, whose name it bears (pl. 173). It is topped by pyramidal turrets of white stone and a small tent roof, and again has large arched openings for the bells in its upper storey.

The bell-gable and Filaret's extension were blown up by the retreating Napoleonic troops in 1812. The great bell-tower remained standing, although a vertical crack appeared in the drum. They were rebuilt by Y. Gilardi in 1814–15, according to plans by I. V. Yegotov and L. Ruska, essentially in their old form, apart from Neo-Classical elements in the articulation of the walls and Neo-Gothic details in the roof of the Filaret tower.

At present 21 bells hang in the bell-tower and bell-gable. The largest, the Resurrection bell, weighing 4000 pud (63 tons), is in the middle arch. It was cast in the nineteenth century by the bell-founders Savyalov and Russinov. The 'Reut' ('euphonious') bell, also in the bell-gable, weighs 1200 pud (nearly 19 tons) and was made by Andrey Chokhov in 1622. The eighteenth-century bell in the Filaret tower, weighing 798 pud ($12\frac{1}{2}$ tons), was cast by Ivan Motorin. All the bells are decorated with subtle designs in low relief, symbols and inscriptions.

The Chapel of St Nicholas of Gastunsk was set up in the second storey of the bell-gable in 1772, after the demolition of the church of that name on Ivan Square. The demolished church is interesting for having been built by Alovisio Novo in 1516, on the orders of Ivan III, to symbolize the completion of the liberation from the Tartar yoke, and for having been the place where Ivan Fyodorov set up the first printing press in Russia around 1553. Ivan Square is to the east of the bell-tower and was used at one time for the public punishment of offenders.

On a pedestal at the foot of 'Ivan the Great' stands the gigantic 'Tsar Bell' (pl. 173, left), cast by the son of Ivan Motorin in 1733–35. It weighs 12,327 pud (195 tons), is 20 feet high and has a diameter of $21\frac{1}{2}$ feet. In the devastating fire of 1737 it was still in the pit where it was being cast, and the uneven heating and the cooling while the fire was being put out caused numerous cracks in it, to the extent that a large piece (nearly $11\frac{1}{2}$ tons) fell away. It remained in the ground in this broken state and was a popular attraction for the curious. In 1836 it was hauled up under the supervision of O. Montferrant and for a time served as a chapel. Low reliefs on its outer surface depict Tsar Alexey Mikhailovich and Tsarina Anna Ivanovna, as well as five icons and some delicate ornamentation by the sculptors V. Kobelov, P. Galkin, P. Kokhtev and P. Serebryakov who were trained in Italy at the expense of Peter I. There are also two inscriptions giving the history of how the giant bell came to be made.

7, 176–190, 371   Moscow   Москва

Cathedral of the Annunciation in the Kremlin, 1484–89

Благовещенский собор в Кремле

Blagoveshchensky sobor v Kremle

Soon after the completion of the Cathedral of the Assumption, work started on alterations to the Cathedral of the Annunciation, an integral part of the palace structure which served as the Great Prince's domestic chapel. It had fallen into a dilapidated condition under Vasily I, the son of Dmitry Donskoi. The chronicler noted in 1482 that its ceiling vaults had been demolished and a temporary roof built. The work was not resumed in 1483, for unknown reasons. It was not until 1484 that Great Prince Ivan III and Metropolitan Photius entrusted the task to the Pskov architects who had been consulted about the collapse of the Cathedral of the Assumption. They kept the relatively high cellar-storey, built of stone, and erected a brick structure over it which, it seems, may have united stylistic elements of various different schools of early Russian architecture, with early Muscovite and Pskov forms perhaps being the most in evidence. As it gathered the reins of power to itself, so Moscow centralized all the Russian architectural traditions to create from them a new, monumental, all-Russian style, which was taking shape at this very period, at the end of the fifteenth century. The new palace church was finished in 1489.

Today the Annunciation differs considerably from the original church built by those Pskov architects. Even the expert eye cannot distinguish the areas and individual elements of the building that date from different periods. Each of the architects who subsequently worked here showed his skill by incorporating his alterations or additions organically into the existing structure. It was originally a small cube with three domes, three apses and four pillars,

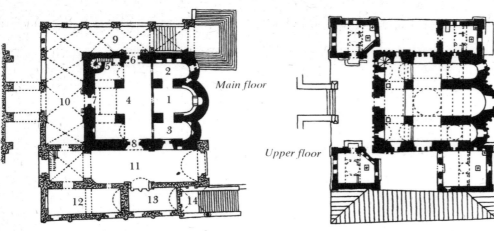

Main floor

Upper floor

1 *Sanctuary* 2 *Prothesis* 3 *Diakonikon* 4 *Nave* 5 *Stairs to the tribune* 6 *North door* 7 *West door* 8 *South door* 9 *North gallery* 10 *West gallery* 11 *Chapel of St Nicholas the Miracle-worker* 12 *Sacristy* 13 *Gallery* 14 *Ivan IV's staircase*

surrounded on three sides by a terrace. Even then it did not look so much like a cube as an upright oblong block, especially from the east side, since it must have been raised by its cellarage to the same level as the Royal Palace *(pl. 178)*. The walls were divided vertically by lesenes into three sections, terminating in ogee gables, and horizontally by a frieze of blind arcading. In other words, the Pskov architects employed the earlier Vladimir and Moscow system of articulation and followed another Moscow pattern (for example the Cathedral of the Saviour in the Andronikov Monastery) in that they arranged two tiers of gables round the main dome to disguise the corbelled arches within *(pl. 177)*. Since the gables do not correspond to the form of the arches, they perform a purely decorative function as kokoshniki *(pl. 176)*. The architects may already have been familiar with this technique from their home-town, because the interior was entirely in accordance with Pskov traditions. One of the three original, limestone doorways has been preserved in the south gallery, the columns flanking it decorated with 'melons' and 'wheatsheaf' capitals *(pl. 371)*. This form of architrave, slicing into the walls at a very extreme angle and finishing in concentric ogee arches, is typical of the entrances to the other fourteenth- and fifteenth-century cathedrals in the Kremlin. The only reminders of Pskov forms among the decorational elements are the triple friezes on the drums, combining round arches, porebrik and begunets.

Inside the building there are four square pillars supporting the corbelled arches which rise successively to form the ceiling *(pls 177, 182)*. The vertical, dynamic movement, which is only hinted at in the exterior appearance of the cathedral, dominates its interior. The confined nature of the space draws the eye upwards. The nave is compressed between the iconostasis, which reaches up to the roof, and the tribune stretching across the west end. The two smaller domes are over the prothesis and the diakonikon. The tribune is reached from below by a spiral staircase let into the thickness of the wall in the

north-west corner of the cathedral, but a passage also led directly from it to the Royal Palace over an archway. This passage was renovated in the middle of the nineteenth century when the Great Kremlin Palace was being built. Thus the tsar was able to go directly from his apartments into the relatively small palace church, the dimensions of which suited the personal requirements of himself and his family: it was used, for instance, for the baptism of the imperial children. It is likely that the female members of the family normally stayed in the tribune. The small vaults in the cellar, preserved from the fourteenth-century cathedral, were used as a treasure-house.

Very soon after the cathedral was completed, possibly in the first decade of the sixteenth century, while Vasily III was still on the throne, the terraces surrounding it were roofed over to form enclosed galleries. It is no longer possible to ascertain whether the fire of 1547 made more alterations necessary: what is certain is that Ivan IV instigated major rebuilding involving substantial alterations, made between 1562 and 1564. The east pair of domes was offset by a new pair, placed on top of the existing roof of the west corners; since these corner cells are wider than the side apses, the new domes have a greater diameter than the older pair, which are also closer to the middle dome. Terraces were constructed on the roofs of the exterior galleries and small domed chapels dedicated to church festivals were erected in each of the four corners. So the three-domed composition was replaced by one with nine domes, and the cathedral's original, classical simplicity transformed into something much more painterly and complex and much more to Ivan IV's taste (as exemplified by the Cathedral of the Virgin of the Intercession on Red Square). The tsar also had the domes and the roof covered with lead and gilded, which resulted in the building's becoming known as the cathedral 'with the Golden Roofs'. Ivan IV's fourth marriage in 1572 was a transgression of church law, for which he was declared excom-

South elevation

formity, since the various models followed by the architects were all related to each other. The ornamental friezes on the drums, and the ceramic balusters running round the tops of the apse walls both derive from similar elements on Pskov churches of the fifteenth century. Influences from Vladimir and Moscow itself can be seen in the blind arcades, with their long supporting columns, resting on consoles and interrupted by 'wheatsheaves'. The panels resembling door panels and caissons that articulate the walls of the four chapels recall the Renaissance façades of the Cathedral of the Archangel Michael. In spite of its small dimensions, the felicitous proportions, the pyramidal composition and the homogeneity of the decorational forms make this cathedral the standard to which all the other buildings in Cathedral Square conform.

In the interior, the later north and west doorways attract as much attention as the original south one. Both possess limestone surrounds, beautifully carved with plant motifs *(pl. 188)*. They are flanked on each side by pairs of columns with Corinthian capitals, the splayed surfaces of the walls on each side of the door are treated as single panels, the cornices are prominent and the moulding on the archivolts takes the form of thick, cylindrical bundles. The entire surround is covered in the Renaissance style with arabesques in low relief, which have been picked out in gold against a blue background. These elegant portals probably replaced the more austere, fifteenth-century doorways during the alterations of 1560, and their decoration is modelled on the doorways in the Faceted Palace and the Cathedral of the Archangel. The columns between the Chapel of St Nicholas and Ivan IV's staircase date from 1572. The nineteenth-century brickwork filling in the arches was cleared away from one of them in 1950. The column has preserved its original form and the striking freshness of the reds and blues in its painting. Ivan IV spared no expense in the decoration of the cathedral. He replaced the old floor with a new one of polished jasper, which was taken from Rostov Cathedral and has survived to the present day. The reddish-brown that is its basic colour complements the colouring of the old wall paintings *(pl. 185)*. It was also Ivan who had the doors with engraved panels brought to the north and west entrances, just as he transferred the Novgorod doors to Alexandrov. In date and style they are akin to the south door of the Cathedral of the Assumption. Their origin is unknown. They date from the fifteenth century, or perhaps the sixteenth, if they were made specially in Moscow. Each pair of doors has ten damascened panels (engraved in gold on a black lacquered ground), with Old and New Testament scenes paired typologically and commented on in lengthy inscriptions. The depiction of the Sibyl and Christ (the Queen of Sheba and Solomon) on the north door *(pl. 189)* unfolds an animated linear play, combining

municate; he therefore ordered a chapel, dedicated to St Nicholas, to be built at the east end of the south gallery, and an exterior staircase in the southeast corner. He heard services read in the chapel, as if he wanted to be simultaneously in and outside the cathedral. No further major alterations were made to the building. In the nineteenth century, the line of Ivan's staircase was continued westwards in a gallery and sacristy, the whole of the south front was homogenized by a unifying arch-motif (windows and blind arches), and the west and north galleries were glazed.

The Cathedral of the Annunciation presents a unified appearance today, in spite of the stylistic traits, originating in different periods, that it has accumulated over the years. The impression it makes is dynamic, harmonious and expressive. The symmetrical positioning of the domes and the corresponding gradation of their heights create a pyramidal silhouette, from whichever side the cathedral is viewed. There is not a single dry or static element in the composition. Seen from the east *(pl. 178)*, the vital upward thrust of the three apses, which look more rounded than they actually are, is accented by the columns in the blind arcade and the conical roofs. The painterly roof form continues the vertical movement by means of the ogee-shaped kokoshniki and the lavishly ornamented domes, while the extensions at the sides seem to provide a structural frame. In spite of the different dates at which the decorative members were added they preserve a certain uni-

representational and ornamental compositional elements.

The interior and galleries of the Annunciation were painted in 1508 by a 'fraternity' from the Joseph of Volokolamsk Monastery under the direction of Feodosy (Theodosius), the son of the famous Dionysius. Feodosy was a zealous supporter of the political and social thinking of the feudal ecclesiastical party of the 'Josephites', a ruthless persecutor of heretics, and an Orthodox dogmatist and traditionalist, and helped to prepare the ground for Ivan IV's theocratic absolutism. He had a close personal relationship with Joseph of Volokolamsk. The treatment of the subjects is contained within the strict ecclesiastical canon, but their presentation is discursive, highly imaginative and allegorical. There is a notable preference for miniature forms, crowd scenes and elaborate architectural backgrounds. The frescos were presumably restored soon after the devastating fire of 1547, which swept through almost the whole of Moscow, and again in the late seventeenth century and in 1771 on the orders of Catharine II. After further retouchings in 1801, 1836 and 1860 the painter V. D. Fartusov was commissioned in 1882 to uncover and restore the originals. The result was a catastrophe for him personally and for Russian art. While cleaning the frescos on the west wall of the gallery he discovered an iconography and a style that were totally unknown hitherto in sixteenth-century Russia, perhaps copies of works by Italian Renaissance artists. Fartusov was accused of suffering from hallucinations, and of having faked the paintings himself. He was dismissed and everything he had found was destroyed. The Safonov studio was then employed, and they overpainted all the frescos in the cathedral in a style that the late nineteenth century conceived to be authentic early Russian. In 1935–36, 1946–47 and 1960–61, the remnants of the original 1508 murals were uncovered by knowledgeable artists from the specialist studios in Palekh and Moscow, under the supervision of I. E. Grabar. Unfortunately the tests made to verify Fartusov's hypothesis produced no results, so thoroughly had all the evidence been cleared away. Nor have all the works painted by Feodosy's team survived. It is however certain that the composition of the paintings on the walls and pillars can be attributed to him and his assistants, although the actual paint dates from a wide variety of different periods. The best-preserved are in the apses, on the pillars, in the tribune, and in the north-west corner beneath the tribune. Peter's Release from Prison and a scene from the life of St Basil the Great are particularly fresh. They were not executed in pure fresco, but finished on dry plaster with egg tempera. There is also a series of murals from the eighteenth and nineteenth centuries.

Within the canonical decorative scheme, three main themes stand out. The traditional scenes associated with the Last Judgment appear on the walls and ceiling of the west part of the cathedral, underneath the tribune. This is a more complete Apocalypse than any of the earlier examples in Russia. Its interest for the early sixteenth century was doubtless linked with the increasing intensity of the conflict between the Josephites, for the state church, and the heretical Judaizers. Abraham's Bosom, earth and sea giving up their dead, Christ as the 'Faithful and True' rider on a white horse (pl. 186), are all compositions employing many figures, small elements and a strong narrative line, in which the subjects from the Revelation are given a contemporary gloss. The second main theme can be termed dynastic. The paintings in question are those on the pillars and walls of the tribune. Since the Kievan ancestry of the Muscovite royal house no longer seemed adequate to their purposes, the legend of their descent from the Byzantine emperors was propagated, to make the 'third Rome' the legitimate successor of the second and therefore of the first also. The aura of divine authority with which Joseph of Volokolamsk invested Vasily III, who had been reigning since 1505, was transferred by Feodosy and his fellow-artists to their portraits of the royal ancestors of the Muscovite dynasty: the Byzantine emperors and empresses (Constantine, Helena, Michael, Theodora, Irene), the Kievan princes (Olga, Vladimir, Boris and Gleb, Yaroslav the Wise and others), Alexander Nevsky and Ivan Kalita (pl. 184), Dmitry Donskoi, his son Vasily and other forebears appear as noble, sublime figures, grouped among their patron saints (such as St George and St Demetrius on the south-west pillar, cf. pl. 185). These alleged 'portraits' of the ancestors of the rulers of Moscow were intended by the artists to illustrate the legend of the transfer of the power of the Basileus by inheritance to the Great Princes—a legend that was invented in the fifteenth century. The third main theme covers the lives of the Virgin and of Christ, and takes up the south and north walls and the apses. The Forty Martyrs of Sebaste on the ceiling in the north-west corner (pl. 187) and the Miracle of the Archangel Michael at Khonae, and other scenes, on the north-west pillar (pl. 182), as well as paintings in the main apse and on the south-west pillar, are attributed to Feodosy himself. The figures have a courtly elegance in their posture and small heads, gestures are measured (even in the martyrdom) and garments flow, and the colouring is light, airy and festive. V. N. Lazarev has pointed out the mastery in the team of artists' treatment of space: the murals add definition to the forms of the domes, vaults, arches, window embrasures, niches and pillars. The tiers of archangels, patriarchs and prophets in medallions in the central drum, the evangelists in the pendentives, the Old Testament characters on the soffits of the arches, the Judgment with the attendant apostles on the cor-

Ornament in the stone floor of the upper chapels

Assumption. The west and north portals were also renovated at this period, in brick in the typical seventeenth-century manner. Two chapels were added to the church in the eighteenth and nineteenth centuries: one (no longer extant) at the west end of the south side, and one at the south end of the west side. Other substantial changes to the fifteenth-century form, such as a new roof, were reversed by the restorations carried out between 1920 and 1960.

Inside the church, four rectangular pillars support the arches on which the drum rests, unusually, without the aid of any intervening pendentives. The walls and ceilings were painted in 1644 by S. Osipov, I. Borisov and other members of the 'Tsarist' School, who had previously worked in the Assumption. The main theme of the frescos was the Glorification of the Virgin. Their scale and arrangement in four zones were determined by the small size of the building. The painting was reminiscent of an Oriental carpet, dominated by deep and light blues, ochre and pale yellows and browns. The old iconostasis of 1627, made up of small icons, was replaced at the end of the nineteenth century by a new one with 'baroque' carving and gilding, and the miniatures of the first and second tiers were exchanged for others of similar dimensions but inferior quality. In 1963 work started on the restoration of the iconostasis as it originally was, reproducing both the icons that Nazari Istomin and his assistants first painted and the sequences in which they were arranged.

193–199, 372   Moscow   Москва

Cathedral of the Archangel Michael in the Kremlin, 1505–08

Architect Alovisio Novo

Архангельский собор в Кремле
Архитектор Алевиз Новый

Arkhangelsky sobor v Kremle
Arkhitektor Aleviz Novyy

In 1505, on the command of Ivan III, Alovisio Novo (Aleviz Fryazin the younger), who had arrived in Moscow from the Crimea the year before, started work on the construction of this, the second-largest cathedral in the Kremlin. The previous church dedicated to the archangel had been built in 1333 by Ivan Kalita to commemorate the end of a famine in Moscow. The new cathedral was finished in 1508, under Great Prince Vasily III, with the collaboration of Russian architects. Like its predecessor it was the burial place of the ruling house, and shelters the remains of a total of fifty-four Great Princes, heirs to the throne and tsars, from Ivan Kalita to Alexey Romanov. The building's present-day appearance is the outcome of numerous alterations and accretions. We have to bear in mind that Alovisio Novo sur-

rounded it on the north, west and south sides with an open arcaded gallery with pillar supports (where guests of honour were accommodated during ceremonies on Cathedral Square), that each round gable was crowned with an ornamental pyramid carved of limestone, that the central dome was approximately the same shape as the other four and that the roof was of black tiles, laid directly on the vaulting. All these characteristics were swept away in the eighteenth century. How the cathedral looked originally can only be judged today from seventeenth-century miniatures, and from the reconstructional plans drawn by Soviet restorers in recent years. The immense difference between the early sixteenth-century cathedral and its present form is obvious at a glance.

Alovisio Novo came from either Milan or Rimini. In Moscow, like his compatriots and fellow-architects, he was faced with the necessity of making allowance for his employer's aesthetic preconceptions, but he found a different solution to the problem. In the actual structure of the cathedral he followed the traditional plan of the domed cruciform church with six pillars, but the composition of the façades was entirely in the style of the northern Italian Renaissance. In spite of the cathedral's sepulchral function the effect of the exterior is bright and festive. The west vestibule makes an important contribution to that effect. Novo had to provide a small, separate chamber for the ladies of the tsar's family, so that they could attend services without coming into contact with the mass of the congregation. The tribune served this purpose in the Annunciation and other churches, but Novo devised a means whereby he avoided the loss of interior space that a tribune involved. He built a two-storey extension at the west end, separated from the body of the church, but with a large arch opening on to the interior from the upper storey. A second floor was built in at a later date. The almost square groundplan was further modified by the construction, immediately to the east of the transept, of a separate, tripartite area for the sanctuary. This resulted in the articulation of the north and south walls in five divisions, instead of the four usual when a church had six pillars, and it is for the same reason that the five domes are placed so far to the east. The two western bays were left without domes, which could have been a positive cause of asymmetry in the building's proportions, had not Novo altogether compensated for it by the articulation of the façades and the differences in the diameters of the drums.

A comparison of the Archangel Michael with the Assumption reveals the extent to which Aristotle Fioravanti's view of the native Russian architectural tradition was coloured by his Renaissance ideas: he replaced asymmetrical compositions by symmetry, he made the internal supports columnar, and he went a long way to impose geometrical regularity

on the architectonic articulation of the cathedral. By contrast, Alovisio Novo's concept of all the basic physical and spatial relationships in the Cathedral of the Archangel was fully in accordance with Russian traditions. But he was more than the architect of the cathedral, he was also its decorator, brilliantly creating its stylistic character by the exclusive use of Renaissance ornamental forms. Medieval and more modern elements are combined in a heterogeneous union. With its six pillars, the cathedral's groundplan allows for a broad nave and transept. The dimensions of the central drum and dome correspond to those of the spacious crossing. In the same way, the dimensions of the smaller domes are governed, for one pair, by the narrowness of the eastern divisions of the walls, corresponding to the confined area of the sanctuary, and for the other pair, by the greater width of the western divisions, resulting from the spacing of the middle and west pairs of pillars: the diameter of the east drums (above the prothesis and diakonikon) is smaller than that of the west pair. It is hard to say now whether this was done deliberately or happened by chance, but, although barely perceptible to the eye, it makes a significant contribution to the overall harmony of the exterior. The discrepancy in the sizes of the drums compensates for their easterly positioning, restoring a balance in favour of the west, which is assisted by the tall, central onion dome, constructed at the beginning of the nineteenth century.

The character of the external appearance is determined by the vertical articulation provided by the pilasters, and by the horizontal division into two zones by a broad entablature running round the building at about half its height. The system is modelled on Tuscan palaces. The north and west fronts giving on to Cathedral Square *(pl. 193)* are the more exposed to view and perhaps treated accordingly. The five divisions of the north front, corresponding to the interior construction, with only the middle three relatively similar in width, are all elaborately decorated. The ornament on the capitals of all the pilasters is basically the same: a symmetrical group of two acanthus leaves and two volutes, but the flowers between the volutes are different on each capital. The blind arches and smaller pilasters, which have the appearance at socle level of being arcading, draw most attention to the lower horizontal zone, while the upper one, whose ornamentation consists of rectangular niches in moulded surrounds, is less assertive. The windows in both zones betray the thickness of the wall. The top of the wall is decorated in typical Renaissance fashion, with a strongly defined, richly differentiated entablature, cutting off the scallops in the round gables, a Venetian motif. The doorway leading into the transept is decorated with delicately carved arabesques. Some remnants of the original gallery survive on the south side, though covered by the buttresses built in 1773 and the Palatka of 1826. The east and west ends, unlike

the longer sides, are divided symmetrically into three, corresponding to the three aisles. From the outside the Archangel Michael appears to have five apses, like the Assumption, but they are even smaller and lower seemingly no more than exedras, an impression strengthened by the prominent scallops in the round gables *(pl. 372)*. At the end of the sixteenth century two domed chapels were added at the east end, one against each of the pairs of outer apses: St John the Baptist to the south and St Uar to the north. The middle division of the west front has a porch in the lower zone, a double window on the floor above and circular windows in the gable, which were later to become one of the typical ornamental elements of the Russian School. The white limestone doorway at the rear of the porch is elaborately and playfully decorated with arabesques, flowers, fabulous beasts, candlesticks and urns, all familiar motifs in north Italian Renaissance ornamentation *(pls 195, 196)*. The painterly effect is enhanced yet further by blue and gold paint. The walls of the porch were covered with frescos depicting the mass baptism in the Dnepr under St Vladimir, probably dating

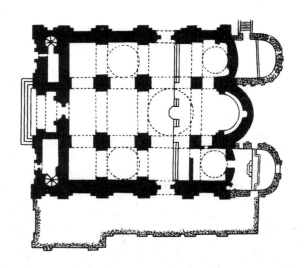

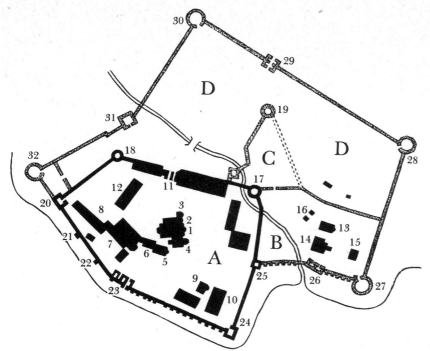

A *Large Monastery of the Assumption* B *Small Monastery of St John* C *Prison* D *New town*
1 *Cathedral of the Assumption* 2 *Church of St Vladimir* 3 *Church of the Epiphany* 4 *Church of St Cyril* 5 *Church of the Archangel Gabriel* 6 *Bell-tower* 7 *Church of the Oblation of the Virgin with refectory* 8 *Kitchens* 9 *Church of St Euthymios* 10 *Large infirmary* 11 *Holy Gate with Gate-church of St John Klimakos* 12 *Archimandrite's house* 13 *Church of St John the Baptist* 14 *Refectory-church of St Sergius of Radonezh* 15 *Small infirmary* 16 *Monuments to St Cyril* 17 *Round Tower* 18 *Faceted Tower* 19 *Prison Tower* 20 Merezhenni Tower* 21 *Kitchen Tower* 22 *Bread Tower* 23 *Water Tower with Tower-church of the Transfiguration* 24 *Svitochny Tower* 25 *Fisherman's house* 26 *Boiler-house Tower* 27 *Kusnechny Tower* 28 *Vologda Tower* 29 *Kazan Tower and gate* 30 *Therapontos (Moscow) Tower* 31 *Scythe Tower* 32 *Belozersky Tower*

appear subordinate to the horizontal articulation: the ornamental frieze of ceramic balusters, tiles, rectangular depressions and a band of saw-tooth, with the addition of a band of begunets on the three apses and on the drum, is unprecedentedly wide. There is no mistaking the influence of the Pskov School here and in other decorational elements *(pls 374, 375),* The walls of the apses are markedly irregular *(pl. 374),* and their roofs were originally the lowest stage in a pyramidal construction. Beneath the new roof there is still a tier of kokoshniki, above the three broad, low gables still visible. They correspond to large corbelled arches inside the cathedral, which took an unusual form, however. The north and south arches were built longer than the west and east ones, so that the west arch is supported not by the pillars but by the side arches *(pl. 376).* The north doorway, with its ogee-shaped archivolts and 'wheatsheaf' capitals to its flanking columns reproduces a decorative formula familiar from fifteenth-century Moscow. Evidently the Rostov architects had served the usual term in Moscow before moving north to develop a new stylistic variant that, in harmony with the milieu, emphasized physical and organic elements.

In spite of numerous later alterations the cathedral has retained its monumental structure. In 1554 the Church of St Vladimir was built alongside the south apse, and the Church of the Epiphany was added against St Vladimir in 1645. There was further replacement of wooden buildings by masonry ones during the course of the sixteenth century: the refectory and Church of the Oblation of the Virgin in 1519, the treasury and the Holy Gate in 1523. The Church of St John Klimakos was constructed over the Holy Gate in 1572. The stylistic influence of the buildings they replaced is discernible in the taut concision of the structures and the rectangular form of the apses. The churches of the Archangel Gabriel and St John the Baptist were built by Vasily III of Moscow in 1531–34 to celebrate the birth of his heir (later Ivan IV). The second half of the century saw the erection of the church over the tomb of St Cyril (forming a north chapel to the cathedral), the Church of St Sergius of Radonezh with its refectory, and the Church of the Transfiguration over the Water Gate, leading out to Lake Siversky. The Monastery of St Cyril was turned into the strongest fortress in northern Russia in the sixteenth and seventeenth centuries. It was one of the most important outposts on the northern frontier of the state. It resisted a prolonged siege by the Lithuanians, Poles and Swedes during the Time of Troubles, 1612 to 1613. A distinction is made between the Old Town of the sixteenth century, and the New Town of the seventeenth. The massive stone walls and towers of the Old Town *(pl. 377)* were built to replace wooden defences in the first quarter of the sixteenth century. Another function devolved on the monastery at the same period: it was made the prison and place of exile for the tsar's political opponents. The Old Town is a rough pentagon and chiefly comprises the original Large Monastery of the Assumption. The extent of its walls was 3,600 feet. The fortifications were in the traditional manner: platforms for defence and the movement of patrols, round towers at the corners, rectangular towers along the sections of wall. As the monastery expanded a substantially larger area had to be enclosed. The wall was extended to include the Small Monastery of St John (centred on the Church of St John the Baptist) at the end of the sixteenth century. Then the massive, frowning walls and towers of the New Town were constructed between 1633 and 1679, the most magnificent defensive system of the seventeenth century, over 4,250 feet in length. It has three tiers of platforms for defence and patrol, up to 23 feet wide. Later on the walls were considerably altered. The line of gunports along the foot was reconstructed as a sequence of interconnecting ground-floor rooms used as casemates, storerooms, cells and living-quarters *(pl. 379).* In spite of their defensive function the upper parts of the towers carry brick and tile ornamentation. The sober, weighty forms of the fortress look particularly imposing from the lake *(pl. 377).*

425

Соловецкий остров Белого моря
Solovetsky Monastery, 16th–17th centuries
Соловецкий монастырь
Solovetsky monastyr

426

A monk called Savvati left the busy, and by now rich, Monastery of St Cyril to find somewhere quieter further north, in order to devote his life to rigid asceticism and meditative contemplation of the divine light (Hesychasmos). In the course of his search he met a hermit called German, and in 1429 they crossed to the largest island of the Solovetsky Archipelago in the White Sea. German did not remain in this isolation after Savvati's death in 1435, but he soon returned there with another Skit monk, Zosima, the son of a Novgorod boyar. Other hermits assembled around the two of them until Zosima was appointed abbot by the archbishop of Novgorod and began to introduce the strict rule of communal life, the Coenobion, probably in the face of opposition from the brothers. The monastery soon acquired considerable economic power, thanks to gifts and the process of feudalization that they inevitably brought in their wake, the proceeds of fishing the well-stocked waters and trapping animals for their skins, and above all the production and sale of salt. In addition it became a centre of the religious opposition to the state church and tsarist rule, as a result of official policy at first, since it was compelled to take in banished rebels, and later as the refuge of the Old Believers, who went to ground there and were only wiped out in a bloody battle by tsarist troops in 1676, after a siege lasting six years. The defence was directed by the Archimandrite Nikonor himself. The monastery benefited in this struggle from having been made one of the strongest fortresses in northern Russia between 1584 and 1594, able to withstand interventionist forays by Swedish forces on several occasions. The Cyclopean walls and towers describe an elongated pentagon around the most important buildings, which are grouped along an axis. They rear up beside the sea like a magnificent, blank cliff-face, offering an untamed, romantic view to anyone approaching by boat.

In the centre stands the Cathedral of the Transfiguration (1558–66), a building remarkable for its combination of the sacred and the military. It is in the form of a huge cube, with smaller cubes at the four top corners, created by four chapels (originally connected by galleries) like watch-towers above the walls, which are thirteen feet thick in places. The roof was originally composed of tiers of kokoshniki (ogee-shaped gables), grouped round a central octagonal tower, tapering towards the top and surmounted by a tent roof or a dome; only a stump of the tower survives. Inside one can see the layers of squinches corresponding to the roof form. The vol-

ume was made up of small cells, divided horizontally by floors as well as vertically. The unrelieved mass of the building represents a complete departure from the architectural canons and in N. I. Brunov's view self-taught builders played a large part in its construction, that is, the monks themselves. The cathedral was obviously built as part of the fortification system.

The monastery includes other sixteenth-century masonry buildings: the Refectory-church of the Assumption (1552–57), and the Church of the Annunciation (1596–1601). The prison, the guard-room and the gate-house with a beautiful frieze of ceramic inlay (1642), all date from the seventeenth century. Many more buildings—the abbot's house, the bell-tower, the archbishop's palace, the churches of St Philip and of the Trinity, monks' cells—date from the eighteenth and nineteenth centuries. A fire destroyed the roofs and domes of all the buildings in 1925. New roofs were built, but it was not possible at the time to observe historical accuracy in their construction. Systematic restoration began in 1962. In drawing up the plans for the work O. D. Savitskaya discovered a large number of unusual architectural features, for instance, the slight inclination of the cathedral's walls, and their construction of rubble and granite blocks weighing up to eight tons.

201-204 Vladimir Владимир

Cathedral of the Assumption in the Convent of the Duchesses, early 16th century
Успенский собор Княгинина монастыря
Uspensky sobor Knyaginina monastyrya

The Convent of the Assumption, for noble ladies, was founded by Maria Shvarnovna, the wife of

Prince Vsevolod III, at the turn of the twelfth century, and thus became known as the Princesses' or Duchesses' Convent. It originally formed a small fortress within the city of Vladimir. A brick cathedral was built in its midst in 1200–01. There is no documentary evidence as to when or why it was destroyed. The exact date of construction of the present cathedral is also unknown. Details of its style and construction, deriving from the Moscow traditions of the fifteenth century, permit a dating at the end of that century or the beginning of the next. Excavations have revealed that it stands on its predecessor's foundations. The plinth is also constructed of the same small bricks as these, behind a cladding of larger bricks. The level at which the new fabric, also all brick, begins is still visible on the apses, where the wall abruptly becomes thinner, accentuated by a moulding (pl. 202). The new cathedral is almost square in plan, and it has one massive dome, three wide aisles, three apses and four pillars. The walls are each divided by pilasters into three wide sections, all with ogee gables. The distinguishing characteristic of the building is its pyramidal roof form, which was reconstructed in 1959–60. A tier of false gables, concealing the corbelled arches within, rises above the gables of the walls, and a third tier decorates the cylindrical pedestal of the drum. This system was used in variant forms from the twelfth century onwards in Russia (the Paraskeva in Chernigov, St Michael in Smolensk, the Paraskeva-Pyatnitsa in Novgorod, the Church of the Saviour in the Andronikov Monastery in Moscow). The cathedral is surrounded on three sides by a gallery with funerary chapels at both east ends, which were altered several times, most recently in 1823.

in 1647–48, on the instructions of Patriarch Joseph, by a team of Moscow painters led by Mark Matveyev. The predominant theme at the east end is the Eucharist, the north and south walls are devoted to the Glorification and the life of the Virgin, and the west wall is filled by a spectacular Last Judgment, composed of a large number of parts. The prophet Daniel's vision of an angel, before whom he falls on his knees, is one of these (pl. 201). The Pantocrator looks down upon the congregation from the dome, not as an inexorable judge but rather as an elegant and wise prince, wearing a turquoise himation and a richly embroidered brown chiton. The background picks up the same shades of ochre as dominate the colouring of the figure (pl. 204). The pillars bear the traditional figures of saintly warriors and princes of Vladimir-Suzdal, including Andrey Bogolyubsky, Vsevolod III, Yury and Konstantin Vsevolodovich. They make no pretensions to individual portraiture, but are all conceived according to the schema illustrated by plate 203: curly hair, large eyes with thin, arched brows, thin noses, sparse, straggling beards. The only distinctions are in the rich embroidered garments and the headdresses. All the figures seem small and delicate and slightly mannered in their expressions and gestures. These murals, painted in a mixed technique, have recently been restored, and present one of the most complete and earliest iconographic programmes of the first half of the seventeenth century, a period which saw the rise of a narrative and instructive style, inspired by a love of both life and colour, which resulted in realistic depiction of everyday things, but also led to comprehensive, allegorical interpretations of matters of faith and hagiographical representation.

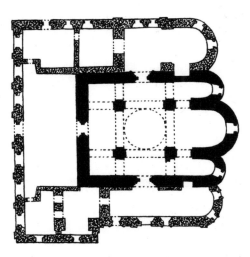

The interior has no tribunes and makes a lofty, spacious and free impression, because the arches supporting the dome are stepped above the level of the barrel vaults over the arms of the central cross. The corner cells are groin-vaulted, and the ribs are supported on the walls by consoles, corresponding to the position of the cruciform pillars. The walls and vaults are almost dissolved by the frescos painted

205-208   Moscow   Москва

Cathedral of the Icon of Our Lady of Smolensk in the New Convent of the Virgin, 1524-25
Собор Смоленской Богоматери
Новодевичьего монастыря
Sobor Smolenskoy Bogomateri Novodevichego monastyrya

The ring of monastery-fortresses around Moscow was added to in the sixteenth century. Vasily III founded the strong and wealthy New Convent of the Virgin (cf. also *pls 286-290*) in 1524 to improve the capital's defensive system to the south and west. The first building to be erected was the Cathedral of the Icon of Our Lady of Smolensk, in celebration of the liberation of the town of Smolensk from Polish-Lithuanian suzerainty and in fulfilment of a vow that Vasily had made in 1514 at the inception of his campaign. The Refectory-church of St Ambrose and the apartments of Tsarina Irina Godunova were built at the end of the sixteenth century, the defensive walls and towers during the course of the sixteenth and seventeenth centuries, and all the conventual buildings at the end of the seventeenth century.

The cathedral belongs to the type of domed cruciform church with six pillars and five domes. As another symbol of growing tsarist authority it was meant to imitate the Cathedral of the Assumption in the Kremlin, but differs from it in certain significant features. The Renaissance system of simple relationships preferred by Fioravanti gives way to the Russian traditions of vertical articulation and vertical flow, that had predominated in the previous stylistic period. As N. I. Brunov has shown, merely to compare the proportionate width and height of a division of the walls of the two buildings demonstrates the difference: with the Assumption the ratio is 2 : 5, here it is 1 : 7. The vertical movement is accentuated by a high cellar-storey. The cathedral is surrounded on three sides by a gallery, with chapels at both its east ends (pls 205, 207). The walls are articulated by broad lesenes with triple capitals and each division has a round gable. The horizontal articulation consists of a band of cylindrical mouldings. There is no blind arcading as such, but an arched moulding surrounds each of the relatively wide windows in the lower zone and extends across the apses, which project a considerable distance. The undulating roof form is also conservative. While the walls are built of brick, the details are of limestone. The ornamentation shows the influence of not only the Assumption but also the Cathedral of the Archangel. The resemblance to the latter becomes particularly clear when the articulation of the two interiors by pillars and pilasters is compared. The interior also expresses an upward movement, with very tall pillars drawing the gaze up into the main dome. The eastern pair of pillars merges with the walls separating the apses. The ceiling consists of barrel vaults. The domes were reconstructed in onion form in the seventeenth century.

The walls and ceilings are completely covered with frescos executed in the 1530s, but entirely overpainted at the end of the sixteenth century, in the reign of Boris Godunov (1598-1605). N. Y. Mneva considers them to be the most interesting monument of the so-called Godunov School, the principal characteristic of which is the effort made to reproduce the austere, sublime style of the end of the fifteenth century and to revert to the religious figures of the time of Dionysius. The compositions follow the Akathist, a hymn that was sung standing, primarily devoted to the praise of the Virgin and the miracles of the icon of Our Lady of Lida. The clarity of construction and the rhythmic movement of the figures recall the frescos in the Monastery of Therapontos, but the liking for architectural backgrounds, realistic details taken from everyday life and iridescent colours illustrates a much more recent trend.

Plate 208 shows some of the figures of saints painted on the pillars, which were intended to be impressive and elegant, but cannot disguise a certain mannered quality. The photograph also includes the massive basin for holy water covered with a relief ornamentation of large tulips and roses, executed in chased copper and painted in bright, strong colours, a masterpiece of craftsmanship, dating from about 1685, probably made under Dutch influence.

The huge, imposing iconostasis also looks as though it was cast or chased in a precious metal, with its five tiers of elaborate, gilded ornamentation, which demands as much attention as the paintings themselves. It is in fact made of wood, carved between 1683 and 1685 by fifty craftsmen from the Imperial Armoury, led by the famous masters Klim Mikhailov, Osip Andreyev and Stepan Zinovev. The eighty-four small columns, carved with vines in high relief, support cornices consisting almost entirely of ogee mouldings. The swelling movement of all the forms, informing even the composite capitals, the cartouches and the tracery, and accentuated by the metallic effect of the heavy gilding, dissolves the traditional two-dimensional style which persists, however, in the arrangement of the icons in strict horizontal lines. The ornamental framework leads a life of its own, governed by a penchant for the three-dimensional and spatial and for the bombastic. The trend marks the inception of the baroque on Russian soil. The iconostasis was commissioned and paid for by the Tsarevna Sophia, who was banished to the New Convent of the Virgin by her half-brother Peter I in 1689, after the failure of the palace revolution. The icons of the feast-day tier, which belong to the Godunov School like the frescos, were transferred from the previous iconostasis

(1598). All the other icons are in the same late seventeenth-century baroque style; some are the work of Simon Ushakov, the principal artist of the 'Tsarist School'.

There are abundant examples of sixteenth and seventeenth-century applied art in the cathedral, embroidery in gold and silk threads, silver crosses, bibles, chalices and woodcarvings. One of the finest specimens of woodcarving is the ciborium made by Kirill Kondratyev in 1653, which stands in the central apse (pl. 206). Its elegant columns, the shafts encircled by band upon band of various kinds of ornamentation, support a tent-like canopy, the kokoshniki on which take a curious disc form, with upright spindles on them.

209, 210, 380   Suzdal   Суздаль

Convent of the Virgin of the Intercession, 16th–18th centuries
Cathedral of the Virgin of the Intercession, c1518
Holy Gate with the Church of the Annunciation, c1518
Refectory-Church of the Conception of the Virgin, 1551
Покровский монастырь
Покровский собор
Святые ворота с церковью Благовещения
Церковь Зачатия Богоматери
Pokrovsky monastyr
Pokrovsky sobor
Svyatye vorota s tserkovyu Blagoveshcheniya
Tserkov Zachatiya Bogomateri

The Convent of the Virgin of the Intercession lies at the north-west end of the city, opposite the Monastery of the Saviour and St Euthymios, on the low-lying right bank of the Kamenka (pl. 209). It was founded in 1364 by Prince Andrey Konstantinovich, the ruler of the state of Suzdal-Nizhegorod which prospered for a time in the fourteenth century. Nothing has survived of the original wooden buildings. Most of the masonry buildings date from the period in the first half of the sixteenth century when Vasily III of Moscow had the intention of banishing his wife Solomoniya to the convent. He wished to divorce her because the marriage was childless. The violent opposition of the nobility and the clergy made him postpone the decision from 1510 onwards, but in 1525 Solomoniya was finally forced to take the veil. Other women of noble birth were banished to the convent on several subsequent occasions.

It was Vasily III who ordered the construction of the stone walls (the surviving sections are to be ascribed to the seventeenth and eighteenth centuries), the stone Cathedral of the Virgin of the Intercession, that replaced the wooden one c1518, and the Holy Gate with the Church of the Annunciation. The Refectory-church of the Conception of the Virgin dates from 1551, and the bell-tower with a church inside it from the seventeenth century.

The cathedral stands at the centre of the monastery complex (pl. 380). It is square in plan and has four pillars, three massive apses, a cuboid structure above a high socle, a gallery surrounding it on three sides, and three domes. The large middle dome rests on a cylindrical pedestal; the two smaller domes are over the prothesis and diakonikon and grow almost organically out of the gables on the east front. The asymmetrical composition with the three domes placed well to the east of centre derived from Moscow influences (cf. the original form of the Annunciation) and, like the more common five-dome composition, constituted a symbol of the central authority of the tsar. An effect of sublimity and austerity is achieved by the mass of the overall appearance and the sparing application of ornament. Pilasters divide the walls into three sections, terminating in ogee gables, and the ogee form is echoed by the arcades of the galleries. The horizontal articulation of the nucleus of the building is by means of the traditional frieze of blind arcades. The cornice of the plinth recurs as an articulating element on the apses. The apses and domes are encircled at the base of their roofs by a frieze of saw-tooth and ceramic balusters. The socle contains the vault where many of the noblewomen banished to the convent in the sixteenth, seventeenth and eighteenth centuries were buried (members of the boyar families of the Nagi, Shuisky and Gorbati, as well as the Tsarina Solomoniya).

An open, arcaded passage was built out from the south-west corner of the cathedral in the eighteenth century, to connect it with the massive octagonal bell-tower and church. The two lower storeys, which also served as a mausoleum, with narrow demishafts on the broad corner lesenes and arched windows, are dated 1518 by N. N. Voronin, while he ascribes the tent-shaped upper part, with the little church and the bell-chamber, to the seventeenth century. The stairs suggest fairly clearly that the structure belonged to the type of tent-roof church 'under bells' from the very start.

The Church of the Conception of the Virgin, of 1551, is attached to a refectory, square in plan and with a single pillar (pl. 209). The actual dining-room was in the upper storey, approached by an external staircase, and the lower storey contained the storerooms and kitchens. This large main building was adjoined by the small, rectangular church on the east side and slightly to the south, and by the nuns' cells on the west side. In the second half of the sixteenth century a clock-tower was built at the refectory's south-west corner, which has a curious formal composition, apparently influenced by wooden architecture: the high square base supports, not the usual octagon, but two irregular hexagons, one above the other.

The cornice of the refectory is decorated with a brick ornament of narrow rhomboids, which is familiar from a number of Polish buildings. It is possible that Vasily III's second wife, Yelena Glinskaya, sent to Poland or Lithuania for architects.

The Holy Gate with the Church of the Annunciation (*pl. 210*) of 1518 is in the south wall, and is the principal entrance to the convent. Compared to the majestic cathedral it makes a graceful, welcoming impression. The ground floor contains two arched passages, a lofty one to the east for carts and carriages, and a low one to the west for people on foot. The staircase is in the wall between them. The little church in the centre of the upper storey is surrounded on the south, west and north sides by a narrow gallery with open arcades, with small chapels at both east ends. The form of the roof follows the three ogee gables on each of the walls and is surmounted by a dome resting on a pedestal decorated with more gables. The kokoshniki and domes on the two chapels give the building as a whole an asymmetrical silhouette. The apses are indicated only faintly both inside and out. The brick decoration of the south front of the Holy Gate is typical of the period. The square shirinki indentations, the friezes, the cylindrical shafts and mouldings and bands of porebrik completely cover it in an apparently arbitrary arrangement which is both painterly and yet subject to the logic of the structural articulation. This kind of ornamentation resembles elaborate woodcarving and it is believed to have influenced the decorational style, first of Moscow, and then of the whole of Russia, during the seventeenth century.

211   Rostov.   Ростов

Cathedral of the Assumption, early 16th century
Bell-gable, 1682-87
Успенский собор
Звонница
Uspensky sobor
Zvonnitsa

The exact date at which the existing cathedral was built cannot be ascertained, but details of the style and construction indicate that it was near the beginning of the sixteenth century. Archaeological investigations by N. N. Voronin between 1954 and 1956 established the presence in the foundations of fragments of masonry surviving from both the two earlier churches on the site, that of 1161-62 built by Andrey Bogolyubsky, and that of 1213-31 built by Prince Constantine of Rostov. There is justification for the assumption that the twelfth and thirteenth-century cathedrals had almost exactly the

same groundplan as the present one, but for being a little shorter. As now, they had six pillars and three apses. It appears that they resembled churches of Vladimir-Suzdal of the twelfth and early thirteenth centuries, but there are few tangible remains of them: the fragments of masonry mentioned above, some arched tombs, the graves of St Leonti and St Ignatius in the south apse, and two animal masks in bronze, with rings in the jaws, which were the

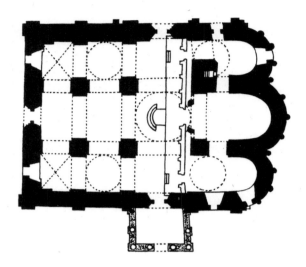

handles on the west doors. The excavations further uncovered fragments of flooring, made up of coloured majolica tiles, and the consoles of the columns of the kind of blind arcading that usually decorated the exterior of such buildings. A block of stone with a relief carving found embedded in the masonry also belongs to the earlier period. There is an account in one of the chronicles of the collapse of the roof of the second cathedral during the fire in 1408, and of its rebuilding in 1411, but there is no mention of the building's later history.

The next documentary information does not crop up until the seventeenth century. The episcopal chronicle of Rostov records that the cathedral was the citizens' last stronghold in the struggle against the interventionist Poles in 1609. The same source reports that it was robbed of its valuables, but there is no mention of any serious damage. That the cathedral remained unharmed is further borne out by the fact that it was there that Tsar Michael Romanov met the townspeople on his journey from Kostroma to Moscow in 1613. The manuscript sources record the decoration of the cathedral walls in 1659, 1670 and 1671. The only structural change they mention is the building of the north and south vestibules.

On the basis of this evidence, B. Eding and S. Bezsonov date the construction of the present-day cathedral in the years between 1509 and 1533. N. N. Voronin, however, dates it at the end of the sixteenth century, after 1587, when the episcopal see of Rostov was elevated to a metropolitanate.

The roof and windows have been reconstructed in their original forms, as established by the researches of V. S. Banige, and the nineteenth-century vestibules to the north and west have been demolished, so the cathedral now appears in its sixteenth-century shape. The dignity and calm of its broad mass, its monumental construction, the harmonious proportions of all the individual parts, and not least the ornamentation, all make a deep impression. Pilaster-like lesenes with horizontal mouldings divide the west wall into three vertical sections, the north and south into four each. There are three relatively low apses at the east end. Each division of the wall ends in an ogee gable, and these gables lend the roof an agreeable, undulating outline, surmounted by the five imposing domes. Circular and rectangular string courses at several levels give the walls a clear horizontal articulation, with the appearance of actually marking the divisions between floors. The tall plinth on which the building stands also carries prominent mouldings, emphasizing the horizontal. At each intersection by a string course the lesenes suffer a decrease in width and thickness, and the intervening sections of wall are also changed, to give the surface of the building a massive substantiality. The decisive factor is the relative height of each section: the first and the third zones (from the bottom) exercise a contracted force, the second and fourth an expanding force. The second zone, containing the lower row of windows, is taken into the third dimension by the frames. The third zone is filled by a blind arcade of ogee arches let into the thickness of the wall, with all the shafts decorated by two 'melons'. A penchant for geometry dominates the whole system of articulation. It is possible to discern, in spite of the thick coat of whitewash, that the plinth, the lesenes, the string courses and other details are of limestone, while the walls themselves are of brick.

The architect was undoubtedly influenced by the Cathedral of the Assumption in the Moscow Kremlin: he repeats its imposing five-dome composition and the proportional relationship of the area and the height are the same. The growing tsarist centralizing power was anxious to erect symbols of its power in the provinces as well as in the capital, in accordance with the schema produced by its own architectural school. N. I. Brunov thinks it is even possible that one of the Italian architects was in charge of the project, but at the same time he draws attention to the decisive part played by Muscovite builders. The treatment of the wall surfaces—the sectional articulation, the intersection of the lesenes by the string courses rather than vice versa—recalls the Cathedral of the Archangel. The wheatsheaf capitals on the blind arcading also demonstrate an inspiration originating with the Kremlin cathedrals. On the other hand, the upper row of windows are not inserted in the blind arcade in Rostov, as they are in the Moscow Assumption, but follow the Vladimir tradition in occupying a fourth zone above. The south and north fronts are altogether more reminiscent of the Cathedral of the Assumption in Vladi-

mir than the one in Moscow, because of the varying widths of their vertical divisions. The south porch, with its pairs of arches supported by pillars and pendant girki, dates from the seventeenth century, and is the work of the architects employed by the Metropolitan Jonas Sysoyevich. The three apses are articulated by means of demi-shafts with simple bases but no capitals, and horizontal cylindrical mouldings that seem to mark different storeys. At the top of the apse walls there are shallow niches, which evoke associations with Novgorod buildings of the fourteenth to fifteenth centuries. The embrasure of the west doorway is lined with columns with wheat-sheaf capitals and rings on the shafts in the style of 'melons' (dynki). The building does not appear to have been painted until 1671, when it received an undercoat of chalk and lime wash and a polychrome decoration, remnants of which still gleam like jewels today.

The interior resembles that of the Moscow Cathedral of the Archangel. Its height and additive constuction are astonishing. The breadth of the middle aisle and the transept accentuates the central cross. There are pilasters to correspond to the four cruciform pillars that stand to the west of the crossing. The form of the east pair of pillars is governed by functional requirements. The crossing under the main dome is well lit, not least because its supporting arches start at a higher level. It is on record that the Yaroslav artists Sevastyan Dmitriyev and Josef Vladimirov began painting the frescos in 1659, continued them in 1669 with Vasily and Konstantin Ananin, Ivan and Fyodor Karpov, Dmitry Grigoryev, Gury Nikitin from Kostroma, Sila Savin, Vasily Kuzmin and other artists, and started to renovate them in 1670-71, after large sections of them had been damaged by fire. The frescos have not, however, survived. They are assumed to have been totally destroyed in the course of the 'renovation' of the cathedral in 1779 and a second painting in oils in 1843.

V. G. Bryusova's research in the 1950s brought to light a fragment of a fresco on the wall behind the iconostasis (at the level of the third tier), which proved to be part of a Wedding at Cana. A torso of St Stephen (unfortunately without the head) was discovered on the north side of the north-east pillar. Bryusova ascribes these fragments, the figures of Christ Emmanuel and the angel on the Triumph Arch, and the exquisitely beautiful decorations in the so-called Palatka to the sixteenth century (c1589). The cleaning of an area of well over two square yards on the east side of the north-east pillar uncovered a well-preserved fresco painting of Metropolitan Epiphanius of Cyprus, which is ascribed to the series of 1659.

The carved, gilded iconostasis and the icons of its top tier date from 1730-40, after the previous iconostasis had been destroyed by fire. According to the report of the Rostov city administration, it was only possible to save some of the icons from the bottom tier; of those, the icons of the Saviour (1649), of the apostles Peter and Paul and of the Tsarevich Peter Ordinsky have survived to the present day. The carving of the iconostasis with its columns and cartouches is in the swelling forms of the Russian Baroque style.

Like every cathedral of the subject principalities and metropolitan sees, the Rostov Assumption contains the tombs of secular and ecclesiastical princes, the most noteworthy among them Metropolitan Jonas Sysoyevich, who built the kremlin in Rostov.

The bells are housed in two adjacent structures built between 1682 and 1687. The four-storeyed gable with three arches, standing on a north-south axis, was built first, and then the tower with one arch holding the largest bell. The white walls, articulated by lesenes and string courses create a monumental impression. The decoration borrows heavily from the articulation of the façades of the cathedral. While the walls of the ground floor are interrupted only by doors and an archway, the two floors above are pierced by narrow window slits to permit daylight to enter the interiors. The stairs leading up to the bell-platform are in the thickness of the wall, and tiny windows giving on to them indicate their course on the façade. The wide arches in which the bells are hung are covered by a roof that follows the line of their gables. A small dome on a circular drum surmounts each of the arches. Examples of this type of bell-gable are found in sixteenth and seventeenth-century architecture in Novgorod, Kostroma (Ipatyev Monastery) and Suzdal. The actual model for it is likely to have been the Ivan the Great bell-tower in Moscow. Metropolitan Jonas ordered thirteen bells, four of which have incised inscriptions referring to their Rostov origin. The largest bell, with the name of Sysoy, weighs 2000 Pud (32 tons) and was cast in 1681 by Fyodor Terentyev; the Poliyeleiny bell of 1000 Pud (16 tons) was cast in 1683 by Philip Andreyev and his son Kyprian; the 500 Pud (8 tons) 'Swan' was also cast by Andreyev, in 1682; and the 'Wether' bell, of 80 Pud (a little over 1 ton), was cast by Yemelyan Danilov in 1684. The Golodar bell, weighing 144 Pud (2 ¼ tons), was cast in 1807 from old bells that had been melted down, the 'Beauty', weighing 30 Pud (9.6 cwt), and the 'Goat', 20 Pud (6.4 cwt), were cast together in the seventeenth century. The remaining six bells have no names, and there is no precise information about them. The thirteen bells can play a number of tunes, which were heard on specific occasions. One tune, used for ceremonials, was called Jonas, another Georgiyev. A third, called Kolyazin, was based on a dance rhythm. Rostov Museum has a collection of tuning-forks, made at the end of the last century, which reproduce exactly the pitches of the bells.

381   Moscow   Москва

Cathedral of the Nativity of the Virgin in the Convent of the Nativity of the Virgin, 1501-05
Рождественский собор Рождественского монастыря
Rozhdestvensky sobor Rozhdestvenskogo monastyrya

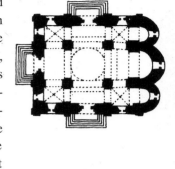

The Convent of the Nativity of the Virgin was founded in 1386, and its little principal church was built in 1501-05 to replace a wooden one. It belongs to the type of domed cruciform church with four pillars, corbelled arches and one dome. Its design follows on from the Moscow traditions of the fifteenth century, and its roof is in the form of three tiers of ogee gables, with the gables in each tier being set across the angles of the adjacent tier. The drum and dome rise on the pedestal that these gables surround at a height way above the gable ends of the transept and middle aisle. The corner cells of the building are still lower, and roofed with groin vaults, which are rare in Moscow. The cornices separating the arches of the gables from the wall below are a new feature.

Although the building retains the traditional structure of monastic cathedrals, with its four pillars, three aisles and apses, and the surrounding galleries, it also exhibits forms which are due to the influence of the new churches rising in the suburbs, with a special emphasis falling on the decorational elements. The taste of the middle-class inhabitants of the suburbs (the Posad) reveals itself in the concentric framing of the gables, like archivolts, and in the delicately moulded and ornamented cornices. The ogee moulding of the cornices is also reminiscent of the exactly contemporary Cathedral of the

Archangel, a sign that Alovisio Novo looked for ideas for his Renaissance façades among the work of his Russian colleagues. The pyramidal form of the roof, composed of corbelled arches inside and blind gables outside, had been current since the fourteenth century; in this conventual cathedral it finally comes into its own, relieving the cuboid form of its four-square mass and giving it a dynamic vitality.

The interior decoration has not survived. Numerous alterations and additions were made to the cathedral between the seventeenth and the nineteenth centuries. It was restored in its original form in 1970–71, according to plans drawn up by I. V. Ilenko.

382 Volokolamsk Волоколамск

Cathedral of the Nativity of the Virgin in the Vozmishchensky Monastery, early 16th century
Рождественский собор Возмищенского монастыря
Rozhdestvensky sobor Vozmishcenskogo monastyrya

Volokolamsk was the oldest of the Russian towns on the frontier between the Muscovite principality and the territory of Novgorod. It was founded on the Lama river in the twelfth century, at the point where ships had to be conveyed a short distance across land, in order to leave the system of waterways that descended towards Moscow and enter the system that descended to Novgorod and Pskov. The final phase of the town's political and economic importance fell in the years 1462-1513, the reign of Prince Boris Volotsky, the brother of Ivan III of Moscow.

The Vozmishchensky Monastery is one of several that were built on the hills surrounding Volokolamsk. It was dissolved in the eighteenth century. The Cathedral of the Nativity of the Virgin, dating from the early sixteenth century, is the only one of its masonry buildings to survive. In the eighteenth century its roof was rebuilt with four faces, two domes and drums flanking the main dome were demolished, and a vestibule was added at the west end. The cathedral is a domed cruciform church with four pillars and three apses, but like many other monastic cathedrals of that period and type it originally had three domes. The walls are divided into the traditional three vertical sections, with round gables. The lesenes have capital-like mouldings that support the arches of the gables. The horizontal division consists of a narrow ogee moulding about halfway up the walls, which continues as a cornice on the apses. In the wider middle division of each wall, directly under the arch of the gable, there is a circular niche, made to hold an icon. This motif, which derives from the roundels on the west front of the Moscow Cathedral of the Archangel, is also found on many other churches and cathedrals. Master Povelik of Tver, who built

the refectory in 1545, may also have been responsible for the cathedral. As well as the archaic forms originating in the architecture of Novgorod, it offers evidence of influences emanating from the cathedrals of the Moscow Kremlin. Master Povelik's name is on a plaque in the wall of the monastery's gate-church.

383 Mozhaisk Можайск

Cathedral of the Nativity of the Virgin in the Luzhetsky Monastery, 1520
Рождественский собор Лужецкого монастыря
Rozhdestvensky sobor Luzhetskogo monastyrya

The Cathedral of the Nativity of the Virgin in the Luzhetsky Monastery founded by Therapontos at the end of the fourteenth century is a typical structure of the early sixteenth century. It is one of the churches that are closely associated with the concept of the central power of Moscow and reflect the architectural influence of the Kremlin cathedrals. It was built at the time of the final victory of the Josephites and of the monasteries who supported the tsar and were eager to enrich themselves, over the Skit monks and the hermitages whose inmates fixed their thoughts on their individual sanctity and turned their backs on all possessions. The monasteries propagated the ideology of 'Moscow, the third Rome', the identity of the interests of Church and State. This cathedral is the godchild of several of the Kremlin cathedrals. It was built with five domes (like the Assumption and the Archangel), façades divided into three, four supports, a cellar-storey and exterior galleries (like the Annunciation; the galleries are to be reconstructed), columns rather than pillars inside (like the Assumption), and a cornice of round arches and cylindrical mouldings across the foot of the arches of the gables (like the Archangel). There is a large number of other ornamental elements reminiscent of the Archangel, but they have a different significance, more akin to the medieval concept of monumentality: their purpose is to show off the strength and thickness of the walls they adorn. The tall, narrow windows in the fronts and the niches in the three apses serve the same end, and at the same time, in combination with the cellar-storey, the massive pilasters, the doorway flanked by columns and the cylindrical pedestals beneath the drums, they accentuate the vertical lines of the building.

The ensemble of the Luzhetsky Monastery has a painterly silhouette that fits superbly well into the surrounding countryside. In addition to the cathedral, the following buildings survive: the refectory (1577, with seventeenth and nineteenth-century alterations), the gate-church (1673), the monks' cells (1681-92) and the stone perimeter wall and towers (1681-92).

Cathedral of the Holy Trinity in the Monastery of
the Assumption, 1513

Троицкий собор Успенского
монастыря

Troitsky sobor Uspenskogo monastyrya

In the early sixteenth century the settlement of
Alexandrov, to the north-east of Moscow, the precursor of the modern town of the same name, belonged to the Great Prince of Moscow, Vasily III.
He built the Church of the Virgin of the Intercession,
later consecrated as the Cathedral of the Holy
Trinity, in 1513. In 1565 Ivan IV moved his household from Moscow to Alexandrov, which gave rise
to the construction of a large number of masonry
buildings between that date and 1582, including
the tent-roof bell-tower *(pl. 392),* the large refectory
and the Church of the Assumption. In the seventeenth century the palace was converted into the
Monastery of the Assumption.

The Cathedral of the Holy Trinity has a cellar,
exterior galleries, four pillars, three apses, one dome
and a roof form that follows the silhouette of the
round gables. It symbolized the Prince of Moscow's
concept of rule and was therefore based on models
in the capital. In spite of rather heavy proportions
it exhibits a realistic and popular freshness and
vigour appropriate to the growth of the state. Its
ornamentation is reminiscent of the cathedrals in
the Moscow Kremlin. Pilasters divide the walls into
equal sections, all the round gables are the same
size and shape, the capitals are delicately ornamented and the gables moulded like archivolts, a
triple frieze adorns the drum and the apses and div-
ides the walls into two horizontal zones: all these
details reflect the decorational principles applied by
the Italian architects who worked in the Moscow
Kremlin in the early sixteenth century. In addition
to those elements, the cathedral acquired a polychrome decoration which became typical of a large
number of ecclesiastical buildings. The bricks were
painted black, white, yellow and gold and decorated
with crosses, and according to Peter Jerlesunda's
account of his travels even the domes were painted
with alternate stripes of black and gold.

The south door, dating from 1336 and brought
from Novgorod by order of Ivan IV, is one of the
sights of the cathedral. It is covered with illustrated
panels, engraved by the same damascening technique which we have already met in Suzdal, but the
hatching of the surfaces makes a more painterly
effect. Beside the west doorway there is a plaque
with a picture of the Old Testament Trinity, be-
lived to have been made in Tver in the middle of
the fourteenth century. The iconostasis has some
valuable icons of the fifteenth to seventeenth centuries.

Cathedral of St Sophia, 1568-70

Софийский собор

Sofysky sobor

The brick cathedral built by order of Ivan IV imitates the structural layout of the Moscow Assumption. Ivan also commanded its dedication to divine
wisdom, like the chief cathedrals of Constantinople
and Kiev, as an assertion of the tsar's ideological inheritance and the divine approval of his rule. In the
second half of the sixteenth century, after the construction of the first monumental tent-roof churches
in stone and brick, such a reversion to the formal
models of the Kremlin cathedrals, entailing as it did
an act of homage to tsarist Moscow and its autocrat,
necessarily implied a conscious conservatism. As
with every retrogressive stylistic development, the
original vigour of the model is weakened in the
successors.

St Sophia is of the type of domed cruciform church
with three aisles, three apses, six pillars and five
domes. The façades are divided vertically by pilasters: the north and south fronts into four sections,
the west into three. The capitals of the pilasters
support the arches of the round gables at the top of
each division of the walls. There is no horizontal
articulation, except insofar as the windows are placed
directly above each other, in horizontal rows, with
the upper row right up in the semi-circles of the
gables. This form of articulation and the absence
of decorative elements give the building a laconic
severity in keeping with north Russian architectural
principles, but the simplification of the clear, majestic
forms of the model results in an integrated, stone
mass. The doorways in the west, north and south
fronts are in the traditional style, the embrasures
lined with columns and the archivolts in ogee form.

A hipped roof was built in the seventeenth and
eighteenth centuries in place of the undulating form
dictated by the round gables, and the onion domes
typical of the seventeenth century were constructed
at the same time. A small vestibule was built outside
the west door in the seventeenth century, and similar
ones at the north and south doors in 1850. The interior is dominated by the massive pillars and is divided
into small spatial cells. There is an impressive carved
and gilded wooden iconostasis, made in 1737-41.
The walls and ceilings were covered with frescos
between 1686 and 1688, painted in the traditional
Yaroslavl style of the seventeenth century, by a team
of thirty artists from Yaroslavl led by Dmitry Plek-
hanov. Soviet restorers replaced the original roof
form and cleaned the frescos in the 1960s.

Nikita Monastery 16th–17th century

Никитский монастырь   *Nikitsky monastyr*

the process. The Russian Primate's fears were well-founded: the tent roof did allow a secular element to penetrate ecclesiastical architecture. It invigorated the means of artistic expression and structural logic, and imparted plasticity and dynamism to formal composition, thereby aggravating the differences between this and the type of one, three or five-domed cathedral, with wavy roof following the outline of its round gables, a schema which by that time was a static conception. The new type, which could be absorbed organically into the surrounding rural or urban landscape, appealed to the taste of the time and was frequently repeated, with plentiful variations.

The French composer, Hector Berlioz, wrote about the church in a letter to Prince Vladimir Odoyevsky: 'Nothing has aroused me to such a pitch of enthusiasm as the monument of early Russian architecture in the village of Kolomenskoye, I have seen very many things, have liked many, and have fallen under the spell of not a few, but this epoch, this very ancient epoch in Russia, which has left its monument in this village, has been the most marvellous thing of all for me. I have seen Strasbourg Cathedral, which was built over a period of many centuries, I have stood outside Milan Cathedral, but apart from their ornamentation I could see nothing in them. But beauty itself stood before me here. Every part of me started to tremble. It was mysterious stillness. It was the beauty of perfect formal harmony. I saw a new kind of architecture. I sensed its upward straining, I stood there for a long time, quite unable to move.'

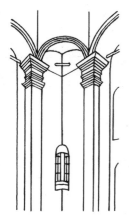

Interior pilasters and segmental vault

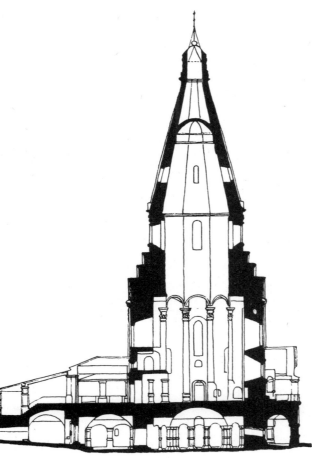

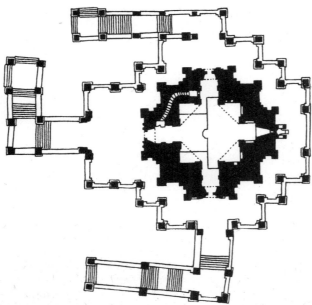

216   Moscow   Москва

Church of St John the Baptist in Dyakovo, 1547
Церковь Иоанна Предтечи в Дьякове
Tserkov Ioanna Predtechi v Dyakove

The church at Dyakovo stands up like a castle keep above the steep bank of the Moskva. Dyakovo is now part of the city of Moscow, but in the sixteenth century it was still a village, bounded on one side by the tsar's summer residence at Kolomenskoye. N. I. Brunov has said that if the term 'Russian Renaissance' has any meaning at all, it applies to this church. While the Church of the Ascension reaches dynamically upwards, the total impression of St John the Baptist is static, integrated, massive, although it does not lack decorational elements. It may have been built to mark the official coronation of Ivan IV and his marriage to Anastasia Romanov in 1547. It is dedicated to the tsar's name-saint. M. A. Ilin, P. N. Maximov and V. V. Kostochkin support a different theory, namely that it was built in 1553–54 as a memorial to Ivan's son, Dmitry, who died after living only a few months.

The groundplan consists of a central octagon, the body of the church, with four octagonal chapels on the diagonal edges. The semi-circular apse on the east side, and the enclosed galleries on the remaining three sides unite these separate cells in an integrated complex, in which the dominating principle is the subordination of relatively independent elements to the central octagon, but without any interpenetration. The construction of this plan is appropriately expressed by the shape of the building that rises on it. The central octagon is given great prominence, while the four chapels are significantly lower and smaller. The bottom stage of the drum of the central octagon is encircled by one tier of semi-circular and one tier of triangular kokoshniki, while the corresponding stage on the chapel roofs carries three tiers of progressively diminishing triangular kokoshniki, like zigzag friezes. The four low towers press very closely around the central one, and all five are surmounted by heavy-looking, shallow domes. The central drum takes an unusual form, being surrounded by eight massive semi-cylinders, one on each of the corners of the short second octagonal stage. Like the machicolation inside the tower they may derive from French fortress architecture. It is even possible that originally each supported an individual cupola. The galleries and the apse take up the whole of the space between the four small towers, thereby concealing the bottom part of the central octagon. The positioning of the chapels on the diagonals of the groundplan is an innovation in Russian architecture, and anticipates the subsequent, far more complicated composition of the Cathedral of the Virgin of the Intercession (St Basil the Blessed) in Moscow.

The decoration of the exterior makes use of all the elements current in Moscow architecture in the late fifteenth and early sixteenth centuries, exhibiting an extraordinary prodigality and formal variety. The massive walls are articulated with shallow niches with moulded surrounds and caissons, the cornices are made up of narrow fillets, there are both semi-circular and triangular gables, enclosing round windows, the blind arcading on the gallery walls has straight-sided triangular arches, the windows are narrow slits, and there is a triangular bell-gable on the west front. The interior is completely divided up into individual cells. In the central octagon, the transition from the walls to the drum is effected by the use of machicolation, a feature of French castle architecture.

Original though St John the Baptist is, it is possible to point to the separate precursors of many of its features: the system of corbelled arches to lift the dome pyramidally, the composition with one dome towering up from a cluster of four lower domes, the pillar-shaped churches 'under bells' (cf. the Church of the Holy Spirit in the Monastery of the Trinity and St Sergius), the vertical construction in a series of graduated stages (cf. the Ivan the Great bell-tower in the Kremlin), the Renaissance style of decoration taken from the Cathedral of the Archangel, and decorative details deriving from the Pskov style (e. g. the alternation of triangular and semi-circular gables). Some of the formal elements make the relationship to wooden architecture very clear: among other things, the central octagon, the octagonal drums of the diagonal towers, the triangular gables.

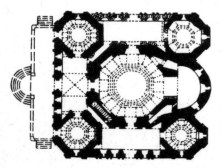

Like the Ascension in Kolomenskoye, St John the Baptist represents a defeat for the traditional canon. On the one hand the building techniques of the various provincial schools can be seen here to be merging to form a unified all-Russian style. On the other hand, totally new elements were revolutionising the old domed cruciform plan, and moulding a national style, closely associated with the political ambitions and growing power of the tsars, but also an expression of the ideals and dreams of the common people.

217 Moscow Москва

Church of St George 'under bells' in Kolomenskoye, early 16th century

Церковь-колокольня Георгия в Коломенском

Tserkov-kolokolnya Georgiya v Kolomenskom

There was a large number of very fine buildings in the old summer palace of the tsars at Kolomenskoye. Its position high up on the banks of the Moskva gave it both scenic charm and strategic importance. It experienced an Indian summer in the seventeenth century under Alexey Mikhailovich (1645–76), who built the large wooden palace (demolished in the eighteenth century), the Falcon tower, the Church of the Icon of Our Lady of Kazan, and the outer gate (1672–73; *pl. 217,* right background), the entrance to the palace grounds, which were enclosed by moats and low walls. The passage through the gate leads directly towards the Church of the Ascension. The gate played a leading role in the development of a new type of public masonry building. The low, widespread structure, surmounted by an eight-faced tent roof, the graduation of the storeys and the columnar decoration occur together again in a number of later buildings. The adjoining domestic and residential wings were added at the end of the seventeenth century.

The Church of St George 'under bells' dates from the early sixteenth century, and shows the influence of the pillar-shaped buildings of the period, of which the most important example is the Ivan the Great bell-tower in the Moscow Kremlin. In point of fact it differs somewhat from that particular model in having a circular, not polygonal, groundplan, and its ornamentation recalls Alovisio Novo's Renaissance style. Its low ground floor supports a lofty upper storey, with tall, round-arched openings for the sound of the bells, and the small drum and low dome are topped by another little cupola. The articulation is in the form of broad pilasters supporting an elaborate cornice, on which delicately moulded, semi-circular gables rest. A blind arcade, similar to the one on the Cathedral of the Archangel, runs round the ground floor. The transition to the drum, and again to the cupola, is effected by kokoshniki.

The symmetrical repetition of the ornaments, the simulated Triumphal Arch, and the geometrical regularity of the separate wall surfaces, create an almost classical impression of order. Both decoration and composition compel comparison with the nearby Church of St John the Baptist in Dyakovo.

218–221, 389, 390   Moscow   Москва

Cathedral of the Virgin of the Intercession 'by the Moat' (St Basil the Blessed),
1555–60/1588/17th century
Architects Barma and Posnik
Покровский собор «что на рву» (Василий Блаженный)
Архитекторы Барма и Посник
Pokrovsky sobor 'chto na rvu' (Vasily Blazhennyy)
Arkhitektory Barma i Posnik

With its bizarre, painterly play of forms, St Basil's Cathedral at the south end of Red Square looks like a fantastic creation from the Tales of a Thousand and One Nights. Its actual dedication is to the Virgin of the Intercession, after the feast falling on the day in 1552 (Pokrov: 1 October) when Ivan IV's troops took Kazan, one of the last strongholds of the Golden Horde, and freed the Russian state from the Tartar menace. The birth of the Tsarevich Dmitry also fell on the same day. A wooden church was built before the end of 1552, succeeded by the stone building on the same site, erected between 1555 and 1560. It is essentially a monument and a symbol. Ivan IV deliberately had it built on the chief market place, the economic and political heart of the city, where people thronged from morning to night. Repeating the many domes of the Kremlin, from which it was separated by a moat (no longer there) and the walls, but quite different in appearance, it formed a pendant to the palace in the city, without setting up in opposition to it. As a symbol of the victory over the age-old enemy, it was intended to be a constant reminder to the people of the might and strength of the tsarist state. The central pillar structure is dedicated specifically to the feast of the Virgin of the Intercession, the eight encircling tower-chapels to saints and other feasts celebrated on the days of the most important battles round Kazan. But the cathedral became known popularly by the name of Basil the Blessed (Vasily Blazhennyy), a 'Holy Fool' (Yurodivy) who became famous for his fearless denunciation of the atrocities of Ivan IV. Holy Fools were unusually numerous at that period, and were held in great veneration by the people, because the mask of idiocy surrounded them with a kind of charisma, within which they castigated both the weaknesses and errors of the ruling classes, of whom nobody would otherwise dare to speak in such a way. After Ivan IV's death Basil was canonized and a church dedicated to him built beside the cathedral.

Just as St Sophia in Kiev must be regarded as the proud symbol of the Russian state before the Tartar invasions, the Virgin of the Intercession is the most splendid, stately monument of the age of Ivan IV. It is the outstanding example of the new Russian, national architectural type, an example that was never surpassed by any later expression. It is an embodiment in stone of the idea of theocratic absolutism as the legacy of the Christian empire of Byzantium, which had been made a political reality by the despotic character of Ivan IV and the Josephite theology of Metropolitan Makary. The tsar's triumphal entry into Moscow after the fall of Kazan resembled the 'Bringing in of the Lord', a Byzantine ritual celebrated on Palm Sunday, when the emperor represented the person of Christ. Moscow itself was frequently hailed as the 'City of God' and the 'New Jerusalem', and Ivan played the – liturgical – role of the Saviour. He introduced the feast of the Procession of the Ass in memory of the occasion, which was celebrated annually by the whole population, until Peter I abolished it, and he had the west chapel of the Virgin of the Intercession, which was simultaneously the main entrance, dedicated to the feast of the Entry into Jerusalem. Like the capital city itself, the cathedral was to represent the Heavenly Zion to which the literature of the period devoted so much attention. The two architects, Barma (perhaps a native of Pskov) and Posnik, were originally commissioned, on the advice of Metropolitan Makary, to build a group of 'eight altars dedicated to the holy Testament'. But they laid the foundations of 'nine altars, by divine providence, not because they were so ordered, but through God's wisdom, which was vouchsafed to them when they were measuring out the foundations'. The number is a reference to the heavenly hierarchy. But it is quite clear that the two architects were influenced by Dyakovo in planning a symmetrical group of eight, tower-like chapels around a central pillar structure, not least because it enabled them to subordinate the traditional domed cruciform scheme to the new tent roof. The rhythm of the nine elements, the exploitation of all the architectonic means evolved in the past, produced a complex ensemble with a fairy-tale beauty that, according to legend, moved the tsar to blind the two architects, so that they should never build another, comparable church.

The groundplan resembles an eight-pointed star, the centre a square with its north-west and south-west corners cut across, and a large, trapezoid sanctuary on the east side. Four separate octagonal chambers adjoin the central square on the north, south, east and west sides, forming a cross, in the angles of which, that is on the extended diagonals of the central block, there are four separate chambers, square but for the slanting of the corners adjacent to the centre; so much of these corners has been cut off in the two western cells, indeed, that they are nearer heart-shaped. The dimensions of the central cell, the Church of the Virgin of the Intercession, which appears like a pillar from the outside, determine the arrangement of the eight tower-chapels. The size of the sanctuary pushes the church west of centre, and the three western chapels press much closer to it than the corresponding ones on the east side. If the area of the central cell is squared, a square is produced whose corners coincide with those of the four square or heart-shaped chapels; if this larger square is turned through 45 degrees, its corners settle on the octagonal chapels. An inner and an outer ring of galleries, with interposed support arches, run between these nine cells, giving access to them, and approached by two symmetrically placed exterior staircases at the two west corners. The whole ninepart complex stands on a socle or undercroft, formed by stout pillars and open arches under the exterior galleries, which were originally laid out as terraces.

The nine separate structures give the groundplan of the cathedral a lively, painterly shape. Most of it is built in brick, though the undercroft and some of the mouldings on the upper part of the building are of limestone. The original helmet domes were covered with tin-plated sheet iron. Ornamental details garnered from both ecclesiastical and fortress architecture were applied with prodigal abundance. The basic octagon appears at almost every important part of the complex and even disguises the shape of the central square and the chapels on the diagonals. The often complicated transitions make use of the motif of a semi-circle: from the arcading in the socle to the blind gables of the drums. The liturgical importance of the east-west axis is acknowledged by the displacement of the central tower to the west and by the more ornate decoration of the east Chapel of the Trinity and the west Chapel of the Entry into Jerusalem, which are also larger and higher than the other six.

The central tower-church is in the form of an octagonal pillar, divided horizontally into several zones by various forms of ornamentation (pl. 218). The first zone is encircled by a narrow gallery, with a vaulted roof supported by arches on small octagonal pillars, and terminating in triangular kokoshniki. There follows, somewhat inset, a band of blank niches with triangular tops and shirinki. The second zone has three-quarter shafts at each of the corners of the octagon, rusticated in the Renaissance manner, each of the intervening sections of the wall has three tall, narrow niches, with a window in the middle one, and the top of the zone consists of an overhanging, undercut cornice of shirinki. Above that there rise three tiers of semi-circular blind gables, with pronounced mouldings, each stepped behind the one

below. The lowest tier contains a row of small round windows. The blind gables effect the transition to the pedestal of the tent roof, which recapitulates the unusual form of the groundplan, an eight-pointed star, with its points projecting out beyond the angles of the tower below. The relatively small tent roof, lavishly decorated with gables round its foot, with coloured ceramic inlay on its faces, and with gilded chains on its ribs, supports a miniature octagonal drum and a small cupola.

Each of the four octagonal chapels is individually decorated, though the diversity is subordinated to a rhythmic unity. All their corners are accentuated by lesenes, but they are differently shaped on each chapel. The tall arrow-points, reaching up through the ogee moulding, and the narrow niches or windows within them, that appear on all the faces of the octagons provide a strong unifying motif. The arrow-points were intended to recreate the vertical effect of the tent roof on the chapels, which are all domed. The walls are finished off by a cornice in the form of a band of shirinki, machicolation or saw-tooth. The transition to the octagonal drums is effected by tiers of various forms of blind gables: round arches with moulded archivolts, ogee arches and frontons (repeated on a miniature scale round the bases of the domes). The actual top of the drums is marked by a cornice with circular, rhomboid or square indented panels. Each dome is a different size, has an individual silhouette and its own ornamental covering.

The four square or heart-shaped chapels are lower, but like the octagons they rise through a series of horizontal zones. Their walls are concealed by the galleries, and only their drums and domes can be seen from outside, resting on tall octagonal pedestals. Each pedestal is decorated with three tiers of blind gables, those in the middle tier being set across the angles of the upper and lower tiers, and diminishing in size from bottom to top. The principal articulation of the drums is by means of narrow windows. Again, each of the domes differs in size and casing. The narrow exterior gallery encircling the entire complex on the roof of the undercroft was originally an open terrace. Its balustrade supports an arcade of low pillars, strongly moulded, trapezoid capitals and round arches, which together create the effect of a broad ornamental frieze.

The basic structure of St Basil's Cathedral has remained essentially unchanged, but numerous additions and decorative modifications were made to it during the second half of the sixteenth century and throughout the seventeenth century. In 1588 a chapel was built on the north-east corner in honour of Basil the Blessed, and the little Church of St John was built alongside that in 1672. These two detracted but little from the clarity and symmetry of the original ensemble. A bell-gable with three arches was built at the south-east corner of the cathedral at the end of the sixteenth century, but remodelled at the end

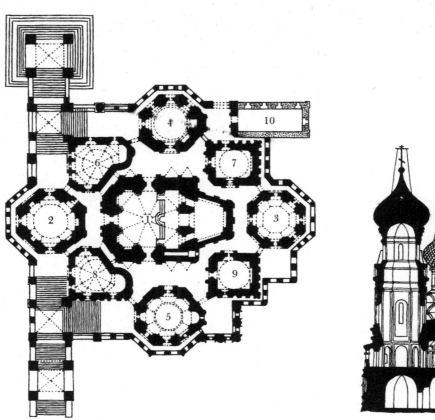

1 *Central tower-church of the Virgin of the Intercession* 2 *West tower-chapel of the Entry into Jerusalem* 3 *East tower-chapel of the Trinity* 4 *North tower-chapel of SS Cyprian and Justinian* 5 *South tower-chapel of St Nicholas the Great* 6 *North-west tower-chapel of St Gregory the Armenian* 7 *North-east tower-chapel of the Three Patriarchs* 8 *South-west tower-chapel of St Varlaam Khutynsky* 9 *South-east tower-chapel of St Alexander Svirskovo* 10 *Chapel of St Basil the Blessed*

of the seventeenth in the style of the time: a cuboid base is surmounted by an octagonal arcade, supporting a sharp-pointed tent roof with small windows in its faces, and a cupola at the apex *(pl. 218)*. The seventeenth century also saw the construction of the onion domes, each with its different pattern of ribs or facets, the arcading and roofing of the exterior galleries and staircases, the tent roofs over the staircase landings, and the entrance porches at the northwest and south-west corners, with squat pillars with caisson mouldings on their faces and girki on the low arches *(pls 218, 390)*.

The outstanding alteration to the cathedral's appearance as a result of the renovation during the 1670s and 1680s was the painting of it in bright colours, creating an effect of rich folk embroidery. It took the original ornamentation into account, but had an independent life of its own, further invigorated by the addition of 560 tiles in 1682, which decorated the façades and bore inscriptions about the various stages of the building. The inscriptions refer, among other things, to the contemporary murals. The investigation of the cathedral carried out in the 1950s established that the fronts and domes were not originally as brilliant in their colouring as they are today. The building was plainer and more austere. The seventeenth-century architects were working in the spirit of their age when they brightened the exhilarating polychrome decoration and created the slight degree of asymmetry which, rather than de-

stroying the composition, lends it even greater tension and dynamism.

The interior of the cathedral consists, not of a single, unified area, but of small, confined, gloomy cells, the individual churches, 'piazzette' and corridors, like catacombs or the dark rooms of ordinary houses. They symbolize the buildings, squares and streets of the Holy City. As is the case with other tower-like buildings, the interior has nothing like the formal variety and grandeur of the exterior. The central church is an exception to that rule. Its interior measurements are $26\frac{1}{4}$ x $26\frac{1}{4}$ feet, with a height of 150 feet. Although it is basically a square ground-plan, the cutting of the west corners and the tripartite arcade in front of the apse provide a foundation for the octagon that develops from the first stage of the tower. The transition is effected by squinches. The eight angles are accentuated by demi-shafts, and by lesenes at a higher level. The separate zones are distinguished by elaborate cornices. The numerous windows provide more and more light towards the top, so that it is possible to see all the way to the apex of the tent *(pl. 221)*. There are no figure paintings in the church, only some very restrained ornaments and commemorative inscriptions (at the base of the upper octagon and of the tent roof). The interior walls of the chapels, originally simply whitewashed, are articulated with pilasters, arches, niches, machicolation and cornices, often performing structural functions, and in varying combination in each separate chapel. The masonry of some domical vaults, in the form of ribbed stars that appear to revolve, shows an astonishing virtuosity. The decoration of the eight chapels and the church was redone in 1847. The sixteenth-century iconostases were all replaced by new ones in a baroque style, which incorporated just a few of the old icons; the other have not survived.

Systematic restoration of the cathedral began in 1921, at first under the direction of D. P. Sukhov, and under that of N. N. Sobolev since the war. The masonry filling in the arches of the galleries has been removed, the profile of the socle, the exterior paintwork and the unusual ornamentation of the portals have been restored (pl. 389). The restorers also discovered that the roof of the gallery between the west chapel and the central church was not a vault, but flat, built of brick and strengthened with iron braces. Elements have been found in the brick decoration reminiscent of timber construction, such as the vertical friezes of circular protrusions, suggesting the ends of the logs at a corner of a wooden building (pl. 219). Fragments of ornamental murals of the second half of the seventeenth century have been discovered in the galleries. They have been cleaned, and supplemented by new paintings in the same style, restoring the artistic atmosphere of the seventeenth century to these areas (pls 219, 220).

St Basil's Cathedral represents the creative fulfilment of the new ideas that were born in the Ascension at Kolomenskoye and in St John the Baptist at Dyakovo. It lacks their formal clarity, it is true, and it does not make the impression of a fortress as they do, but it shares with them the transference of forms from wooden architecture, and the use of Renaissance ornamentation as it had been assimilated in Moscow. Persian, Indian and other Oriental motifs have also been established. But its artistic originality is a result not least of the tension between the appearance, painterly, fantastic, almost bewildering, and the construction, complex, but with every element carefully considered and thoroughly thought out. The geometrical and symmetrical rules governing it are made particularly clear if one looks frontally at the east or west front. The decoration is concentrated on the upper part, thereby accentuating the relentless, pyramidal upward thrust. It soars into the realm of the limitless. Just as the corridors inside draw the visitor irresistibly from one cell into the next, so the exterior appearance enforces motion. Walking round the cathedral brings a new, enchanting, different prospect at every angle. The views from the north and south, particularly, present the impression of organic, asymmetrical growth. The total composition of the cathedral was never reproduced in any subsequent buildings, but its individual elements played an important role in architecture, especially in the remainder of the sixteenth century and the beginning of the seventeenth.

391 Ostrov Остров

Church of the Transfiguration, 16th century
Преображенская церковь
Preobrazhenskaya tserkov

The church rises like a fortress on the steep banks of the Moskva, not far from Moscow. It must have been built by order of a member of the tsar's family, since the village of Ostrov belonged to the crown in the sixteenth and seventeenth centuries, but the exact date of construction is not known. Some scholars date it in the first half of the sixteenth century, others nearer the end. The fact that it was reconsecrated in 1646, in the presence of Tsar Alexey Mikhailovich, indicates that there was a later rebuilding. The hypothesis that the entire upper part of the building, with the tent roof, and the apses and two side chapels all date from the seventeenth century is not, however, acceptable to all scholars. There is no doubt that the basic structure is a product of Moscow architecture of the sixteenth century, a godchild of the Ascension at Kolomenskoye, but unique in itself. Like the Ascension, it has a cruciform groundplan and the central cross is transformed into an octagonal tower (the transition being concealed by blind gables), on which the tent roof rests. But there are some significant differences as well. In the Transfiguration the vertical lines are balanced by semi-circular forms, the mass of the walls is softened, the building is rooted more firmly in the ground (there is no undercroft). Two chapels adjoin the semi-circular apse symmetrically at the north-east and south-east corners, and a wide gallery leading from one to the other embraces the body of the church. The walls of the central, cruciform nucleus terminate in an ogee moulding, and the next horizontal stage consists of four tiers of ogee gables, stacked pyramidally. A low octagon grows out of the gables, ending in a frieze of round arches, above which three tiers of kokoshniki (the top tier in the form of angular frontons)

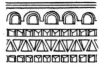

Frieze of round arches with niches, and a triple band of begunets

Window, with rose embrasure

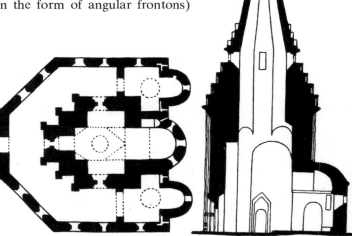

form the base of the blank, octagonal tent roof. A frieze of triangular ornamental gables separates the roof from the drum and dome. The profiles of the protruding stepped lesenes at the corners of the cruciform nucleus, the vigorous frieze of round arches which start by slanting up from the surface of the wall, and the tall niches formed in the angles emphasize the plasticity of the composition. These features are reminiscent of Western European Romanesque, and they are unusual in Russian architecture of this period. It is possible that architects from Pskov had a hand in the work, the more likely since the central apse and the apses and drums of the two side chapels are decorated with the characteristic triple band of rectangular and triangular indentations. The ceiling of each of the relatively low chapels is vaulted without pillars by means of the Pskov system of corbelled arches, giving rise to a pyramid of three tiers of blind gables on the outside, surmounted by a slender drum and dome. Additional decoration is provided by slender lesenes and beautiful round windows with embrasures moulded in a rose form.

The church is built of Moscow limestone, which is an unusual material for the first half of the sixteenth century. The only bricks in evidence are large ones in the interior, whereas normally at that period brick was used exclusively for construction, and limestone only for ornaments. The use of stone enabled the carving of the begunets frieze in the Pskov manner.

In the nineteenth century the arches of the gallery were glazed and a Neo-Gothic bell-tower was added to the west.

392   Alexandrov   Александров

Church of the Crucifixion 'under bells' in the Monastery of the Assumption, second half of the 16th century

Церковь-колокольня Распятия Успенского монастыря

Tserkov-kolokolnya Raspyatiya Uspenskogo monastyrya

When Ivan IV moved his household to Alexandrov in 1565, he built, in addition to the Cathedral of the Trinity (cf. *pl. 384*), this bell-tower church. It occupies a dominating position. It was considerably altered in the seventeenth century, when the palace was being converted into a monastery. In composition it resembles the central tower-church of St Basil's Cathedral. It rises in three stages on an octagonal groundplan: a lofty ground floor with powerful pillars at the corners, each with three attached lesenes, creating a blind arcade of deep niches out of the intervening walls; a low gallery with a real arcade, with broad piers decorated by engaged demi-shafts; and a bell-chamber supporting a tent roof, drum and cupola, and with a pedestal covered by three diminishing tiers of semi-circular moulded kokoshniki. The vehemence of the tower's upward thrust is almost without equal, and receives an especially strong impulse from the prominent openings, which, however, do nothing to relieve its mass.

393   Pereslavl-Zalessky

Переславль-Залесский

Church of Peter the Metropolitan, 1585

Церковь Петра митрополита

Tserkov Petra mitropolita

The political ideas embodied in the tent-roof construction, the tsarism that was both popular and progressive at that period, influenced a large number of new buildings in the provinces, which did not, however, equal their Moscow models in quality. In the brick Church of Peter the Metropolitan, the influence of the traditional domed cruciform plan results in a simplification of the type, modelled on the Ascension at Kolomenskoye, that was prevalent in the sixteenth and early seventeenth centuries.

The groundplan is cruciform, with proportionately large arms to the cross. The body of the church is thus of imposing dimensions with a relatively small octagon, surmounted by an octagonal tent roof, an octagonal drum and a dome. The whole structure is raised by a cellar-storey and is surrounded by galleries on three sides. The walls are divided into three by pilasters and terminate in round gables, in the traditional manner. The horizontal articulation imitates that of the Cathedral of the Archangel in Moscow. The architect used the same frieze (including saw-tooth and cylindrical moulding) to mark the level of the roof of the cellar round the plinth, as he did to separate the walls from the panels within the round gables. Lesenes emphasize the corners of the low octagon. The transition to the tent roof is effected by a tier of blind gables which looks like a frieze of round arches. The ceilings of the nave and transepts are in the form of two corbelled arches over each arm, leaving clear the square of the crossing, which has the octagon immediately over it.

The bell-tower to the west of the church was built in the nineteenth century. The sixteenth-century decoration of the interior has not survived.

394   Krasnoye, near Kostroma

Красное близ Костромы

Church of the Epiphany, 1592

Церковь Богоявления   *Tserkov Bogoyavleniya*

In the sixteenth century the village of Krasnoye near Kostroma belonged to the Godunov family, and it was clearly they who directed the church to be built. The groundplan resembles the Transfiguration at Ostrov. The cruciform body of the church is almost square. There are three apses to the east, flanked symmetrically by north and south chapels. A two-storeyed gallery with low arcading surrounds the nucleus on three sides, running from one chapel to the other. The transition from cube to octagon on the pillar-shaped central block employs simple, pitched gables, but each of the three diminishing tiers of the octagon is encircled by semi-circular gables and a pronounced ogee moulding. The base of the tall tent roof is surrounded by triangular blind gables, each of which contains six smaller kokoshniki. The side chapels have wavy roofs, following the silhouette of their ornamental round gables and small domes.

This church in the northern region of the Muscovite state is built on a smaller scale than the great tent-roof churches of the mid-sixteenth century in central Russia. But its decoration already hints at the transition to the painterly Moscow style of the seventeenth century. The building was restored in its original form in 1963 by the Kostroma restoration workshop. The seventeenth-century bell-tower adjoining the west front belongs to an unusual type. Its base consists of four pillars, connected by arches at two levels and supporting a vault. The bell-chamber above is octagonal and is surmounted by a tent roof with two rows of apertures for the sound to pass through.

222, 223 Yaroslavl Ярославль

Cathedral of the Transfiguration in the Monastery of the Saviour, 1506–16/1564

Преображенский собор Спасского монастыря
Preobrazhensky sobor Spasskogo monastyrya

The monastery was founded at the end of the twelfth century, and its first masonry cathedral was built between 1216 and 1224. The present building was built between 1506 and 1516 by architects sent to Yaroslavl from Moscow by Great Prince Vasily III. The town, standing at the point where the road from the White Sea to Moscow crosses another major trade route, the Volga, was no longer the capital of an independent principality in the sixteenth century, but belonged to the newly formed, united Russian state. The cathedral therefore shows the influence of the Moscow School.

The structure belongs to the type of the domed cruciform church with three aisles, four pillars and three apses *(pl. 222)*. It stands over a cellar-storey.

There were adjoining galleries on the north, west and south sides, built over open arches, which were partly rebuilt in 1564 and again in the seventeenth century. The walls are divided vertically by lesenes, in the usual way, and finish in round gables. The cathedral has three domes, the largest over the crossing and smaller ones over the prothesis and dia-

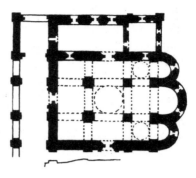

konikon. The building is in fact typical of the early Moscow School up to this period, but there are features of the decoration which establish a connection with the exactly contemporary Cathedral of the Archangel. The groundplan and the actual structure both make use of a uniform module of measurement (the Russian sazhen). The laying and bonding of the brick masonry is of an unusually high standard. The round gables are separated from the walls by a broad cornice, that also runs across the lesenes, giving them capitals. There are round windows in the gables of the north, west and south fronts. The wide architraves of the doorways were decorated in relief. The four pillars inside the church have unusually formed capitals. They stand squarely in the centre of the room, giving the body of the church relatively great importance vis-a-vis the sanctuary.

The interior of the cathedral and the Holy Gate were painted with frescos during 1563–64 by Larion Leontyev and Tretyak and Fyodor Nikitin from Moscow, and by Afanassi and Demont Isidorov of Yaroslavl. Their subject matter was taken from the bible and the ecumenical councils. The scenes from the Old Testament, Christ's parables and the Last Judgment are particularly fine. They were overpainted in 1781–82 and 1814, and restoration is cur-

370	371	372
373		374
375	376	377
		378
379		380

370 *Zvenigorod, Cathedral of the Assumption 'in the little town', 1399: view from the north-east* **371** *Moscow, Kremlin, Cathedral of the Annunciation, 1484–89: doorway from the south gallery to the interior* **372** *Moscow, Kremlin, Cathedral of the Archangel, 1505–08: view from the north-east* **373** *Kirillov, Therapontos Monastery, Cathedral of the Nativity of the Virgin, late 15th century: view from the north-east; bell-tower, 18th century*
[*374–377, 379*] *Kirillov, Monastery of St Cyril Belozersk, founded c. 1397* **374** *View from the east of the Cathedral of the Assumption, 1497 (left); Church of St Vladimir, 1554; and Church of the Epiphany, 1645*
[*375, 376*] *Cathedral of the Assumption, 1497* **375** *View from the south-west* **376** *View through the nave, showing iconostasis and vaulting* **377** *View of the fortifications from Lake Siversk: (from left to right) Church of the Archangel Gabriel, 1531–34; bell-tower, 1757–61; refectory and Church of the Presentation of the Virgin, 1519; Cathedral of the Assumption, 1497; Church of St Cyril, 16th century; Church of St Euthymios, 1653; Svitochny tower, 16th century*
379 *Three-storeyed ramparts and Belozersk tower in the New Town, 1633–79* **378** *Solovetsky Island in the White Sea, Solovetsky Monastery: general view, showing the Cathedral of the Transfiguration, 1558–66, fortifications and towers, 1584–94*
380 *Suzdal, Convent of the Virgin of the Intercession, Cathedral of the Virgin of the Intercession, c. 1518: view from the east, showing bridge and bell-tower, 16th–18th centuries*

rently in progress. The compositions are simple and well-balanced, the frontal figures combine monumentality with elegance, the chromatic range of silvery, nacreous shades seems restrained, muted and monochrome. The exquisitely delineated head of the God of Sabaoth *(pl. 223)* on the concha of the diakonikon is fascinating. The subject is one that artists did not dare to depict before the end of the fourteenth century. Yahweh, the Lord of Hosts, is represented as the Ancient of Days, after Daniel 7 : 9: 'whose garment was white as snow, and the hair of his head like the pure wool.' Great and terrible, he appears as the angry and just judge of all law-breakers and sinners. The colours underline the gloomy ascetic atmosphere, which may also be a reflection of the ruthless conflict waged in the early sixteenth century between the adherents of Nils Sorsky and those of Joseph of Volokolamsk. The popular movement of the hermits, with their rejection of earthly wealth and temporal power and their demands for religious and social tolerance, which the monasteries of northern Russia supported, was violently opposed by the movement representing the official Church and the interests of the tsarist autocracy. What gave the Josephites, the party of loyalty to the authorities and thus the party of nationalism, the victory was the fact that the heretics pursued by the government, often for their utopian social ideas, found refuge in the monasteries beyond the Volga, where the monks were opposed to the use of force for any reason, whereupon those monasteries were charged with heresy and promptly dissolved. The angry God of the Old Testament—on whom might he pass judgment?

The icons from the iconostasis are now kept in the local museum. They date from the beginning of the sixteenth century and are typical of the flourishing Yaroslavl School of that period.

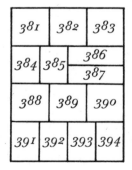

224, 225   Zagorsk   Загорск

Cathedral of the Assumption in the Monastery of the Trinity and St Sergius, 1559–85
Успенский собор Троице-Сергиевой Лавры
Uspensky sobor Troitse-Sergiyevoy Lavry

The Monastery of the Trinity, forty-five miles north of Moscow, originally founded by St Sergius as a hermitage, was gradually transformed by its close patriotic allegiance to the ruling house during the 'Gathering of the Russian Land' into a bulwark of theocracy. The Skit monks had to yield to the strictly regimented activities of a coenobitic community, whose economic wealth and political influence were continually growing as a consequence of the process of feudalization. The aggressive social and nationalist policies of Josephism overwhelmed the ideology of the individualist hermit life preached by Nil Sorsky. By the middle of the sixteenth century the monastery employed some 100,000 peasants on its estates, and had become a thriving centre of trade, education and art.

The fortress of God became a fortress of the tsar, with defences built between 1540 and 1550 on the model of the Kremlin in Moscow. The new stone walls took the position of the older buildings into account *(pls 9, 156-158)* and enclosed a wider area, roughly trapezoid in form, which conditioned all later building projects *(pl. 224)*. The length of the sections of the wall was dictated by the range of the artillery positioned on the towers, of which there were nine in all. During the Time of Troubles, from 1608 to 1610, the monastery successfully withstood a sixteen-month-long siege by a Polish army of 30,000 men, led by the second False Dmitry. The walls reached their present thickness and height around the middle of the seventeenth century, and the towers were altered and many new buildings were erected in the course of the same century (cf. *pls 279–285* and the plan on p. 492).

The largest church in the monastery, the Cathedral of the Assumption, was built by order of Ivan IV, and took a relatively long period to finish (1559-85). It was modelled on its namesake in the Moscow Kremlin and was intended to express the power and wealth of the monastery and of its royal patron. Being built of brick and then whitewashed, its appearance is actually even more imposing than that of its prototype. The monumental square block seems to have been designed to dominate all the surrounding buildings, but the defective ordering of the ensemble detracts considerably from the impression made by its sheer size. This applies above all to the

449

381 *Moscow, Convent of the Nativity of the Virgin, Cathedral of the Nativity of the Virgin, 1501–05: view of pyramidal blind gables and dome with drum*   **382** *Volokolamsk, Vosmishchensky Monastery, Cathedral of the Nativity of the Virgin, early 16th century: view from the north-east*   **383** *Mozhaisk, Luzhetsky Convent, Cathedral of the Nativity of the Virgin, 1520: south front*   **384** *Alexandrov, Cathedral of the Holy Trinity, 1513: view from the north-east*   **385** *Vologda, Cathedral of St Sophia, 1568–70: view from the south-east*   **386** *Pereslavl-Zalessky, Nikita Monastery, 16th–17th centuries: general view*   **387** *Moscow, Nikita Church on Shviva Hill beyond the Yausa, 1595/1684 to 85: view from the south-west*   **388** *Suzdal, Monastery of the Saviour and St Euthymios, refectory Church of the Assumption, c. 1525: view from the north-east* [**389, 390**] *Moscow, Cathedral of the Virgin of the Intercession 'by the Moat' ('St Basil the Blessed'), 1555–60/1588/17th century*   **389** *West portal leading to the main church*   **390** *North front*   **391** *Ostrov, Church of the Transfiguration, 16th century: view from the east*   **392** *Alexandrov, Monastery of the Assumption, Church of the Crucifixion 'under bells' second half of the 16th century: north front*   **393** *Pereslavl-Zalessky, Church of Peter the Metropolitan, 1585: view from the north-west* **394** *Krasnye, near Kostroma, Church of the Epiphany, 1592: view from the north-east*

south front, which is more elaborately decorated than the other fronts, as it is on the Moscow Assumption. But whereas in the Kremlin this front is exposed to view from across the expanse of the square that is the normal approach to the cathedral, in the monastery the south front can be seen only from close to, and does not have to stand up to prolonged scrutiny. In winter there is an impressive view of the east end for a person entering the monastery and looking across at the cathedral through the bare branches of the trees, but even in these circumstances there is no vantage point at an adequate distance. The composition of the front closely follows that of the Moscow Assumption, with five apses articulated by demishafts and windows, and projections, in the form of broad corner pilasters, to conceal the apses from the

merge with the walls between the apses, whose depth corresponds to a whole division of the outside wall. The walls and ceilings were covered with frescos in 1684 by a team of thirty-five artists assembled from Yaroslavl and various monasteries, led by Dmitry and Vasily Grigoryev. They were overpainted in the eighteenth and nineteenth centuries and restored in 1940. The elegant solemnity of the interior is enhanced by an immense carved wooden iconostasis, dating from the end of the seventeenth century. A vault containing the remains of Tsar Boris Godunov (died 1605) and his family lies outside the west doorway, on the left.

The roof was restored to its original form, following the silhouette of the round gables, in 1960 under the direction of V. I. Baldin.

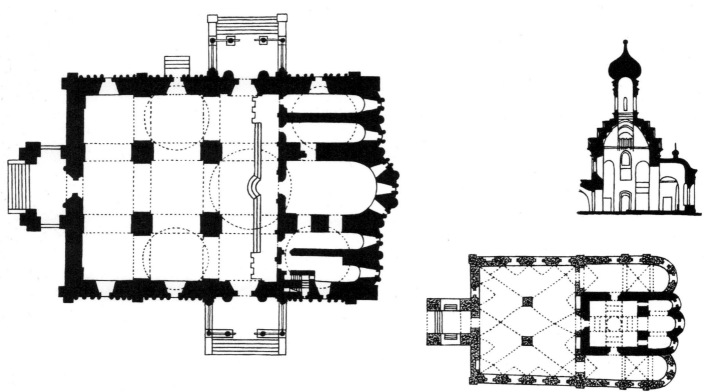

north and south sides. The effect of this articulation, which is more abundant than that of the other fronts, is enhanced by the five majestic domes, the gilding on which reflects the clear winter sunlight.

The groundplan of the Zagorsk Assumption is a rectangle with three aisles, six pillars and five apses, which provide ample room for chapels. The façades are subdivided by prominent pilasters, with plain capitals supporting wide semi-circular gables, the outline of which is followed by the roof. The north and south fronts have four divisions, the west three, and each division is pierced by two narrow windows, one above the other. The horizontal articulation is provided by a wide blind arcade, with small arches resting on demi-shafts adorned with dynki. The windows of the apses are framed by columns in the same form.

The sublimity, unity and height of the interior take one's breath away. The monumentality of the portals is repeated in the pillars, which are basically square in section, but indented at the corners. The east pair

11, 226   Moscow   Москва

Old Cathedral of the Icon of the Virgin of the Don in the Monastery of the Don, 1591–93/1678–79
Старый собор Донской Богоматери Донского монастыря
Stary sobor Donskoy Bogomateri Donskogo monastyrya

The Monastery of the Don was founded in 1591, during the period when Boris Godunov was acting as regent for Tsar Fyodor, on the site where Russian forces had successfully resisted a sudden attack by the Crim-Tartars in 1571. It is part of the southern section of the ring of monastery-fortresses around Moscow. Its construction may well have been under the supervision of the office set up by Ivan IV in 1583–84 to control masonry architecture, which introduced standard sizes for bricks and blocks of stone, among other measures. The fortifications of the present day actually date from a century after

Our Lord and of Isidore the Miracle-worker was built under Nikander, Bishop of Rostov; the church is the work of the Great Prince's architect, Master Andrey Maly.' The tsar's architect chose to use the pillarless type of suburban parish church, prevalent in the cities and towns of Muscovy at the beginning of the sixteenth century. The kreshchaty vault, a Russian invention not found in any other country, is a typical feature of the type. It is made up of four barrel vaults with a shallow arc over the arms of the central cross, giving the highest part of the outside walls, and intersecting the domical vault, a quarter of which roofs each corner. A drum with windows and a small dome rise above the crossing. The kreshchaty vault makes the virtually square groundplan and the trefoil roof obligatory.

Andrey Maly's version of the system is strictly consistent to type. The rectangular surfaces of the four exterior walls are divided into three by lesenes. The middle division is wider than the other two and terminates in an ogee gable, while the two outer divisions end in quadrant arcs. The trefoil silhouette of each façade creates the impression over the building as a whole of vertical thrust, which is emphasized by the drum. The articulation of the north and south walls is symmetrical, the axis of symmetry underlined by the portal with its simple surround and the window above it. Three apses adjoin the nucleus on the east side, which, though low, are fairly extensive in area. At the west end there is a vestibule, apparently built in the seventeenth century. The delicate frieze marking off the trefoil gables from the basic cube is another typical element. The design, intended to meet the practical requirements of city-dwellers, met with great approval from the people of Rostov, on account of its unassuming elegance and comfortable dignity. It was taken as a model by the seventeenth-century builders of the Church of the Saviour in the kremlin and the churches in the Abraham and Belogostitsky monasteries.

The Church of the Blessed Isidore contains some murals of the 1760s and 1770s which are unusually interesting. Although they retain the traditional schemata, especially in the scenes from the life of Christ, they have strong elements of baroque style, with its love of movement and of elaborate architectural backgrounds. The paintings in the lower zone depict the life of the Blessed Isidore, a Holy Fool who may have been German in origin and died in 1474. The representations in them of buildings of Rostov, especially of the Cathedral of the Assumption and the Church of the Resurrection without their late eighteenth and nineteenth-century additions, are extraordinarily valuable.

The carved wooden Royal Door must surely be regarded as a work of the highest artistic significance. It, and a 'gilded Deesis' (i. e. the iconostasis), were made by order of Ivan IV on the occasion of his last visit to Rostov in 1572. Both are in the Rostov Museum at present.

The Period of Transition: the Seventeenth Century

395   Uglich   Углич

Church of the Assumption in the Alexey Monastery, 1628

Успенская церковь Алексеевского монастыря

Uspenskaya tserkov Alekseyevskogo monastyrya

The monastery was founded in 1371 by one of the most influential figures in Moscow's political life, Metropolitan Alexey, but did not have any masonry buildings before the early sixteenth century. It was razed to the ground during the Intervention of Poland and Lithuania at the beginning of the seventeenth century. The Church of the Assumption built after the Time of Troubles, in 1628, received the popular nickname of 'the Miraculous'. Its most interesting feature is the row of three tent roofs on the north-south axis, harbingers, in a structure that otherwise abides by the traditions of the sixteenth century, of the transition to the seventeenth.

The church consists of three structural parts: the refectory, with a single, central pillar, the actual church and the apses. All three rest on a basement-storey which, beneath the church and apses, rests in its turn on a cellar. For this reason there was originally an exterior staircase on the north side, which no longer survives. The best angle at which to see the church is from the south-east, where the three apses and the three tent roofs above them, pressed close together on octagonal bases, can all be seen together. The broad, rectangular block formed by the fusion of the three square pedestals on which the octagons stand is articulated vertically by pilasters, each division terminating in an ogee gable, two under each of the small tent roofs, three under the larger one. The walls of the low octagons are blank and finish with a simple brick cornice. The middle octagon also has a row of small ornamental gables. The tent roofs are of stone, with broad, ornamental bands on the eight edges, and bear small drums and domes covered with small rhomboids of sheet iron, and a cross on each. The total composition is distinguished by its harmony and balance, its structural logic and its restrained decoration. The blind arcade on the apses has alternately long and short columns, which present an appearance reminiscent of the twin arches with

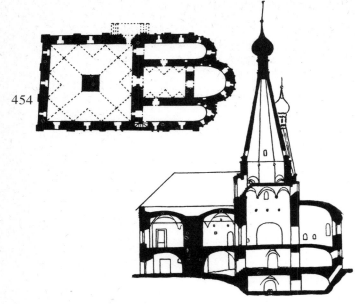

pendant girki which were a popular motif in the seventeenth century. The elongated proportions intensify the overall impression of verticality. The simple, shallow relief moulding of the window surrounds accentuates the building's elegance.

The church had got into a state of advanced dilapidation, but has been restored by a number of measures in recent years. The series of wooden braces in the outside walls, for instance, which had rotted, have been replaced by braces of ferro-concrete. The repair of the nalichniki surrounding the doors and windows, the roofs of the apses and the blind gables, was another priority. The refectory at the west end of the church has also been restored to its original impressive form. Its walls are articulated vertically in the usual fashion with lesenes, and horizontally with circular mouldings and two rows of windows, the simple surrounds of which are surmounted by triangular gables.

396   Zagorsk   Загорск

Church of SS Zosima and Savvati in the infirmary of the Monastery of the Holy Trinity and St Sergius, 1635–37

Церковь Зосимы и Савватия при больничных палатах Троице-Сергиевой Лавры

Tserkov Zosimy i Savvatiya pri bolnichnykh palatah Troitse-Sergiyevoy Lavry

The infirmary church, dedicated to the founders of the Solovetsky Monastery, is characteristic of the stylistic transition from the sixteenth to the seventeenth centuries. Its plan takes the form of a square, without spatial subdivisions, plus a single apse occupying the entire width on the east side. The apse is separated from the body of the church by a screen with two doorways through it, to the diakonikon and to the main altar. There is an basement-storey below the church. At the level of the main floor the

church is surrounded by a vaulted gallery on the west side and terraces on the south and north sides, the latter with a flight of steps. The walls of the central cube terminate in ogee gables, above which rise the traditional octagon, ringed with kokoshniki, and a tall tent roof with a dome on a polygonal drum. This type of groundplan and overall structure became the rule for tent-roof churches in the seventeenth century.

The decoration is dualistic in character, employing motifs both of the fifteenth and sixteenth centuries (for instance, the garlands on the apse are borrowed from the monastery's own Church of the Holy Ghost) and of the mid seventeenth century. The window surrounds in the form of frames with little pediments, the ornamentation of the upper part of the structure and of the apse, seem rather conservative for the middle of the seventeenth century. The new painterly style makes its mark in the use of coloured tiles in the cornice and in the small dimensions of the individual ornamental elements. The main fabric is brick, but the capitals, the pilasters, the girki on the arches of the gallery, the dynki on the portals and apse and a few other details are of limestone.

The infirmary itself occupied two wings, each of two storeys, extending to the north and south of the church. This method of composition was influenced by wooden architecture, and we have already come across it in the refectory-church in the Monastery of the Saviour and St Euthymios in Suzdal. The

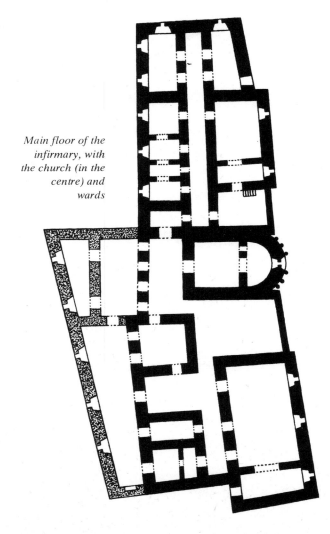

Main floor of the infirmary, with the church (in the centre) and wards

whole complex was much altered during the eighteenth and nineteenth centuries, but was restored to its original form in 1946–50, on the basis of P. V. Trofimov's thorough study.

397   Yaroslavl   Ярославль

Gate-church of the Nativity of Christ 'under bells', 1644

Надвратная церковь-колокольня Рождества Христова

Nadvratnaya tserkov-kolokolnya Rozhdestva Khristova

Yaroslavl, one of the most important trade centres of the Muscovite state, reached the peak of its prosperity in the seventeenth century. The foundation of the port of Arkhangelsk in 1584 enabled the merchants of the Posad to increase their activities as middlemen in the trade along the Volga and to and from Moscow, and to concentrate large amounts of capital in their own hands. It was they who commissioned the many churches whose imposing dimensions and lavish ornamentation are a reflection of the new urge the middle classes felt to state their self-confidence, and of the taste of a population to whom life was good. The merchants also played an important political role in the Time of Troubles, when the popular army recruited by Kusyma Minin and Dmitry Pozharsky in Nizhni Novgorod armed for the 'holy war' against the invading Poles and Lithuanians, and a new governing assembly, the Zemsky Sobor, was formed.

The provincial school, which can only be understood in the light of the social background, is not really expressed by the Church of the Nativity, in

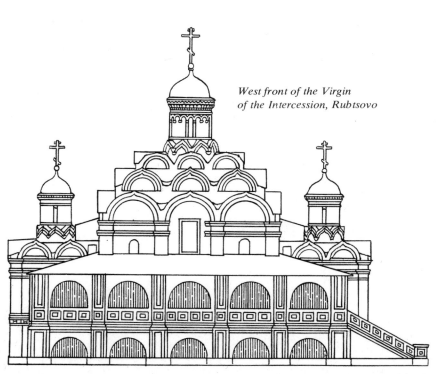

West front of the Virgin of the Intercession, Rubtsovo

fact. Its asymmetrical composition, its playful ornamental forms, made up of small elements, are entirely in the style of the architecture of the capital city. It originally constituted the entrance to a monastery. The church itself is almost square in plan, with four pillars and five domes, flanked by chapels on the north and south sides, and surrounded by a gallery on three sides. At the west end there is an exterior staircase and a third chapel, placed asymmetrically at the south-west corner. An arcaded passage, which no longer exists, led from here to the church itself. At ground level a wide gateway and two passages for pedestrians pass through the building. The pairs of twin arches with pendant girki and finely moulded archivolts are supported by squat engaged columns, modelled like a stack of barrels, and encircled by bands of ornamental relief. The rhythm is quite different in the arcading of the galleries on the level above, where the arches rest on pillars shaped like plump vases. Two small towers with low, four-faced tent roofs stand at the east corners, completing a group of three. The body of the church itself is a small cube, rising above the galleries, with small pylons at the west corners, and merging with the small, square towers at the east end to form a wide, high, blank wall. It supports the octagon, with open, arcaded sides for the bells and there are three tiers of further openings in the tall tent roof above. The decoration is provided by moulded bricks, a technique which anticipates the church in Moscow-Putinki, but the motifs are traditional ones such as shirinki, archivolts, bead moulding and saw-tooth frieze.

455

398   Moscow   Москва

Church of the Virgin of the Intercession in Rubtsovo, 1619–28

Церковь Покрова в Рубцове

Tserkov Pokrova v Rubtsove

The church, built on one of the tsar's country estates, is an example of the further development of the mixed type that emerged towards the end of the sixteenth century, in which the pyramidal construction with one dome came under the influence of the Posad. It is modelled on the Old Cathedral in the Don Monastery *(pls 11, 226)*. The kreshchaty vault over the square, pillarless body of the church takes one step down during the length of the arms of its central cross, and appears on the façades in the form of groups of blind gables, arranged in three tiers. The central cube is joined on the east side by three apses, the middle one of which is larger than the other two, while the apses of the north and south chapels alongside are even wider. The side chapels are linked by a gallery that runs round the three sides of the church and rests on a line of powerful arches, as the church itself has a high basement used for services in winter. All the walls are divided vertically by pilasters and horizontally by a moulding at the level of the top of the basement, a string course composed of a frieze of balusters and a circular moulding, and a cornice at the top; all three elements intersect the pilasters.

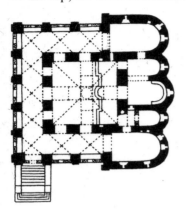

The proportions of the central cube, the kokoshniki and the drum seem ill-judged, creating a somewhat coarse effect. The side chapels are surmounted by two tiers of blind gables and a dome that rises organically above them. The two storeys of the gallery have groin-vaulted ceilings and are decorated by a horizontal band of shirinki and by lesenes with shallow inset niches, a motif which was undoubtedly influenced by the Kremlin Cathedral of the Archangel. The bell-tower at the west end was built in the nineteenth century. The church was restored in 1960–64 under the direction of A. V. Okh.

230, 399 Moscow Москва

Church of the Nativity of the Virgin in Putinki, 1649–52

Церковь Рождества Богородицы в Путинках
Tserkov Rozhdestva Bogoroditsy v Putinkakh

The new baroque style first appeared in the new type of urban churches commissioned by the mercantile and craft guilds. It originated in the higher standards in decoration and domestic comfort that the middle classes were now demanding. The church at Putinki, towards which Tsar Alexey Romanov (1645–76) contributed three sums, amounting to a total of 800 roubles, is a characteristic example. The process of secularization is evident in the shift of attention

towards the exterior, which added emphasis to the decoration of the façades, differentiation of the roof forms and the unusual conjunction of separate parts of the building. Artistic expression, a sense of temporal joy and the demands of social self-advertisement take precedence over the religious function. The interior's loss of significance and cohesion is symptomatic of the same shift of emphasis. The tent roofs, for instance, are no longer open to the space below, but solid structures. The church is composed in such a way as to provide a series of delightful aspects for a passerby, but to walk right round the building brings as abrupt a change as to step behind the scenery on a stage. The rear side was not properly composed at all, which was something quite new, analogous to the contemporary situation in icon painting, where the details of the painting were often neglected altogether while the oklad (frame) became more and more elaborate. The original sacred significance of the content was submerged in eye-catching spectacle.

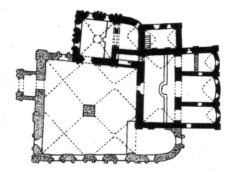

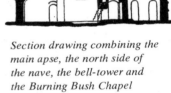

Section drawing combining the main apse, the north side of the nave, the bell-tower and the Burning Bush Chapel

The building consists of four separate parts, grouped together asymmetrically: the church itself, whose nearly square plan includes the three apses, the curvature of which is hardly visible; the rectangular bell-tower adjoining the western part of the church's north side; the 'Burning Bush' Chapel, another square block with an apse encroaching on the tower; and the large refectory, again almost square with groin vaults and a central pillar, standing to the west of the church and the south of the chapel, and probably built a little later. These parts are all totally unrelated in their dimensions, and small, additional chambers are formed where they join. The complex presents a no less complicated multiform appearance. The church, like the refectory-church at Suzdal and the Assumption at Uglich

395	396	397	398
399	400		401
402	403		404
405			

395 *Uglich, Alexey Monastery, Church of the Assumption, 1628: view from the south-east* **396** *Zagorsk, Church of SS Zosima and Savvati, 1635–37, near the hospital of the Monastery of the Holy Trinity and St Sergius: view from the south-east* **397** *Yaroslavl, Gate-church of the Nativity of Christ 'under bells', 1644: west front* **398** *Moscow, Church of the Virgin of the Intercession, Rubtsovo, 1619–28: view from the south-east* **399** *Moscow, Church of the Nativity of the Virgin, Putinki, 1649–52: view from the south-west* **400** *Murom, Monastery of the Holy Trinity, Church of the Annunciation, 1555/1644: view from the south-east* **401** *Moscow, Church of St Simeon the Stylite, mid 17th century: east front* **402** *Vladimir, Church of the Assumption, 1649: view from the north-east* **403** *Moscow, New Monastery of the Saviour, 15th–18th centuries: general view from the River Moskva* **404** *Istra, Monastery of the New Jerusalem, Cathedral of the Resurrection, 1658–66/1679–85 (restored 1748–59 by K. Blank to a design by B. Rastrelli): east front*
[405, 406] *Volokolamsk, Monastery of St Joseph of Volokolamsk, 15th–17th centuries* **405** *General view from the south-east*

Nalichnik

(pls 388, 395) is surmounted by three tent roofs on a north-south axis, with the middle one somewhat larger than the other two. The roofs in turn support slender drums, onion domes and filigree crosses. Half the area of the virtually square plan is a nave, considerably wider than it is long, with a barrel vault, intersected by segmental vaults at the short ends, and the other half is occupied by the three separate apses with similar vaults, which are, however, only one-third as high as the nave, so that from the outside the nave appears as a wide oblong block, and the number of kokoshniki above the broad cornice is greater on the east and west sides than on the north and south sides. The blind ogee gables round the bases of the drums, the tent roofs and the octagons, the prominent cornices, the arrowhead motifs, the corner lesenes which continue upwards along the angles of the roofs, the elaborate ornamentation and mouldings on all these elements—all this recurs, with appropriate modifications, on the other parts of the complex. Even so the decoration of the chapel, which belongs to the Posad type of church and has a domical vault, enables it to stand out: its roof is in pyramidal form with three tiers of reciprocally interposed kokoshniki, which support a drum decorated by a blind arcade and separated from the usual onion dome by a small tent roof. The top of the bell-tower, high above the rest of the complex, is finished in the same way, only here the eight faces of the tent roof have openings, framed like windows, to assist the spread of the sound. The octagonal bell-chamber is open-sided, and the base of the tower is square, the bell-tower unites the disparate parts of the building, drawing them towards itself, performing on the periphery an architectonic function more usually assigned to a central element. The low-roofed refectory is entered through a porch (later rebuilt) with open-arched sides divided by girki, and surmounted by a sixth tent roof which is the first stage in the upward-surging, baroque dynamic. The complex of roofs seems to flicker like candle flames.

The varying compositions of the individual parts of the building, the intersections caused by the lack of symmetry, the elaborate articulation, the horizontal members at different levels, the multifarious vertical members, prepared for by semi-circles, ogee

arches and arrowheads, the bizarre roof forms, the tapestry of the smaller ornamental elements, the archivolt mouldings of the kokoshniki, the nalichniki and other forms of window surround, the broad, complex friezes – all this amounts to a painterly exterior appearance, which presents a different outline to every vantage point. The combination of advancing members, projecting lesenes and columns, and the various forms of small, deep niches inset between them is characteristic, breaking up the surface of the walls in a play of chiaroscuro contrasts. By contrast with Western European Baroque, however, the elements retain their physical substance and real volume, and the three-dimensional movement-in-depth is articulated by means of self-contained compartments. The optical play only ornaments the surfaces, it does not dissolve them. All the decoration was executed in bricks made in a range of standard moulds, and dressed individually as need arose. The standards were fixed by the tsar's supervisory office for masonry architecture, which also laid down the standard size of the ordinary bricks.

The church was finished in 1652, at the beginning of the patriarchate of Nikon, during which the attempt was made to retrieve ecclesiastical architecture from the secular path it had started to follow, and guide it back to the sober, austere monumentality it had owned at the time of the rise of the Muscovite state, in the late fifteenth and early sixteenth centuries.

The church was restored 1954–60, under the direction of N. Sveshnyakov.

231–237 Moscow   Москва

Church of the Holy Trinity, Nikitniki, 1634–53
Церковь Троицы в Никитниках
Tserkov Troitsy v Nikitnikakh

Immediately to the east of the Red Square, the chief market-place of Moscow, lay the Kitai-Gorod, a quarter densely populated by small tradesmen and craftsmen. (The name, which means 'basket town' derives from the baskets of earth used to strengthen the wooden palisades when the city was attacked by the Tartars.) The houses of feudal lords and well-to-

406	407	408
409	410	411
412	413	414	415
416	417	418	419	420

[405, 406] *Volokolamsk, Monastery of St Joseph of Volokolamsk, 15th–17th centuries*   **406** *Gate-church of SS Peter and Paul and tower of the Resurrection, 1678: view from the south-west*
[407, 408] *Borisoglebsk, Monastery of SS Boris and Gleb*   **407** *Gate-church of the Purification of the Virgin, 1680: south front*   **408** *Gate-church of St Sergius, 1545/1680: view from the south-east*   **409** *Veliky-Ustyug, Church of the Ascension, from 1648: east front*   **410** *Kostroma, Church of the Resurrection of Christ 'in the forest', 1650–52: north front, with Chapel of the Three Saints, 1680*   **411** *Tutayev, Cathedral of the Resurrection, 1652–78: view from the north-west*   **412** *Kolomna, Cathedral of the Assumption, 1672–82: east front*   **413** *Moscow, Church of the Virgin of Tikhvin at Alexeyevskoye, c. 1680: south-east aspect*   **414** *Ryazan, Cathedral of the Assumption, 1693–99, by Jakov Bukhvostov: view from the south-west*
[415, 416] *Gorky, Church of the Nativity of the Virgin, 1697–1718*   **415** *View from the north-west*   **416** *Detail of the facade*
417 *Moscow, Monastery of the Don, Gate-church of the Ikon of the Virgin of Tikhvin, 1713–14: view from the south-west*
418 *Vologda, Alexander Kushtsky Monastery, Church of the Assumption, first half of the 16th century: east front*   **419** *Island of Kizhi, Lake Onega: bell-tower, 1874*   **420** *Kondopoga, Church of the Assumption, 1774: staircase*

do merchants began to appear in the quarter from the end of the sixteenth century, and gradually the lower ranks of society were pushed out, beyond the walls. In 1622 the rich merchant and manufacturer Grigori Leontyevich Nikitnikov moved into the Kitai-Gorod from Yaroslavl, with his family and a full complement of employees. He had his extensive business premises built next door to the wooden church of Nikita the Martyr, not far from the Red Square, where he had four shops. Paul of Aleppo reports that his house and his premises were not inferior in magnificence to the palaces of the tsar's own ministers. The properties of other wealthy merchants stood in the vicinity: Vasily Shorin, Grigori Tverdikov, Foma Bulgakov.

The wooden church burned down in 1626, and in 1634 Grigori Nikitnikov commissioned a new one on the site, which was by then part of his property. The new stone and brick church was a large, beautiful building, dedicated to the Trinity and also known as the Church of the Georgian Virgin. Its structural and decorative innovations reflect the taste and requirements of the wealthy merchant who paid for it. It consists of a complex of several buildings. The groundplan has a square nave as its central unit, with one semi-circular apse taking up the whole width of the east wall, the Chapel of St Nicholas to the north-east, the Chapel of Nikita the Martyr to the south-east, and a low vestibule at the west end. The line of the north-east chapel is continued westward by a refectory which forms a common west front with the vestibule. Galleries on the north and west fronts of the complex converge on the bell-tower in the north-west corner, which also contains the Chapel of St John the Evangelist, and a porch and exterior steps in the south-west corner give access to the west gallery *(pl. 233)*.

This additive method of composing a building derives ultimately from wooden architecture and has some connections with the processes of the sixteenth and early seventeenth centuries, but the Nikitniki Trinity is both a culmination of the historical development and an original new departure. A number of earlier buildings have an additive composition: the Transfiguration at Vyazema (late sixteenth century), the Transfiguration at Ostrov *(pl. 391),* the Old Cathedral of the Don Monastery *(pl. 226),* and the Virgin of the Intercession at Rubtsovo *(pl. 398).* All these churches have symmetrical side chapels with separate entrances to the gallery which connects them to each other and surrounds the central cube of the church. This equilibrium is missing in the Trinity. As if its position on a hill was not enough, the whole complex is raised up on a massive plinth of limestone blocks, enclosing a high, spacious basement used as a storeroom. The oblong block of the nave of the church itself towers up in the centre, slender in its proportions, and surmounted by three tiers of reciprocally interposed blind gables and five

domes. This block must have been the dominant architectural element in an area of relatively low wooden structures. Only the main dome has a drum with windows in it, the other domes are placed directly upon the roof without openings and without access to the interior. The additional cells making up the complex are grouped round the central block in a completely new structural form and a new interior arrangement.

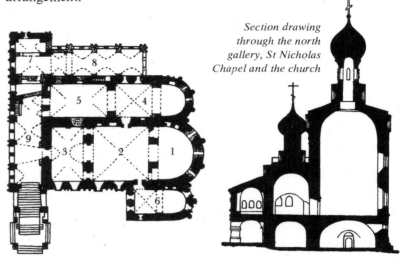

Section drawing through the north gallery, St Nicholas Chapel and the church

1 *Sanctuary* 2 *Nave* 3 *Vestibule* 4 *St Nicholas Chapel* 5 *Refectory* 6 *Chapel of Nikita the Martyr* 7 *Bell-tower and Chapel of St John the Evangelist* 8 *North gallery* 9 *West gallery*

The two side chapels are asymmetrical. The large north chapel, the refectory at its west end and the gallery beyond it on its north side together extend the total complex by a solid block. The miniature south chapel, on the other hand, is exposed on three sides, projecting from the complex as an isolated entity. Both chapels are connected directly to the main church by interior doors *(pls 236, 237),* which is new. The only way into the church from the outside is up the steps and through the vestibule. Another structural innovation is the construction of the roof of the tall, square nave as a domical vault with a small round opening at its apex giving on to the central dome. As a result the room is free of pillars and there are no obstructions to the light entering through two rows of windows, so that the murals can be seen without difficulty. The two side chapels also have domical vaulting, while the other rooms have barrel vaulting with segmental webs at the shorter ends.

The exterior appearance of the complex owes much to the nicely calculated, pleasant proportional relationship between the vertical blocks of the main church and the tent-roofed bell-tower, and the low, horizontal blocks (the chapels, galleries and the stairs). The arches and thick pillars supporting the north and west galleries, the tent roof of the porch and the numerous semi-circular and ogee-shaped motifs all function as intermediaries between the two directions. So in places the building reaches upwards; in others its vertical force dissolves and it stretches out sideways. The variety of form, the com-

plexity and the asymmetry create a magical, painterly outline, reminiscent of wooden palaces. But the most remarkable thing of all is the elegant ornamentation *(pl. 233)*. The porch gives a magnificent foretaste of the whole, its columns adorned with niches, torus mouldings and jutting capitals, the delicately moulded arches with girki, the archivolts of the kokoshniki, with inset green tiles in their panels, the vertical semi-circular ribs on the tent roof, and other details. Bricks shaped in standardized moulds play a less prominent part in the decoration than versatile limestone. The west and south façades of the church are each divided into three equal sections by pairs of massive engaged columns and finished by a broad and elaborately moulded entablature, presenting a continuous sequence of projecting elements and rectangular or heart-shaped sunken panels. It is linked with a frieze of green tiles ornamented with plants and forms like gingerbread moulds or the wood-blocks used for printing fabrics. The south front has, in addition, two string courses, the lower marking the level of the plinth, both on the church and on the side chapel, and the upper running on from the church to be the chapel's cornice. The lower has 'Attic' mouldings.

The cornices and string courses, the tiers of blind gables, the blind arcading on the drums, the nalichniki, the whole complex of the articulation and the totality of the limestone and the elaborate forms it is worked into, create a bizarre chiaroscuro play. The detailed ornamentation on the two street façades entices the passerby to take a closer look. The side overlooking the courtyard of Nikitnikov's business premises has simpler decorations (principally on the window surrounds and the apses of the St John Chapel), closely related to the sixteenth-century style of the Moscow Posad (cf. the Triphon Church at Naprudnoye). Two large stone window frames on the south front are especially original. They are placed side by side and boldly infringe the laws of symmetry. One has a semi-circular arch at the top

of the opening, the other arch comprises five lobes. On this one, the dominant ornamental motif in the high-relief frame consists of sprays of flowers and pomegranates, with two parrots in the spandrels. Fragments of the original paint in red and gold on a blue background survive in a few places. The surrounds are supported by pilasters and terminate in Renaissance-style pediments. The other windows also display an astonishing formal variety in their moulded surrounds and their ogee-shaped, roll-moulded archivolts, which appear to be attempting to smooth the transition of the walls into the gables above *(pl. 234)*.

The Trinity's architectonic and decorational innovations exercised a persistent influence on the whole of the stylistic development of the second half of the seventeenth century. It is very plain in churches of the Moscow Baroque, such as St Nicholas at Bersenevka *(pl. 260)* and Holy Trinity at Ostankino *(pl. 264)*, but there are provincial churches, too, which show a close affinity: the Annunciation at Murom *(pl. 400)* and the Ascension at Veliky Ustyug *(pl. 409)* are but two examples.

The elegant decoration of the windows is a preparation for the even more luxuriant treatment of the doorways, for which Moscow limestone is again the material chosen. From the west gallery the vestibule is entered through a doorway flanked by columns and with an absolutely plain, unstepped architrave, but with cast-iron doors and screen that are masterpieces of Muscovite craftsmanship, the surfaces covered with delicate engravings: various kinds of rosette, elves, fabulous beasts, owls, peacocks, griffins, boars, horses and lions. The way from the west vestibule into the nave is through a low, wide, semi-circular doorway with a stepped architrave *(pl. 236)*, which gives a superb idea of the excellence of Russian stone carving in the second quarter of the seventeenth century. The beautiful reliefs were originally painted in gay colours. The exotic flowers and plant motifs resemble those on the ornamental tiles, the carved wooden frame of the iconostasis and the mural paintings, but in each medium the motifs are translated anew into the appropriate 'language', not on their own terms but subordinated to the architectonic composition. The portals in the north and south walls of the nave are tall and narrow by comparison with the west door. All three are totally different in their composition and their relief ornamentation. The new shape of the north and south doorways underlines the innovatory nature of their function as the direct connections between the nave and the side chapels. The north doorway *(pl. 236)* has a rectangular frame, covered with a low relief design of closely entwined tendrils with roses and pomegranates. A huge but delicately formed palmette in the gable dominates the entablature which is decorated with a wavy ribbon motif. The south doorway *(pl. 237)* is rectangular at its base, but its arch has five lobes. The jambs have elaborately profiled capitals. Most of the relief carving on the frame is of plant motifs, but there are small parrots in the spandrels, whose heads and plumage still show traces of red and blue paint. The pediment is open, in the baroque manner. The stone carving on all three portals, characterized by the same painterly vitality and abundance as the wood carving on the iconostasis, must be the work of highly gifted artists from Moscow and Yaroslavl.

The whole of the interior is agreeable and welcoming in atmosphere but is every bit as representative of the aspirations and standards of the *haute bourgeosie* as the sumptuous exterior. The mural paintings, for instance, do not lag behind the best products of the Tsarist School in artistic quality, and indeed some of the masters of the school were probably among the team of artists that executed them between 1652 and 1653. Their rhythmic construction, wealth of movement and vivid colouring, due to the use of tempera, are astonishing. They are concentrated in the central nave, the south chapel, the apses and the St John Chapel in the bell-tower, where they are spread like tapestries over the walls, ceilings and window soffits. In the nave they are divided between four horizontal zones, marked off by red lines. Each zone contains four scenes, except where windows take up some of the space. There are no vertical divisions: scenery or architectural elements are used to separate the scenes, so that each horizontal zone is perceived as a unified composition. The subjects are Christological cycles bearing on the dogma of the Trinity. Some scholars believe that Western European engravings (such as those in the Piscator Bible) served as the models, but if that is really the case the models were fundamentally reworked.

Each wall bears a complete cycle taken from the Gospels, with the Passion cycle on the south wall taking pride of place. The scenes run in strict historical sequence from left to right and from top to bottom, so that the narrative begins in the top left-hand corner with the Last Supper, while the Crucifixion is the penultimate scene in the bottom zone *(pl. 231)*. The various emotional nuances, suffering, astonishment, reflection, perturbation and anger are represented dynamically through mime and gesture, making every scene comprehensible without tituli. The Crucifixion is highly dramatic. The depiction of Christ, the body sagging, the head drooping on the breast, the resigned expression of the face – all are permeated with a profound sensitivity. The scene vividly contrasts the mortal torment being inflicted on the victim with the rude vigour and energy of the four soldiers impatiently hammering nails into his hands and feet. Their figures and gestures form a curious oval frame within which the cross and the crucified figure stand out compositionally. The cycles on the walls are co-ordinated

with the representations of the feasts of the Church on the ceiling, which serve either to conclude or to introduce the cycles.

The paintings on the west wall are a logical continuation of the Passion cycle. The first and second zones illustrate scenes from the gospels about Christ's appearances after the Resurrection. The third zone is devoted to some of the miracles. The Marriage at Cana deserves particular attention: the artist transposed the scene to seventeenth-century Russia. The wedding feast is taking place in a stone palace, with an open wall affording a view of the interior: the bride, the bridegroom and a group of guests – including Christ, but he is by no means the centre of attention – are seated at a richly decked, rectangular table, and all are elegantly dressed in the clothes of the seventeenth-century merchant class, so that this religious painting has the air of a contemporary drinking party. The bottom zone of the west wall, traditionally the position of the Last Judgment, has three of the parables: Dives and Laz-

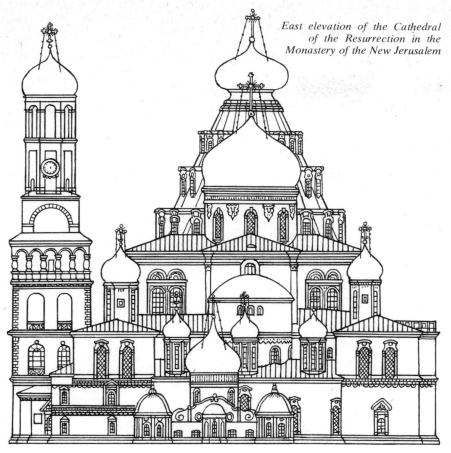

*East elevation of the Cathedral
of the Resurrection in the
Monastery of the New Jerusalem*

with the five domes of the cathedral compose an ensemble typical of Russian architecture of the seventeenth century. The four-storey, 256-feet-high bell-tower of 1759, designed by I. Zherebtsov, provides the group with an essential visual accent. It forms the main gate to the monastery. Although it was nearly twenty-five years in the building its top storey remained unfinished. Its wealth of slender columns, open pediments and ornamental members is representative of the Russian Baroque of the mid eighteenth century. The Neoclassical Church of Our Lady of the Sign was built in 1791–95 by the Moscow architect Y. Nazarov to a commission from Count Sheremetyev, whose family vault occupies the ground floor. Although some substantial buildings went up in the eighteenth century, the ensemble is dominated by the stylistic traits of the seventeenth-century buildings, which are particularly evident when the monastery is seen from the Moskva.

404   Istra   Истра

Monastery of the New Jerusalem, 17th–18th centuries
Cathedral of the Resurrection, 1658–85
Воскресенский Новоиеруcалимский монастырь
Собор Воскресения Христова
Voskresensky Novoierusalimsky monastyr
Sobor Voskreseniya Khristova

When Nikon became patriarch in 1652 he tried to counteract secularization in ecclesiastical architecture as elsewhere, by a series of regulations. While he attempted to uphold the austere formal traditions of the fifteenth and sixteenth centuries in the first two monasteries commissioned by him and built according to his prescriptions, the Monastery of the Iberian Virgin in the Valdai region and the Monastery of the Cross on the Kii Islands in Onega Bay in the White Sea, in the last of his projects, the Monastery of the New Jerusalem, founded in 1658, he was prepared to use the painterly, decorative style of his day, in order to compete with the monastic foundations of the tsar. Even his plans could not evade the process of secularization. The site of natural beauty which he repeatedly recommended in his official decrees and in his literary commentaries was never more carefully chosen than here. On the banks of the Istra he found one of the most picturesque spots in the vicinity of Moscow, on which to build a new City of God.

He stipulated the Church of the Holy Sepulchre in Jerusalem as the model for the monastery's cathedral, an idea that had already attracted him in 1649, when he was still archimandrite of the New Monastery of the Saviour. It may have been already at that period, or else it was when the building of the cathe-

workmen began to knock down the masonry that had blocked the arches of the exterior gallery since the eighteenth century, and in doing so discovered a piece of the gallery of the fifteenth-century building. The fragment consists of three octagonal pillars with limestone capitals and bases, resembling the ornamental members of the Cathedral of the Archangel in the Kremlin. It has proved impossible to identify any other elements of fifteenth-century origin.

The Cathedral of the Saviour of 1645–47 is constructed according to the typical domed cruciform scheme of the late fifteenth and early sixteenth centuries, with three aisles, five domes and a gallery surrounding the central block. It stands above an undercroft, used as the burial vault of the boyar family of the Romanovs, the tsar's kin. The powerful cuboid structure, its imposing proportions and restrained articulation and decoration were deliberately conceived in the spirit of the earlier traditions, to impart an impression of solemnity and sublimity. It is likely that Nikon was already taking the opportunity to put his conservative ideas on architecture into practice. The interior is decorated with frescos painted in 1689 by artists from the tsar's Armoury studio, and the carved wooden iconostasis is in the Moscow Baroque style. The refectory built in 1673–75 was much altered in the nineteenth century. The infirmary Church of St Nicholas and two blocks of monks' cells were put up at the end of the seventeenth century.

Walls and towers with all the provisions necessary for effective defence were erected in 1640–42. The fortifications are truly impressive and together

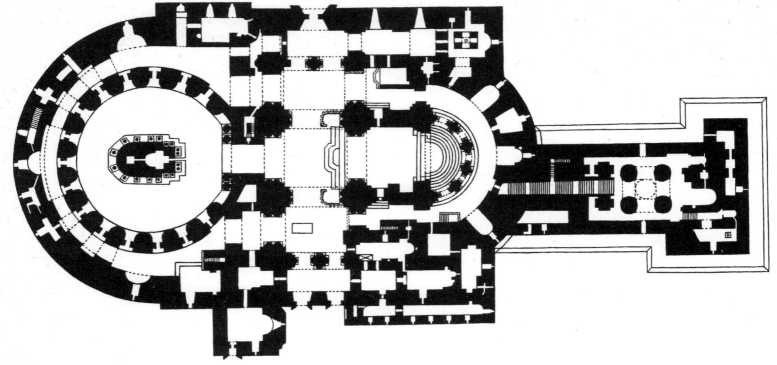

dral was being projected, that he procured a model of Constantine's rotunda (now in the museum) as well as Bernardino Amico's treatise of 1609 with its faithful sketches and drawings. His intention was that the cathedral should actually be still larger, in accordance with his political claims to be ranked above the tsar as the spiritual ruler of Russia, and the first, the *primus inter pares,* of the patriarchs of the whole world. He originally planned the bulding with 365 chapels (one for each day of the year), but only twenty-nine were built (compared with fourteen in the prototype, even so) as work on the building was suspended when Nikon fell from grace and lost his office in 1666. It was not resumed until 1679 and the cathedral was finally completed in 1685. It is a complex of numerous heterogeneous units, and completely of the seventeenth century in its style. One church with a single dome, constructed in part below ground level, stood to the east of the Church of the Resurrection, which also had one dome and a kreshchaty vault. It was adjoined to the west by the immense rotunda, surmounted by a tall, nearly circular tent roof, which enclosed the 'Holy Sepulchre'. Ambulatories and chapels broke up the interior into numerous cells. The tent roof was so large that it collapsed in 1723. In addition a fire broke out in 1726. It was restored 1748–59 by K. Blank in an opulent baroque style, after a design by B. Rastrelli. The rotunda was blown up during the last war. The whole of the baroque ornamentation was destroyed by the flames, and the explosion also brought down the bell-tower. Only the subterranean church to the east and the Church of the Resurrection survived. The most remarkable feature of the Resurrection is its elaborate decoration in multi-coloured, glazed tiles. The door and window surrounds, the cornices and the iconostasis are

aglow with the radiant chromatic combinations of the ceramics, which play the major part in the decoration of these elements. They are the work of the Belorussian artists Stepan Polubes, Ignati Maximov and Pyotr Zaborsky.

The restoration of the monastery began in 1950. So far the perimeter walls, towers and seventeenth-century gate-church have been completed.

405, 406   Volokolamsk   Волоколамск

Monastery of Joseph of Volokolamsk, 15th–17th centuries
Gate-church of SS Peter and Paul, 1678
Иосифов-Волоколамский монастырь
Надвратная церковь Петра и Павла
Iosifov-Volokolamsky monastyr
Nadvratnaya tserkov Petra i Pavla

Although the primary factor determining Nikon's ecclesiastical and artistic policies was his conflict with the temporal power, they nevertheless followed in the mainstream of the tradition of 'Josephism', and it was precisely in that light that the ordinary people saw them. The people regarded the patriarch's monumental churches as symbols of secular authority. Joseph of Volokolamsk himself (1439–1518) had at first wanted to strengthen the church against the Great Prince, and had yielded first place to him only because he believed the centralized Muscovite state was the best means of preserving the purity of the faith and the inviolability of ecclesiastical property. Nikon's disagreement with Alexey Romanov was only about precedence in the state church, not about the basic conception, and there-

screen, and is echoed by a canopy of similar construction over the altar in the main apse (cf. also *pl. 253*). When the Royal Door is open the effect is of a ceremonial golden colonnade passing through it. The use of columns, unlike an iconostasis, accentuates the possibility of movement in depth. This kind of organization of the interior is exclusive in Russia to the architecture of Rostov. Architectonic means of considerable expressive potential – the lighting, the arcade and the portico – served to focus attention on the positions of liturgical significance.

The frescos were executed in the mid 1670s by the best artists of the time, including Dmitry Grigoryev of Yaroslavl, who is listed in the registers of the tsar's Armoury workshop as a master of the first rank. There are five thematic cycles. The chief cycle narrates Christ's life on earth and occupies the north, west and south walls. The second cycle on the altar screen consists of the usual iconostasis programme. The third cycle, in the sanctuary, is concerned with the Christian sacraments. The fourth is a series of portraits of saints and other venerable figures, painted on the window embrasures. The fifth and last embraces biblical myths and apocalyptic visions and is found in the gallery. Even the pairs of columns along the walls are painted with archangels, cherubim and seraphim. The Passion scenes are extremely dramatic. The Crucifixion on the south wall *(pl. 245)* displays a multiple rhythmic animation in the composition and a lively realism in the details, especially in the positions of the bodies and in the expressions. But the conventional linear clarity and two-dimensionalism are preserved, in spite of all the intersections and distancing. Against a detailed architectural background, two clusters of figures are grouped round Christ on the cross: the group on the left, in the foreground in front of the redeemed thief, includes Mary and John, whose calm composure contrasts with the violent gesture of Stephanton offering the sponge soaked in vinegar on a hyssop branch, while on the right, below the damned thief, is a turbulent group of soldiers, three of them throwing dice for Christ's robe. The cross stands above the skull of Adam, according to the tradition of the Eastern Church. The style of the frescos combines the conservative tradition of linearism, especially evident in the clear, integrated contours, with the courtly, graceful flow of line and movement and bright, delicate colouring of the painterly formal language of the seventeenth century. The principal figures and content of each scene always stand out clearly. There is a felicitous wedding of the figurative paintings with ornamental designs, which are not schematized, and therefore not repetitive. The simulated 'drapes' on the bottom zone, for instance *(pl. 247)*, carry medallions with individually conceived birds, fishes, flowers and vines.

Church of the Saviour 'above the Entrance Hall' in the Kremlin *c*1675
Церковь Спаса на сенях в Кремле
Tserkov Spasa na senyakh v Kremle

The Church of the Saviour was built at the same time as the Red Palace and the White Hall, in about 1675, to be the private church of the metropolitan, whose apartments it adjoins on the south side. It is a unique variant of the refectory-church developed by Russian architects since the beginning of the sixteenth century. Surmounted by a single dome, the unadorned structure rises above a high, simple base, the broad lesenes dividing whose walls have no relationship to the articulation of the church itself. The positioning of the windows also seems quite unsystematic *(pl. 248)*. The existence is recorded of a wooden church on a massive plinth which stood on the site until burning down after being struck by lightning in 1671. It is likely that the stone plinth survived and became the base of the existing church. Again, the zone between the plinth and the blind arcading is not made to correspond with the two zones above. It is possible that the original plan was to build a very small church, commensurate with the existing three apses, which have the blind arcading continuing in a smaller form beneath the eaves, and that the rest of the structure would have been the refectory. In fact the windows are very large, even at the level of the apses, and framed by rectangular surrounds, without the traditional pediments.

But it would appear that while the building was still in progress the idea of a larger refectory – the White Hall – was conceived and realized. All the discrepancies in the articulation of the façades are in any case hardly perceptible as a result of the unified treatment of the upper zones as an integrated structure. The form of the roof recalls the Novgorod system with gables embracing trefoil blind arches, which govern the division of the walls into three sections, with the middle one wider and higher than the other two. The three apses have separate plank roofs, each with a politsa and shaped ends to the planks. They form a relatively large integrated block, from which the usual semi-circular ends hardly project at all. The arcade of ogee arches and thin, ringed columns takes up the decoration from the Cathedral of the Assumption, which also provides the model for the graduation of the structure, the proportions of the apses, the pilaster-like lesenes and the string courses of roll mouldings and fillets. The arched windows accentuate the calm impression of the walls. The graduation of the thickness of the walls and of the width of the lesenes, the eight faces of the roof, corresponding to the shape of the gables, the ridges converging on the cuboid pedestal of the round drum, the ornamental columns and gables on the pedestal, and the aspiring onion dome itself give the composition its pyramidal and vertical character. The entrance is marked by a small porch with a bochka and barrel-shaped supports. It is on the north side, unusually, since the White Hall adjoins the church on the west side and for some unknown reason direct access by means of a connecting door was not wanted.

The decoration of the church's interior is unique in its richness, in deliberate contrast to the austerity of the exterior. The dynamic height, taken in conjunction with a relatively small ground area, the colonnade with twin arches and girki above the parapet of the dais in front of the stone altar screen *(pl. 250)*, the brightly coloured tapestry-work of frescos spread out over every wall and ceiling surface, create a ceremonial and monumental impression which has pronounced aesthetic accents as well. The dais is almost as wide as the area for the congregation a few steps below it. The sanctuary behind the screen is again approximately the same in area, so that the interior is divided across its width into three rectangles. This unusual division is the outcome of Metropolitan Jonas's preference for services in the ceremonious Byzantine rite, sometimes involving some dozens of priests and large choirs, taking up two-thirds of the space and leaving only one-third for the small number of chosen guests.

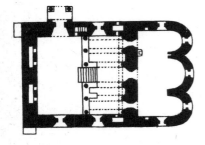

The stone altar screen is covered with frescos, like the one in the Church of the Resurrection (cf. *pl. 247*). The only icons on it are two local ones in its first tier. The Royal Door is framed by magnificent copper-gilt columns which give it a visual prominence equal to its liturgical importance. The south and north doors are also flanked by columns, but decorated only with paintings. The painting on the first tier of the screen and on the dais achieves an amazingly successful decorative and aesthetic effect. The curious holes in other walls are the mouths of the golosniki, helping to improve the acoustics.

The Church of the Saviour was probably the first of all the churches in the kremlin to be decorated. The traditional view is that the frescos were painted in the seventies, as soon as the building was finished, by Popen Timofey of Rostov, Dmitry Stepanov of Vologda and Ivan and Fyodor Karpov of Yaroslavl. Christ's life on earth, from the calling of the apostles to his death on the cross is narrated in a sequence of separate scenes in five zones on the

north and south walls. The whole of the west wall was given over to the traditional Judgment. The altar screen carries the programme usually found in the iconostasis. The walls of the sanctuary are painted with liturgical subjects, themes from the story of the Creation and the Fall, and the figures of Christian patriarchs, archdeacons and ordinary saints. The Crucifixion, Deposition, Entombment, Resurrection and the Descent of the Holy Ghost are represented on the ceiling. The subjects that appealed most to the artists were evidently those in which revelation was by means of actions and images, such as the miracles of healing and raising the dead, the feeding of the five thousand, the parable with the coin concerning the kingdoms of God and of Caesar. The Passion scenes in the two lower zones, wider than those above, are depicted with a sense of drama that arouses sympathy and involvement in the spectator. The judgment of Pilate is made to relate to the Mos-

Section drawing, showing the arcade in front of the solea and the altar screen

cow Synod of the winter of 1666–67 which condemned Nikon and in which Jonas Sysoyevich took part, as a secret supporter of the patriarch. No other Last Judgment in the whole of Russian art is as detailed, expressive and sumptuously coloured as this one. The ranks of the sinners are notably swollen by numbers of foreigners (pl. 249). The Russian merchant class, which played a prominent role in society in the seventeenth century and also influenced artistic taste and choice of subjects, here finally disposed of the unwelcome foreign rivals who had forced their way into Russia's internal trade after the Time of Troubles. The figures include orientals, adherents of other faiths, Muslims in striped and ornamented killuts and kaftans and often wearing white turbans. The largest group is of Western Europeans, the women wearing dresses of western cut with lace collars and cuffs, the men dressed like Dutch burghers with ruffs and belts, knee-breeches, top-boots and tall hats. Transgressing monks and nuns and old men swell the motley throng. Angels with trumpets and balances, the dead risen in white shrouds, the fiery mouth of hell, Satan with Judas on his lap, apocalyptic monsters, all are part of a magnificent spectacle that arouses less terror and fear than aesthetic pleasure.

251, 253   Rostov   Ростов

Gate-church of St John the Evangelist in the kremlin, 1683

Надвратная церковь Иоанна Богослова в Кремле

Nadvratnaya tserkov Ioanna Bogoslova v Kremle

St John the Evangelist is built over a gate in the west wall of the kremlin, flanked by two round towers in the wall, with a gallery running between them. There is an obvious resemblance to the Church of the Resurrection, but this later building of c1683, probably the last element in the ensemble, is distinguished by especial skill in the management of the proportional relationships, giving it an exquisite harmony that is the sum and culmination of all the architectural

experience behind it. The visitor to the kremlin is impressed right here at the entrance with the sense of ceremony evoked by the painterly splendour that Metropolitan Jonas loved.

The main façade (pl. 251) is presented to the city's Moscow Street. Although the construction is similar to the Church of the Resurrection there are some distinguishing characteristics. The relationship of the two towers to the central cube is asymmetrical, and they do not press so closely to it. The three gateways – the middle one significantly wider than the other two – are overhung by elaborately moulded arches, supported on pairs of columns with barrel-shaped rings on their shafts. The whole front of the gate below the gallery is studded with shirinki with inset tiles, forming vertical and horizontal rows. A small niche for an icon and the varying depths of the shirinki create a certain variety. The gallery is lit by five large windows with twin arches and pendant girki, and the form of their surrounds, with the delicately moulded, undulating outline of the pediment, introduces a new ornamental motif, that has been described as the 'form of a popular terem'. The cube of the church rising above the gallery is divided on all four sides into three equal sections by pilasters, thus revealing a square groundplan, unlike that of the Resurrection. There is a window, without an ornamental surround, in each of the divisions of the north, west and south walls, except the middle division of the west wall, which has a large niche for a fresco. Above the windows, between horizontal bands of fillet and roll moulding cutting across the pilasters, there is a blind arcade which, like those on the other churches in the kremlin, derives from the influence of the Cathedral of the Assumption, but which is not usually found in Russian architecture by this date. Each division of the wall ends at the top in a blind arch beneath an overhanging triangular gable, which determines the beautifully assured line of the roof. The cube is crowned by the traditional five domes of which only the middle one rests on a drum with windows in it. The round towers, which have mob-cab domes with shimmering silver shingles, strengthen the impression of a ceremonial welcome. The small bell-tower with a steep tent roof is supported by eight columns on top of the wall to the north of the church, in a conception that recalls the Tsar turret in the Moscow Kremlin.

It is only after passing through the gateway that one realizes that the church stands on a high basement-storey. One theory is that it was taken over from an older building that formed part of the Ivanov Monastery that formerly occupied the site. It accommodates several storerooms and, of course, the three passages, which make only one right-angled bend, unlike those under the Resurrection. There are only two archways on the east side, and not three as on the west, where the composition meets the demands of symmetry. The gallery is also more prominent from inside the kremlin, although its decoration is less elaborate. It encloses the church on three sides. The exterior staircase with barrel-shaped supports leading up to it on the south side was built at the end of the nineteenth century. The three apses, like those of the Church of the Saviour 'above the Entrance Hall', form a relatively large, independent block, with the rounded ends barely projecting from the mass; each has its own wooden roof with a politsa, and a wide frieze of ornamental bands and a row of shallow niches, with triangular tops, similar to the frieze on the Assumption, decorate the three.

Since the body of the interior is square it has a domical vault, with spandrels across the line of the groins. It gives an impression of height and light, since it is well-lit by eight windows on three sides. As in the two other churches in the kremlin, there is no iconostasis, but an altar screen with frescos painted directly on its surface. The bottom tier is in the form of a blind arcade with gilt engaged columns. There is a portico in front of the Royal Door, aligned with the similar columns supporting the canopy over the metropolitan's throne in the middle apse *(pl. 253)*, resulting in a colonnade like the one in the Resurrection. The two gate-churches thus resemble each other inwardly as well as outwardly, but St John's is more intimate in character, thanks to its smaller size and the lack of a dais raising the sanctuary high above the floor of the nave. It evidently served the Red Palace as domestic chapel, and is connected to it by a single-span bridge. An inscription on the altar screen behind one of the local icons tells us that the frescos in the church were painted in 1683, but it does not give the artist's names. S. S. Churakov attributes them to Dmitry Grigoryev and his assistants. The programme is divided between six zones, not five as in the other churches in the kremlin, and comprises three thematic cycles. The two top zones have a Christological programme, the next three narrate the life of the church's patron, St John the Evangelist, and the bottom zone that of St Avraam of Rostov. The sanctuary has the appearance of a pantheon of the early church fathers and saints, underlined by the position of paintings of the Last Supper and Christ Washing the Disciples' Feet beside the Royal Door and of the Crucifixion and medallions depicting the sacraments in the roof. The style is soft, elegant and colourful, without weakening the contours. All the colour combinations are based on the principle of increasing tonal intensity or of the contrast of complementary colours. The paintings in the gallery, devoted to the lives and deeds of the apostles, are of an equally high artistic standard, but they have suffered some damage and it has not yet been possible to restore them. The doors leading from the gallery into the church are flanked on each side by five alternately semi-circular and rectangular shafts in carved, richly ornamented bricks. This kind of door frame became widespread in Muscovite architecture from the middle of the seventeenth century onwards and is particularly apt in this church, where it marries harmoniously with the splendid colouring of the murals.

Monastery of SS Boris and Gleb, 16th–17th centuries
Gate-church of the Purification of the Virgin, 1680
Gate-church of St Sergius, 1545/1680
Борисоглебский монастырь
Надвратная церковь Сретения
Надвратная Сергиевая церковь
Borisoglebsky monastyr
Nadvratnaya tserkov Sreteniya
Nadvratnaya Sergiyevaya tserkov

The monastery dedicated to Russia's two national saints was founded at the end of the fourteenth century by two monks from the Monastery of the Trinity and St Sergius, Fyodor and Pavel. It lies in the middle of a pine forest, twelve miles from Rostov, on the road to Uglich. The first masonry buildings were erected in the early sixteenth century. The ensemble of the monastery as it now exists consists of the defensive walls, laid out in a rectangle, with fourteen towers, dating from the sixteenth and seventeenth centuries, and two gate-churches, St Sergius (1545, refurbished *c*1680) and the Purification of the Virgin (1680). The other buildings, placed at random inside the walls, are the Cathedral of SS Boris and Gleb (1522–24, by Master Boris), the Church of the Annunciation with refectory and the abbot's apartments (1524–26/1690–1710), the bell-tower (late seventeenth century) and domestic and residential quarters of the sixteenth and seventeenth centuries.

The north gate and Church of the Purification *(pl. 254)* give on to the Uglich road, and the front is accordingly spectacular. The cuboid form of the church, surmounted by five domes, and the gallery linking the two towers placed asymmetrically in front of it, repeat the pattern of the gate-churches of the Rostov Kremlin, and Jonas Sysoyevich was again the builder. But the forms are refashioned in a quite original manner and accorded individual value by a painterly sense of movement. There are two passages beneath the church, already asymmetrical in that they are of different widths. The main cube is divided vertically by lesenes, but into two sections, not the usual three, and the lesenes do not reach to the top of the wall but only to the foot of the shallow blind arcade with pendant columns, which goes all the way round the building instead of a cornice. Each wall, except the east, contains two windows, accented by their ornamental surrounds in seventeenth-century style. The uniform wide brick friezes on the slender drums make the domes look extremely decorative. The hipped roof is quite plain. Structural challenges also receive a decorative answer in the composition of the towers, which are clearly articulated by roll mouldings at the levels of the floors, and have a large

476

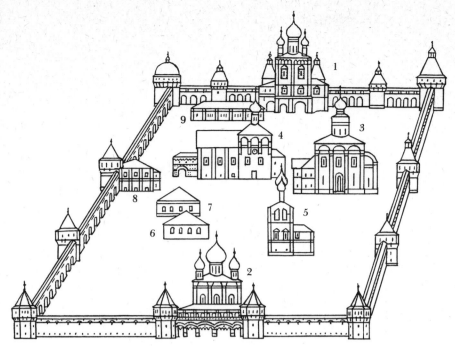

1 *Gate-church of the Purification of the Virgin* 2 *Gate-church of St Sergius* 3 *Cathedral of SS Boris and Gleb* 4 *Church of the Annunciation, refectory and abbot's apartments* 5 *Bell-tower* 6 *Treasurer's house* 7 *Kitchens* 8 *Old apartments of the abbot* 9 *Monks' quarters*

form of vaulting, the south and north walls are articulated by pairs of engaged columns, and the sanctuary is separated from the body of the church by a stone screen. The screen itself is somewhat different, however, with only its bottom zone with the three doors treated architectonically, while the usual wooden iconostasis is fixed to the upper part of the wall instead of frescos.

The Gate-church of St Sergius in the south wall (*pl. 408*) unites architectonic forms from two centuries, from its first building in 1545 and from the alterations made to it c1680. Its blank walls and sparing articulation give it a sober, serene appearence. The walls are divided into three by the traditional flat, wide pilasters which run on up to form a row of round gables. Since the apse is not prominent the overall form is an integrated cuboid block. The five domes are arranged symmetrically over the corners and in the middle. The three gateways are the only elements to disrupt the symmetry. The narrowest, now walled up, was intended for use by those on foot. The arches and vaulted roofs were painted in the seventeenth century. The two double gates are a rare survival, and a monument to their makers' craftsmanship; the leaves are made up of a grid of small panels of pinewood. The south façade yields a clear example of how the linear architecture of the sixteenth century, with its blank surfaces, clear articulation and narrow window apertures, was replaced at the end of the seventeenth century by an elegant, painterly style which used brick ornamentation as its principal formal medium. The slight asymmetry of the arches, with their row of girki, the pillars, all decorated with a regular pattern of little brick 'barrels', the shirinki with inset coloured tiles, and the arcading of the gallery combine in a unique symphony of ornament. Like the north gate, the ensemble includes two tent-roofed towers, flanking the gallery of the church asymmetrically, and hexagonal in plan. The top floor of each has narrow windows, and below them there are apertures at three levels: machicolation at the top, roundels in the middle and arches at ground level, giving the impression that the towers were built for serious defensive purposes. They were evidently added in the seventeenth century in acknowledgment of the Rostov architectural school. It was at that date that the church acquired its four-faced roof, cutting off the tops of the round gables, and the interior and exterior staircases leading into the spacious gallery. The interior has four pillars and only one entrance and its whitewashed walls give it a simple, archaic air.

The perimeter walls of the monastery are furnished with continuous platforms along their length and properly equipped for defence. They date from the middle of the sixteenth century, though they were not all built at one time. Many sections were renovated or rebuilt in the seventeenth century.

number of elegantly framed windows, as well as machicolation on the upper string course and round firing-holes on the lower.

The combined façade of the gate and the gallery draws attention to itself by the uninterrupted expanses of ornamental elements and their uniform chiaroscoro play, characteristic of Moscow architecture of the mid seventeenth century (cf. the Nativity of the Virgin at Putinki and the gate of the Goritsky Monastery at Pereslavl-Zalessky). The treatment of the surface is not so much a matter of subdividing its area as physically articulating it. The supports, arches, ledges and shirinki are subject to a strict geometrical arrangement, for all their apparent lack of order, and all the painterly variety is achieved by the permutations of a limited number of standard shapes of moulded bricks. The line of pendant girki across the mouths of the arches, and their recurrence in the windows of the gallery, make an effective stroke. Seen from the courtyard the structure seems even taller and more imposing (*pl. 407*). The sanctuary forms a small, rectangular block, separately roofed, added at the east end in a manner forbidden by Nikon, and another gallery at the west end contains the staircase. This façade presents the contrast of a blank wall surface with a frieze of shirinki, an ornamented arcade and a string course of begunets and porebrik motifs in brick. The proportions of the low, wide arches and the low relief of the brick ornamentation recall the Pskov style of the sixteenth century. The church is entered by two magnificent portals from the west and south galleries. Each is flanked by four pairs of engaged columns, with bead moulding on the archivolts and each is decorated with different reliefs. The interior resembles the Gate-church of the Resurrection at Rostov, in that it has the same

Walls and gate-tower of the Monastery of the Saviour and St Euthymios, second half of the 17th century

478

Крепостная стена и башня над главным входом Спасо-Евфимиева монастыря

Krepostnaya stena i bashnya nad glavnym vkhodom Spaso-Yevfimiyeva monastyrya

We have already looked at some of the older buildings in the monastery (cf. *pls 212, 213, 388*); the gate-tower of *c*1660 at the main entrance is an outstanding example of fortress architecture put to decorative use *(pl. 256)*. It looks like a great square-cut monolith, its upper part decorated with imagination and refinement. The roof is a low, four-faced tent, surmounted by a tiny onion dome on an octagonal drum. As well as window slits and firing embrasures the upper zone of the façades carries a wide band of friezes of various motifs typical of the seventeenth-century Moscow style: shirinki, niches and blind arcades with ogee arches. The moulded bricks were made in the local brickworks on the banks of the Kamenka. The unusually low archways of the gates, resting on short 'barrel' supports, seem to have been pressed down by the immense weight of the superstructure. The two arches of different widths (one for vehicular traffic and one for pedestrians), the two icon niches and a few firing embrasures are the only features to relieve the blank walls of the lower part of the tower. The massive gate-tower, about 72 feet high, stands halfway along the south section of the monastery's outside wall, and is set diagonally to the line of the road. It indicates the principle axis of the whole ensemble. Its importance is underlined by the far less elaborate decoration on the two corner towers on the south-west (water tower) and south-east extremities. Although it no longer had a military role to play the appearance of fortification is as much a part of the effect it makes as the decoration. In the Time of Troubles the monastery was held by the Poles and Lithuanians and in 1634 it fell to the Crim-Tartars. But it must have been above all the principle of the superiority of the spiritual authority, championed by Patriarch Nikon and the Metropolitan of Rostov, Jonas Sysoyevich, that inspired the replacement of the massive wooden palisades between 1660 and 1690 by the stone defences that still stand today. The wealthy and ambitious monastery, owning more than 10,300 serfs at the time, built itself a 'kremlin' to rival Moscow's, surrounded by a wall nearly 4,000 feet long. The walls and the twelve towers, which are variously rectangular, polygonal or round, according to the lie of the ground, together form a painterly ensemble which gains an additional scenic charm from its position spread out along the bank of the Kamenka. While the side facing towards the town is richly decorated in a deliberate attempt to make an artistic effect, the other towers and sections of wall seem relatively sober and bare.

The monastery-fortress was founded on the north side of Suzdal in 1352. Its other seventeenth-century buildings include the infirmary church of St Nicholas and the prison; the Gate-church of the Annunciation *(pl. 212)* and the bell-tower *(pl. 213)* were greatly modified in the painterly style of the age.

Terem Palace and the Terem Churches in the Kremlin, 1627/1635–37/1680–81

Теремной дворец и Теремные церкви в Кремле

Teremnoy dvorets i Teremnye tserkvi v Kremle

It was a characteristic of seventeenth-century architecture to strive to unite as many separate buildings as possible in a single complicated complex and to cover the façades with a multitude of ornament. The trend originated in secular architecture, in the timber houses in the traditional style, with ornamental carving, that the boyars lived in in the country and their mansions in the Posad, as well as the ornate stone houses built by the wealthy middle classes from the 1630s onwards, obviously reflecting popular taste. Features of composition and ornamentation evidently garnered from these sources

large windows, and is considerably higher than the other four. The group stands on a pedestal set back somewhat from the top of the walls, and pedestal and parapet are decorated with two tiers of gables quite unlike anything seen in the middle of the seventeenth century. Their elaborately curved outlines are interrupted by sturdy little pillars with panelled sides, and decorated with volutes, scallops and finials. They look like coxcombs and became a characteristic detail of the new style, employed on parapets, cornices and window surrounds. The twisted columns with Corinthian capitals standing on consoles, and the curved, open gables over the windows also became regular traits of the style. The strong pilasters and clustered columns at the corners, and the ornate moulding, often including sawtooth and zigzag motifs, on the cornices (cf. *pl. 261,* bottom right) intensify the plasticity and differentiation of the ornamentation and the buoyancy of the composition as a whole. The roofs of the galleries and vestibule on the ground floor form a terrace surrounding the upper floor on three sides. The body of the church is lit by two zones of windows, and the three apses project from the mass in a trefoil-shaped bay.

As N. I. Brunov remarks: 'the upward thrust of the whole of the upper part of the building is created by the contest between the strong horizontal lines marking the top of the main block and the dynamic forces embodied in the convoluted ornamentation.' The plain, regular brickwork provides a painterly background to the dainty limestone decoration and its play of forms.

The bell-tower – a square base supporting several stepped octagons – has a tent roof whose impressive proportions earned it the nickname of 'the candle'. It is narrow and steep, and its cupola and cross can suggest the shape of a flame.

Both the winter church and the upper church have shallow domical vaults without supports, and the enlargement of the windows in the walls and in the octagon fills the upper church with swathes of light. The decoration of the interior is in a poor state of preservation. The wrought-iron door and the baroque iconostasis, both in the upper church, are the most interesting features.

262, 263   Moscow   Москва

Church of the Assumption in Gonchari (the Potters' suburb), 1654–1702

Церковь Успения в Гончарах

Tserkov Uspeniya v Goncharakh

The church was commissioned by the guild of potters and ceramics workers who had settled in this extensive quarter of Moscow in the seventeenth century, and its members saw to it that the building

was abundantly decorated with examples of their skills. The south chapel was built in 1702. Alterations were made to the refectory in the eighteenth and nineteenth centuries, but without affecting the superb tile frieze of the seventeenth century. The bell-tower dates from the middle of the eighteenth century.

The main structure of the church belongs to the type of five-domed church without pillars usual in suburban Moscow in the middle of the seventeenth century *(pl. 263)*. The groundplan, as with St Nicholas at Bersenevka, is an oblong with its longer axis from north to south. The ornamentation in dressed bricks is carried out in the traditional style, with engaged columns at the corners and an entablature as the dominant horizontal feature, separating the façades from the elaborately detailed gables and roof. A frieze of blind arches runs between the cushion capitals and the actual cornice. The first zone above the cornice is formed by a pedestal below the actual roof, with a row of blind ogee gables on its vertical faces. The second zone consists of the five separate square pedestals that support the drums and domes. The small square recesses on their sides may originally have contained inset coloured tiles. The tops of the pedestals are in the shape of kokoshniki, above which rise the drums, decorated with the characteristic blind arcades and not open to the interior, and the onion domes. The middle dome and the large filigree crosses are gilded, and the four smaller domes are painted midnight blue and sprinkled with gold stars. Although there is nothing unusual for the period in the form of the roof, or in the brick mouldings on the window surrounds and cornice, the church has nonetheless a markedly individual character. One of its most obvious features is the size of the upper part, the height from the cornice to the crosses being as great as that from the ground to the cornice. The ornamental details are also somewhat large and overstated in proportion to the structural elements. The low apse, perfunctorily divided into three, is the same width as the body of the church, and occupies approximately the same area.

The chapel of Tikhon Amafuntsky the Miracleworker on the south side of the wide refectory has an octagonal drum, with a circular neck at the base of the dome consisting of six rows of coloured tiles with plant patterns on them. Four of the octagon's sides bear low relief representations of the four evangelists. Plate 262 shows St Matthew, without his symbol, as a Russian peasant type, holding his robe with his right hand and his gospel in the left. The relief is on three tiles of fired clay with a coloured glaze. The tile frieze on the refectory, the neck of the dome of the chapel and the four evangelists were evidently made for the church in a pottery in the neighbourhood, though the style is also reminiscent of the Belo-Russian artist Stepan Ivanov

Polubes, who worked on the Monastery of the New Jerusalem. Rebuilding and alterations done in the nineteenth century robbed the interior of its original artistic value, though the somknuty vault survives.

264 Moscow Москва

Church of the Trinity at Ostankino, 1678–92

Церковь Троицы в Останкине

Tserkov Troitsy v Ostankine

The Trinity was built over a period of fourteen years on the estate of Prince Cherkassky (later of Prince Sheremetyev) outside Moscow, by Pavel Potekhin, who was also the architect of the churches at Nikolskoye-Uryupino and Markovo. It was consecrated in stages: the north Chapel of Our Lady of Tikhvin in 1683, the south Alexander Svirsky Chapel in 1691, and the central Church of the Trinity in 1692. The complex is a typical example of Moscow architecture in the second half of the seventeenth century.

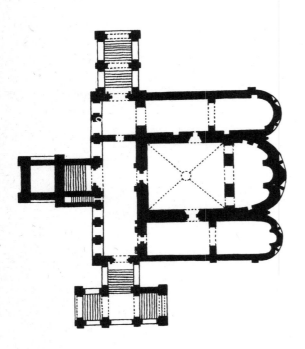

All the separate components stand on a common high basement-storey and are unmistakably oriented towards the central structure housing the body of the church. This is virtually a cube, though just oblong in plan, with a low, massive apse separated from it by two pillars. It is surrounded symmetrically by the two chapels at its east corners, both constructed in two zones and surmounted by a dome, the tent-roof bell-tower and external staircase to the west, a low gallery running round the cube on three sides linking the parts, and two ceremonial staircases at the north and south ends of the west section of the gallery, leading up to the main floor of the building from ground level. The roof consists of two tiers of blind gables, with five 'inflated' onion domes set close together on thin drums, and not opening on to the interior. The drums rest on square pedestals decorated with ogee gables. The two side chapels have the same roof form as the central block, and their domes are related to the central group. The bell-tower, which is connected to the west gallery and the north and south stairs by a bridge, plays an essential part in the composition. The stairs, both double flights, have low tent roofs over their landings and enrich the overall painterliness of the effect. The entire decoration is treated with extraordinary virtuosity and imagination. Potekhin and his workmen handled the moulded bricks as if they were wood. A dense ornamentation of brick, limestone and majolica covers every surface like tapestry. Even the lesenes are fashioned as vertical columns of shirinki, with tiles or terracotta reliefs at their centres. But for all their multiformity and delicate scale proportions, these small-scale forms, shirinki, heart-shapes, niches, small columns, balusters, barrel-shapes, ornamental gables, chains and girki, with their complicated decorations, are all subject to a prescribed rhythmic order. Their density increases from the bottom towards the top of the building. The window surrounds and the roll mouldings and ledges that provide the horizontal articulation play the major organizing part.

The interior of the main church is tall and light, with a domical vault and no pillars. The original iconostasis and icons have survived. The murals date from the end of the nineteenth century. The church was restored by N. V. Sultanov in 1877–78.

409 Veliky Ustyug Великий Устюг

Church of the Ascension, from 1648

Церковь Вознесения

Tserkov Vozneseniya

The strong influence that the capital exercised on provincial taste is very plain to see in this parish church commissioned by the merchant Nikifor Revyakin and probably built by masons from Moscow. The 'ornamental' style evolved by the Moscow School in the middle of the seventeenth century, with its complex, multiple composition and elaborate brick ornamentation, exemplified by the Trinity in Moscow-Nikitniki and the Assumption in Vladimir, spread to the distant towns of northern Russia (Veliky Ustyug is north-east of Vologda).

The Church of the Ascension was not built all at once, but in at least three phases, though within a time-span of not more than twenty to thirty years. The whole complex, which contains eight altars, stands on a basement-storey. The main church in the centre is square in plan and has a domical vault, without pillars. Of its five domes only the middle one has a drum with windows. The middle section of the low, semi-circular apse is marked out by

that of the main church. The complicated form of the pediments of the upper windows is especially attractive. The painting intensifies the ornamental character. The chapel retains, in its interior, frescos of the 1680s and a baroque iconostasis, also of the seventeenth century, with panels and a richly carved Royal Door, which is framed by alternate vertical mouldings of roll, bead and intricate ribbon patterns.

411 Tutayev Тутаев

Cathedral of the Resurrection, 1652–78
Собор Воскресения Христова
Sobor Voskreseniya Khristova

The monumental cathedral in Tutayev (formerly Romanov-Borisoglebsk), a town on the Volga, about thirty miles above Yaroslavl, was built on the site of an earlier tent-roofed refectory church, in which the weight of the roof had produced a number of fissures. It is likely that the groundplan was taken over from the earlier church, an oblong on an east-west axis which is a departure from the traditional Yaroslavl pattern of churches with four pillars. The ground floor has three apses of about the same height as itself, which project some distance, while the apses of the main church on the upper floor are contained within the outline of the overall structure, and hardly protrude on the outside. The middle one of the upper apses is surmounted by a small dome, but they rise no higher than the side chapels. Apart from this unusual feature, the exterior appearance is in the style of the Yaroslavl School of the seventeenth century. The building was made as large, and decorated as richly, as possible. The tall central structure is surmounted by five domes, surrounded on three sides by two levels of vaulted, arcaded galleries and flanked on the north and south sides by chapels with ornamental domes on them. The positioning of the two exterior staircases introduces an unusual note of asymmetry. Each consists of two flights of steps and the stone roofs in the form of bochki reveal the influence of wooden architecture.

The ornamentation is considerably more elaborate than on other buildings of the Yaroslavl School, evidently under the influence of Moscow. In particular, the treatment of the central structure is as lavish as that of the drums, the galleries and the staircases. The north and south façades are divided into four, the west into three. All the articulating elements – the complicated columns at the corners, the three demi-shafts ringed with bead mouldings placed against each pilaster, the entablature and the ornamental window surrounds – are delicately modelled in dressed brick to stand out from their surroundings. The upper storey of the gallery is even more elegant, the parapets decorated with a frieze of square sunken panels filled with coloured tiles, the pillars of the arcade surrounded with clusters of dainty columns. The cathedral's builders understood perfectly how to combine the Yaroslavl type with the Moscow style of brick ornamentation, and to enfold the entire structure in a baroque chiaroscuro play.

The interior decoration is equal in artistic quality to that of the Church of the Prophet Elijah in Yaroslavl. All the wall and ceiling surfaces are covered with frescos executed in the years following 1679 by artists from Yaroslavl. In addition to the usual subjects there are some relatively rare themes, especially in the galleries, taken from the Russian 'Books of the Fathers', hagiology and chronicles, and depicted in a decorative, narrative style. The carved wooden altar canopy and the shrine with the wooden figure of St Nicholas of Mozhaisk are from the same school, though earlier in date (1654). The two founders' pews with brightly painted carved lions are slightly later.

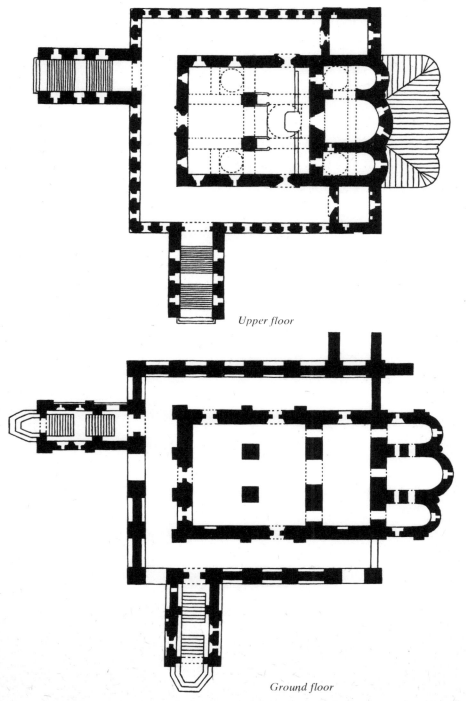

Upper floor

Ground floor

Monastery of the Holy Trinity and St Sergius
Church of St Sergius of Radonezh with refectory, 1686–92
Well Chapel, late 17th century
492 Gate-church of St John the Baptist, 1693–99
Duck Tower, 16th–17th centuries
Bell-tower, 1741–70

Троице-Сергиева Лавра
Церковь Сергия Радонежского с трапезной
Подкладезная часовня
Надвратная церковь Иоанна Предтечи
Уточья башня
Колокольня

Troitse-Sergiyeva Lavra
Tserkov Sergiya Radonezhskogo s trapeznoi
Podkladeznaya chasovnya
Nadvratnaya tserkov Ioanna Predtechi
Utochya bashnya
Kolokolnya

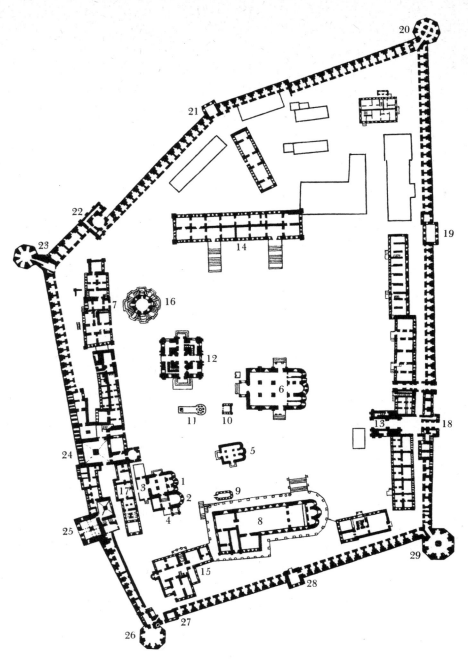

1 *Cathedral of the Trinity* 2 *Nikon Chapel* 3 *West vestibule* 4 *Serapion Palace* 5 *Church of the Holy Ghost* 6 *Cathedral of the Assumption* 7 *Church of SS Zosima and Savvati and the Infirmary* 8 *Church of St Sergius of Radonezh and refectory* 9 *Mikheyevskaya Church* 10 *Well chapel* 11 *Ciborium* 12 *Bell-tower* 13 *Gate-church of St John the Baptist* 14 *Tsar Charterhouse* 15 *Metropolitan's Palace* 16 *Church of the Icon of Our Lady of Smolensk* 17 *Sacristy* 18 *Red Tower and Holy Gate* 19 *Drying-room Tower* 20 *Duck Tower* 21 *Sounding Tower* 22 *Gate-tower* 23 *Wooden Tower* 24 *Cell Tower* 25 *Brewery Tower with cold cellar* 26 *Water Tower* 27 *Water gate* 28 *Onion Tower* 29 *Pyatnitsa Tower*

At the end of the seventeenth century, and throughout the eighteenth, the old Monastery of the Holy Trinity and St Sergius (*pls. 9, 156–8, 224, 225*) was enriched by a large number of new buildings in the baroque style. The old refectory of 1469 which was no longer adequate for its purposes was replaced between 1686 and 1692 by a new, spacious hall suitable for lavish receptions, attached to a church dedicated to St Sergius. The long rectangular building stands on a high plinth, surrounded by a terrace, and its ornamentation is unusually elegant (*pl. 281*). It is structurally simple. The walls of the plinth are pierced by wide, squat arches, corresponding to the vaulting of the basement-room within, and surmounted by a limestone balustrade running round the terrace that is its roof. Two wide ceremonial flights of steps were built up to the porches on the north façade which was treated as the main front. The church and its one small dome tower over the east end of the refectory. It has three apses rising to about half the height of the wall and projecting a considerable way, and its upper storey is stepped slightly inwards above the lower storey. The façades are articulated by engaged columns (pairs of them at the corners) with unusual capitals of a Corinthian type. The west wall of the refectory has three divisions, corresponding to the three apses, and the north and south walls have fifteen each, three on the church and the rest on the refectory. An attic storey decorated with stone scallops rises above the massive entablature. The stone window surrounds in each division of the walls have columns with a vine carved in relief spiralling up them and an open pediment with curved sides, adorned with baroque flourishes. The open staircases that used to lead directly from ground level up to the church and the vestibule of the Great Hall have not survived. The original porches at the east and west ends of the north front remain, however, with columns supporting twin arches with the ornamental carved *girki* invariably found at this period. The portals within the porches have ornate architraves featuring pairs of columns. A regular, chequered pattern of triangles is painted on the façades, rustication on the apse walls, and vines on the large columns. This architectonic-cum-decorative system, representing a new stylistic trend of the late seventeenth and early eighteenth centuries, is termed Moscow Baroque, or sometimes called by the name of Prince Naryshkin, the rich

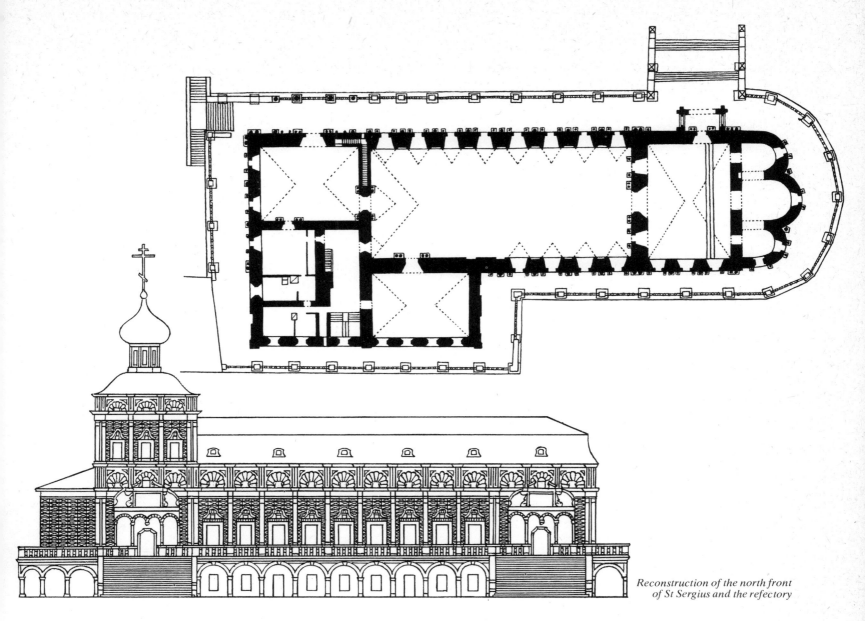

Reconstruction of the north front
of St Sergius and the refectory

aristocratic patron of architecture, and it introduced the formal terminology of the age of Peter I, which led to the final break with the national tradition.

The huge Great Hall of the refectory is 112 feet long and 49 feet wide. Its roof is formed by an arc of a barrel vault, without supports, and with spandrels over the windows *(pl. 280)*. At the west end the barrel is intercepted by a segmental vault with spandrels over the door and portal. It may well have been modelled on the Hall of the Cross in the Patriarch's Palace in Moscow. The Church of St Sergius is an extension of the hall to the east, separated from it by a wall pierced by three doorways flanked by columns *(pls. 279, 280)*. The elegance of the exterior is matched by the interior decoration. The graceful screen and the romantic murals, executed in oils, date from the end of the nineteenth century and the beginning of the twentieth. The ornate baroque iconostasis in the church is contemporary with the building. Service rooms lead off the west vestibule to the south and east.

The Well Chapel, as exquisite in its ornamentation as in its form, was built at the end of the seventeenth century, possibly by the same architects who built the refectory *(pl. 282)*. There is an affinity in their execution and both are in the same Moscow Baroque style. The characteristic stepwise construction, with a square base supporting three octagons of appreciably decreasing diameters, makes use of the inward curving roofs of the octagons, the topmost of which is crowned by a cupola and filigree cross. The decorative columns, the window surrounds, with a different form of gable in each zone (those of the ground floor windows are similar to the

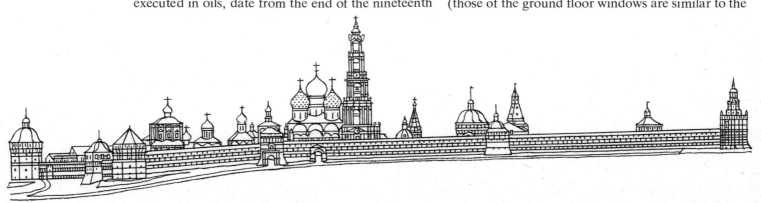

ones on the refectory), the recurrent vine motifs, and the bright, cheerful painting of the walls are all typical. A holy water basin beside the chapel is shaded by a late nineteenth-century ciborium in an eclectic style.

494   The Church of St John the Baptist over the monastery's main east gate dates from 1693–99 *(pl. 285)*. It was paid for by the Stroganovs, a family of merchants who had been the financially soundest of all the middle-class patrons since the turn of the sixteenth century and even generated an individual style (notably in icon painting). The gate-church belongs to the Moscow Baroque movement, but displays idiosyncracies derived from the Stroganov School. Three rectangular blocks, progressively smaller in size, rise one above the other, surmounted by an octagonal drum and dome. The brick masonry is painted red, which shows off the white stone ornamentation very effectively. The latter includes engaged columns with Corinthian capitals, a prominent entablature with a frieze of blocks shaped like consoles, the scallop niches below the roof and the octagonal window surrounds. Until the fire in 1746 the walls were painted in a geometrical pattern similar to the painting on the refectory.

The monastery's fortifications, which suffered severely from the Polish siege during the Time of Troubles (cf. the commentary on *pl. 224*), were repaired between 1620 and 1650. By the end of the century the monastery had lost its strategic military importance, and its towers were refashioned to present a less forbidding, more ceremonious appearance. The transformation of the Duck Tower at the north-east corner into something highly ornamental is typical *(pl. 283)*. The parapet was reconstructed as a pierced arcade with pinnacles and stone balls placed at regular intervals along its top, and an octagonal bell-tower, several storeys high, and with a typical baroque profile, was built on top of the platform. Its lavish stone ornaments, including a balustrade, contrast well with the red brick fabric.

Other seventeenth-century structures include the long, rectangular, two-storey block of the Tsar Charterhouse, built in the eighties to replace a wooden palace, and the Metropolitan's Palace adjoining the refectory to the west (1640 and 1687–92).

The 320-feet-high bell-tower is one of the most impressive creations of Russian architecture on the boundary between the Baroque and Classicism, and as the dominant vertical element of the ensemble it provides the organic link between the old and the new buildings *(pl. 284)*. The design by the St Petersburg architect A. Shumakher was approved by the Tsarina Anna Ivanovna, and the monastery commissioned the Moscow architect I. Michurin to build it. He decided to build it on a site a little to the north of the one originally chosen, that was on the axis of the Cathedral of the Assumption, in order to clear a greater space round the tower. Michurin

supervised the construction from the laying of the foundation stone in 1741 until he was obliged to take up a commission in Kiev in 1747, when he handed over to his pupil D. Ukhtomsky. Ukhtomsky altered the plan by adding two more storeys and he took until 1770, a relatively long time, to complete it. The tower rises in four stages pierced by large arches, above a massive base. The ornamentation is governed by the Composite orders with their elongated proportions, though the plan to complete it with thirty-two allegorical statues was not carried out. A total of forty-two bells hang in the four storeys.

286–290   Moscow   Москва

New Convent of the Virgin
Church of the Assumption with refectory, 1685–87
Gate-church of the Transfiguration, 1687–89
Lopukhin Palace, 1687–89
Bell-tower, *c*1690
Fortifications, 16th–17th centuries

Новодевичий монастырь
Успенская церковь с трапезной
Надвратная Преображенская церковь
Лопухинский корпус
Колокольня
Крепостные сооружения

Novodevichy monastyr
Uspenskaya tserkov s trapeznoy
Nadvratnaya Preobrazhenskaya tserkov
Lopukhinsky korpus
Kolokolnya
Krepostnye sooruzheniya

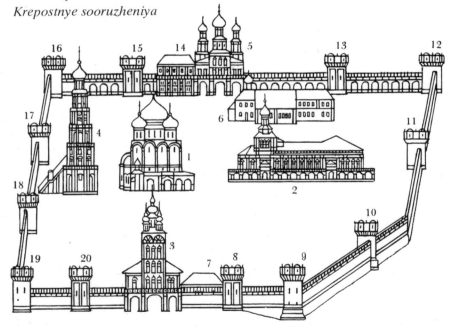

1 *Cathedral of the Icon of Our Lady of Smolensk* 2 *Church of the Assumption and refectory* 3 *Gate-church of the Transfiguration* 4 *Bell-tower* 5 *Gate-church of the Virgin of the Intercession* 6 *Church of St Ambrose and palace of Irina Godunova* 7 *Lopukhin Palace* 8 *Lopukhin Tower* 9 *Naprudni Tower* 10 *Savvinsky Tower* 11 *Refectory Tower* 12 *Setunsky Tower* 13 *John the Baptist Tower* 14 *Maria Palace* 15 *Virgin of the Intercession Tower* 16 *Shoemaker Tower* 17 *Tailor Tower* 18 *Joseph Tower* 19 *Nicholas Tower* 20 *Tsarina Tower*

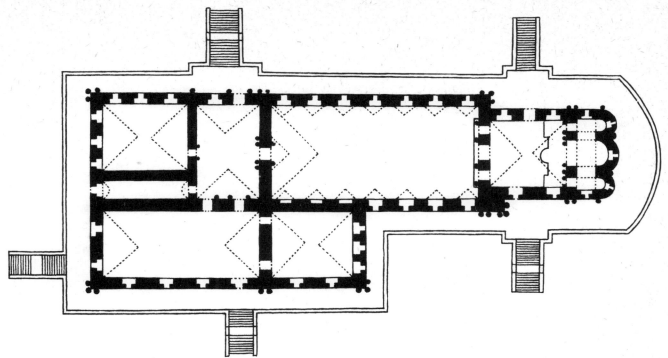

The convent dedicated to the Virgin, with the Cathedral of the Icon of Our Lady of Smolensk (cf. *pls 205–08*), on the south-west boundary of Moscow, founded in 1524 to form part of the ring of fortresses round the city, was badly damaged during the Wars of Liberation in 1612. Its rebuilding took place in stages. It enjoyed its period of greatest flowering under the patronage of the clever, ambitious Tsarevna Sophia, who was made regent for her young half-brother Peter I in 1682, but was deposed by him and banished to the convent in 1689, after she had hatched a new conspiracy with the Streltsy guards. The layout of the convent already had an east-west longitudinal axis intersecting a north-south axis at the point where the Cathedral of Our Lady of Smolensk stands. The refectory and Church of the Assumption (1685 to 1687) were now placed to the west of the cathedral, and the bell-tower (*c*1690) to its east, on the same longitudinal axis. Raising the height of the two main gates produced the Gate-church of the Trans-

figuration (1687–89) and the Gate-church of the Virgin of the Intercession (1683–88) at the north and south ends respectively of the transverse axis. The Lopukhin Palace (1687–89), where Peter I's first wife Eudoxia Lopukhina, whom he married in 1689, lived from 1727 to 1731, forms one section of the north perimeter wall, and the Maria Palace (1683–88), where another half-sister of the tsar, Maria Alexeyevna, lived, is similarly connected with the south wall. The palace of Irina Godunova dates from 1598. The new buildings and the construction at the same period of ornamental tops to the twelve towers (with machicolation, arcades, gables and pinnacles) gave the convent a delightful, painterly silhouette *(pls. 288, 289)*. The new layout was frequently copied and was even the model for Rastrelli's plan for the Smolny Convent at St Petersburg.

The long refectory building (1685–87), raised on a basement-plinth, recalls the refectory in the Monastery of the Holy Trinity and St Sergius *(pls.*

279–81). The original terrace and five open-air staircases were not restored after the fire of 1796, and the somewhat narrower Church of the Assumption at the refectory's east end, with its three prominent apses, did not get its five domes back. Its square main structure, with the upper storey stepped slightly inward, is surmounted by a low octagon and a slender drum and dome *(pl. 286)*. The façades are decorated with the kind of ornament usual in the Moscow Baroque style, but in distinctly simpler forms. The engaged columns and pilasters supported by massive pedestals lack Corinthian or Composite capitals, for instance, and the cornices lack complicated friezes or mouldings. The window surrounds are also plainer, topped by open pediments with acroteria at the top and sides. The covered staircases leading into the church and the vestibule of the refectory date in their present form from the nineteenth century. The nave of the church has a domical vault. The Chapel of the Descent of the Holy Ghost in the upper storey has been accessible only through the attic of the refectory since the fire. The area of the immense dining hall is approximately 4,200 square feet. The ceiling is a shallow barrel vault, without supports, meeting the end wall of the church perpendicularly, while a segmental vault curves up from the west wall to intercept the barrel vault. There are spandrels above all the windows and the west door. Anterooms and service rooms adjoin the vestibule to the west and south.

The Church of the Transfiguration was built in 1687–89 on top of the immense, wide rectangular block that encloses the three archways of the convent's main gate *(pls 288, 290)*. There is room for a terrace with parapet round the church, the bottom zone of which includes the refectory and the sanctuary, while the nave in the centre – a square room with a domical vault – towers above to a height allowing for two more zones. The large windows light the interior well. The elaborate columns, the window surrounds with their baroque open pediments, the fluting and the plant ornamentation, the cornice, the scallop niches in the blind gables, the decoration on the five octagonal drums below the two-tier domes – all testify to the skill of the stone-masons, and make the church one of the most handsome monuments of the Moscow Baroque. The tall, narrow, five-tier iconostasis is also characteristic of the end of the seventeenth century.

The Lopukhin Palace (1687–89) consists of a single, imposing block, whose north front, windows and all, takes the place of the convent's outer wall between the Gate-church of the Transfiguration and the Lopukhin Tower *(pl. 288)*. The royal apartments were on the upper floor, and the magnificent stone window surrounds on the south front distinguish them very clearly from the servants' accommodation and kitchens on the ground floor *(pl. 287)*. The carved and moulded pediments must be almost

without equal. Only the pedestals and abaci remain of the columns, whose articulating function has passed to the wide lesenes.

The king-pin of the whole ensemble is the 236-feet-high octagonal bell-tower of 1690 *(pl. 289)*. It rises in six steps, and each storey has its own type of ornament. Alternate storeys are made up of arcades and solid walls decorated with window surrounds that lack windows. The elaborately moulded cornices and the little terraces with balustrades surmounting the four lower tiers intensify, by contrast, the vertical dynamic of the elegant tower, which is also expressed by the slender columns at every corner. As the drawing, right, illustrates, the arcade on the third tier is particularly appealing, for its logical assembly and the artistry of its ornamentation. The bell-tower served as a prototype for a large number of later towers of this type.

Detail of the façade of the third tier of the bell-tower

291 Moscow Москва

Church of the Virgin of the Intercession at Fili, *c*1693
Церковь Покрова в Филях
Tserkov Pokrova v Filyakh

Baroque forms in composition and ornament reach their peak of perfection in the last decade of the seventeenth century. The painterly asymmetry of various buildings of the earlier phase of the style is replaced by a more refined, symmetrical assemblage, which creates a unified vertical dynamic by pyramidal construction. The church at Fili, a former suburb now absorbed into the modern city, has been

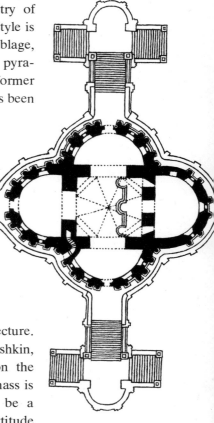

called the swan-song of early Russian architecture. Commissioned by Prince Lev Kirillovich Naryshkin, it simultaneously overthrows and rests upon the medieval traditions. The way the structural mass is differentiated and dematerialized seems to be a subtle expression of a courtly, aristocratic attitude to life, but at the same time one senses in it the organic vigour and – via Ukrainian and Belo-Russian influences – the formal vocabulary of the wooden architecture of the Russian people. The best examples of this type, in which its potentialities were most fully realized, proliferated in the many properties in the vicinity of Moscow belonging to the respected Naryshkin family, who were closely related to Peter I on his mother's side. The characteristic traits include the symmetrical, multifoil layout of the groundplan, the many tiers of stepped, diminishing storeys, the centripetalism and differentiation, the decoration governed by specific groupings, and the parapets of open pediments in the form of coxcombs (cf. also the Church of the Resurrection at Kadashi).

The church at Fili stands on a high base surrounded by a narrow arcaded loggia, the roof of which forms a terrace round the church itself. Identical broad, open staircases lead up to the terrace from ground level on the north, west and south sides, each with double flights to a first landing at right angles to the single upper flight. The outline of the principal floor of the church repeats that of the ground floor, a square centre with semi-circular apsidal arms on each side, producing a Greek cross with rounded ends. The east arm is the sanctuary and the other three serve as vestibules. Each is surmounted by an octagonal drum with a pot-bellied dome, placed close to the central tower. Inside, the semi-circles open on to the square by means of arches occupying almost the whole width and height of its sides, so that a regular, if relatively small room is formed. The walls of the square are continued above the semi-circles providing a base, which looks rather squat from the outside but draws the proportions of the interior upwards, for three successively diminishing octagons. The lowest, massively proportioned, accentuates and lights the central cube with its huge windows. The two upper octagons are pierced with arches and were intended to house the bells. The dome on the top one is exactly the same size and shape as the four on the apsidal arms below, providing a new variation on the traditional group of five. The proportions and outlines of the constituent parts of the pyramidal structure create a dynamic and harmonious impression. The central room is not large, but looks tall and light, a typical characteristic of court churches in the seventeenth century. The opulent decoration of the interior is both ceremonial and elegant. The richly carved, baroque 'Imperial boxes' on the west wall correspond interestingly to the wooden iconostasis on the facing wall, which is carved in the same style.

All the significant details of the exterior decoration converge on the third tier of the building, the upper part of the church proper, and grow steadily more attenuated from bottom to top. The forms are the usual corner columns, window surrounds with curvaceous open pediments, consoles, pinnacles and, not least, the coxcombs replacing the traditional kokoshniki; together they unfurl a fascinating play of light and shade. Slender columns in groups of three across the very short slanting faces that cut off the corners of the square third tier replace angularity with an agreeable roundness. The tallest octagon with its ornamental gables and disproportionately long columns finally resolves the battle, fought on

many fronts between verticals and horizontals, in favour of the vertical dynamic. The unusual thickness (over six feet) of the exterior walls is not only able to cope with the numerous downward and outward thrusts, but also to accommodate a staircase leading up to the bell-chamber in the middle octagon. The walls are of brick, and all the ornamentation is of limestone. The natural colours were intensified with red paint and whitewash in the nineteenth century. Restoration began in the 1960s and still continues in the interior, under the direction of I. V. Ilenko.

The church at Fili is stylistically close to the church in the village of Ubory outside Moscow, built by Yakov Bukhvostov in 1694–97.

292   Moscow   Москва

Church of Peter the Metropolitan in the Upper Monastery of St Peter, 1690
Bell-tower 1694

Церковь Петра митрополита
Высокопетровского монастыря
Колокольня

Tserkov Petra mitropolita Vysokopetrovskogo monastyrya
Kolokolnya

The Upper Monastery of St Peter was founded at the end of the fourteenth century. All its buildings in stone and brick date from the end of the seventeenth century, however, and were financed by generous gifts from the Naryshkin family and Tsar Peter I, who took refuge in the monastery during the Streltsy uprising stage-managed by his sister Sophia. The Church of Peter the Metropolitan, the bell-tower, the sprawling two-storey palace (Terem Palace) and the residential wings were built in the Moscow Baroque style. The Church of the Icon of the Virgin of Bogolyubovo and the Church of St Sergius of Radonezh survive in addition.

The Church of Peter the Metropolitan was originally planned with three storeys, with an eight-lobed outline to the first two floors and an octagon on top. It seems to have anticipated the ornate, symmetrical pyramidal churches built by the Naryshkin family on their estates around Moscow. As at Fili (*pl. 291*) the square nucleus is disguised by a wreath of apsidal outer cells: semi-circular to the east and west, trefoil to the north and south. The compositional principle was that of the 'octagon on the square' dominating wooden architecture of the same period. Unfortunately the original ground floor, which was surrounded by an arcaded gallery, has been buried as the level of the ground has risen. That is one reason for the church's present top-heavy appearance; the other is the fact that instead of the usual stone surrounds to the doors and windows, plant motifs in yellow and brown have been painted directly on to the brick surfaces. The pilasters on the corners of the octagon, the cornice and frieze of round arches, the wide dome with its shallow curvature, the polychromaticism, have a harmonious total effect that is appropriate to the Baroque style. The relatively constricted but lofty interior is flooded with light.

The bell-tower, which found many imitators in the eighteenth century, was erected on the spacious terrace roof of a broad gate-house, which embraces the usual three archways, flanked by columns. The bottom tier of the tower, which contains a church, is a cube and supports two octagonal tiers with open arches for the bells and a drum surmounted by an onion dome and cross. The exterior ornamentation includes elements typical of the Moscow Baroque: corner columns, shirinki on the parapets, ornamental window surrounds with tall, lobed pediments, and string courses in various forms.

293 Moscow Москва

Church of the Archangel Michael in the Andronikov Monastery of the Saviour, 1691–1739

Церковь Михаила архангела Спасо-Андроникова монастыря

Tserkov Mikhaila arkhangela Spaso-Andronikova monastyrya

This tower-church was built against the east wall of the refectory *(pl. 159)*. Its construction stretched over a relatively long period. It climbs in several stages, acknowledging the 'octagon on a square' principle. The first floor above the high plinth-storey is a rectangular block containing the sanctuary and the lower half of the nave. The upper part of the nave forms a second rectangle, which supports three diminishing octagons, surmounted by a small cupola. The articulation by means of columns and pilasters and an entablature in which bands of zigzag and saw-tooth are linked to the cornice by a frieze of wedge-shaped motifs, the scallop niches acting as blind gables, the columns flanking the windows and the open pediments above them, the consoles and the fillets – all amount to a simplified version of the Moscow Baroque style, which harmonizes well with the stern, monumental style of the fifteenth and sixteenth-century buildings and is appropriate to the monastic setting in general. The church was restored between 1948 and 1960.

294 Moscow Москва

New Cathedral of the Icon of the Virgin of the Don in the Don Monastery, 1684–93

Новый собор Донской Богоматери Донского монастыря

Novy sobor Donskoy Bogomateri Donskogo monastyrya

A new building programme was undertaken in the Don Monastery in the last years of the seventeenth century, under the patronage of the young Peter I (cf. the commentaries on *pls 11, 226, 417*). The area enclosed by the monastery was enlarged to form a large square with strongly fortified walls, and the New, or Great, Cathedral which was built in the exact centre of the square, is massively proportioned, as if to reflect the military character of its surroundings. I. E. Grabar records that the people of Moscow regarded it as an architectural wonder. The five towering, monumental domes, the four square pillars and the extreme paucity of ornament appear to revert to the austere traditions of the sixteenth century. But it is just as strongly influenced by the new baroque stylistic principles governing the virtually contemporary churches at Fili and the Upper Monastery of St Peter *(pls 291, 292)* and the later church at Dubrovitsy *(pl. 301)*: centripetalism, symmetry and apsidal forms. The architect was probably Ukrainian.

The four smaller domes are spaced well apart from the central one, near the edges of the roof, corresponding to the semi-circular bays of the groundplan. The plan is basically a square with the addition of large apsidal vestibules on three sides as well as the three apses on the east side, producing a Greek cross with rounded ends. The tall, weighty structure, divided into two zones horizontally, and the gallery that completely and symmetrically surrounds it, reproducing its outline in an angular variant, stand on a basement storey which has an apse and an arcade of single arches echoing the double arches of the gallery above. The basement contained the winter church as was customary. Broad open staircases lead up to the gallery on three sides. It may well be the case that the influence that Ukrainian Baroque exercised on the composition also brought an indirect influence of wooden architecture to bear upon it. The interior, restored in 1782–85, is excellently lit by the numerous large windows, and contains an iconostasis by artists of the tsar's Armoury workshop (1693–99). The cathedral now houses the A. V. Shchusev Museum of Architectural Research.

412   Kolomna   Коломна

Cathedral of the Assumption, 1672–82
Успенский собор
Uspensky sobor

The first civic cathedral in Kolomna was built of limestone in 1379–82 on the orders of Great Prince Dmitry Donskoi, and it symbolized the victory over the Tartar hordes of Mamai at Kulikovo (1380). It had three aisles, six pillars, three apses and three domes, and even at this early date the roof took the form of graduated tiers of blind gables. It stood above a cellar-storey and was surrounded by an open arcaded gallery. The surviving fragments of the façades indicate that a relief frieze ran round the building halfway up the walls. These are all characteristics of the Moscow School which began to develop at the beginning of the fourteenth century.

That cathedral was partly demolished in the second half of the seventeenth century. The present cathedral was built on the old foundations in 1672 to 82, in the style of the Moscow School of the period, specifically in the more conservative variant favoured by government circles. Its revival of the forms of the period when the power of Moscow was rising to its zenith was in conscious conformity with the building reforms introduced by Nikon and upheld by the tsar even after the patriarch had been dismissed. It has five massive domes and a simple four-faced roof. The one idea behind its composition is to make a monumental, majestic, ceremonial impression. The ornamentation is surprisingly modest: the greatest extravagance is the widening of the windows and their arrangement in two tiers, with surrounds that are typical of the seventeenth century, albeit in a very restrained fashion. The architrave mouldings round the doors are alternately rectangular and semi-circular in profile and are ornamented in dressed brick.

A massive bell-tower was built beside the cathedral at the end of the seventeenth century, the bells being hung in an octagonal chamber with arched openings in the sides, and the whole crowned by a tent roof.

413   Moscow   Москва

Church of the Icon of the Virgin of Tikhvin at Alexeyevskoye, *c*1680
Церковь Тихвинской Богоматери в Алексеевском
Tserkov Tikhvinskoy Bogomateri v Alekseyevskom

The church is one of the last of Tsar Alexey Romanov and has the five domes prescribed by Nikon, but it combines the austere conservative type of composition with the refined, stylistic decorative details and the verticalism of the court school. It was erected at the side of a wooden palace (no longer extant) that lay on the road from Moscow to the Monastery of the Holy Trinity and St Sergius. It stands on a basement-storey which is surrounded by an arcaded open gallery. The three apses project some distance, forming an integrated block. Two tiers of unusually high windows with ornamental brick surrounds pierce the façades, which are articulated by columns and clustered columns at the corners, and are terminated by a vigorous entablature incorporating a saw-tooth frieze. The roof is magnificent, a pyramid formed by two tiers of blind gables, with a third tier on the pedestals of the five drums. The interior is square in plan, vaulted without pillars, and makes an impression of height and light like one of the commemorative tower-churches. It is embraced at the west end by a refectory that was at one time linked to the wooden palace by a bridge. It is unusual in that the inner room is surrounded on three sides by a passage of the width of the sections that protrude on the north and south sides. It opens on to the nave of the church by way of three tall, wide arches, thereby considerably enlarging it. The passage round the refectory consists of a tribune built over a kind of peristyle. The bell-tower was built in 1824.

414   Ryazan   Рязань

Cathedral of the Assumption, 1693–99
Architect Yakov Bukhvostov
Успенский собор
Архитектор Яков Бухвостов
Uspensky sobor   Arkhitektor Yakov Bukhvostov

The generous scale of the conception of both plan and structure develops from the weighty, conservative type of civic cathedral that was widespread in the sixteenth and seventeenth centuries. Yakov Bukhvostov, the architect, adopted all the type's principal characteristics: the three aisles, the six supports, the three apses and the five domes, placed close together. He differed in placing the whole building on top of a massive basement-storey that gives the impression of being pressed down by the weight. The basement consists of the winter church, surrounded by a gallery whose outer wall was originally a line of open arches. The roof of the gallery provides a terrace round the church. The essential artistic character of the building is certainly in accordance with the period when it was built, depending as it does on the pleasing proportions and the ornamentation. The vertical articulation of the façades (the west in three equal divisions, the north and south in four) is by means of extremely thin columns, arranged in pairs on small pedestals. In place of round gables a cornice in the form of brick pendants, which are also found on the capitals, finishes the walls at the top. A horizontal articulation is suggested by the three lines of windows, which nevertheless do more to accentuate the vertical dimension. A relatively inconspicuous string course runs between the second and third zones, and rings on the shafts of the columns seem to want to suggest the presence of another between the first and second zones. The drums of the domes are polygonal, and their corners are marked by thin demi-shafts with 'melons'.

500

The fabric of the walls is brick, but all the details are in white limestone, a characteristic of the Moscow Baroque. The main ornamental elements are the surrounds, with two or four columns, of the doors and windows. The columns in the first zone are decorated with a subtle relief pattern, which covers only the bottom third of the columns of the second zone, while there is no relief on the windows of the third zone, though the spiral form of the top two-thirds of the columns is a compensation for it. The pediments are treated equally systematically: the amount of ornamentation decreases with the distance from the ground. The recessed doorways, with their various shapes of pillar and scalloped pediments are particularly fine illustrations of the architect's talent. The relief carving accentuates the three-dimensional element of the splay. In spite of the variety of the ornament, all the motifs are subordinated to the fundamental architectonic idea: monumentality, with the function of every structural element clearly defined. The interior is spacious and well lit. The nave is about 92 feet high, with four round supports, and there are two rectangular pillars behind the iconostasis. The iconostasis, carved and gilded by S. Khristoforov and his assistants, is one of the best examples of the Moscow Baroque style. It occupies the full height of the church, and its imposing structure is based on columns in the classical orders.

Technical errors crept into the construction of the cathedral. As a result cracks appeared in the masonry during work on the roof in the eighteenth century, and subsequently the open gallery and terrace collapsed in 1728. This stately building was given a thorough, authentic restoration in the 1950s, under the direction of Y. V. Mikhaylovsky and I. V. Ilenko.

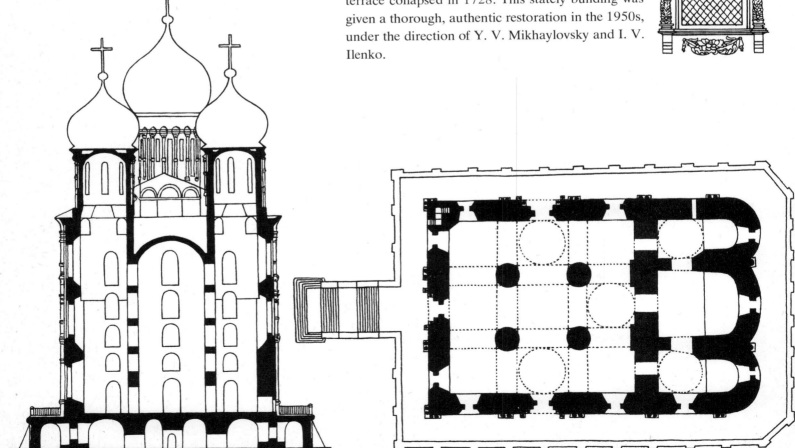

415, 416 Gorky Горький

Church of the Nativity of the Virgin, 1697–1718
Церковь Рождества Богоматери
Tserkov Rozhdestva Bogomateri

The church and its adjunct structures were commissioned by the powerful and influential Stroganov family, to stand on a commanding hill above the Volga, next door to their palatial business premises. The reason why it took over twenty years to finish, from the date of the laying of the foundation stone in 1697, was that the Stroganovs left Nizhni Novgorod (now Gorky) in 1705, when no more than the shell had been built, and took no further interest in it.

The whole complex is on two floors. The upper storey consists of the sanctuary, the cuboid nave, the long refectory and a small anteroom, aligned one after another on an east-west axis. It is a variant of the type of church built by middle-class patrons after Nikon's reforms, with a simpler, more regular composition (cf. *pls 259–64*). The regularity is relieved in this case by the bell-tower, a completely independent structure to the south-west of the church, and set at an angle to its line. The refectory is unusual, perhaps unique, both for the separate anteroom across the whole of its width at the west end, and for being narrower, rather than wider, than the nave. This particular form of the refectory, the reduction of the external dimensions of the nave in its upper part, and the cruciform base provided for the four smaller drums, reflect the influence of wooden architecture.

The three apses, projecting as a barely differentiated block at the east end, are no higher than the refectory at the west, and the nave rises above them both by a full zone, while the four rectangular bases of the drums, pointing due east, west, north and south, are a zone higher still. They form a Greek cross, with a low octagon at the centre, supporting the octagonal drum of the main dome. The four smaller domes, also on octagonal drums, are level with the central drum. All the octagons are pierced on every face. The systematic use of columns and the virtuosity of the ornamentation may well also be unique. The principle behind the ornamentation is the continuous repetition of the same, compositionally integrated units, each one centred on a window and its surround (*pl. 416*). The ringed, fluted or spiral columns with their Corinthian capitals, the consoles, pediments, friezes, balustrades, the rows of wedges suspended below the cornices, all combine to compose a multiform, subtle ornamentation, frequently supplemented by a

pattern of low relief. The building is wrapped in this way in a ceaseless play of forms and chiaroscuro, which yet does not detract from the clearly discernible regularity of its composition. Most of the ornament is of carved stone, but brick and tiles are also used.

The interior has remained in its original form and is remarkable for the contrast between the refectory and the church. Apart from the east wall, the walls and ceiling of the refectory are smooth and painted white. The east wall, pierced by the door into the church and two windows giving on to it, is covered with an opulent limestone relief. The tall, cuboid nave has a domical vault of four cells, each of which is interrupted by an opening admitting light from one of the four smaller domes. The apex of the vault is the octagonal opening below the main dome. The light flooding into the square room from above draws the eye upwards, but it is held above all by the baroque iconostasis, its carved wooden frame glowing with the rich colours of the icons. The niches, pilasters and frescos on the walls, together with the windows, enlarge the space by their various different kinds of outline. The tribune is constructed like a small balcony.

The bell-tower stands on somewhat higher ground than the rest of the complex and can be reached from the west anteroom by a passage built over an arcade. It consists of seven steadily diminishing storeys, the first two square in plan, the remainder octagonal. The ornamentation is also in the Moscow Baroque style.

13, 295 Pskov Псков

Cathedral of the Holy Trinity, 1682–99
Троицкий собор
Troitsky sobor

As explained (in the commentary on pls 137 and 146) the fortifications of the city of Pskov were among the most extensive and strongest systems in medieval Russia. They consist of four circles: the central, oldest part (the Krom), the adjoining section (the Dovmontov town), and the walls surrounding the Middle Town and the Okolny Town. The city began to build walls of stone as early as the late thirteenth and early fourteenth centuries, using the local Permian limestone, though it was a soft, easily weathered material. The only sections to survive were the Krom section, the towers and walls overlooking the Lower Grid, and fragments of the wall round the Okolny Town, including the tower of the Virgin of the Intercession. These were all carefully restored or rebuilt in their original form – one of the outstanding Soviet achievements of its kind. In the foreground of plate 13 is the Flat tower by the Lower Grid (1500), so called because there was a grid that could be used to bar navigation between the Pskova and the Velikaya in time of war. The tall tower with a lookout platform in the middle ground is the Kutekrom tower (*c*1400/1701). The sturdy, conical shape, the simple, narrow embrasures and the form of the tent roof reflect the style of the turn of the fifteenth to the sixteenth century.

The Cathedral of the Holy Trinity is the most impressive building in the Krom. Hardly anything is left of the original twelfth-century building, which was altered in the fourteenth and fifteenth centuries, and again at the beginning of the sixteenth. The present, five-domed cathedral was built in 1682–99 *(pl. 295)*. It rises in three tiers above a tall basement-storey, is surrounded on three sides by a gallery, with chapels at each east end, and has three wide apses. In other words, it represents the type which predominated in central Russia in the seventeenth century. The nucleus of the building is very high in relation to the other parts. The façades are articulated by the traditional lesenes, and separated by a cornice from a line of blind twin arches. Although every feature of the architectonic structure belongs to the Moscow School, the unusual restraint and austerity of the decoration is entirely in the spirit of the Pskov tradition. The window surrounds, the lesenes on the drums, the sober plaster ornaments all date from restoration work done in 1894–95. The builders paid this much tribute to Moscow ornamental forms of the late seventeenth century, that they decorated the gallery with a frieze of shirinki and coloured tiles and gave some of the windows carved stone surrounds in the baroque style. The whole building sank at the end of the eighteenth century, and the fabric cracked in a number of places, making it necessary to fill in the arches of the gallery and to build brick buttresses. Alterations were also made to the characteristic staircase and porch.

The interior is amazingly high and light, and the six pillars supporting the ceiling vaults and domes are surprisingly slender. The walls are whitewashed, which enhances the effect of the huge carved and gilded wooden iconostasis, with the large icons typical of the end of the seventeenth century. It is one of the best works in the Moscow Baroque style.

The contemporary bell-tower is distinguished by its weighty proportions, which were clearly dictated by the military character of the wall in which it stands. The upper storey, with the classical roof form, dates from the nineteenth century.

296   Pechory   Печоры

Sacristy of the Pskov Monastery of the Caves, late 17th century

Ризница Псково-Печерской Лавры

Riznitsa Pskovo-Pecherskoy Lavry

The 500-year-old Monastery of the Caves near the Latvian border still retains its massive sixteenth-century fortifications, the Gate-church of St Nicholas, built in 1565, and a large number of other churches and domestic and residential buildings from the seventeenth to nineteenth century *(pls 148–54)*. Of these, the sacristy and library building offers one of the most interesting examples of the influence of Moscow Baroque on the Pskov style. The wall, painted red and as uneven as if modelled by hand, is divided into two zones by three whitewashed semi-circular mouldings. The linear surrounds to the nearly square windows combine elements reminiscent of the traditional Pskov motifs with the columns and little gables of the Moscow style. The curious dormer windows and dome on the roof add a fitting final touch to this naive, but delightful building.

297-299   Suzdal   Суздаль

Convent of the Miracle of the Veil
Cathedral of the Miracle of the Veil,
16th century/1688
Holy Gate, 1688

Ризположенский монастырь
Собор Ризположения Богоматери
Святые ворота

Rizpolozhensky monastyr
Sobor Rizpolozheniya Bogomateri
Svyatye vorota

The convent, founded in 1207 according to tradition, stands at a street corner, and stretches over the highest ground in the old part of the town. It is in harmonious accord with the natural lie of the land and the buildings in the vicinity. Its earliest stone buildings were erected in the sixteenth century, but all were later either demolished, altered or substantially enlarged. The present appearance of the convent dates from the end of the seventeenth century, and is governed by the architectural traditions of Suzdal and the decorative style of that period. The names of three architects who nearly always worked together crop up in this context: Ivan Mamin, Andrey Shmakov and Ivan Gryaznov. It was they who built the ornate gallery on the west and south sides of the early sixteenth-century Cathedral of the Miracle of the Veil, and the Holy Gate.

The cathedral is small by comparison with other monastic cathedrals, and is one of the earlier instances in Russian architecture of a church without pillars, with a ceiling in the form of a domical vault with spandrels. It has three apses, the traditional round gables at the base of the roof, and three domes. The walls are plain, pierced only by windows and articulated only by a frieze of large pentagonal niches, which recurs on the drums. The north chapel was built in 1586, to celebrate the canonization of St Euphrosyne of Suzdal. A century later, in 1688, the three architects built the two galleries, the ornamentation of which presents one of the best extant examples of provincial Russian art. The principal façade of the west vestibule *(pl. 298)* is especially fine, decorated with shirinki, window surrounds, pilasters, saw-tooth friezes, ogee arches and glazed coloured tiles. The motifs on the tiles are stylized sunflowers, buds and leaves, evidently of folk-art origins *(pl. 297)*. The portal is magnificent, with its five concentric stepped arches and pairs of supports, carved to form chains of 'casks', pyramidal wedges, balusters and rings.

The Suzdal architects Mamin, Shmakov and Gryaznov also built the Holy Gate in 1688, which gives directly on to an old street *(pl. 299)*. This is an oblong building, on an east-west longitudinal axis, with two archways of different size and different forms of ornamentation, and two low octagons supporting octagonal tent roofs and cupolas. The façades are decorated with columns of vertical shirinki and a frieze of horizontal ones, all of which have colourful glazed tiles in them. Shirinki are found again on the octagons, alternating with small windows in rectangular niches. The windows in the right-hand octagon have ornamental surrounds, emphasizing that the archway on that side is the main entrance. The cornice consists of a projecting fillet and a frieze of consoles. A staircase in the thickness of the wall leads up to the small rooms in the octagons, which are connected to each other. The tent roofs are decorated with two tiers of blind windows of the kind usually found on bell-towers, though there they are real openings of course. The composition and ornamentation of the Holy Gate are characteristic of such buildings in the seventeenth century, but through the use of forms of folk-art origin and its simple, pleasing proportions it displays an amazing and unique artistic perfection.

300   Kiev   Киев

Church of All Saints over the Gate in the Monastery of the Caves, 1696–98

Церковь Всех святых на воротах Киево-Печерской Лавры

Tserkov Vsekh svyatykh na vorotakh Kiyevo-Pecherskoy Lavry

The Church of All Saints is one of the most significant examples of Ukrainian Baroque. Its cruciform groundplan, with polygonal ends to the arms of the cross, is the same shape as the Ukrainian type of wooden church with five domes. The external form draws attention to the plan, with the central block

rising a tier higher than the four arms. The whole building is in two storeys. The ground floor is disproportionately low, and the gateway runs through the middle of it. Each of the five cells of the upper floor, which comprises the actual church, is an octagon with a shaped roof surmounted by a wide, octagonal drum with a mob-cap dome and lantern. The vaulting and the roofs also illustrate the influence of wooden architecture. The transition to the drums was accomplished by the use of segments of vaulting cut off short. The junction of the inclined surfaces of the roof of the octagon with the vertical walls of the drum is called a zalom. The number and the combinations of zalomy determine the silhouette of the roof. Stone buildings do not usually have more than three zalomy, and All Saints has only two. The lavish ornamentation on the façades is typical of the Ukrainian Baroque style of the late seventeenth century. The dominant motifs are the wide corner pilasters articulated by numerous horizontal ledges and mouldings. The inverted volutes give the capitals an individual form. The narrow sections of wall between the pilasters contain windows framed by pediments and engaged columns, and niches with swirling baroque contours.

301   Dubrovitsy   Дубровицы

Church of the Virgin of the Sign, 1690–1704

Церковь Богоматери Знамения

Tserkov Bogomateri Znameniya

The church, dedicated to the feast of the apparition of the Virgin in the Church of the Blachernae in Constantinople (later known as the Virgin of the Sign in Russian iconography), stands on a tall high river bank at the confluence of the Pakhra and the Desna. It was built for Prince B. A. Golitsyn, the tutor of the future Peter I, on his estate near Podolsk, southwest of Moscow. Only a person of such eminence would have dared so open a break with the Russian traditions, anticipating in some respects the reforms introduced later by his pupil, who is believed to have taken a direct interest in the building and to have been present at its consecration. I. E. Grabar believes the church to have been inspired by the work of Ivan Zarudny, the architect of the Menshikov Tower in Moscow; he draws parallels with the Church of the Virgin of the Intercession at Fili *(pl. 291)* and the New Cathedral in the Don Monastery *(pl. 294)*, and points to the evidence of the influence of Ukrainian Baroque. Other scholars surmise that the architect was Italian. It is beyond dispute that the church, which remained a unique specimen, shows the impact of Western European forms that could no longer be excluded from Russian architecture.

The groundplan is similar to that of Borromini's Sant' Ivo in Rome (1660). The central area is a square, surrounded by compartments in a tretoil form on all four sides, so the complete plan could be described as a Greek cross, with curving sides to the arms. The outer compartments give on to the central square by means of tall arches and give the interior space great complexity. The character of the building as a three-dimensional structure is determined by the imposition of a vertical dynamic, the octagonal three-tiered tower, on the cruciform base, specifically on the central square. The fabric is limestone, and the outer surface of the tower is completely covered with a relief ornament, which creates the impression of a heavy opulent brocade. The church and narrow terrace surrounding it are supported on a socle, whose walls, steeply sloping rather than vertical, give it the air of a stylobate, and are covered with another dense ornament imitating an expensive cloth, turning into trailing acanthus foliage on the parapet. Statues of eight of the apostles stand on plinths at the top of the broad flights of steps approaching the terrace from below on all four sides, the four evangelists are at ground level in the angles of the socle (which exactly reproduces the outline of the church), while the figures of other saints and angels are placed round the edge of the roof and against the bottom tier of the octagon. This was the first occasion when a Russian church of any kind was decorated with stone statues, which had hitherto been strongly condemned as 'Latin' by the Orthodox hierarchy. I. E. Grabar attributes them to stonemasons from Kostroma, A. Eliasberg to the German artist Konrad Osner (1669–1747). The façades are rusticated. Twelve Corinthian columns, placed at the corners of the square and the trefoil arms, support the entablature of the lower part of the church, which is topped by an ornate parapet, fashioned to look like an attic storey with a line of lucarnes. The transition to the octagon also involves the use of ornamental lucarnes, alternately upright and following the curve of the vaulting. The columns flanking the curved ones look as though they are about to slide down. The relief ornament on the top zone of the tower, where the windows are also octagonal, is particularly elaborate. The dome is totally new and original, eight cartouches form the base of an open crown of gilded wrought iron, an emblem of the 'King of Heaven'.

Inside the church, there is the original iconostasis and the tribune at the west side, the prince's 'Royal Box', both of carved wood. The decoration is every bit as splendid as that of the exterior, and also includes statuary. The figures, the ornate flourishes, the festoons of fruit and flowers, the swelling forms all exhibit the hand of an experienced artist who must have been familiar with Western European Baroque. The low reliefs on the ceiling, the Latin inscriptions, all the many painterly stylistic traits which are quite unique in Russian architecture, serve to underline the building's debt to foreign models, and testify to

504

Detail of the façade of the Church of the Virgin of the Sign, Dubrovitsy

the interest that Western European architecture aroused in some members of the Russian aristocracy. Nonetheless, this outstanding building inspired no

direct imitations. In St Petersburg in the first half of the eighteenth century, Russian architecture began to develop along a completely different path.

Gate-church of the Icon of the Virgin of Tikhvin in the Monastery of the Don, 1713–14

Надвратная церковь Тихвинской Богоматери Донского монастыря

Nadvratnaya tserkov Tikhvinskoy Bogomateri Donskogo monastyrya

The delightful Church of the Virgin of Tikhvin, built in the early eighteenth century above the North Gate (1693) of the Don Monastery (cf. commentary on *pls 11, 226),* was one of the last products of the Moscow Baroque. Its composition is obviously indebted to the rounded forms of the New Cathedral finished some years earlier *(pl. 294).* Its bottom tier is approximately oval in plan, with eight curved sections of wall, the next tier is a true oval, while the bell-chamber and the slender turret (later topped by the mob-cap dome) are circular. The building stands, surrounded by a terrace, on the base provided by the flat roof of the gate, a broad, powerful-looking structure with three archways through it. The forms of the columns, pilasters, window surrounds, ledges and cornices accentuate the light, airy charm of the composition. I. E. Grabar suggests the architect may have been a Ukrainian from the circle of Ivan Zarudny.

Typology of the Wooden Churches

302   Island of Kizhi on Lake Onega

Остров Кижи на Онежском озере

Church of St Lazarus from Murom, *c*1390 (in the open-air museum)

Церковь Лазаря Муромского монастыря в музее под открытым небом

Tserkov Lazarya Muromskogo monastyrya v muzeye pod otkrytym nebom

The Church of the Raising of Lazarus belongs to the simple type of log-built church, composed additively of three rectangular cells in a straight line from east to west. It stands directly on the ground, without any kind of plinth. The three areas with separate functions into which the interior is divided are clearly distinguishable from the outside: the vestibule and the sanctuary are lower than the nave in the middle, and all three have separate pitched roofs of planks. The differences in the height of the three roofs and their angles of inclination constitute one of the chief means whereby the building acquires its expressive silhouette. The body of the nave is a perfect cube, with length, breadth and height all just over 9 feet. The rafters of the steep roof rest on small corbels along the tops of the side walls. The onion dome is covered with shingles of aspen wood. One of the most interesting features of the building is the simple way the logs interlock at the corners, each one resting in a notch cut in the log below, obviating the need to cut tenons.

According to the local tradition St Lazarus was built during the lifetime of the monk Lazar, the founder of the monastery at Murom, who died in 1391. It originally stood close to the point where the little River Muromka flows into Lake Onega. Its construction and composition are appropriate to the simple needs of a hermit community. The condition it was in made restoration necessary in the 1880s, and in 1961 it was moved to the architectural museum on the island of Kizhi. The west vestibule was rebuilt with uprights and planks.

303   Island of Kizhi in Lake Onega

Остров Кижи на Онежском озере

Chapel of the Archangel Michael from Lelik-Ozero, 18th century (in the open-air museum)

Часовня Михаила архангела из Лелико-озера в музее под открытым небом

Chasovnya Mikhaila arkhangela iz Leliko-ozera v muzeye pod otkrytym nebom

The chapel, dating from the second half of the eighteenth century, belongs to the simple cell type of church, but shows a greater complexity in its details. The three compartments of the interior are indicated by the two vertical lines of the ends of logs in the long walls. Observe that the vestibule and nave have one pitched roof in common, while the sanctuary has a separate, higher, pitched roof, surmounted by a shingled dome. The tent-roofed bell-tower over the vestibule provides an architectonic counterpoise. Since the rectangular cells are raised on a high plinth an exterior staircase was added on the north side. Interesting features of the building include the construction of the sanctuary roof in two stages, and the tent roof of the balcony-like bell-tower, with the two wide collars or flanges of planks (politsa), intended to deflect water. Among the relatively small amount of ornament, the carved bargeboards and the frame round the double window in the west wall stand out as typical elements of wooden architecture.

Church of St Nicholas from Tukhola, 17th century
(in the open-air museum at the Yuryev Monastery)
Никольская церковь из села Тухола в музее
под открытым небом

*Nikolskaya tserkov iz sela Tukhola v muzeye pod
otkrytym nebom*

The church consists of three rectangular, log-built
cells on a line from east to west, with their different
liturgical functions represented by the different
heights and forms of their roofs. The vestibule is
wider than the nave and has a simple pitched roof.
The nave is higher and the roof is an unusual form,
rising in two pitched stages and surmounted by a
beautiful union dome. The shape of the roof was
achieved by laying progressively shorter logs in
the east and west walls, as the beginning of a gable,
then progressively longer ones to produce a gradual
overhang comparable to a cornice (poval). Eventually the length of the logs is again gradually shortened
to form the gable for the upper layer to the pitched
roof. The aesthetic effect the building makes is the
result of the harmony in the relationships between
the different heights of the roofs of the separate parts
of the building. The exterior staircase, with its two
flights, is an integral part of the artistic composition.
This was the village church of Tukhola, in the region
of Novgorod, and dates from the seventeenth century.
It was transferred to the architectural museum at the
Yuryev Monastery in Novgorod when the museum
was being set up in the early 1960s.

Church of St Nicholas from Glotovo, 1766
(in the open-air museum near the kremlin)

Никольская церковь из села Глотово в музее
под открытым небом

*Nikolskaya tserkov iz sela Glotovo v muzeye pod
otkrytym nebom*

The village church of Glotovo in the district of Yuryev-Polsky belongs to the type made up of three
cells, but its structure is quite complex and painterly
in appearance. It stands on a relatively high cellar-
storey and is surrounded on the north, west and
south sides by a gallery supported on projecting logs
which have the function and something of the form
of consoles. A roofed exterior staircase leads up to
the church in the middle of the west front. The
carved ends of the planks of the gallery roof, the tall
log gable ends, and the different heights of the plank
roofs of the three cells create an artistically sucess-
ful effect. The roof of the nave supports a small
octagonal drum with a shingled dome. While the

nave and vestibule have steep pitched roofs, the pentagonal apse also has an unusually high plank roof,
but supported on trusses.

Church of St John the Evangelist, by the River
Ishna, 1689

Церковь Иоанна Богослова на реке Ишне

Tserkov Ioanna Bogoslova na reke Ishne

The old village church still stands on its original site
(pl. 306). It is a 'storeyed church', a type that
emerged during the seventeenth century in the attempt to create verticality by pyramidal construction. The groundplan consists of three cells: a central
square, flanked to east and west by two smaller
squares. The building rests on a tall cellar and is surrounded by a gallery on consoles on the north and
west sides (there was also a gallery on the south side,
which has not survived). Attention is drawn to the
nave in the centre by the height of the square block,
which is added to by three elements of diminishing
size, two octagons and a dome. The drum rests on
a curious base like a cushion. Dome, drum and
'cushion' are covered with shingles. The upper of the
two octagons gradually widens towards the top, with
its sides leaning outwards, as each successive frame
is made of slightly longer logs. This kind of construction is called a poval, and was employed in
timber architecture to deflect rain water away from
the lower part of the building. The vestibule and
sanctuary are appreciably lower than the nave, and
their roofs are in the semi-cylindrical shape with an
ogee point at the ridge called a bochka (barrel, keg).
They may originally both have been kubi, the form
produced by the conflation of two bochki. A line of
planks inclined at a moderate angle, called a politsa,
was placed at the base to assist the deflection of rain
water.

The gallery *(pl. 307)* was a place where the congregation could gather before and after services, but
it also served for secular functions, such as judicial
proceedings, the collection of taxes, government
proclamations, and assemblies of the villagers to
discuss important local issues. This allowed the west
vestibule to be kept for its proper liturgical function
of accommodating catechumens and excommuni-
cates. Its use by the public is the reason for the benches with carved legs lining the inner walls of the
gallery. These benches were found in every part of
northern Russia, decorated with various distinctive
forms of carving, from the simple to the elaborate
and elegant. Often there was also a stove in the gallery, which resembled the living room of a house in
many ways. The gallery walls are of planks or logs.
There are grooves in the window posts, allowing the
shutters to be pushed up to admit daylight.

The interior has been preserved in a good condition. The west doorway is surrounded by a carved architrave *(pl. 308)*. The recessing, the ogee point, the braided motif, all represent an unsophisticated adaptation of the decorative forms of masonry architecture in linear terms. The ceiling of the vestibule is of planks laid diagonally across the room and resting on beams. In the nave the ceiling is drawn down very low, creating an intimate atmosphere, which is enhanced by the two platforms with carved parapets placed at either side of the altar steps for the church choir. The broad tyabla of the iconostasis are painted with multicoloured plant designs, and the icons date from the seventeenth century. The elaborately decorated Royal Door was made in 1562 by Isaiyey, a monk of the Abraham Monastery in Rostov. The church belonged to the monastery's parish until 1764, and probably acquired the door when the cathedral in the monastery got a new iconostasis in the eighteenth century. The delicate gilt carving looks like goldsmith's work. The pattern of plant motifs stands out vigorously from the red painted background. An exact copy of the door was made in 1883, and it is that that is now in the church, while the original is in the museum in Rostov.

The church was robbed of much of its charm when its walls were covered over with flat planks at the beginning of the twentieth century, and not improved by a coat of the red paint generally used on railway carriages. The bell-tower at the west end was built in the nineteenth century, in imitation of the seventeenth-century tent-roofed type, but the hexagonal second tier is so disproportionately slender that the roof is nearer to a spire than a true tent. The restoration work in the 1950s included re-covering the dome and the bochki over the vestibule and sanctuary with shingles in the original ploughshare shape, and renewing the politsi and the plank roofs of the gallery and the octagons with planks with carved ends, reproducing the original amount of overhang.

309   Novgorod   Новгород

Church of the Assumption from Kuritsko, 1595
(in the open-air museum at the Yuryev Monastery)
Церковь Успения из села Курицко в музее под открытым небом
Tserkov Uspeniya iz sela Kuritsko v muzeye pod otkrytym nebom

This village church belongs to the type of tent church composed of an octagon on a square, a variant of the older type of pillar-shaped tent-roof church with an octagonal base, which developed towards the end of the sixteenth century, and was the more widespread in the seventeenth century. Its basic principle is one of organic verticality. The nucleus of the church is a square nave, with the addition of an apse on the east side and galleries on the other three sides, all built of logs. In this particular case there is no west vestibule, but normally in churches of this type it comes between the nave and an open-sided gallery supported by consoles.

The exterior reflects the organization of the interior: the spread of the galleries is succeeded by the higher, but still wide, central cube, which in turn supports a low, sturdy octagon. There is no mistaking the pyramidal intention of this construction, but the essential vertical pull is exerted by the tall, eight-sided tent roof surmounted by a drum and dome. There is hardly any ornament on the building; its artistic effect is created by the harmony of the proportional relationships between the individual components and by the upward dynamic. The 'beautiful' planks (that is, planks with their overhanging ends shaped by carving) of the povale and politsi, throwing a rhythmic pattern of serpentine shadows on the walls, and the shingles on the dome and drum, constitute the only formal decorative elements. As the building stands on a plinth, as was usual, a symmetrical staircase of two flights was built against the west front, which is adorned with some simple carving, notably on the pillars.

The church was transferred from Kuritsko to the architectural museum at the Yuryev Monastery in Novgorod in 1964.

310, 311, 420   Kondopoga   Кондопога

Church of the Assumption, 1774
Церковь Успения
Tserkov Uspeniya

This is the most important example of the log-built tent-church type of the Onega School. It towers up on a low spit of land reaching out into Lake Onega, like a natural feature of the Karelian landscape. It expresses the self-confidence and the conservative outlook of a prosperous, relatively independent peasant community. The square base below the octagon is something of an innovation, even so. In an earlier church the octagon would have been the bottom stage – instances have been traced as far back as the eleventh and twelfth centuries – but this construction follows the 'octagon on a square' principle, which had been gaining ground in wooden church architecture since the end of the sixteenth century. The building consists of the usual three cells, but with some interesting variations. Their area increases from east to west. The small, square sanctuary leads off a nave 22 feet square. The west vestibule is larger still, 26 feet 3 inches square, and has a narrow anteroom (26 feet 3 inches by 9 feet 10 inches) attached to it, which corresponds to a gallery. The cells all rest on a very high plinth, so there are staircases leading up to the gallery on the north and south sides, sheltered by flat plank roofs but open at the sides *(pl. 420)*. The steps are supported by logs projecting from the wall of the plinth like consoles.

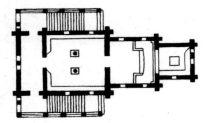

The exterior appearance adequately expresses the interior organization. The tall rectangular block of the nave gives place directly to an octagon, which goes straight up for the thickness of fourteen layers of logs before starting to slant outwards for the first poval, then for another seven before forming the second poval which supports the politsa. The four corners left at the point where square stops and octagon starts are covered by small pitched roofs. A carved zigzag frieze runs round the lower poval. The octagonal tent roof is finished by a short drum and small cupola. The west cell is lower than the central one and carries an ordinary pitched roof with a cupola in the middle of the ridge. The sanctuary is actually the same height as the vestibule, but looks much higher from the outside because of the shape of the roof and the vertical bias of its proportions. In this way it vitalizes the composition as a whole, providing a touch of asymmetry which stimulates a sense of movement towards the east, appropriate to its liturgical role. The roof takes the form of politsi at an angle of 45 degrees and a bochka with a dome. The outcome is painterly but perfectly balanced, a superb artistic achievement, surpassed only by the basic architectonic idea of achieving an unusually strong vertical dynamic by simple, linear, prosaic means. At 148 feet, the Assumption is the tallest wooden tent church in northern Russia. There is probably no other wooden building which so successfully marries the 'open form' predominant in seventeenth-century architecture with an austere archaism.

The interior of the vestibule makes a strong impression. Benches with a simple pattern carved on them line the walls. The roof is supported by two columns, each ringed by three bands of a braid motif and suggesting a human figure with raised arms *(pl. 310)*. The nave occupies only a small part of the total volume of the tall central block, and is ceiled off by an eight-faced 'sky', of the kind that became common in the seventeenth century. The carved and gilded iconostasis retains the tyabla of the previous one, which have a lively plant ornament painted on them.

There is little ornament on the church, but it appears in effective contrast to the surface of the log walls. The carved ends of the planks of the politsi, the different shapes of the roofs, the elegant supports and carved fillets trimming the roofs of the staircases, are all typical elements, found all over northern Russia. The zigzag frieze on the first poval, suggesting the blind gables of a stone church, is the only motif peculiar to the Onega School.

418   Vologda   Вологда

Church of the Assumption in the Alexander Kushtsky Monastery, first half of the 16th century

Успенская церковь Александро- Кушстского монастыря

Uspenskaya tserkov Aleksandro-Kushtskogo monastyrya

This tent church belongs to the type of 'round church with twenty walls', mentioned in the Legend of Ustyug. People commonly spoke of the shape formed by octagonal and polygonal frames of logs as 'round', and arrived at a total of twenty by adding the eight sides of the central octagon to the three outer sides of each of the four protruding additional cells. In the course of developing from initial simplicity of construction towards greater complexity, the area of the central cell was enlarged by being made octagonal instead of square, and as the octagon grew taller it became necessary to buttress it on all sides. The apse on the east side and the vestibule on the west side were augmented by compartments on the north and south sides producing a cruciform groundplan. The Legend of Ustyug, really a chronicle of the building of a new cathedral in Veliky Ustyug at the end of the fifteenth century, refers to the centuries-old tradition behind the type, whose descent can be traced back to the simple octagonal tower-church with tent roof known at least since the eleventh century. The 'round churches with twenty walls' were larger than the square ones, and the structure was more stable. Their shape was moreover a close approximation to the cruciform schema approved by the Orthodox church.

There is nothing out of the ordinary about the forms of the Assumption. The roofs of the four square additional cells are bochki with politsi. The central octagon has a poval with a pronounced outward slant, surmounted by an octagonal tent with a small drum and dome. The circle of 'beautiful' planks (i. e. with their ends carved) and the politsi above the poval create a well-proportioned transition from octagon to roof. The shingles on the dome, drum, tent roof and bochki contrast effectively with the logs composing the walls. The harmonious outlines of all the parts and the elegance of the overall shape give rise to a certain air of solemnity.

Standing in the middle of the nave, one can look up to the base of the tent: in other churches of this type it was often possible to look to the very top of it, though it was always dark, since the only light in the church came through the small windows of the square compartments and the door.

The Assumption originally stood beside Lake Kubenskoye and belonged to a small Skit monastery, which burned down before the sixteenth century was out. In order to preserve the church it was moved a few years ago to Vologda and rebuilt on the site of the Prilutsky Monastery of the Saviour, where an open-air museum has recently been founded.

14, 312-315   Island of Kizhi on Lake Onega
Остров Кижи на Онежском озере
Church of the Virgin of the Intercession, 1764
Покровская церковь
Pokrovskaya tserkov

A unique group of buildings with a fairy-tale beauty was erected in the eighteenth century amid the lakes and forests of northern Russia, where they harmonize with the landscape as if part of the natural scenery. The Church of the Transfiguration (1714)

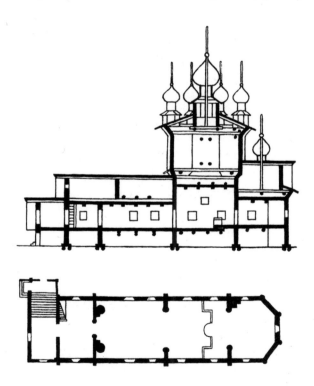

and the Church of the Virgin of the Intercession (1764) stand on the island of Kizhi on Lake Onega. This was the administrative centre for the economy of a large area, although it gradually lost its importance with the transference of increasingly large shares of trade and production to the bigger cities. Kizhi was also the religious and cultural centre of an extensive parish that included a large number of villages scattered over several of the islands. After

the people had gone, the large wooden churches were all that was left on the island. They are surrounded by a low wall of roughly cut stones and courses of timber with a wooden coping. The tent-roofed bell-tower stands on its own between the two churches, which translate the painterly decorative style of the seventeenth century into the rich forms of the traditional language of wooden architecture. They represent the last links in an evolutionary chain that had been centuries in the growing, and belong to the most complicated type of all, the 'many-domed' church. The carpenters from Kizhi used to be esteemed as the most skilful and competent in all Russia. They handled their axes with astonishing dexterity – saw, puncheon and auger were used only for ornamental details – and with the simplest of techniques, 'following their eye' as the Russians say, they put together structures of the utmost formal variety. The local church records of 1616 describe two earlier churches of the same names, which later burned down.

Beside the proud splendour of the Church of the Transfiguration, the Church of the Virgin of the Intercession looks almost simple and modest. The groundplan repeats the schema of three rectangular cells lined up on an east-west axis, the elevation repeats the schema of the octagon on a square base, surmounted by tent roof and domes. The building stands on a high plinth. The pentagonal apse is the same width as the nave and relatively high; its roof form is a bochka with a dome and politsi (*pl. 312*). The low, oblong west vestibule has a simple pitched roof. A separate anteroom is partitioned off at its west end, although there is a gallery, also with a pitched roof, beyond that, approached by an outside staircase on the north side. The walls of the tall central cube bend outwards in a poval, and then the central part of each is carried straight up as four of the walls of the ensuing octagon, which is thus actually wider than the cube below the poval. The octagon is proportionately quite tall, by comparison with tower-churches, has a poval of its own, and supports nine domes on its low tent roof, standing on octagonal pedestals, each with a politsa. All the drums and domes are covered with shingles in the shape of ploughshares. Eight of them straddle the eight ridges of the roof, and a larger one stands in the centre (*pl. 14*).

The interior has been well preserved. The iconostasis has the traditional tyabla, with a stylized flower pattern painted on them (*pl. 315*). The tier of prophets touches the ceiling and is slightly inclined towards the nave. Ornament is sparse inside and out, and the greatest concentration of it is on the exterior staircase and the gables. Plate 314 shows some of the prichelini, the carved fillets decorating the ends of the plank roof, and a polotentse, a 'towel', both decorated with geometrical motifs. The zigzag frieze typical of the Onega School runs below the poval of the octagon, looking like a line of small blind gables. Many of the ornaments have a perfectly sober function as well: the politsi and the spouts on the zigzag frieze serve to divert rain water from running down the walls, and prichelini protect the boards from rotting.

Systematic restoration has been in progress since 1944. During the war the more valuable parts were removed to Finland for safety and some of these were lost, but have been replaced since. In recent years the plank casing has been removed from the walls, the shingles have been restored to the domes, and the exterior staircase has been thoroughly renewed, down to the ornamentation. The work has been under the direction of A. V. Opolovnikov. Structural repairs are still being made. Simultaneously with the restoration of the churches, the Open-air Museum of the Wooden Architecture of Karelia has been established on the island, which already comprises twenty-eight exhibits at the time of writing.

312, 316–319   Island of Kizhi on Lake Onega

Остров Кижи на Онежском озере

Church of the Transfiguration, 1714

Преображенская церковь

Preobrazhenskaya tserkov

The Church of the Transfiguration, built in 1714 to replace a simple tent-roof church destroyed by fire, is probably the most famous wooden building in north Russia, the consummate example of the complex type of 'many-domed' churches. Its fairy-tale appearance is due to a formal variety that could only be achieved by drawing on every architectonic and decorative resource developed by wooden architecture in Russia over centuries. But at the same time it has stylistic traits that had only developed during the secularization of art in the seventeenth century: the pronounced differentiation of silhouette, the tendency towards asymmetry, the liking for ornament, the eye-catching ostentation, the false ceiling ('sky') in the nave. It is also characteristic of the seventeenth century that the ornamental elements accumulate from the bottom to the top of the building, instead of being concentrated on the upper parts. M. A. Ilin points out the close relationship to the Church of the Virgin of the Intercession at Fili in this respect. Clearly the conservatively inclined farmers of northern Russia clung to the old, strict, formal language, but were unable to resist some incursions of the new, painterly style. The carpenters, working by eye, without blueprints or measuring instruments, created a synthesis of the old and the new with a unique artistic beauty that is still a delight to the eye. According to legend, when the church was finished one of the master-builders, named Nestor, threw his axe into Lake Onega with the words: 'Master Nestor built this church, there is not another like it, and there never will be.' Others of the kind were built, in fact, but none were of the same artistic standard.

In spite of the dynamic composition and the 'open', fluid, complex forms, the church displays above all an astonishingly integrated monumentality. The outline of the strongly differentiated pyramid, climbing in five tiers and crowned by twenty-two domes, could be contained within an isosceles triangle *(pl. 319)*. The groundplan is cruciform, with

a central octagon, four very nearly square arms, and a gallery which runs from the north to the south arm, by way of the west front. All the cells are built over a plinth. The only entrance is by way of the symmetrical, double flight of stairs built on outside the gallery. The landing and both the flights are roofed, and at the foot of each flight there is a little porch, facing west, with a pitched roof *(pl. 318)*. In order to accentuate the sanctuary a low, small, trapezoid apse was added to the east arm of the cross. The plan is the traditional one of the 'church with twenty walls' (the octagon accounting for eight and each of the four additional cells contributing three more), but the form of the structure erected on the plan is unique. The tall octagonal nave supports two further octagons, each diminishing in size, while the four arms rise in two stages. The two lower octagons, the steps of the arms and the apse all terminate in bochki, which have politsi at their base and support short drums and onion domes. In this way the church, whose total height is 115 feet, accumulates twenty-two domes, stacked up its sides: the four square cells support one on each of their two steps; the bottom octagon has eight, one over each face; the middle octagon has four, one on each of the faces that the four square cells are built against. The small octagon at the top is the pedestal of the central dome, larger than any of the others, supporting the uppermost cross. The bochka motif is used again up here, purely as ornament, four of them appearing round the drum. The twenty-second dome is lower than all the rest, on the roof of the apse *(pls 316, 319)*.

In spite of the bewildering formal abundance, the church was plainly thought out very carefully. The complicated composition, with its multiplicity of tiers and domes is nonetheless a unified architectonic organism, like the Cathedral of the Virgin of the Intercession in Moscow. By stacking the domes pyramidally and constantly repeating the outlines of the bochki and the domes the architects showed an awareness of their form-giving potentialities that enabled them to create the impression of uninterrupted vertical movement and of compulsive formal rhythm. Although the ornamental motifs gradually multiply towards the top of the building they have a solid tectonic base in the plain walls of the base, which enhances, rather than weakens, their painterly charm.

The interior of the church has been well preserved. The log frames, the sloping ceilings, the beams round the doors and windows, and the traditional benches along the walls for the congregations to rest on, create an atmosphere of dignified simplicity in the gallery. The nave is more ostentatiously decorated. The 'sky ceiling is formed by sixteen slightly curved beams converging on a circular area in the middle. These ribs are painted with a distinctive pattern, while the planks filling the cells between them were originally painted with religious subjects *(pl. 317)*. The 'sky' was a seventeenth-century innovation, prompted by people's liking for decoration and for comfort. Previously the central octagon was open as far, or nearly, as the tip of the tent roof, not that it was possible to see up so far in the darkness, since the only light was through low windows. The four-tier iconostasis, which even spreads on to the east walls of the north and south arms of the building, is an outstanding local interpretation of the baroque style. It is believed to date from 1759. Its magnificent gilt carvings and the Royal Door, flanked by pillars and covered with a convoluted vine relief, give the nave a festive air. The icons are good examples of the art in the eighteenth century. There is a large stall for the choir on each side of the altar steps, and a large wooden crucifix in the form of a Russian cross stands in front of the one on the north side, with God the Father above the figure of an emaciated Christ, and with inscriptions and monograms carved on the ends of the arms. It dates from the same period as the church itself *(pl. 317)*.

There is not a single element on the church's exterior that does not have a structural, practical function in addition to its ornamental role. The pattern of domes, bochki, politsi, the ogee gables on the diagonal faces of the octagon, the eaves, water spouts, and prichelini amounts to an efficient system for draining water from the building. Rain, melting snow, damp and humidity, all prevalent in this northern latitude, had to be deflected from the wooden fabric. There is even a second false ceiling above the 'sky' over the nave, with two faces draining into two internal gutters along which water can run away. Functional forms and artistic forms coalesce here to a quite unusual degree.

The same harmony reigns in the church's relationship to the landscape, which has already been referred to in connection with the Church of the Virgin of the Intercession. The Transfiguration rears up like a tall pine tree on the low hillock, visible from far away across the reflecting surface of Lake Onega for the visitor approaching Kizhi by boat. Restoration work, under A. V. Opolovnikov, has followed a course exactly parallel to that of the Virgin of the Intercession (the iconostasis and the 'sky' were sent to Finland during the war), and has preserved the building's organic vigour. All the twenty-seven other wooden buildings from Karelia, which have been assembled in the open-air museum on the island, give the same impression of natural organic growth.

419   Island of Kizhi on Lake Onega

Остров Кижи на Онежском озере

Bell-tower, 1874

Колокольня

Kolokolnya

The bell-tower is a reasonably faithful reproduction of the earlier tower on the site. A square base supports an octagon with a bell-chamber and an eight-faced tent roof. The lower room is divided into three compartments by two log walls, with a ladder up to the bell-chamber in the west compartment. The tent rests on eight pillars at its corners, which are supported by a special interior scaffolding, as well as by the walls of the octagon. The whole structure stands on stone foundations. Although the schema is traditional, there are also signs of the influence of masonry architecture, in the shape of the arches over the windows and the door, for instance. The tower forms a harmonious ensemble with the churches of the Transfiguration and the Virgin of the Intercession.

GLOSSARY

512

Acheiropoietos: Iconographic type, the 'Image (of Christ) not made with hands'; similar to the 'Veil of St Veronica' (Greek: mandilion)

Acroterion: Three-dimensional ornament placed at the apex, and sometimes also at the lower corners, of a pediment

Ambo: In a domed cruciform church, the area in the middle of the solea, in front of the Royal Door, from which the readings and the sermon are given, and the singing is directed

Apse: Semi-circular or polygonal end of the bema and the pastophoria

Arcade: Line of arches with supports (columns, pillars)

Arched tomb: Form of tomb, wherein a tomb-chest rests in an arched niche, flush with the wall

Archimandrite: Arch-abbot, the head of a large Orthodox monastery (Lavra), or of a group of monasteries with special traditions

Architrave: The moulded or carved surround of a door or window

Archivolt: The arched surround above a door or window opening; the moulding on an arch

Attic base: Base of Ionic column consisting of two large rings of convex moulding joined by a spreading concave moulding

Basileus: Title of the Byzantine emperor (Greek: the king)

Bay: Compartment of a vaulted ceiling, defined by transverse arches; also, the compartment of a building roofed by one ceiling bay, defined by its supports

Begunets: Brick ornament usually formed by tilting the bricks on a short edge, alternately to left and right, with a long side flush to the wall surface, resulting in a line of triangular depressions, with the apexes pointing alternately up and down (in Pskov it is done in stone, and sometimes used to form alternate square depressions and bosses)

Bell-arcade: Arches replacing the wall on a tower at the level of the chamber where the bells are hung

Bell-gable: Gabled arcade, with any number of openings, with a bell hung in each, usually on top of a wall

Bema: Sanctuary; the area, usually raised, at the east end of the nave, containing the altar and the clergy benches

Blind arcade: Articulation or decoration of a wall in the form of an arcade, without the wall being pierced

Cantharus: Pool outside a church, often canopied, where the congregation wash before entering

Capital: Projecting head of a column or pillar, usually decorated

Catechumen: Candidate for baptism

Chetverik: Compartment of a building with a square plan

Ciborium: Canopy supported by columns, usually above an altar

Coenobion: The order of life in an Orthodox monastery under an abbot, governed by a 'typikon', a collection of liturgical and disciplinary ordonnances (as opposed to the life led by hermits)

Console: Support for a pilaster etc., projecting from the wall

Crossing: Area in the centre of a church where the transepts and the nave intersect; usually square in plan

Deesis: Christ enthroned between the Virgin and John the Baptist; the central picture, or group, of an iconostasis

Diakonikon: Room to the south of the main altar where vestments, liturgical vessels and books are kept and where priests robe; similar to a sacristy (Russian: riznitsa)

Drum: Cylindrical or polygonal structure supporting a dome, usually pierced by windows (Russian: baraban)

Dynka: Ornamental band in the shape of a melon, found encircling the shaft of a column or pillar, usually on door or window surrounds

Embrasure: Opening in a wall (as a window, or slit used by archers and riflemen to fire through); splayed side of such an opening

Emmanuel: Iconographic type of Christ as a young man, the Incarnation of the Word

Fresco: Wall painting done on fresh damp plaster, usually mixed with 'secco' paintings, executed on the dry plaster

Fronton: pediment

Gallery: In the context of this book, usually an exterior passage, along one or more sides of a building, with an open arcade on its outer side (cf. tribune)

Girka: Conical boss, usually of carved stone, which is suspended on an iron bar, concealed in the masonry, to form the centre of a pair of twin arches

Glava: The outer part of the roof of a dome

Golosniki: 'Resonators': small clay vessels, let into the upper zones of a wall, with the mouth open to the interior of the building, as an aid to resonance

Dynki

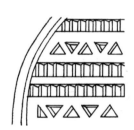

Begunets and porebrik

Girka

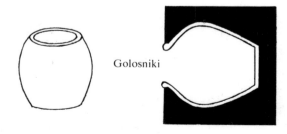

Golosniki

Gont (Lemekh): Thin pieces of wood (shingles) used for roofing in the same way as tiles, usually the shape of a ploughshare

Gulbishche: Terrace surrounding a building on more than one side

Iconoclasm: Rejection of icons as objects of veneration; also, destruction of icons for that reason

Iconostasis: Screen between the sanctuary and the nave, carrying rows of icons on shelves

Igumen: Abbot of an Orthodox monastery

Imposts: The blocks, usually the ends of a cornice, or the tops of capitals, supporting an arch

Izba: Log house

Izrazets: Tile of fired clay, glazed on the obverse, which may be smooth or have a relief on it, and with a hollow in the back, whereby it is fixed to the wall surface

Katholikon: Church of a monastery

Klet: Basic rectangular compartment in log houses: a 'cell' or 'module'

Kokoshnik: Ornamental or blind gable, semicircular or ogee-shaped, most often arranged in two or three tiers round the drum; but also used to improve the outer appearance of the roof in other ways, by covering the vaulting, or finishing the walls

Kolokolnya: Bell-tower

Kremlin: Social and administrative centre of a medieval Russian town, surrounded by a defensive wall; by extension, castle or citadel (Russian: detinets)

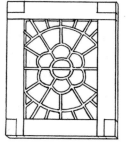

Mica window

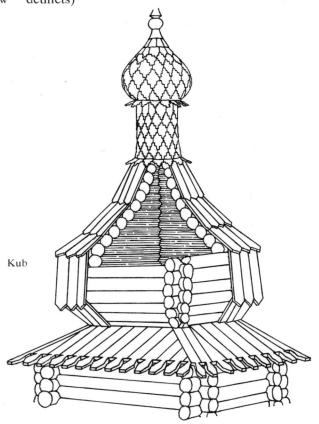

Kub

Kub (Kubovatoye pokrytiye): From of roof on wooden buildings over a square plan, conflating two bochki, so that all four faces are the same; the shape suggests a squared-off onion dome

Lapa: One of the methods of joining logs at the corners of wooden buildings, with the ends

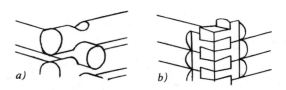

a)   *b)*

Two methods of shaping the corners of log buildings: a) interlocking b) dovetailing

shaped so that they dovetail without projecting beyond the joint

Lesene: Vertical rectangular member, projecting only slightly from the surface of a wall, without base or capital; usually a decorative means of articulating the surface; see also lopatka

Leshchad: Thin stone slabs, used on floors and sometimes on roofs or for ledges, string courses etc.

Lopatka: Lesene with impost block, often with a structural function, or a pilaster without a capital

Lucarne: Dormer window, or window in a spire of tent roof, usually with an eleborate surround and pediment

Lukovitsa: Onion dome

Machicolation: Projecting edge of the platform on top of a fortress wall, supported by brackets, with holes between the brackets through which to pour hot liquids or to fire at besiegers; also used here of a similar construction, on a smaller scale, used to form the transition to a drum on the inside

Maphorion: Virgin's robe

Melon: see dynka

Nalichnik: Ornamental surround to a door or window, generally with columns and a pediment (like an aedicule)

Naos: Nave, aisles; the part of a church occupied by the lay (baptized) congregation

Narthex: Anteroom, vestibule of a church, occupied by non-communicants

Ogee gable: Arched gable in a double curve made by convex and concave parts

Okonchina: Bars of a window, the framework for small pieces of glass or mica

Pantocrator: Iconographic type of Christ as the ruler and judge of the universe

Papert: Roofed area outside the entrance to a church, a kind of porch

Pastophoria: Collective term for the diakonikon and prothesis, the side apses

Pechura: Niche in a stone or brick wall

Pendentive: Segment of vaulting or spandrel in the form of a spherical triangle, effecting the transition to a circular base for a dome from a square groundplan

Pilaster: Engaged pillar, consisting of a base, shaft and capital, projecting only slightly from the wall's surface, usually with a structural function; also found without base or capital but with an impost block, when it is called a lopatka

Pinnacle: Ornamental column, turret, obelisk

Piscator Bible: A collection of copper engravings on biblical subjects by various artists, published in Holland in the mid seventeenth century by Piscator (Claes Visscher or Jan de Vischer)

Podest: Landing of a staircase

Podklet: Ground floor of a house, usually the rooms serving domestic purposes

Podzor: Carved boards decorating the overhang of a roof; also found on masonry buildings as a band of iron with pierced ornament

Pogost: Trading post outside a settlement

Politsa: Lower, less steep part of a roof rising in two stages with different angles of inclination, or of a tent roof, supported by the poval

Porebrik: A frieze of bricks (sometimes blocks of stone) laid at forty-five degrees to the plane of the wall, so that an edge is flush with the plane. The effect is like the cutting edge of a saw

Portico: Porch with columns, in front of a main entrance

Posad: Suburb, tradesmen's quarter outside the kremlin of a town

Poval: Upper part of the wall of a log building, which is gradually bent outwards by corbelling the ventsi, to form a kind of cornice

Pridel: Secondary altar in a chapel specially added to, or partitioned off from, the main body of a church

Prothesis: Room to the north of the main altar, where the altar of preparation, or offerings, stands; the altar itself (Russian: zhertvennik)

Refectory: see Trapeznaya

Riznitsa: Diakonikon, sacristy; it may consist of several rooms in cathedrals and large monasteries (Lavry), used for storing church treasures

Roof forms:

Bochka: Roof, or section of roof, in the form of half a cylinder raised to a point at the ridge (like an ogee arch) (Interpenetration of two bochki produces the 'crossed bochka': kubovatoye pokrytiye)

Bochka

Four-faced roof: Hipped roof on a building with a square plan, in which all four faces would meet at a central point (but for the presence of a dome)

Eight-faced roof: Formed by two pitched roofs intersecting at right angles, usually on a building with a square plan

Hipped roof: With sloping rather than vertical ends

Tent roof: Steep pyramidal roof; see Shater

Trefoil roof: The shape dictated by the vaulting of the interior with barrel vaults over the central cross, and quadrants over the lower corner cells, producing a trefoil (cloverleaf) shape at the top of each wall

Undulating, or Wavy roof: Follows the outline of the zakomari (semi-circular gables)

Royal Door: The middle of the three doors in the iconostasis, leading directly to the main altar; also called Paradise, or Tsar Door

Sarcophagus: Tomb of wood, stone, metal or earthenware in the shape of a casket, not sunk in the ground or the thickness of a wall

Saw-tooth: see Porebrik

Shater (Shatrovoye Pokrytiye): Roof in the form of a pyramid with four or more surfaces

Sheya: Blind, windowless drum supporting a dome

Shirinka: Small square or oblong depression in the wall or parapet of a masonry building, with a moulded frame, and sometimes with an inlaid tile or ornament of brick or stone at the centre

Skit: Community of hermits

Socle: Base or pedestal

Soffit: The underside (intrados) of an arch

Solea: Altar steps, or dais before the iconostasis, stretching its full width; during services the choir is positioned on both sides, and readings and the sermon are given from the middle (ambo)

Spandrel: Triangular area of a wall beside an arch: (a) right-angled triangle, with the hypotenuse formed by the arc of the arch (b) area between two adjacent arches (e. g. in an arcade) (c) area between the arc of a vaulted ceiling and a vertical window

Springing line: The imaginary line between imposts; the base line of the semi-circle or other form of an arch

Squinch: Fan-shaped niche, or segment of vaulting in the shape of part of a hollow cone with the point downwards

Terem: Attic, visually distinct from the shape of the main building

Titulus: Verse or prose caption on or below a picture, assisting the interpretation of its iconography

Trapeznaya: Refectory, in a monastery the dining room with ancillary rooms attached to a church; later a low, large room built on the west end of any church, often put to secular use

Tribune: Gallery or balcony inside a church, usually supported by pillars or columns and overlooking the interior (Russian: khory)

Triumph Arch: Arch between the east supports of the crossing, marking the boundary between the nave and the bema

Tsemyanka: Broken and crushed brick added to lime mortar

Tyabla: Horizontal wooden beams with rimmed edges, supporting the icons on an iconostasis

Undercroft: Vaulted underground room

Shirinka

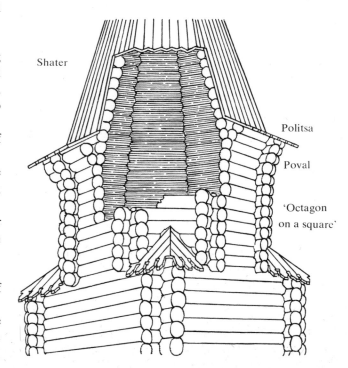

Shater

Politsa

Poval

'Octagon on a square'

Vault forms:

    Basket vault: Vault whose section is a partial ellipse or parabola; like a barrel vault but less than half a circle

    Corbelled vault: Method of vaulting small rooms with progressively higher transverse arches supporting arches at right angles to them; in churches a square opening is left at the centre below the drum and dome

Domical vault: Construction of segmental cells rising to a common apex over a polygonal, usually square, groundplan

Groin vault: Formed by the intersection of two barrel vaults at right angles, producing four pairs of right-angled spherical triangles

Kreshchaty vault: Method of vaulting a domed cruciform church without pillars, with a kind of basket vault over the arms of the cross, and segments of domical vaulting over the corner cells

Quadrant vault: Vault with both a horizontal and a vertical section of a quarter of a circle; used to roof small cells at the corner of a building

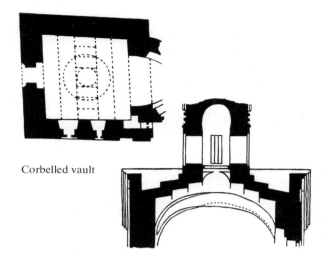

Corbelled vault

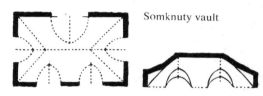

Somknuty vault

Somknuty vault: Vault of four or more cells above. a square, oblong or polygonal base, in which the weight rests on the supporting walls (and not on the corners alone as with groin vaulting); it differs from a domical vault in that it has a ridge rib

Venets: Polygonal log frame, laid horizontally; the basic unit of log construction

Vosmerik: Compartment of a building with octagonal plan

Web: One of the four compartments of a groin vault, also called a cell

Zakomara: Semi-circular gable finishing a division of a wall, usually corresponding to the form of the vault, but also found as a purely ornamental element (pozakomara)

Zalom: Means of transition from a curved section of roof to a flat section, developed in wooden architecture in the Ukraine in the seventeenth century, under the influence of the baroque

Zone: Horizontal division of a wall, usually corresponding to the level of a floor within, but also decorative (Russian: yarus)

Zvonnitsa: Bell-gable

Kreshchaty vault

BIBLIOGRAPHY

516   *General Works*

Всеобщая история архитектуры. Под ред. Н.
Я. Колли. ТТ. 5 и 6. М. 1968 (General History
of Architecture. Ed. N. Ya. Kollya. Vols 5 and
6. Moscow 1968)

Всеобщая история искусств. Т. II. Искусство
средневековья. Под ред. А. Д. Чегодаева. М.
1956 (General History of Art. Vol. II: The Art of
the Middle Ages. Ed. A. D. Chegodayev. Moscow
1956)

Allgemeine Geschichte der Kunst. Bd. II: Die Kunst
des Mittelalters. Red. A. D. Tschegodajew. Dtsch.
Red. U. Kuhirt. Leipzig 1963 (German edition of
the above)

Памятники древнерусского искусства. Вып.
1–4. СПБ. 1908–1912 (Monuments of Early
Russian Art. Nos 1–4. St Petersburg 1908–12)

История русской архитектуры. Краткий
курс. Издание 1. М. 1951. Издание 2. М.
1956 (History of Russian Architecture. Short
outline. 1st ed. Moscow 1951, 2nd ed. Moscow
1956)

История русского искусства. Под ред. И. Э.
Грабаря. Т. I–VI. М. 1909–1915 (History of
Russian Art. Ed. I. E. Grabar. Vols I–VI. Mo-
scow 1909–15)

История русского искусства. Под ред. И. Э.
Грабаря, В. Н. Лазарева и В. С. Кеменова.
Т. I–IV. М. 1954–59 (History of Russian Art.
Ed. I. E. Grabar, V. N. Lazarev and V. S. Keme-
nov. Vols I–IV. Moscow 1954–59)

Geschichte der russischen Kunst. Red. I. E. Grabar,
W. N. Lasarew und W. S. Kemenow. Bde. I–IV.
Dresden 1957–65 (German edition of the above)

Очерки истории СССР. Период феодализма
IX до XV вв. Под ред. Б. Д. Грекова, Л. В.
Черепнина и В. Т. Пашуто. Ч. I–II. М. (His-
tory of·the USSR. Feudal period, 9th to 15th
centuries. Ed. B. D. Grekov, L. V. Cherepnin and
V. T. Pashuto. Pts. I–II. Moscow)

Geschichte der UdSSR. Feudalismus 9.–15. Jahr-
hundert. Bd. I (I,1 und I,2), Bd. II. Red. B. D.
Grekow, L. W. Tscherepnin und W. T. Paschuto.
Berlin 1957, 1958 (German edition of the above)

Историческая выставка архитектуры. 1911.
СПБ. 1912 (Historical exhibition of architecture
1911. St Petersburg 1912)

O Bojan, du Nachtigall der alten Zeit – Sieben
Jahrhunderte altrussischer Literatur. Berlin 1967

Русская архитектура. Доклады, прочитан-
ные в связи с декадником по русской архитектуре в Москве в апреле 1939 г. М.
1940 (Russian Architecture. Lectures given in
connection with the Decade of Russian Architecture, Moscow, April 1939. Moscow 1940)

Русское зодчество. Вып. 1–6. М. 1953 (Russian Architecture. Nos 1–6. Moscow 1953)

Ainalov, D.: Geschichte der russischen Monumen-
talkunst der vormoskovitischen Zeit. Berlin, Leipzig 1932

Ainalov, D.: Geschichte der russischen Monumen-
talkunst zur Zeit des Großfürstentums Moskau.
Berlin, Leipzig 1933

Алпатов, М. В.: Всеобщая история искусств.
Т. III. Русское искусство с древнейших
времен до начала XVIII в. М. 1955 (Alpatov,
M. V.: General History of Art. Vol. III. Russian
Art from the Earliest Times to the Beginning of
the 18th Century. Moscow 1955)

Alpatow, M., und *Brunov, N.:* Geschichte altrussischer Kunst. Augsburg 1932

Bandmann, G.: Mittelalterliche Architektur als Be-
deutungsträger. Berlin 1951

Behrens, E.: Kunst in Rußland. Ein Reiseführer zu
russischen Kunststätten. Köln 1969

Benz, E.: Geist und Leben der Ostkirche. Hamburg
1957

Benz, E.: Das Buch der heiligen Gesänge der Ostkirche. Hamburg 1962

Вунин, А. В.: История градостроительного
искусства. Т. I. М. 1953 (Bunin, A. V.: History
of Urban Architecture. Vol. I. Moscow 1953)

Bunin, A. W.: Geschichte des russischen Städte-
baues bis zum 19. Jahrhundert. Berlin 1961

Buxton, D. R.: Russian Mediaeval Architecture
Cambridge 1934

Demus, O.: Byzantine Mosaic Decoration. London
1947

Dittmar, H.: Der Kampf der Kathedralen. Düssel-
dorf 1964

Дмитриев, Ю.: Теория искусства и взгляды
на искусство в письменности древней Руси. – В кн.: Труды Отдела древнерусской
литературы Института русской литературы Академии наук СССР. Т. IX. М.-Л. 1953,
с. 97–116 (Dmitriyev, Yu.: Theory and Concepts of Art in Early Russian Literature. In: Proceedings of the Department of Early Russian
Literature in the Academy of Sciences of the
USSR. Vol. IX, Moscow–Leningrad 1953, pp.
97–116)

Döpmann, H.-D.: Der Einfluß der Kirche auf die
moskowitische Staatsidee. Berlin 1967

Donnert, E.: Rußland an der Schwelle der Neuzeit.
Berlin 1972 (seen in manuscript)

Eliasberg, A.: Russische Kunst. München 1915

Grabar, A.: Byzanz. Baden-Baden 1964

Gudzij, N. K.: Geschichte der russischen Literatur.
11.–17. Jahrhundert. Halle 1959

Hamilton, G. H.: The Art and Architecture of Russia. Harmondsworth 1954

Kitschelt, L.: Die frühchristliche Basilika als Dar-
stellung des himmlischen Jerusalem. München
1938

Косточкин, В. В.: Русское оборонное зодчество конца XIII – начала XVI вв. М.

1962 (Kostochkin, V. V.: Russian Fortress Architecture from the End of the 13th Century to the Beginning of the 16th. Moscow 1962)

Лавров, В.: Монастыри и крепости XVI–XVII вв. – Форпосты Московского государства. – В кн.: Русская архитектура. М. 1940, с. 36–39 (Lavrov, V.: Monasteries and Fortresses of the 16th and 17th Centuries – the Outposts of the Muscovite State. In: Russian Architecture. Moscow 1940, pp. 36–39)

Lichatschow, D. S.: Die Kultur Rußlands während der osteuropäischen Frührenaissance vom 14. bis zum Beginn des 15. Jahrhunderts. Dresden 1962

Lukomski, G. K.: Alt-Rußland. Architektur und Kunstgewerbe. München 1923

Lukomski, G. K.: L'architecture religieuse russe du XIe au XVIIe siècle. Paris 1929

Мартынов, А. А., и Снегирев, И. М.: Русская старина в памятниках церковного и гражданского зодчества. Т. 1–6. М. 1848–60 (Martynov, A. A. and Snegirev, I. M.: Old Russia, in Monuments of Ecclesiastical and Secular Architecture. Vols 1–6. Moscow 1848–60)

Мартынов, А.: Русские достопамятности. Т. I–IV. М. 1877–1883 (Martynov, A.: Russian Memorials. Vols I–IV. Moscow 1877–83)

Максимов, П.: Опыт исследования пропорций в древнерусской архитектуре. В кн.: Архитектура СССР. М. 1940. Ho. I, с. 68–73 (Maximov, P.: Exploratory Study of Proportion in Early Russian Architecture: In Architecture of the USSR. Moscow 1940, no. 1, pp. 68–73)

Некрасов, А. И.: Очерки по истории древне-русского зодчества XI–XVII веков. М. 1936 (Nekrasov, A. I.: Notes on the History of Early Russian Architecture between the 11th and 17th Centuries. Moscow 1936)

Nemitz, F.: Die Kunst Rußlands. Baukunst, Malerei, Plastik vom 11. bis 19. Jahrhundert. Berlin 1940

Norberg-Schulz, Chr.: Logik der Baukunst. Berlin, Frankfurt/M., Wien 1965

Onasch, K.: Ikonen. Berlin 1961

Onasch, K.: Grundzüge der russischen Kirchengeschichte. Göttingen 1967

Ouspensky, L.: Symbolik des orthodoxen Kirchengebäudes und der Ikone. Stuttgart 1962

Потапов, А. А.: Очерк древней русской гражданской архитектуры. Вып. 1–2. М. 1902–1903 (Potapov, A. A.: Outline of secular architecture in Early Russia. Pts 1–2. Moscow 1902–03)

Réau, L.: L'art russe des origines à Pierre le Grand. Paris 1921

Рихтер, Ф. Ф.: Памятники древнего русского зодчества. Тетр. 1–5. М. 1851–56 (Richter, F.F.: Monuments of Early Russian Architecture. Fascs 1–5. Moscow 1851–56)

Рыбаков, Б. А.: Ремесло древней Руси. М. 1948 (Rybakov, B. A.: Craftsmanship in Early Russia. Moscow 1948)

Sauer, J.: Symbolik des Kirchengebäudes. Freiburg i. Br. 1924

Schubert, O.: Gesetz der Baukunst. 2 Bde. Leipzig 1954

Schweinfurth, Ph.: Die byzantinische Form. Berlin 1943

Sedlmayr, H.: Epochen und Werke. Bd. 1. Wien 1959, S. 80–140

Шквариков, В. А.: Очерк истории планировки и застройки русских городов. М. 1954 (Shkvarikov, V. A.: Outline of the History of the Planning and Building of Russian Towns. Moscow 1954)

Сперанский, А. Н.: Очерки по истории Приказа каменных дел Московского государства. М. 1930 (Speransky, A. N.: Notes on the History of the Office for Masonry Architecture of the Muscovite State. Moscow 1930)

Strzygowski, J.: Kleinasien, ein Neuland der Kunstgeschichte. Leipzig 1903

Strzygowski, J.: Die Baukunst der Armenier und Europa. Wien 1918

Суслов, В. В.: Очерки по истории древнерусского зодчества. СПБ. 1889 (Suslov, V. V.: Notes on the History of Early Russian Architecture. St Petersburg 1889)

Суслов, В. В.: Памятники древнего русского зодчества. Вып. 1–7. СПБ. 1895–1901 (Suslov, V. V.: Monuments of Early Russian Architecture. Parts 1–7. St Petersburg 1895–1901)

Суслов, В. В.: Памятники древнерусского искусства. Вып. 1–4. СПБ. 1908–12 (Suslov, V. V.: Monuments of Early Russian Art. Parts 1–4. St Petersburg 1908–12)

Talbot Rice, D.: Byzantine Art. Melbourne, London, Baltimore 1954

Talbot Rice, T.: Russian Art. London 1949

Talbot Rice, T.: A Concise History of Russian Art. London 1963

Толстой, И., и Кондаков, Н.: Русские древности в памятниках искусства. Вып. 1–6. СПБ. 1889 до 1899 (Tolstoy, I. and Kondakov, N.: Old Russia in Artistic Monuments. Parts 1–6. St Petersburg 1889–99)

Тверской, Л. М.: Русское градостроительство до конца XVII в. (Планировка и застройка русских городов). Л.-М. 1953 (Tverskoy, L. M.: Russian Urban Architecture up to the End of the 17th Century [The planning and construction of Russian towns]. Leningrad–Moscow 1953)

Weidhaas, H.: Einiges Grundsätzliche zur Formenwandlung in der russischen Baukunst. Dresden 1935

Воронин, Н. Н.: Древнерусские города. М.-Л. 1945 (Voronin, N. N.: Early Russian Towns. Moscow–Leningrad 1945)

Забелин, И. Е.: Русское искусство. Черты самобытности в древнерусском зодчестве. М. 1900 (Zabelin, I. Ye.: Russian Art. Original traits in early Russian architecture. Moscow 1900)

For a fuller bibliographical list, see the Geschichte der Russischen Kunst, Bde. I–V, Dresden 1957–1970

518

Архітектурні пам'ятникі. Київ. 1950 (Architectural monuments. Kiev 1950)

История культуры древней Руси. Домонгольский период. I. Материальная культура. Под ред. Н. Н. Воронина, М. К. Каргера и М. А. Тихановой. II. Общественный строй и духовная культура. Под ред. Н. Н. Воронина и М. К. Каргера. М.-Л. 1948–51 (History of the Culture of Early Russia. Pre-Mongol Period. Vols I and II. Ed. N. N. Voronin, M. K. Karger and M. A. Tikhanova. Moscow–Leningrad 1948–51)

Geschichte der Kultur der alten Rus. Red. N. N. Woronin, M. K. Karger und M. A. Tichanowa. Bd. 1. Berlin 1959, Bd. 2. Berlin 1962 (German edition of the above)

Орнамент Софії Київської. Київ. 1949 (The Ornamentation of St Sophia in Kiev. Kiev 1949)

Ainalow, D.: Die Mosaiken des Michael-Klosters in Kiew. Belvedere 1926 (9–10), S. 201–216

Асеев, Ю. С.: Спасский собор в Чернигове. Київ. 1959 (Aseyev, Yu. S.: The Cathedral of the Saviour in Chernigov. Kiev 1959)

Асеев, Ю.: Новые данные о соборе Дмитровского монастыря в Киеве. — В кн.: Советская археология. М. 1961. III, с. 291–296 (Aseyev, Yu.: New findings about the Cathedral of the Demetrius Monastery in Kiev.
In: Soviet Archaeology. Moscow 1961, III, pp. 291–96)

Айналов, Д., и Редин, Е.: Древние памятники искусства Киева. Софийский собор, Злато-верхо-Михайловский и Кирилловский монастыри. Харьков. 1899 (Aynalov, D. and Redin, Ye.: Early Artistic Monuments of Kiev. St Sophia, the Monastery of St Michael with the Golden Roofs and the Monastery of St Cyril. Kharkov 1899)

Айналов, Д.: Архитектура черниговских церквей. – В кн.: Труды XIV Археологического съезда. III. М. 1909, с. 67 (Aynalov, D.: The Architecture of the Churches of Chernigov. In: Proceedings of the XIV Archaeological Congress. III. Moscow 1909, p. 67)

Барановский, П. Д.: Собор Пятницкого монастыря в Чернигове. – В кн.: Памятники искусства, разрушенные немецкими захватчиками в СССР. М.-Л. 1948, с. 13–34 (Baranovsky, P. D.: The Cathedral of the Pyatnitsa Monastery in Chernigov. In: Artistic Monuments Destroyed by the German Forces of Occupation in the USSR. Moscow–Leningrad 1948, pp. 13–34)

Бережков, Д. Н.: О храмах Владимиро-Суздальского княжества (XII–XIII вв.). Владимир на Клязьме. 1903 (Berezhkov, D. N.: The churches of the Vladimir-Suzdalian principality [12th–13th centuries]. Vladimir on the Klyazma 1903)

Безсонов, С. В.: Архитектура Западной Украины. М. 1946 (Bezsonov, S. V.: The architecture of the western Ukraine. Moscow 1946)

Бобринский, А. А.: Резной камень в России. Вып. I. Соборы Владимиро-Суздальской области XII до XIII ст. М. 1916 (Bobrinsky, A. A.: Stone Carving in Russia. Pt. 1: The Cathedrals of Vladimir-Suzdalia in the 12th and 13th Centuries. Moscow 1916)

Брунов, Н. И.: К вопросу о первоначальном виде древнейшей части Киевской Софии. – В кн.: Известия Государственной Академии истории материальной культуры. Т. V. Л. 1927 (Brunov, N. I.: On the question of the original form of the oldest parts of St Sophia in Kiev. In: Publications of the State Academy for the History of Material Culture. Vol. V. Leningrad 1927)

Брунов, Н.: О хорах в древнерусском зодчестве. – В кн.: Труды секции теории РАНИОН. М. 1928. II, с. 93–97 (Brunov, N.: Tribunes in Early Russian Architecture. In: Proceedings of the Theory Section of the RANION. Moscow 1928, pp. 93–97)

Брунов, Н. И.: Белорусская архитектура XI до XII вв. Сборник Артык – белорусской культуры. 1928 (Brunov, N. I.: Belo-Russian Architecture of the 11th and 12th Centuries. Collected Articles on Belo-Russian Culture, 1928)

Брунов, Н.: К вопросу о самостоятельных чертах русской архитектуры X–XII вв. – В кн.: Русская архитектура. М. 1940, с. 106 до 126 (Brunov, N.: The Question of Independent Characteristics in Russian Architecture in the 10th to the 12th Centuries. In: Russian Architecture. Moscow 1940, pp. 106–126)

Брунов, Н. И.: Киевская София древнейший памятник русской каменной архитектуры. Византийский временник. III. М.-Л. 1950 (Brunov, N. I.: St Sophia in Kiev – the Earliest Monument of Russian Masonry architecture. Byzantine Journal. III. Moscow – Leningrad 1950)

Чиняков, А. Г.: Архитектурный памятник времени Юрия Долгорукого. – В кн.: Архитектурное наследство. Сб. 2. М. 1952, с. 43–66 (Chinyakov, A. G.: An Architectural Monument of the Time of Yury Dolgoruky. In: Architectural Heritage. No. 2. Moscow 1952, pp. 43–66)

Durczewski, Z.: Stary Zamek w Grodnie w swietle wykopanisk dokananych w latach 1937–38. Grodno 1939 (The Old Castle in Grodno, in the Light of the Excavations of 1937–38. Grodno 1939)

Грабовский, С. Я., и Асеев, Ю. С.: Дослідження Софії Київсько. – Сборник Архітектурні пам'ятникі. Київ. 1950 (Grabovsky, S. Ya. and Aseyev, Yu. S.: Further Examination of St Sophia in Kiev. Collection of Architectonic monuments. Kiev 1950)

Grekow, B. D.: Die russische Kultur der Kiewer Periode. Moskau 1947

Halle, F.: Die Bauplastik von Wladimir-Susdal. Russische Romantik. Berlin 1929

Каргер, М.: Зодчество Галицо-Волынской земли XII–XIII вв. В кн.: Краткие сообщения о докладах и полевых исследованиях Института истории материальной культуры Акад. наук СССР. М. 1940. Вып. III, с. 14–21 (Karger, M.: The Architecture of Galicia-Volynia in the 12th and 13th Centuries. In: Summaries of Lectures and Research of the Institute for the History of Material Culture in the Academy of Sciences of the USSR. Moscow 1940, No. III, pp. 14–21)

Каргер, М.: К вопросу об убранстве интеръера в русском зодчестве домонгольского периода. – В кн.: Труды Всерос. Акад. художеств. Т. I. Л. 1947, с. 17–20 (Karger, M.: On the Question of Interior Decoration in Russian Architecture of the Pre-Mongol Period. In: Proceedings of the All-Russian Academy of Arts. Vol. 1. Leningrad 1947, pp. 17–20)

Каргер, М.: Археологические исследования древнего Киева. Киев. 1950 (Karger, M.: Archaeological Investigation of Old Kiev. Kiev 1950)

Каргер, М.: Памятники переяславского зодчества XI–XII вв. в свете археологических на Берестове. – В кн.: Советская археология. М. 1951. XV, с. 44–63 (Karger, M.: Architectural Monuments of the 11th and 12th Centuries in Pereslavl in the Light of Archaeological Research. In: Soviet Archaeology. Moscow 1951, XV, pp. 44–63)

Каргер, М.: К истории киевского зодчества XI в. Храм-мавзолей Бориса и Глеба в Вышгороде. – В кн.: Советская археология. М. 1952. XVI, с. 77–99 (Karger, M.: On the History of Architecture in 11th-century Kiev. The Sepulchre of Boris and Gleb in Vyshgorod. In: Soviet Archaeology. Moscow 1952, XVI, pp. 77–99)

Каргер, М.: К истории киевского зодчества конца XI – начала XII вв. Церковь Спаса на Берестове. – В кн.: Советская археология. М. 1953. XVII, с. 223–47 (Karger, M.: On the History of Kievan Architecture at the End of the 11th century and the Beginning of the 12th. The Church of the Saviour at Berestovo. In: Soviet Archaeology. Moscow 1953, XVII, pp. 223–47)

Каргер, М. К.: Древний Киев. Т. II. М.-Л. 1961 (Karger, M. K.: Old Kiev. Vol. II. Moscow-Leningrad 1961)

Касаткин, В.: Дмитриевский собор в г. Владимире. Владимир. 1914 (Kasatkin, V.: St Demetrius in Vladimir. Vladimir 1914)

Казаринова, В. И.: Архитектура Дмитровского собора во Владимире. – Памятники русской архитектуры. М. 1959 (Kazarinova, V. I.: The Architecture of the Cathedral of St Demetrius in Vladimir. Monuments of Russian Architecture. Moscow 1959)

Холостенко, Н.: Неизвестные памятники монументальной скульптуры древней Руси. (Рельефы Борисоглебского собора в Чернигове.) – В кн.: Искусство. 1951. № 3, с. 84–91 (Kholostenko, N.: Unknown Monumental Sculptures of Early Russia [Reliefs in the Cathedral of SS Boris and Gleb in Chernigov]. In: Art, 1951, No. 3, pp. 84–91)

Холостенко, Н. В.: Исследования Пятницкой церкви в Чернигове. – В кн.: Советская археология. М. 1956. XXVI (Kholostenko, N. V.: Examination of the Pyatnitsa Church in Chernigov. In: Soviet Archaeology. Moscow 1956, XXVI)

Холостенко, Н.: Архитектурно-археологическое исследование Успенского собора Елецкого монастыря в Чернигове. – В кн.: Памятники культуры. 1961, с. 56 (Kholostenko, N.: Architectonic and Archaeological Examination of the Cathedral of the Assumption in the Yeletsky Monastery in Chernigov. In: Monuments of Culture, 1961, p. 56)

Хозеров, И. М.: К исследованию конструкции Спасского храма в Полоцке. Смоленск. 1928 (Khozerov, I. M.: An investigation of the Construction of the Cathedral of the Saviour in Polotsk. Smolensk 1928)

Котов, Г.: Очертание арок во владимиро-суздальском зодчестве. – В кн.: Сообщения Гос. Академии истории материальной культуры. М. 1929. II, с. 450–79 (Kotov, G.: The Shape of Arches in Vladimir-Suzdalian Architecture. In: Publications of the State Academy for the History of Material Culture. Moscow 1929, II, pp. 450–79)

Кресальний, М. И.: Софіиський заповідник у Киіві. Киев. 1960 (Kresalny, M. I.: The St Sophia Conservation Area, Kiev. Kiev 1960)

Лазарев, В. Н.: Новые данные о мозаиках Софии Киевской. Византийский временник. Т. X. М. 1956 (Lazarev, V. N.: New Information About the Mosaics in St Sophia in Kiev. Byzantine Journal. Vol. X. Moscow 1956)

Лазарев, В. Н.: Мозаика Софии Киевской. М. 1960 (Lazarev, V. N.: The Mosaics of St Sophia in Kiev. Moscow 1960)

Лазарев, В. Н.: Михайловские мозаики. М. 1966 (Lazarev, V. N.: The Mosaics of St Michael's Monastery. Moscow 1966)

Логвин, Г. Н.: Киево-Печерская Лавра. М. 1958 (Logvin, G. N.: The Kiev Monastery of the Caves. Moscow 1958)

Логвин, Г. Н.: Чернигов. Новгород-Северский. Глухов. Путивль. М. 1965 (Logvin, G. N.: Chernigov. Novgorod-Seversky. Glukhov. Putivl. Moscow 1965)

Логвин, Г.: Киев. М. 1967 (Logvin, G.: Kiev. Moscow 1967)

Макаренко, М.: Чернигівський Спас. Киев. 1929 (Makarenko, M.: The Church of the Saviour in Chernigov. Kiev 1929)

Моргилевский, И. В.: Изучение собора св. Софии в Киеве (об обмерах Софии Киевской). Київська Софія в Світи нових спостережень. Київ та його околиця в історіі і пам'ятках. Київ. 1926 (Morgilevsky, I. V.: Study of St Sophia in Kiev [on the cathedral's dimensions]. St Sophia in Kiev in the Light of New

Knowledge. Kiev and its Environs in History and Monuments. Kiev 1926)

Новицкий, Олекса: Спроби реконструкціі Киівськоі Софіі. Киев. 1932 (Novitsky, Olexa: Attempted Reconstruction of St Sophia in Kiev. Kiev 1932)

Огнев, Б.: О позакомарных покрытиях (К вопросу реставрации позакомарных храмов северо-восточной Руси XII–XV вв.) – В кн.: Архитектурное наследство. Сб. 10. М. 1958, с. 43–58 (Ognev, B.: On the Forms of Roofs Governed by Round Gables [On the question of restoring roofs in accordance with the line of the round gables on churches in north-eastern Rus dating from the 12th to 15th centuries]. In: Architectural Heritage. No. 10. Moscow 1958, pp. 43–58)

Романов, К. К.: Вновь открытые рельефы Суздальского собора. – В кн.: Сообщения Гос. Академии истории материальной культуры. М. 1931. III (Romanov, K. K.: The Newly Discovered Reliefs in Suzdal Cathedral. In: Publications of the State Academy for the History of Material Culture. Moscow 1931, III)

Rose, K.: Grund und Quellort des russischen Geisteslebens. Berlin 1956

Рыбаков, Б.: Именні написи XII ст. в Киівському Софііському соборі. Археологія. Т. I. Киев. 1947 (Rybakov, B.: Twelfth-century Inscriptions of Names in St Sophia in Kiev. Archaeology. Vol. I. Kiev 1947)

Рыбаков, Б. А.: Древности Чернигова. – В кн.: Материалы и исследования по археологии СССР. Вып. XI. М.-Л. 1949, с. 7–93 (Rybakov, B. A.: The antiquities of Chernigov. In: Materials and Research in the Archaeology of the USSR. No. XI. Moscow–Leningrad 1949, pp. 7–93)

Рзянин, М. И.: Покров на Нерли. — Памятники русской архитектуры. Вып. III. М. 1941 (Rzyanin, M. I.: The Virgin of the Intercession on the Nerl. Monuments of Russian architecture. No. III. Moscow 1941)

Щероцкий, К.: София Полоцкая. Сборник в честь Айналова (Shcherotsky, K.: St Sophia in Polotsk. Essays in honour of Aynalov)

Шмит, Ф.: Заметки о поздневизантийских храмовых росписях. I. Киевский Михайловский Златоверний собор. – В кн.: Византийский временик. 1915–16. XXII, с. 71 (Schmit, F.: Notes on Late Byzantine Mural Paintings in Churches. 1. St Michael's Cathedral with the golden roof in Kiev. In: Byzantine Journal, 1915–16, XXII, p. 71)

Столетов, А. В.: Инженерные укрепления и реставрация Дмитровского собора в Владимире. – В кн.: Практика реставрационных работ. Сб. 2. М. 1958, с. 33–62 (Stoletov, A. V.: The Structural Repairs and the Restoration of St Demetrius in Vladimir. In: Restoration practice. No. 2. Moscow 1958, pp. 33–62)

Варганов, А. Д.: Фрески XI–XIII вв. в Суздальском соборе. – В кн.: Краткие сообщения о докладах и полевых исследовани-
ях Института истории материальной культуры Акад. наук СССР. М. 1940. Вып. V, с. 38–40 (Varganov, A. D.: The frescos of the 11th to the 13th centuries in Suzdal Cathedral. In: Summaries of Lectures and Research of the Institute for the History of Material Culture in the Academy of Sciences of the USSR. Moscow 1940, No. V, pp. 38–40)

Варганов, А.: Суздаль. М. 1944 (Varganov, A.: Suzdal. Moscow 1944)

Варганов, А.: К архитектурной истории Суздальского собора. – В кн.: Краткие сообщения о докладах и полевых исследованиях Института истории материальной культуры Акад. наук СССР. М. 1945. Вып. XI, с. 99–106 (Varganov, A.: On the Architectural History of Suzdal Cathedral. In: Summaries of Lectures and Research of the Institute for the History of Material Culture in the Academy of Sciences of the USSR. Moscow 1945, No. XI, pp. 99–106)

Виноградов, А.: История владимирского кафедрального Успенского собора. Владимир. 1905 (Vinogradov, A.: History of the Cathedral of the Assumption in Vladimir. Vladimir 1905)

Власюк, А.: Первоначальная форма купола церкви Покрова на Нерли. – В кн.: Архитектурное наследство. Сб. 2. М. 1952, с. 67–69 (Vlasyuk, A.: The Original Form of the Dome of the Virgin of the Intercession on the Nerl. In: Architectural Heritage. No. 2. Moscow 1952, pp. 67–69)

Воронин, Н. Н.: К вопросу о взаимоотношении галицо-волынской и владимиро-суздальской архитектуры XII–XIII вв. – В кн.: Краткие сооообщения о докладах и полевых исследованиях Института истории материальной культуры Акад. наук СССР. М. 1940. Вып. III, с. 22–27 (Voronin, N. N.: On the Relationships between the Architecture of Galicia-Volynia and Vladimir-Suzdalia in the 12th and 13th Centuries. In: Summaries of Lectures and Research of the Institute for the History of Material Culture in the Academy of Sciences of the USSR. Moscow 1940, No. III, pp. 22–27)

Воронин, Н. Н.: Памятники владимиро-суздальского зодчества XI–XII вв. М.-Л. 1945 (Voronin, N. N.: Monuments of Vladimir-Suzdalian Architecture of the 11th and 12th Centuries. Moscow–Leningrad 1945)

Воронин, Н. Н.: Владимир. М. 1945 (Voronin, N. N.: Vladimir. Moscow 1945)

Воронин, Н. Н.: Основные вопросы реконструкции Боголюбского дворца. – В кн.: Краткие сообщения о докладах и полевых исследованиях Института истории материальной культуры Акад. наук СССР. М. 1945. Вып. XI, с. 78–86 (Voronin, N. N.: The Most Important Aspects of the Reconstruction of the Palace at Bogolyubovo. In: Summaries of Lectures and Research of the Institute for the History of Material Culture in the Academy of Sciences of the USSR. Moscow 1945, No. XI, pp. 78–86)

520

Воронин, Н. Н.: Раскопки в Гродно. – В кн.: Краткие сообщения о докладах и полевых исследованиях Института истории материальной культуры Акад. наук СССР. М. 1949. Вып. XXVII, с. 138–48; там же, М. 1951. Вып. XXXVIII, с. 25–33 (Voronin, N. N.: The Excavations at Grodno. In: Summaries of Lectures and Research of the Institute for the History of Material Culture in the Academy of Sciences of the USSR. Moscow 1949, No. XXVII, pp. 138–48; Moscow 1951, No. XXXVIII, pp. 25–33)

Воронин, Н. Н.: У истоков русского национального зодчества. (Из истории зодчества периода феодальной раздробленности XI–XV вв.) – В кн.: Ежегодник Института истории искусств. 1952. М. 1952, с. 257 до 316 (Voronin, N. N.: The Birthplace of Russian National Architecture. [From the history of architecture in the period of feudalism, 11th–15th centuries.] In: Yearbook of the Institute for the History of Art 1952. Moscow 1952, pp. 257–316)

Воронин, Н. Н.: Древнее Гродно. М. 1954 (Voronin, N. N.: Old Grodno. Moscow 1954)

Воронин, Н. Н.: Зодчество Северо-восточной Руси XII–XV вв. Т. I. XII стол. М. 1961. Т. II. XIII–XV стол. М. 1962 (Voronin, N. N.: The Architecture of North-Eastern Rus from the 12th century to the 15th. Vol. 1: The 12th Century, Moscow 1961; Vol. 2: The 13th to the 15th Centuries, Moscow 1962)

Вагнер, Г. К.: Скульптура Владимиро-Суздальской Руси. Г. Юрьев-Польской. М. 1964 (Wagner, G. K.: The Sculpture of Vladimir-Suzdalian Rus. The Town of Yuryev-Polskoy. Moscow 1964)

Вагнер, Г. К.: Мастера древнерусской скульптуры. М. 1966 (Wagner, G. K.: Masters of Early Russian Sculpture. Moscow 1966)

Вагнер, Г. К.: Скульптура Древней Руси XII в. Владимир-Боголюбово. М. 1969 (Wagner, G. K.: The 12th-century Sculpture of Early Rus. Vladimir-Bogolyubovo. Moscow 1969)

Woronin, N. N.: Wladimir, Bogoljubowo, Susdal, Jurjew-Polskoi. Leipzig 1962

The City-States of Novgorod and Pskov

Архитектура Софийского собора в Новгороде. Новейшие исследования. Сообщения Института истории и теории архитектуры Академии архитектуры СССР. Вып. 7. М. 1947 (The Architecture of St Sophia in Novgorod. Recent research. Publications of the Institute for the History and Theory of Architecture at the Academy of Architecture of the USSR. No. 7. Moscow 1947)

История культуры древней Руси. Домонгольский период. I. Материальная культура. Под ред. Н. Н. Воронина, М. К. Каргера и М. А. Тихановой. II. Общественный строй и духовная культура. Под ред. Н. Н. Воронина и М. К. Каргера. М.-Л. 1948–51 (History of the culture of Early Rus. Pre-Mongol period. Ed. N. N. Voronin, M. K. Karger and M. A. Tikhanova. 2 vols. Moscow–Leningrad 1948–51)

Geschichte der Kultur der alten Rus. Red. N. N. Woronin, M. K. Karger und M. A. Tichanowa. Bd. 1. Berlin 1959; Bd. 2. Berlin 1962 (German edition of the above)

Афанасьев, К. Н.: Новый вариант реконструкции храма Софии в Новгороде. – В кн.: Сообщения института истории искусств Акад. наук СССР. Вып. 2. М. 1953, с. 91 до 111 (Afanasev, K. N.: An Alternative Reconstruction of St Sophia in Novgorod. In: Publications of the Institute for the History of Art at the Academy of Sciences of the USSR. No. 2. Moscow 1953, pp. 91–111)

Алферова, Г.: Собор Спасо-Мирожского монастыря. – В кн.: Архитектурное наследство. Сб. 10. М. 1958, с. 3–32 (Alferova, G.: The Cathedral of the Mirozh Monastery of the Saviour. In: Architectural Heritage. No. 10. Moscow 1958, pp. 3–32)

Бранденбург, Н. Е.: Старая Ладога (Рисунки и техническое описание акад. В. В. Суслова). СПБ. 1896 (Brandenburg, N. Ye.: Staraya Ladoga [Drawings and technical description by V. V. Suslov of the Academy]. St Petersburg 1896)

Дмитриев, Ю.: К истории Новгородской архитектуры. – В кн.: Новгородский исторический сборник. Вып. 2. Новгород. 1937, с. 116–23 (Dmitriyev, Yu.: On the History of Architecture in Novgorod. In: Novgorod Historical Miscellany. No. 2. Novgorod 1937, pp. 116–23)

Дмитриев, Ю.: Церковь Николы на Липне в Новгороде. – В кн.: Памятники искусства, разрушенные немецкими захватчиками в СССР. М.-Л. 1948, с. 57–76 (Dmitriyev, Yu.: The Church of St Nicholas on Lipna, Novgorod. In: Artistic Monuments Destroyed by the German Forces of Occupation in the USSR. Moscow–Leningrad 1948, pp. 57–76)

Дмитриев, Ю.: Стенные росписи Новгорода, их реставрация и исследование (работы 1945–48 гг.). – В кн.: Практика реставрационных работ. Сб. I. М. 1950, с. 135–54 (Dmitriyev, Yu.: Mural Paintings in Novgorod, Their Restoration and Research [work of the years 1945–48]. In: Restoration Practice. No. 1. Moscow 1950, pp. 135–54)

Гладенко, Т. В., Красноречьев, Л. Е., Штендер, Г. М., и Шуляк, Л. И.: Архитектура Новгорода в свете последних исследований. Церковь Параскевы Пятницы. – В кн.: Сборник Новгород к 1100-летию города. М. 1964, с. 201–14 (Gladenko, T. V., Krasnorechev, L. E., Shtender, G. M. and Shulyak, L. I.: The Architecture of Novgorod in the Light of the Latest Research. The Paraskeva-Pyatnitsa Church. In: Collected Essays about Novgorod for the City's 11th Centenary. Moscow 1964, pp. 201–14)

Гладенко, Т. В., Красноречьев, Л. Е., Штендер,

Г. М., и *Шуляк, Л. М.:* Архитектура Новгорода в свете последних исследований. Церковь Благовешения на торгу. – В кн.: Сборник Новгород к 1100-летию города. М. 1964 (Gladenko, T. V., Krasnorechev, L. E., Shtender, G. M. and Shulyak, L. I.: The Architecture of Novgorod in the Light of the Latest Research. The Church of the Annunciation in the Market place. In: Collected Essays About Novgorod for the City's 11th Centenary. Moscow 1964)

Каргер, М.: Новгород Великий. М. 1946 (Karger, M.: Great Novgorod. Moscow 1946)

Каргер, М.: Раскопки и реставрационные работы в Георгиевском соборе Юрьева монастыря (1933–35). – В кн.: Советская археология. М. 1946. VIII, с. 175–244 (Karger, M.: The Excavations and Restoration Work in St George's Cathedral in the Yuryev Monastery [1933–35]. In: Soviet Archaeology. Moscow 1946, VIII, pp. 175–224)

Каргер, М.: Основные итоги археологического изучения Новгорода. – В кн.: Советская археология. М. 1947. IX, с. 137–68 (Karger, M.: The Major Archaeological Findings in Novgorod. In: Soviet Archaeology. Moscow 1947, IX, pp. 137–68)

Кацнельсон, Р. А.: Древняя церковь в Перынском скиту близ Новгорода. – В кн.: Архитектурное наследство. Сб. 2. М. 1952, с. 69 до 85 (Katsnelson, R. A.: The Old Church on the Place of Perun, Novgorod. In: Architectural Heritage. No. 2. Moscow 1952, pp. 69–85)

Krause, H.-J., and *Schubert, E.:* Die Bronzetür der Sophienkathedrale in Nowgorod. Leipzig 1968

Лавров, В., и *Максимов, П.:* Псков. М. 1950 (Lavrov, V. and Maximov, P.: Pskov. Moscow 1950)

Лазарев, В.: Искусство Новгорода. М. 1947 (Lazarev, V.: The Art of Novgorod. Moscow 1947)

Лазарев, В.: Васильевские врата. – В кн.: Советская археология. М. 1953. XVIII, с. 386 до 442 (Lazarev, V.: The Vasily Door. In: Soviet Archaeology. Moscow 1953, XVIII, pp. 386 to 442)

Lazarev, V. N.: Theophanes der Grieche und seine Schule. Dresden 1968

Максимов, П.: Церковь Николы на Липне близ Новгорода. – В кн.: Архитектурное наследство. Сб. 2. М. 1952, с. 86–104 (Maximov, P.: The Church of St Nicholas on Lipna, Novgorod. In: Architectural Heritage. No. 2. Moscow 1952, pp. 86–104)

Максимов, П. Н.: Церковь Дмитрия Солунского в Новгороде. – В кн.: Архитектурное наследство. Сб. 14. М. 1962, с. 35–46 (Maximov, P. N.: The Church of St Demetrius of Salonika, Novgorod. In: Architectural Heritage. No. 14. Moscow 1962, pp. 35–46)

Монгайт, А.: Софийский собор в Новгороде в связи с новейшими исследованиями. – В кн.: Архитектура СССР. М. 1947. № 16, с. 34–39 (Mongayt, A.: St Sophia in Novgorod in Connection with the Latest Research. In: The Architecture of the USSR. Moscow 1947, No. 16, pp. 34–39)

Некрасов, А.: Древний Псков и его художественная жизнь. М. 1923 (Nekrasov, A.: Old Pskov and Its Artistic Life. Moscow 1923)
N. F.: Guide Through Old Pskov. 2nd ed. Pskov

Окулич-Казарин, Н. Ф.: Спутник по древнему Пскову. Изд. 2. Псков. 1913 (Okulich-Kazarin, 1913)
N. F.: Guide through old Pskov. 2nd ed. Pskov

Onasch, K.: Groß-Nowgorod und das Reich der heiligen Sophia. Leipzig und Wien 1969

Покрышкин, П. П.: Отчет о капитальном ремонте Спасо-Нередицкой церкви в 1903 и 1904 гг. СПБ. 1906 (Pokryshkin, P. P.: Account of the General Restoration of the Church of the Saviour on the Nereditsa in 1903 and 1904. St Petersburg 1906)

Романов, К.: Мелётово как источник истории Псковской земли. I. Проблема истории докапиталистических обществ. 1934. № 9–10, с. 143–56 (Romanov, K.: Meletovo as a Source for the history of Pskov. 1. The Problem of the History of the Pre-Capitalist Social Organization. 1934. Nos 9–10, pp. 143–56)

Рыльский, И.: Гражданское зодчество Пскова. – В кн.: Древности. Труды комиссии по сохранению древних памятников. Т. VI. М. 1915, с. XXXVII до LIII (Rylsky, I.: The Secular Architecture of Pskov. In: Antiquities. Publications of the Commission for the Preservation of Ancient Monuments. Vol. VI. Moscow 1915, pp. xxxvii–liii)

Седов, В.: Древнерусское языческое святилище в Перыни. — В кн.: Краткие сообщения о докладах и полевых исследованиях Института истории материальной культуры Акад. наук СССР. М. 1953. Вып. 50, с. 92 до 102 (Sedov, V.: The Early Russian Pagan Temple on the Place of Perun. In: Summaries of Lectures and Research of the Institute for the History of Material Culture in the Academy of Sciences of the USSR. Moscow 1953, No. 50, pp. 92–102)

Штендер, Г. М.: Восстановление Нередицы. – В кн.: Новгородский исторический сборник. Вып. 10. Новгород. 1962, с. 169–205 (Shtender, G. M.: The Restoration of the Nerl Church. In: Novgorod Historical Miscellany. No. 10. Novgorod 1962, pp. 169–205)

Строков, А., и *Богусевич, В.:* Новгород Великий (пособие для экскурсантов и туристов). Под общей ред. Б. Д. Грекова. Л. 1939 (Strokov, A., and Bogusevich, V.: Great Novgorod [Handbook for travellers and tourists]. General editor B. D. Grekov. Leningrad 1939)

Суслов, В.: Материалы к истории древней новгородско-псковской архитектуры. – В кн.: Записки Русского археологического общества. III. Вып. I. 1887, с. 238–73 (Suslov, V.: Materials for the Early History of Architecture in Novgorod and Pskov. In: Publications of the Russian Archaeological Society. III, 1, 1887, pp. 238–73)

522

Успенский собор Московского кремля. М. 1971 (The Cathedral of the Assumption in the Moscow Kremlin. Moscow 1971)

Александровский, М.: Указатель Московских церквей. М. 1925 (Alexandrovsky, M.: Directory of Moscow Churches. Moscow 1925)

Аренкова, Ю. И., и Мехова, Г. И.: Донской монастырь. М. 1970 (Arenkova, Yu. I. and Mekhova, G. I.: The Monastery of the Don. Moscow 1970)

Балдин, В.: Троице-Сергиева лавра. М. 1958 (Baldin, V.: The Monastery of the Trinity and St Sergius. Moscow 1958)

Бартенев, И., и Федоров, Б.: Архитектурные памятники русского севера. Л. 1967 (Bartenev, I. and Fedorov, B.: Architectural Monuments of Northern Russia. Leningrad 1967)

Бартенев, С. П.: Московский Кремль в старину и теперь. Кн. 1–2. М. 1912–16 (Bartenev, S. P.: The Moscow Kremlin, Past and Present. Books 1–2. Moscow 1912–16)

Безсонов, С. В.: Крепостные архитекторы. I. Опыт исторического исследования. II. Словарь крепостных архитекторов. М. 1938 (Bezsonov, S. V.: Fortress Architects. 1. Historical Essay. 2. Alphabetical List. Moscow 1938)

Безсонов, С.: Архитектура Московского государства. – В кн.: Русская архитектура. М. 1940, с. 27–35 (Bezsonov, S.: The Architecture of Muscovy. In: Russian Architecture. Moscow 1940, pp. 27–35)

Безсонов, С.: Из истории переделок и реставрации храма Василия Блаженного в Москве. – В кн.: Русская архитектура. М. 1940, с. 50–53 (Bezsonov, S.: From the History of the Alterations and Restoration of St Basil the Blessed in Moscow. In: Russian Architecture. Moscow 1940, pp. 50–53)

Богусевич, В.: Новый архитектурный тип в русском зодчестве XVI и XVII столетий. – В кн.: Сборник бюро по делам аспирантов. Гос. Акад. истории материальной культуры. Вып. I. Л. 1929, с. 93–100 (Bogusevich, V.: A New Type in Russian Architecture of the 16th and 17th Centuries. In: Miscellany of the Office for Aspirants' Affairs. State Academy for the History of Material Culture. No. 1. Leningrad 1929, pp. 93–100)

Бочаров, Г., и Выголов, В.: Вологда. Кириллов. Ферапонтово. Белоозерск. М. 1966 (Bocharov, G. and Vygolov, V.: Vologda, Kirillov, Ferapontovo, Beloozersk. Moscow 1966)

Brunoff, N.: Due cattedrali del Kremlino construite da italiani. Architettura e arti decorative, 1926, No. 6, pp. 97–100

Брунов, Н. И.: К вопросу о раннемосковском зодчестве. – В кн.: Труды Секции археологии Института археологии и искусствознания РАНИОН. М. 1928. IV, с. 93–106 (Brunov, N. I.: On Early Muscovite Architecture. In: Publications of the Archaeology Section of the Institute for Archaeology and Art History, RANION. Moscow 1928, IV, pp. 93–106)

Брунов, Н. И.: Московский Кремль. М. 1948 (Brunov, N. I.: The Moscow Kremlin. Moscow 1948)

Чиняков, А.: Каменное зодчество в русском централизованном государстве. (Автореферат диссертации). М. 1954 (Chinyakov, A.: Masonry Architecture in the Centralized Russian State [Dissertation synopsis]. Moscow 1954)

Danilowa, I. J.: Dionissi. Dresden und Wien 1970

Давид, Л. А.: Церковь Трифона в Напрудном. – В кн.: Архитектурные памятники Москвы XV–XVII вв. Новые исследования. М. 1947, с. 33–54 (David, L. A.: The Triphon Church at Naprudnoye. In: Monuments of Moscow Architecture of the 15th to 17th Centuries. New research. Moscow 1947, pp. 33–54)

Фуфаев, А. С.: Собор Московского Рождественского монастыря. – В кн.: Архитектурные памятники Москвы XV–XVII вв. Новые исследования. М. 1947, с. 55–75 (Fufayev, A. S.: The Cathedral of the Convent of the Nativity of the Virgin in Moscow. In: Monuments of Moscow architecture of the 15th to 17th Centuries. New research. Moscow 1947, pp. 55–75)

Горностаев, Ф. Ф.: Очерк древнего зодчества Москвы. – В кн.: Путеводитель по Москве. Под ред. И. П. Машкова. М. 1913, с. III до CCI (Gornostayev, F. F.: Outline Account of the Early Architecture of Moscow. In: Guide to Moscow. Ed. I. P. Mashkov. Moscow 1913, pp. III to CCI)

Грабарь, И.: Андрей Рублев. Сборник Вопросы реставрации. М. 1926 (Grabar, I.: Andrey Rublev. Aspects of Restoration. Moscow 1926)

Ильин, М.: Монастыри Московской Руси XVI века, как оборонительные сооружения. – В кн.: Исторический журнал. 1944. № 7–8, с. 75–81 (Ilin, M.: The Monasteries of 16th-century Muscovy and Their Defences. In: Historical Journal. 1944, Nos 7–8, pp. 75–81)

Ильин, М.: Русское зодчество XVI столетия. – В кн.: Краткие сообщения о докладах и полевых исследованиях Института истории материальной культуры Акад. наук СССР. М.-Л. 1946. Вып. XIII, с. 167–70 (Ilin, M.: Russian Architecture in the 16th Century. In: Summaries of Lectures and Research of the Institute for the History of Material Culture at the Academy of Sciences of the USSR. Moscow–Leningrad 1946, No. XIII, pp. 167–70)

Ильин, М. А.: Собор Василия Блаженного и градостроительство XVI в. – В кн.: Ежегодник Института истории искусств Акад. наук СССР. М. 1952, с. 217–56 (Ilin, M.: The Cathedral of St Basil the Blessed and Urban Architecture in the 16th century. In: Yearbook of the Institute for Art History at the Academy of Sciences of the USSR. Moscow 1952, pp. 217–56)

Ильин, М. А.: Подмосковье. М. 1966 (Ilin, M.: The Moscow Region. Moscow 1966)

Ильин, М.: Москва. М. 1969 (Ilin, M.: Moscow. Moscow 1969)

Караваева, Е. М.: Собор Спасского монастыря в Ярославле (исследование и реставрация). – В кн.: Архитектурное наследство. Сб. 15. М. 1963, с. 39–50 (Karavayeva, Ye. M.: The Cathedral of the Monastery of the Saviour in Yaroslavl [Research and restoration]. In: Architectural Heritage. No. 15. Moscow 1963, pp. 39–50)

Красовский, М.: Очерк истории Московского периода древнерусского церковного зодчества (от основания Москвы до конца I-й четверти XVIII в.). М. 1911 (Krasovsky, M.: Outline of the Muscovite Period in the History of Early Russian Ecclesiastical Architecture [from the founding of Moscow to the end of the first quarter of the 18th century]. Moscow 1911)

Лазарев, В. Н.: Андрей Рублев и его школа. М. 1966 (Lazarev, V. N.: Andrey Rublev and His School. Moscow 1966)

Lazarev, V. N.: Theophanes der Grieche und seine Schule. Dresden und Wien 1968

Lebedewa, J. A.: Andrei Rubljow und seine Zeitgenossen. Dresden 1962

Маковецкий, И.: Коломенское. (Автореферат диссертации). М. 1951 (Makovetsky, I.: Kolomenskoye [Dissertation synopsis]. Moscow 1951)

Максимов, П. Н.: Собор Спасо-Андроникова монастыря в Москве. – В кн.: Архитектурные памятники Москвы XV–XVII вв. Новые исследования. М. 1947, с. 8–32 (Maximov, P. N.: The Cathedral of the Andronikov Monastery of the Saviour in Moscow. In: Monuments of Moscow Architecture of the 15th to 17th Centuries. New research. Moscow 1947, pp. 8–32)

Максимов, П. Н.: К характеристике памятников Московского зодчества XIV–XV вв. – В кн.: Материалы и исследования по археологии СССР. Вып. 12. М.-Л. 1949, с. 209 до 216 (Maximov, P. N.: On the Characteristics of Monuments of Muscovite Architecture of the 14th and 15th Centuries. In: Materials and Research Relating to the Archaeology of the USSR. No. 12. Moscow–Leningrad 1949, pp. 209–16)

Машков, И. П.: Архитектура Новодевичьего монастыря в Москве. М. 1949 (Mashkov, I. P.: The Architecture of the New Convent of the Virgin in Moscow. Moscow 1949)

Мордвинов, А. Г.: Колокольня Ивана Великого. Журнал «Академия архитектуры». 1935. № 5, с. 32–37 (Mordvinov, A. G.: The Ivan the Great Bell-tower. In: Academy of Architecture, 1935, No. 5, pp. 32–37)

Некрасов, А.: Возникновение московского искусства. М. 1929 (Nekrasov, A.: The Origins of Muscovite Art. Moscow 1929)

Некрасов, А.: Проблема происхождения древнерусских столпообразных храмов. – В кн.: Труды Кабинета истории материальной культуры. V. Первый Московский государственный университет. М. 1930, с. 17 до 50 (Nekrasov, A.: The Problem of the Origin of the Early Russian Pillar-Shaped Churches. In: Publications of the Cabinet for the History of Material Culture. 5. The First Moscow State University. Moscow 1930, pp. 17–50)

Никольский, Н.: Кирилло-Белозерский монастырь и его устройство до 2-й четверти XVII в. (1397 до 1625). Т. I. Вып. I. СПБ. 1897 (Nikolsky, N.: The Monastery of St Cyril of Belozersk and Its Layout up to the Second Quarter of the 17th Century [1397–1625]. Vol. I, pt 1. St Petersburg 1897)

Овсянников, Ю.: Ново-Девичий монастырь. М. 1968 (Ovsyannikov, Yu.: The New Convent of the Don. Moscow 1968)

Покрышкин, П. П., и Романов, К. К.: Древние здания в Ферапонтовом монастыре Новгородской губ. – В кн.: Известия археологической комиссии. Вып. 28. СПБ. 1908, с. 107–155 (Pokryshkin, P. P., and Romanov, K. K.: Old Buildings in the Therapontos Monastery in the Novgorod District. In: Publications of the Archaeological Commission. No. 28. St Petersburg 1908, pp. 107–155)

Покрышкин, П. П.: Смоленская крепостная стена. – В кн.: Известия археологической комиссии. Вып. 32. СПБ. 1909, с. 17–29 (Pokryshkin, P. P.: Smolensk City Wall. In· Publications of the Archaeological Commission. No. 32. St Petersburg 1909, pp. 17–29)

Раппопорт, П. А.: Русское шатровое зодчество конца XVI в. – В кн.: Материалы и исследования по археологии СССР. Вып 12. М.-Л. 1949, с. 238–301 (Rappoport, P. A.: Russian Tent-Roof Architecture at the End of the 16th Century. In: Materials and Research Relating to the Archaeology of the USSR. No. 12. Moscow–Leningrad 1949, pp. 238–301)

Раппопорт, П.: Очерки хронологии русского шатрового зодчества. – В кн.: Краткие сообщения о докладах и полевых исследованиях Института истории материальной культуры Акад. наук СССР. М.-Л. 1949. Вып. XXX, с. 82–92 (Rappoport, P.: Notes on the chronology of Russian Tent-Roof Architecture. In: Summaries of Lectures and Research of the Institute for the History of Material Culture at the Academy of Sciences of the USSR. Moscow–Leningrad 1949, No. XXX, pp. 82–92)

Роговин, Н. Е.: Церковь Вознесения в Коломенском (XVI в.). М. 1942 (Rogovin, N. Ye.: The Church of the Ascension at Kolomenskoye [16th century]. Moscow 1942)

Рзянин, М. И.: Иван Великий. М. 1946 (Rzyanin, M. I.: Ivan the Great. Moscow 1946)

Сергеева-Козина, Т.: Коломенский кремль (Опыт реконструкции). – В кн.: Архитектурное наследство. Сб. 2. М. 1952, с. 133 до 163 (Sergeyeva-Kozina, T.: The Kolomenskoye Kremlin [Attempted reconstruction]. In: Architectural Heritage. No. 2. Moscow 1952, pp. 133 to 163)

Снегирев, В. Л.: Аристотель Фиораванти и перестройка Московского Кремля. М. 1935 (Snegirev. V. L.: Aristotle Fioravanti and the Rebuilding of the Moscow Kremlin. Moscow 1935)

Снегирев, В. Л.: Памятник архитектуры храм Василия Блаженного. М. 1953 (Snegirev, V. L.: An Architectural Monument – St Basil's Cathedral. Moscow 1953)

Соболев, Н.: Русский зодчий XV века Василий Дмитриевич Ермолин. – В кн.: Старая Москва. Вып. 2. М. 1914, с. 16–23 (Sobolev, N.: A 15th-century Russian Architect – Vasily Dmitriyevich Yermolin. In: Old Moscow. No. 2. Moscow 1914, pp. 16–23)

Соболев, Н. Н.: Василий Блаженный (Покровский собор). Под ред. Д. П. Сухова. М. 1949 (Sobolev, N. N.: St Basil the Blessed [the Cathedral of the Virgin of the Intercession]. Ed. D. P. Sukhov. Moscow 1949)

Сухов, Д. П.: Новое в архитектуре Василия Блаженного. – В кн.: Вопросы реставрации. Т. I. М. 1926, с. 179–85 (Sukhov, D. P.: Architectural Innovations in St Basil's Cathedral. In: Aspects of Restoration. Vol. 1. Moscow 1926, pp. 179–185)

Тихомиров, Н.: Звенигород. М. 1948 (Tikhomirov, H.: Zvenigorod. Moscow 1948)

Тихомиров, Н. Я., и Иванов, В. Н.,: Московский Кремль (Архитектура). М. 1967 (Tikhomirov, N. Ya. and Ivanov, V. N.: The Moscow Kremlin [the architecture]. Moscow 1967)

Виноградов, Н. Д.: Троице-Сергиева лавра. М. 1944 (Vinogradov, N. D.: The Monastery of the Trinity and St Sergius. Moscow 1944)

Виноградов, Н. Д.: Новые материалы по архитектуре древней Москвы. – В кн.: Сообщения Института истории искусств Акад. наук СССР. Вып. I. М.-Л. 1951, с. 69 до 78 (Vinogradov, N. D.: New Material on the Architecture of Old Moscow. In: Publications of the Institute for the History of Art at the Academy of Sciences of the USSR. No. 1. Moscow–Leningrad 1951, pp. 69–78)

Власюк, А.: Новые исследования архитектуры Архангельского собора в Московском Кремле. – В кн.: Архитектурное наследство. Сб. 2. М. 1952, с. 105–32 (Vlasyuk, A.: New Research into the Architecture of the Cathedral of the Archangel in the Moscow Kremlin. In: Architectural Heritage. No. 2. Moscow 1952, pp. 105–32)

Воронин, Н. Н.: Очерки по истории русского зодчества XVI–XVII вв. М. 1934 (Voronin, N. N.: Notes on the History of Russian Architecture in the 16th and 17th Centuries. Moscow 1934)

Евдокимов, И.: Север в истории русского искусства. Вологда. 1920 (Yevdokimov, I.: The North in the History of Russian Art. Vologda 1920)

Забелин, И. Е.: История города Москвы. Ч. I. М. 1902 (Zabelin, I. Ye.: The History of Moscow. Pt. I. Moscow 1902)

Згура, В.: Коломенское. М. 1928 (Zgura, V.: Kolomenskoye. Moscow 1928)

Агафонов, С.: Горький. Балахна. Макарьев. М. 1969 (Agafonov, S.: Gorky, Balakhna, Makarev. Moscow 1969)

Бахромеев, И. А.: Церковь во имя святого и славного пророка божьего Ильи в Ярославле. Ярославль. 1906 (Bakhromeyev, I. A.: The Church of the Holy and Renowned Prophet of God Elijah in Yaroslavl. Yaroslavl 1906)

Баниге, В.: Покрытия ростовских архитектурных памятников XVI–XVII вв. – В кн.: Материалы по изучению и реставрации памятников архитектуры Ярославской области. I. Древний Ростов. Ярославль. 158, с. 47–70 (Banige, V.: The Roofs of 16th and 17th-century Architectural Monuments in Rostov. In: Material for the Study and Restoration of Architectural Monuments in the Yaroslavl Region. 1. Old Rostov. Yaroslavl 1958, pp. 47–70)

Брунов, Н.: К вопросу о так называемом »русском барокко«. – В кн.: Барокко в России. М. 1926, с. 43–55 (Brunov, N.: On the So-Called 'Russian Baroque'. In: The Baroque in Russia. Moscow 1926, pp. 43–55)

Брюсова, В. Г.: Фрески Ярославля. М. 1969 (Bryusova, V. G.: The Frescos of Yaroslavl. Moscow 1969)

Чиняков, А.: Архитектурные памятники Измайлова. – В кн.: Архитектурное наследство. Сб. 2. М. 1952, с. 193–220 (Chinyakov, A.: The architectural monuments of Izmaylov. In: Architectural Heritage. No. 2. Moscow 1952, pp. 193–220)

Давыдов, С. Н.: Реставрационные работы 1951 до 1953 гг. по церкви Богоявления в Ярославле. – В кн.: Практика реставрационных работ. Сб. 2. М. 1958, с. 75–92 (Davydov, S. N.: The Restoration Carried Out, 1951–53, in the Church of the Epiphany in Yaroslavl. In: Restoration practice. No. 2. Moscow 1958, pp. 75–92)

Добровольская, Э.: Новые материалы по истории Ростовского кремля. – В кн.: Материалы по изучению и реставрации памятников архитектуры Ярославской области. I. Древний Ростов. Ярославль. 1958, с. 26–46 (Dobrovolskaya, E.: New Material on the History of the Rostov Kremlin. In: Material for the Study and Restoration of Architectural Monuments in the Yaroslavl Region. 1. Old Rostov. Yaroslavl 1958, pp. 26–46)

Добровольская, Э.: Ярославль. М. 1968 (Dobrovolskaya, E.: Yaroslavl. Moscow 1968)

Эдинг, Б.: Ростов Великий. Углич. Памятники художественной старины. М. 1913 (Eding, B.: Old Rostov. Uglich. Monuments of Early Art. Moscow 1913)

Грог, А.: Дубровицы. – В кн.: Подмосковные музеи. Вып. 4. М.-Л. 1925, с. 70–87 (Grog, A.: Dubrovitsy. In: Museums in the Moscow Region. No. 4, Moscow–Leningrad 1925, pp. 70–87)

Ильин, М. А.: Рязань. Историко-архитектурный очерк. Ч. I. XI – начала XX вв. М. 1954 (Ilin, M. A.: Ryazan. Historical and Architectural Outline. Pt 1. The 11th to the Beginning of the 20th Century. Moscow 1954)

Ильин, М. А.: Зодчий Яков Бухвостов. М. 1959 (Ilin, M. A.: The Architect Yakov Bukhvostov. Moscow 1959)

Иванов, В.: Ярославль. М. 1950 (Ivanov, V.: Yaroslavl. Moscow 1950)

Иванов, В. Н.: Ростов Великий. Углич. М. 1964 (Ivanov, V. N.: Old Rostov. Uglich. Moscow 1964)

Иванов, В.: Кострома. М. 1970 (Ivanov, V.: Kostroma. Moscow 1970)

Машков, И. П.: Архитектура Новодевичьего монастыря в Москве. М. 1949 (Mashkov, I. P.: The Architecture of the New Convent of the Virgin in Moscow. Moscow 1949)

Михайловский, Е.: О национальных особенностях московской архитектуры конца XVII в. (автореферат диссертации). М. 1949 (Mikhaylovsky, Ye.: On the National Peculiarities of Moscow Architecture at the End of the 17th Century [Dissertation synopsis]. Moscow 1949)

Некрасов, А.: О стиле русской архитектуры XVII в. – В кн.: Труды секции истории искусств Института археологии и искусствознания РАНИОН. Т. IV. М. 1930, с. 138–49 (Nekrasov, A.: On the Style of Russian Architecture in the 17th Century. In: Publications of the Art History Section of the Institute for Archaeology and Art History, RANION. Vol. IV. Moscow 1930, pp. 138–149)

Овчиникова, Е. С.: Церковь Троицы в Никитниках. М. 1970 (Ovchinikova, E. S.: The Church of the Trinity in Nikitniki. Moscow 1970)

Овсянников, Ю.: Ново-Девичий монастырь. М. 1968 (Ovsyannikov, Yu.: The New Convent of the Virgin. Moscow 1968)

Павлинов, А. М.: Древности ярославские и ростовские. М. 1892 (Pavlinov, A. M.: Antiquities of Yaroslavl and Rostov. Moscow 1892)

Первухин, Н. Г.: Церковь Иоанна Предтечи в Ярославле. М. 1913 (Pervukhin, N. G.: The Church of St John the Baptist in Yaroslavl. Moscow 1913)

Первухин, Н.: Церковь Богоявления в Ярославле. Ярославль 1916 (Pervukhin, N.: The Church of the Epiphany in Yaroslavl. Yaroslavl 1916)

Подключников, В. Н.: Три памятника XVII столетия. Церковь в Филях. Церковь в Уборах. Церковь в Троицком Лыкове. М. 1945 (Podklyuchnikov, V. N.: Three 17th-Century Monuments. The Church at Fili, the Church at Ubory, the Church at Troitsky-Lykov. Moscow 1945)

Подольский, Р.: Новый Иерусалим на Истре. – В кн.: Архитектура СССР. М. 1942. № 1, с. 9–16 (Podolsky, R.: New Jerusalem on the Istra. In: Architecture of the USSR. Moscow 1942, No. 1, pp. 9–16)

Подольский, Р.: Государев Хамовный двор в Кадашевской слободе в Москве. – В кн.: Сообщения Института истории искусств Акад. наук СССР. Вып. I. М.-Л. 1951, с. 84 до 111 (Podolsky, R.: The Imperial Drapery in the Kadashevskaya Quarter of Moscow. In: Publications of the Institute for the History of Art at the Academy of Sciences of the USSR. No. 1. Moscow–Leningrad 1951, pp. 84–111)

Ширяев, С.: Памятники барокко и влияние зодчества Москвы в архитектуре Смоленска XVII до XVIII века. – В кн.: Труды смоленских государственных музеев. Вып. I. Смоленск. 1924 (Shiryayev, S.: Monuments of Baroque Architecture and the Influence of the Moscow Baroque on the Architecture of Smolensk in the 17th and 18th Centuries. Smolensk 1924, pp. 1–45)

Суслов, А. И., и Чураков, С. С.: Ярославль. М. 1960 (Suslov, A. I. and Churakov, S. S.: Yaroslavl. Moscow 1960)

Тельтевский, П.: Архитектурные памятники конца XVII века связанные с Бухвостовым, М. 1954 (Teltevsky, P.: Architectural monuments of the late 17th century connected with Bukhvostov. Moscow 1954)

Торопов, С.: Ново-Иерусалимский монастырь. – В кн.: Памятники зодчества, разрушенные или поврежденные немецкими захватчиками. Вып. II. М. 1944, с. 3–23 (Toropov, S.: The Monastery of the New Jerusalem. In: Architectural monuments destroyed or damaged by the German forces of occupation. No. II. Moscow 1944, pp. 3–23)

Торопов, С., и Щепетов, К.: Иосифо-Волоколамский монастырь. М. 1946 (Toropov, S. and Shchepetov, K.: The Monastery of Joseph of Volokolamsk. Moscow 1946)

Воронин, Н. Н.: Очерки по истории русского зодчества XVI–XVII вв. М. 1934 (Voronin, N. N.: Notes on the history of Russian architecture of the 16th and 17th centuries. Moscow 1934)

Воронов, Н. В., и Блохина, Н. Б.: Ярославские изразцы. – Краеведческие записки. Вып. I. Ярославль. 1956 (Voronov, N. V. and Blokhina, N. B.: Yaroslavl tiles. – Local studies No. 1. Yaroslavl 1956)

Згура, В.: Проблема возникновения барокко в России. – В кн.: Барокко в России. М. 1926, с. 13–42 (Zgura, V.: The problem of the Origin of the Baroque in Russia. In: The Baroque in Russia. Moscow 1926, pp. 13–42)

Wooden architecture

Holzbaukunst. Eine Geschichte der abendländischen Holzarchitektur und ihrer Konstruktionselemente. Hrsg. von H.-J. Hansen. Oldenb., Hamburg 1969

Остров Кижи. Под ред. Смирновой. Петрозаводск. 1968 (The Island of Kizhi. Ed. Smirnova. Petrozavodsk 1968)

Красовский, М.: Курс истории русской архитектуры. Ч. I. Деревянное зодчество. СПБ. 1916 (Krasovsky, M.: Outline History of Russian Architecture. Pt 1: Wooden Architecture. St Petersburg 1916)

Ополовников, А. В.: Памятники деревянного зодчества Карело-Финской ССР. М. 1955 (Opolovnikov, A. V.: The Monuments of Wooden Architecture of the Karelo-Finnish SSR. Moscow 1955)

Ополовников, А. В.: Лазаревская церковь Муромского монастыря. – В кн.: Архитектурное наследство. Сб. 18. М. 1969, с. 106–11 (Opolovnikov, A. V.: The Church of St Lazarus from the Murom Monastery. In: Architectural Heritage. No. 18. Moscow 1969, pp. 106–11)

Соболев, Н.: Русская народная резьба по дереву. Гл. II–IV. М. 1934 (Sobolev, N.: The Russian Folk Art of Woodcarving. Chapters II to IV. Moscow 1934)

Забелло, С. Я., Иванов, В. Н., и Максимов, П. Н.: Русское деревянное зодчество. М. 1942 (Zabello, S. Ya., Ivanov, V. N. and Maximov, P. N.: Russian Wooden Architecture. Moscow 1942)

527

Index

534

535

Acknowledgements

The majority of the photographs in this book were taken by Klaus G. Beyer, Weimar. Others were made available by: Deutsche Fotothek, Dresden: 8, 15, 17, 38, 114, 345, 349, 350, 355, 356, 358, 367, 368, 371, 390, 396, 413; V. N. Ivanov, Moscow: 394, 415, 416, 418; Novosti Press Agency (APN), Moscow: 94, 101–03, 118, 353, 363, 377–79, 385, 391, 395, 400, 414; A. V. Shchusev State Museum for Architectural Research, Moscow: 67, 71, 75, 96, 97, 155, 200, 209, 210, 244, 248, 257, 274, 301, 329–40, 342–44, 348, 354, 357, 370, 373–76, 380, 382–84, 392, 398, 399, 404–06, 409, 410, 412.

The drawings were copied from publications listed in the Bibliography, the plans, elevations and section drawings, and the map, by Hans-Ulrich Herold, Halle, the views, details and perspective drawings by Rudolf Peschel, Brieselang. The plans and sections are all in the scale of 1 : 500, with the single exception of the plan of the Cathedral of the Resurrection in the Monastery of the New Jerusalem at Istra, which is in the scale of 1 : 535. The genealogical table was taken from *O Bojan, du Nachtigall der alten Zeit,* Berlin 1967.

The transliteration of Cyrillic characters was based on *The Latinisation of Cyrillic Characters* by W.K. Matthews, reprinted from *The Slavonic Review* Vol XXX No 75, June 1952.